THE HANDBOOK OF
POLITICAL
BEHAVIOR

Volume 2

THE HANDBOOK OF
POLITICAL
BEHAVIOR

Volume 2

Edited by

SAMUEL L. LONG

Center for the Study of Business and Government
Baruch College–City University of New York
New York, New York

PLENUM PRESS • NEW YORK AND LONDON

ISBN 0-306-40602-0

CONTRIBUTORS

ROBERT ABRAMS • Department of Political Science, Brooklyn College, City University of New York, Brooklyn, New York

LLOYD S. ETHEREDGE • Department of Political Science, Massachusetts Institute of Technology, Cambridge, Massachusetts

ROBERT T. GOLEMBIEWSKI • Department of Political Science, University of Georgia, Athens, Georgia

SHELDON G. LEVY • Department of Psychology, Wayne State University, Detroit, Michigan

GERALD J. MILLER • Department of Political Science, University of Kansas, Lawrence, Kansas

ROZANN ROTHMAN • Center for the Study of Federalism, Temple University, Philadelphia, Pennsylvania

PREFACE

In the writing of prefaces for works of this sort, most editors report being faced with similar challenges and have much in common in relating how these challenges are met. They acknowledge that their paramount objective is to provide more than an overview of topics but rather to offer selective critical reviews that will serve to advance theory and research in the particular area reviewed. The question of the appropriate audience to be addressed is usually answered by directing material to a potential audience of social scientists, graduate students, and, occasionally, advanced undergraduate students. Editors who are confronted with the problem of structuring their material often explore various means by which their social science discipline might be subdivided, then generally conclude that no particular classification strategy is superior. In elaborating on the process by which the enterprise was initiated, editors typically resort to a panel of luminaries, who provide independent support for the idea and then offer both suggestions for topics and the authors who will write them. Editors usually concede that chapter topics and content do not reflect their original conception but are a compromise between their wishes and the authors' expertise and capabilities. Editors report that inevitable delays occur, authors drop out of projects and are replaced, and new topics are introduced. Finally, editors frequently confess that the final product is incomplete, with gaps occurring because of failed commitments by authors or because authors could not be secured to write certain chapters.

   With these commonalities in mind, then, and, with the advice of past editors of comparable works, the *Handbook of Political Behavior* project was initiated. In some ways, the experiences associated with the genesis and formulation of this series coincide with the experiences cited by editors in the prefaces of previous comparable works; in other respects, the experiences of this project diverge markedly from those same works. For instance, like other social science research, the *Handbook of Political Behavior* was conceived as a vehicle by which selected topics with an interdisciplinary focus might be critically reviewed. At the same time, however, authors were also instructed to "do their own thing" after having dealt with the subject area, preferably by highlighting gaps in theory and research and by indicating how theoretical and empirical deficiencies might be remedied. Moreover, relative to other collections, much more emphasis was placed on securing authors with diverse backgrounds, not only in political science but also in psychology, sociology, and anthropology as well. Another objective concerned the provision of new subject matter not found elsewhere, or at least not readily available to students of political behavior.

The audience envisioned for the handbook is similar to that of other collections, namely, professional social scientists with a special interest in political psychology and political sociology; graduate students, too, particularly those with an interest in the political behavior area; and, given the inquiries to date, it is clear that faculty members in the social sciences will assign chapters from the handbook to advanced undergraduate students in political behavior courses. Such a diverse and comprehensive audience assures that the unique subject matter found in the handbook will be disseminated throughout the social science community.

Although the *Handbook of Political Behavior* was originally planned as a two-volume work, divided between political psychology and political sociology, it quickly became apparent that the material would require more than two volumes and that the simple distinction between political psychology and political sociology was difficult to maintain in categorizing certain topics. This task was made especially difficult because one of the objectives of the handbook was to extend the traditional boundaries of the political behavior field into areas which, although dealt with in the disciplines of psychology and sociology, were not usually considered from a political science perspective. Another problem, similar to categorization of subject matter, concerned the objective of providing new perspectives on relatively traditional material. Attaining these objectives made it particularly difficult to classify a given chapter as clearly falling either within the domain of political psychology or of political sociology. Thus, the handbook was expanded, and a much less rigid categorization scheme was used in assigning specific chapters to different volumes.

The *Handbook of Political Behavior* is unique in that it is comparatively open-ended in structure and is being written by a group of social scientists associated through other professional activities. Continuity is a major attribute of the chapters published here. Many of the authors are associated with a new journal, *Micropolitics*, as either contributors, reviewers, or editorial board members. Some of the material published in the handbook has appeared in abbreviated form in *Micropolitics*. Other chapters in the handbook will shortly appear as expanded monographs in the Topics in Political Behavior Series to be published also by Plenum. Finally, plans are also underway for continuing the *Handbook of Political Behavior* in the form of annual volumes which will focus on additional subjects in the political behavior field. Thus, the omission and incompleteness problems encountered in other collections have been circumvented in the handbook and its related publications.

Editing these volumes has been somewhat analogous to juggling simultaneously a multitude of pins, and many people have assisted me. My family has been especially supportive throughout the project: my wife, Ruth Taylor Long, by maintaining her equanimity in the face of my obsession with the handbook, and my editorial assistant, Samantha Taylor Long, by continually showing me that other activities, such as kindergarten-league soccer, can be as equally diverting as the social sciences. The staff of the Plenum Publishing Corporation, particularly my editor Frank Columbus—an exemplary juggler himself—has contributed to the experience being both enlightening and exciting. The contributing authors have been very cooperative, given the pressures exerted on them by the deadline. My friend and mentor, Donald Gordon, of the Center for the Study of Business and Government, Baruch College, of the City University of New York, has been generous with both his time and Center resources, contributions I greatly appreciate. Helen and Robert Lane provided much encouragement, warm companionship, and liebfraumilch during the earliest stages of this project while I was a postdoctoral fellow in the Psychology and Politics Program at Yale University. Impetus was also provided this project by William Siffin, who repeatedly questioned my sanity for undertaking the editorship of the *Handbook of Political Behavior* and who insinuated it would never be brought to fruition. It is with much satisfaction and glee that I refute the latter contention.

SAMUEL LONG

Alexandria, Virginia

CONTENTS

Chapter 1

SMALL GROUPS IN POLITICAL SCIENCE: PERSPECTIVES ON SIGNIFICANCE AND STUCKNESS
Robert T. Golembiewski and Gerald J. Miller

Introduction 1
Four Basic Small-Group Orientations: Tracing the Literature's
    Major Themes 2
    Social Facilitation or Inhibition: Better or Worse Performance
      in Groups? 3
    Social Attraction: How/Why Do I Love/Like You? 7
    Social Comparison: You're OK—How Am I? 11
    Social Control: How Are Individuals Tied into Broad Purposes? 15
Some Small-Group Dimensions: Toward Differentiating
    the Species 17
A Primer on What We Know about Central Properties:
    Components of a Small-Group Model 18
Five Particulars Disregarding What We Know: Some
    Garden-Variety Misunderstandings 22
Four Cases of Small Groups in Politics: Dynamics/Dimensions
    as Emergent/Contrived 26
    Groups as Engines of Conformity: Groupthink on Kennedy's
    "Best and Brightest" Team 27

Groups as Supports for Deviant Voting Behavior: The Case
    of Republican Auto Workers   28
Groups and One-to-One Control: A Runaway Norm on
    Nixon's "Young Team"   31
Groups and the Development of Truth-Seeking Norms:
    One Deliberate MARTA Intervention   34
Overview of Significance and Stuckness: The Condition of
    Small-Group Analysis Today   37
    Elaborating on Past, Present, and Future Significance: What
        the Small Group Can Do for Political Scientists   37
    Understanding and Escaping Contemporary Stuckness:
        Whatever Happened to Small-Group Research?   53
References   64

Chapter 2

GOVERNMENT LEARNING: AN OVERVIEW
Lloyd S. Etheredge

Introduction   73
    A Model for Theory Development: Medical Diagnosis Capability   75
    Overview and a Preliminary Caution   76
Defining Learning   76
    Types of Individual Learning   79
    Organizational Learning   82
    Learning Agendas   84
Normative Issues   86
Trends   88
Motivation and Cognition—Individual Bases   90
    Three Images of Individual Learning   90
    Selected Additional Issues   109
Organizational Structure and Dynamics   119
    "Smart" Organization Theory   119
    Organizational Memory   121
    Qualitative Differences of Public Bureaucracies   123
    Intelligence Functions and Decision-Making Processes   124
The Washington Political Environment   128
    The Structure of Time in Washington   128
    Lobbying   129
    Accountability and Review Systems: Legitimacy Trade-Offs ...   129
    News Media Effects   130
    Uniqueness and Self-Transforming Capacity   130
Societal, World, and Historical Contexts   133
    Truth Theory   133

Secularization and Orthodoxy Theories 134
Government Learning: A Dependent Variable? 135
Problem Types 135
No Problem 136
Technology-Dependent Problems 136
Resource-Dependent Problems 136
Known-Answer Problems 137
Unproductively Conceptualized Problems 137
Problems Amenable to Full Scientific Method 138
Strong-Norm-System Problems 138
Pluralist, Low-Norm-Salience or Rapid-Change Problems 138
Forecasting with Uncertain Precedents 139
Problems Unanswerable or Unposable from Brain Constraints 139
Secrecy Penetration Problems 139
Different People and Different Cultures Problems 139
Time-Constraint Problems 140
Incoherent-Policy Problems 140
Diagnostic Repertoires 140
Overview 140
Illustrative Individual Diagnoses 140
Concluding Reflections 142
The Design of Institutional-Memory Capabilities 142
Increasing Effective Transitions and Competence of
    Political Appointees 143
Quality of Watchdog and Critic Systems 143
Dependency Theory of Motivational Blockage 143
Good Judgment 144
Overload and How to Cope 144
The Critique of Ideology and Overconfidence 145
References 146

Chapter 3

POLITICAL VIOLENCE: A CRITICAL EVALUATION
Sheldon G. Levy

Introduction 163
Frequency of Conflict 164
Overview 164
Large-Scale Conflict 165
Assassination 174
Conflict in the United States 177
Comment on Periodicity and Randomness 180

Dimensions of Conflict 181
    Selected Studies 181
    A Typology Including Structural Violence 188
Hypotheses About Violence 191
    Introduction 191
    The Feierabend Group 192
    Gurr 198
    Other Studies 201
Summary 215
    Overall Conclusions: Macroanalyses 215
    Some Other Areas in the Study of Political Violence 217
    Concluding Comment 220
References 220

Chapter 4

RATIONALITY AND COLLECTIVE-CHOICE THEORY
Robert Abrams

Introduction 225
Rationality 226
Individual and Collective Choice 227
Axiomatic-Choice Theory 229
    Arrow's Social-Choice Theory 230
    Arrow's Conditions 231
    Arrow's Impossibility Theorem 236
    Probability of the Voter's Paradox 237
    Single-Peakedness and Value Restrictedness 240
    Preference Priority 242
    Cardinal Utility and the Independence Condition 242
    Logrolling and Vote Trading 244
    The Paradox of Vote Trading 247
Economic Theories of Politics—Spatial Models 249
    Information and Rationality 251
    Party Strategies 252
Game Theory 255
    Games in Extensive, Normal, and Characteristic-Function Form   255
    Two-Person Zero-Sum Games 257
    Individual and Collective Rationality in Games 258
    Solution Concepts 259
    Mixed Strategies 259
    Prisoner's Dilemma 261
    N-Person Games 262
    Rationality Conditions 262

Imputations 267
Domination 268
The Shapley Value 269
Nash Equilibrium 271
The Shapley Solution 274
Harsanyi's Risk–Dominance Relations 275
Collective Goods 278
Free Riders 278
Free Rider and Prisoner's Dilemma 280
Problems of Preference Revelation 280
Noncooperation without Prisoner's Dilemma 281
Altruism 282
Conclusion 282
References 283

Chapter 5

POLITICAL SYMBOLISM
Rozann Rothman

Introduction 285
Sources of the Research Focus 290
Philosophic Concepts of Symbolic Systems 291
Linguistic and Anthropological Approaches to Symbolism 298
Theories of Political Symbols 307
A Survey of Applications of Symbolic Theory 314
Law as a Symbol System 328
The Relation of Metaphor and Political Symbolism 330
Conclusion 334
References 338

INDEX 341

INTRODUCTION

Consciousness is painful. A man reminded of himself in a room of mirrors or hearing his own voice on a tape recorder finds his preferred version of himself out of harmony with the actual self he sees or hears. He avoids such "objective self-consciousness" when he can, but when confronted by himself in these ways, he becomes more truthful and more consistent in what he says (Wicklund, 1975). Someone is watching and listening: the inner eye and ear, himself, perhaps even his better self. "That man's self-knowledge is the highest aim of philosophical inquiry appears to be generally acknowledged" (Cassirer, 1944, p. 1), but it is painful for the individual. Nor is societal self-consciousness different. To stand outside the warm circle of the familiar and look at one's customs and beliefs with the eye of an alien is disturbing and, indeed, alienating. It is not quite the case that familiarity arising from "mere exposure" is always attractive (Zajonc, 1968), but societies have protected the familiar for centuries; over the millenia, stasis and orthodoxy have been the common lot of most societies, with pain and brutality being endured because of inhibitions against asking the question, "How might things be otherwise?" That question involves the immediate, but lesser, pain of consciousness. This *Handbook of Political Behavior* is a contribution to societal self-consciousness.

Philosophy, among the Greeks, was the first instrument of societal self-consciousness, and it still performs that function, with literature and art as powerful and often independent allies. Today, and ever since their emergence from the womb of philosophy, the social sciences have borne and must bear an increasing share of the burden of societal self-consciousness. They reflect back to the society the nature of its practices and institutions; they penetrate the myths and rationalizations which justify its institutions; they confront the ideal with one or more versions of what "actually" happens. And they help answer the question of how things might be otherwise by comparing one society with another, one institution with another, one policy with another, and by extrapolation and inference from observed practice.

In their better moments, the social sciences, and especially the behavioral sciences, may help a society to become more *sociocentric* and less *egocentric* in the Piagetian sense. For Piaget, the concept of egocentrism (a term which he found greatly misunderstood) meant not so much selfishness, although that might follow, but rather epistemological "centration," or "taking as the sole reality the one which appears to perceptions" (cited in Battro, 1973, p. 51). It is a characteristic of childish thought, often but not always outgrown; the child's "thought is isolated, and while he believes himself to be sharing the point of view of the world at large he is really still shut up in his own point of view" (Piaget, 1932/1965, p. 36). This centering of thought on the self does not lead to introspection and self-knowledge; because the egocentrism is unconscious, the egocentric individual finds that his "universe would be centered on one's own actions, the subject being all the more dominated by this egocentric point of view because he remains un-self-conscious" (1960, p. 114). In a similar sense we might say that social science is a protection against societal egocentrism; it is a decentering of cognition, a comprehension not only of the points of view of others but also of their practices, institutions, and policies.

Once released from convention, the inquiry into how things might be otherwise can itself become conventional. One can always imagine how things might be better, perhaps in a nostalgic mood for a world we have lost, real or imagined (Arendt, 1958; Ellul, 1965), perhaps in a utopian mood for a world of human brotherhood (the utopian socialists), perhaps leaving blank the picture of the alternatives and specifying only the evils of the world we know (Marx, Touraine, Habermas, Mumford). The world of real alternatives is smaller than that conceivable to the imagination, but larger than the world we know. To construct such a better world, one needs to know how things work today, the causes, contexts, and machinery of human behavior. It has been said that the study of political behavior is a conservative influence, for it requires observations and, so it is argued, cannot go beyond the "is" to that exciting world of what might be, let alone what ought to be. But that confounds the study of experience with being limited by experience, and more profoundly it implies the moral arrogance of believing that one can experiment with other people's lives without learning from experience. There is no one more radical than the person who takes the trouble to discover what is known about political behavior before seeking to reconstruct it. Such a person is invited to learn from this *Handbook*.

The painful experience of societal self-consciousness comes in two varieties: there is the pain of discovering that humans are not so intelligent and virtuous as has been imagined and there is the pain of learning that the costs of reform may be higher than anticipated. On the first count, Freud's revelations of the precarious rationality of the species has been duplicated with better data by cognitive research, for, using Simon's (1957, p. 198) term, our rationality is indeed "bounded." Similarly, the civic virtue and collective conscience of man has been challenged by theory and research in *The Logic of Collective Action* (Olson, 1969)—we are all free riders in one way or another. On the second count, the hopeful world of John Maynard Keynes, where a pyramid here and a motorway there would give us prosperity in a world of underspending and infinite resources, has given way to the harder realities of inflation and resource depletion requiring new interpretations of the human condition. It is a commonplace in the West that people should select their own leaders; in one way or another we all believe in participatory politics. What, then, could be more appealing than universal presidential primaries? It seems a long time ago that V. O. Key (1964, p. 342) explained why primaries would not have the beneficial effects hoped for. Had good will and the spirit of reform been joined to social science, some more expeditious way of enlisting larger numbers in leadership selection might have been invented. Although experience is ambiguous, research now suggests (Coopersmith, 1967) that maximizing children's choice and discretion does not necessarily lead to wiser adult choices and the benefits that go with self-esteem. Part of social science, but only part, is the employment of what C. W. Mills (1959) called "the sociological imagination," the transformation of statements of human problems into statements of political remedy. That transformation is part of societal self-consciousness.

We are more or less plastic human primates shaped by more or less benign cultures; only the social and biological sciences can tell us both the capacities and the limits of our potentials for living well and wisely with each other. And while we must ever go back to the deep well of humanistic learning for concepts of the good society, unless these concepts are permanently vulnerable to the interpreted experience of the social and behavioral sciences, they may lead down the road to dystopia.

In a paraphrase of a minor poet's "Oh World, I cannot hold thee close enough," Hannah Arendt (1958) complains that the "world alienation" of our time arose when Galileo employed instrumentation, the telescope, to observe the cosmos and to report what our unaided sense could not see. For some, the instrumentation of the social sciences, coming between what we can know of our own human experience and what is "out there," is a source of distress. In the laboratory, the survey, and the group experiment, in psychometrics, econometrics, and biometrics, we have complex instrumentation and data analyses which do, indeed, distance the world from the observer. Commenting on what was later to be called "phenomenology," the first great experimental psychologist, Wilhelm Wundt (1874/1904), once suggested that science required that the observer and the thing observed should be separated; instrumentation of these kinds does indeed perform this separation. We do not lose *verstehen* in this process, for that may be reintroduced at any time, and we gain Piaget's *decentration*, the transcendence of the self as the sole source of knowledge; we gain the standardization of observation across persons and situations, making them more comparable, some protection against seeing only what we want to see, and perception of small differences which cumulatively are more than statistically significant. We can uncover commonalities not apparent to the naked eye, uncouple cause and symptom, discover the conditions under which *A* implies *B*, and gain invaluable training in looking for multiple causation and explaining only part of the variance—a training not in the arrogance of science but in humility in the face of contingent and only partial explanation. To bring the world closer to the heart's desire, we must distance it from the heart for a while—but only for a while.

Just as political philosophers can be considered inadequate social scientists, so it may be that social scientists can be considered inadequate political philosophers, but neither inadequacy is necessary. The line between the two is not to be drawn along the familiar "is" and "ought" lines, nor are they separated by the catchwords "fact" and "value." A fact is a theory, or at least an observation in the light of a theory, and it is a rare political theory that is not in some measure evaluative. Observers are secret philosophers. A value is a concept of the desired, and it is also a concept of the desirable—that which ought to be desired. But a thing ought or ought not to be desired in the light of its consequences, and assessing consequences often implies attributions of causal sequences which are less accessible to philosophy than to science. And philosophers are secret social scientists. The world "implication" leads in both directions: defining a good in a given way *implies* that certain other things are to be called good; philosophy will tell us about that. Thus, by some principle of fairness, civic obligation entails certain duties, perhaps participation in civic life in a certain way entailing certain costs. But engaging in the behavior called good by the philosophers *implies* both the personality constellation which prompted it and the social circumstances which facilitated that behavior, together with the social consequences which follow from it. Freud, equity theory and research, and exchange theory all tell us something about the psychological properties of the person under a strong sense of obligation. An overwhelming sense of obligation risks mental illness (Freud); obligations which cannot easily be discharged often lead to derogation of the source of the obligation (Walster, Berscheid, & Walster, 1973) or to deference and loss of self-esteem (Blau, 1964, pp. 106–111). Similarly, participation is facilitated by a social order which provides each individual with the experience of coupling his actions with anticipated and rewarding outcomes. It is affected by stratification and the "culture of poverty." As mentioned above, its consequences depend on the machinery devised to channel and express the various popular wills. Civic obligation, like other philosophical concepts, is at the juncture of philosophy and social science. It may be that behavioral scientists are only occasionally good philosophers, but they might consider that part of their mission is what Wittgenstein (in Ayer, 1959, p. 23) once said is the business of philosophy: to protect us against the "bewitchment of our intelligence by means of language."

It is straining the term to burden "consciousness" with all these requirements, but it is no strain to see that social science in general, and the behavioral sciences in particular, contribute to societal self-consciousness in a rich variety of ways. We understand their caution as a consequence not so much of modesty, perhaps not even failure of imagination; it is in part due to an aversion to self-inflicted pain.

Man, Society, and Politics

The *Handbook of Political Behavior* takes another important step in restoring man and society to the study of politics. "The nature of political things," to use Leo Strauss's (1959, p. 12) term, is not to be understood by limited reference to governments and politics or to constitutions and institutions, nor yet by deeper inquiry into the good life and the good society, although these matters are surely relevant. Rather, political things can only be understood by grounding that understanding in the analysis of human personality and psychological processes, on the one hand, and the social structure and culture, on the other. As one turns the axis of observation, at a given moment politics will be seen as the response in the familiar S-O-R paradigm: the sociocultural stimuli, working through the dispositions of the relevant organisms or personalities, produces the political responses. Another turn, of course, and politics will be part of the stimuli, with policy as the response, or, coming closer to the subject, with the patterned experiences of life as the response. Unless one is a lawyer or an economist, however one approaches the subject of politics, one will find complex personalities acting in complex situations for which society is the container. This *Handbook* has the virtue of recognizing that fact.

The study of political behavior along these lines does not organize itself; some intellectual constructs for the ordering of phenomena are required. Three simple formulas come to mind: the stimulus–organism–response formula already mentioned, systems theory, and maximization theory. Each serves different disciplines and different purposes. The S-O-R formula is best conceived as a reminder of the theme of this book: it is man in society that determines political behavior, but the formula also serves to organize the study of microprocesses, adaptation, learning, and voting. In an exposition of the art of asking why, Lazarsfeld (1935) once reminded us that we must keep separate lists of social factors and individual factors;

they must not be confounded but rather must be systematically and separately related to each other. The early behaviorists, seeking to exorcise the homunculus in psychology, contracted the formula to two terms, "S" and "R"; it is ironic that the term "behaviorism" should now serve political scientists to reintroduce, if not homunculus, at least his representative, "O," and the richly varied human being for which the "O" stands, into the maze of laws and institutions which governed the field not so long ago. With the rise of cognitive psychology, this middle term has flourished, some treatments offering eight rubrics to organize these middle-term processes. For those who like rubrics, these are: exposure, perception, comprehension, agreement or acceptance, retention, retrieval, decision making, and finally, action. These rubrics represent an information-processing approach containing "the gist of the cognitive psychology that has replaced the S-R reinforcement theory (or behaviorism) as the dominant Establishment view" (McGuire, 1977, p. 337).

For the larger purposes of understanding man in society, this more sophisticated S-O-R formula represents a contribution to the "subassemblies" of the "architecture of complexity" (Simon, 1965). But it is lineal, not reflexive. Brewster Smith (1968) once drew a map of a sociopsychological system accounting for political behavior: it included such distal structures and forces as social stratification, the structures and processes shaping the learning of the relevant individuals, their learned dispositions affecting their responses, and the immediate presenting situation in which they were required to act; and the nature of their final actions were themselves sources of change for the distal structures which altered the next round of learning and decision. Increasingly, each outcome of administrative behavior, legislative behavior, electoral behavior and other behaviors treated in this *Handbook* are seen in these reflexive terms—behavior has consequences which affect behavior. Where the study of specified psychological processes has found the S-O-R formula useful, the study of society and the study of whole personalities has found some variant of systems theory more fruitful.

Within the framework of another subassembly, the economic system, market economists have benefited from the principle of maximization, as have utilitarians more generally, including sociologists who see human intercourse as a process of hedonic exchange (Homans, 1961). Facilitated by principles of maximization and optimization (but not "satisficing"), economists have been uniquely successful in enlisting logic; what they yield in realistic description they gain in the theoretical rigor which logic permits. Great wars are fought over this terrain; economic anthropologists divide between formalists (maximizing principles are useful) and substantivists (only a tactile approach to the complex system will do). Now behavioral economics (Becker, 1976) trespasses on ground thought safe for sociologists and psychologists, just as these disciplines have trod on the sacred grounds of psychoanalysis, which in turn intruded on moral philosophy.

The influence of Freud, Lewin, Piaget, and Skinner is easily traced in the chapters of this *Handbook*, and for particular purposes, Erikson, Kohlberg, Maslow, Robert White, McClelland, and more discreetly, Heider, Allport, and that polymath, Herbert Simon. These all suggest models of man: man as a cognitive, information-processing decision maker; man as a motivated, reinforcement-seeking bundle of learning experiences; man in search of himself; man seeking above all to control his own environment; conflicted man; lustful man; man as a moral agent; man guided by the need for optimal arousal; man as persuasible and plastic or purposeful and autonomous; man seeking to fulfill himself, seeking to reassure himself, seeking to lose himself in groups. But do we need a model of man? Could we not make do with such models of processes as the psychologists currently offer?

What is the model of man in medicine? Is it not the case that medicine understands humans as systems of interrelated processes with homeostatic regulators designed to maintain the various processes in working order and so to keep the ensemble functioning? It understands disease as disruptions of these processes impeding the functioning of the various subsystems. In the same way, but with one consideration, might it not be possible to think of human behavior as the product of a set of interrelated processes, regulated not by homeostasis but by a regnant center concerned with self-esteem and pursuing gratification? Perhaps the idea of a model of man derives from an earlier philosophical discourse characterized by the question, "What is Man?" Speaking of science, Victor Weisskopf (1975, pp. 15–16) said that

> about five hundred years ago human curiosity took a different turn: instead of reaching for the whole truth, people began to examine definable and clearly separable phenomena. They asked not what is matter but how does a piece of matter fall or how does water flow in a tube; not what is life but how does blood flow in the blood vessels; not how was the world created but how do the planets move in the sky.

In time, the "renunciation" was rewarded by insights into the larger, partly philosophical, questions, and they could return to the question of what is matter. "By means of this [earlier] detailed questioning, man has created a framework for understanding the natural world, a scientific world view." Not 500, but less than 100 years ago, psychology began this detailed questioning. How do people perceive objects? What makes people remember some things but not others? How are attitudes formed? How is information processed? By this route might we not hope to do as well as medical science, seeking to understand and use what we know about processes rather than comprehending models of wholes? There is much in this *Handbook* that will further such inquiries and apply them to political behavior.

I mentioned a cautionary exception above; it is an important one. The purpose of medicine is not to make better people but to cure illness; the purpose of politics and other social processes might be defined as facilitating human development. There is no other purpose quite so important. True, we can learn to improve cognition, coping, ease of social interaction, self-knowledge, and self-respect, and if public policy does not do these things, however indirectly, it is misdirected. But, as with environmental policy, because of side effects one must know something of the way processes affect each other—the ecological system, the personality system. As the ecologists say, "you can't do just one thing." Without waiting 500 years, prematurely and therefore tentatively, we must work with models of man in models of society. Thus, departing from the linear S-R formula, Bandura (1974) derived "Behavior Theory and the Models of Man"; from his own variant of cognitive theory, Herbert Simon (1957) developed *Models of Man: Social and Rational*; and Jerome Bruner (1976), changing the term, developed "Psychology and the Image of Man."

Models of society, explicit in many of the treatments in this volume, often reveal traces of their metaphoric past: the family (gemeinschaft), the organism (Leviathan), the machine (Mumford), the anthill (mass society), the army (garrison state), the factory (St. Simon), the market (gesellschaft, Homans's and Blau's exchange societies). More antiseptically, their ingredients are primarily roles, institutions, strata (including classes), parties, communities, and groups (including "primordial" ethnic, familial, and communal groups) engaged in such functions as adjudication and resolution of conflict, technology, defense, production and distribution, socialization, and preservation of social and sacred myths. These structural units are coordinated by custom, command, and exchange; they are endowed with and justified by ideologies invoking tradition, the sacred, reason, and ultimate values which need no other justification. Like all systems, they process inputs to create outputs; they adapt well or badly by means of internal and external adaptive mechanisms. The social environments they create stimulate, channel, and sanction the psychological processes we have described. They are teachers of behavior. It is hard to imagine an adequate political explanation which does not understand and employ at least some of these elements of social structure. But yielding to the temptation to rely on any one of them, say class conflict or social exchange, creates a lopsided explanation quite out of keeping with the usual multivariate analysis.

Social structural explanations are favored by two current streams of thought, the psychological situationists and, of course, the sociological and anthropological structuralists. No one doubts that roles and institutions affect behavior and belief, sometimes quite dramatically. Breer and Locke (1965) have shown that subjects engaged briefly in tasks requiring cooperation develop ideologies of cooperation extending to international affairs while subjects engaged in competitive tasks see the world as competitive. More generally, Mischel (1973) and others find that, almost across the board, the stimulus situations mop up more variance than do the dispositions of those who enter the laboratory. Yet since different persons respond differently to similar situations, others (see Blass, 1977; Greenstein, 1975) can show that in other situations the dispositions (personalities) of the participants account for behavior quite as much as do the situations. Obviously, the explanations lie in the interaction; the term "experience" captures both the situation and the person, but "behavior" does almost as well.

Beneath the surface phenomena of bewildering complexity, there lies a comprehensible guiding structure, similar in form if not in content in most, and perhaps in all societies. That is the lesson of Lévi-Strauss (1963). He finds it most explicit in language, but it can be seen in all forms of communication, which includes the exchange of wives as well as words. The particularities of the Lévi-Straussian (e.g., 1963, pp. 83–96) approach are peculiar; the postulated structure requires the definition of oppositional pairs (e.g., endogenous/exogenous, central/peripheral, marked/not marked, maximal transformation/minimal transformation) which may be useful for some inquiries but not for others. One chooses the features of social structure which promise to account for the surface phenomena which are of concern to the inquiring scholar. Marxist structuralism is more familiar: beneath the superstructure of culture lie the imperatives of the modes of production, the way men earn a living; beneath the "legitimacy" of family relations, property, and religion lie the advantages these institutions yield to the ruling class; within the necessary processes of capitalism there are immanent forces which will bring its downfall. For Marx (as for Freud), nothing is what it seems to be on the surface; if one knows the laws of history, then and only then will the surface phenomena reveal their "true meaning."

Does the behavioral approach skim over the surface of phenomena, treating proximate relationships without examining the social structures which "require" these relationships to be as they are? It runs that risk. Judicial behavior, legislative behavior, and electoral behavior may well vary according to the nature of a society's stratification, its degrees of affluence and scarcity, the rationalization of its bureaucracies and other institutions, the individualism of its culture, and its emphasis on agricultural, industrial, and postindustrial modes of production. If it were the case that there is a structural requiredness (determinism) about political behavior, we would see little variation across situations where the relevant structures were similar and much variation where they were different. In analyzing welfare policies, Dye (1966), Hofferbert (1966), and others have shown that the structuralists may be right in some important particulars: levels of affluence affect welfare policies in the American states quite as much as do the more explicitly political variables. Cross-culturally, pastoral communities, as compared to agricultural communities, are more emotional and expressive, have more concern for the social unit, and more respect for authority (Goldschmidt, 1974); hunters are more "field independent" than agriculturalists (Witkin, 1962); the size and affluence of a nation affect the distribution of wealth more than does its political regime (Cutright, 1963; Jackman, 1974; Sawyer, 1967). On the other hand, conservative political regimes protect the middle classes against inflation more than do social democratic or liberal regimes, while the latter protect their constituencies against unemployment more than do conservatives (Hibbs, 1977). Within a sample of American states, the individual ideologies of legislators makes a substantial difference in the policies they support, quite independently of the structural characteristics of their constituencies (Entman, 1977). Among administrators, location in the State Department, the War College, and the Office of Management and Budget affects their foreign policies, but the personality dispositions of the individuals make equally important contributions to an accounting of the policies they support (Etheredge, 1978). The structuralists win some of the honors, but by no means all of them. The proximate variables of electoral success, the varying beliefs of legislators, and the personality differences of administrators also explain political behavior.

The analogical character of the models of society mentioned earlier (gemeinschaft/gesellschaft, mass society, mechanical/organic) invite decomposition into sets of dimensions which may be scored and recombined to give greater flexibility. It is useful to divide these dimensions into subjective characteristics, those things which are part of the mental structures of the members of the society, and objective characteristics, those things which are not. The objective dimensions would include degree of institutionalization, division of labor, communication density and facilities, urbanism, modes of production, levels of technology, levels of literacy, and levels and distribution of affluence. Of course, these greatly affect mental processes and beliefs, but they are not themselves of that character.

The subjective dimensions, what Triandis (1972) calls "subjective culture," represent the norms, attitudes, and values of a society and form the social ingredients which structuralists have most often explored. Parsons (Parsons & Shils, 1951/1962) addressed himself to this question of dimensionality, giving, in effect, five dimensions to the gemeinschaft/gesellschaft typology: ascription/achievement, universalism/particularism, affectivity/affective neutrality, role specificity/role diffusion, and individualism/collectivism. Kluckhohn and Strodtbeck (1961) offer a pentad of value orientations with equal claim to universal relevance and explanatory power: the good/bad, plastic/fixed nature of man; the source of authority (lineal, collegial, individual); the time focus of the society; the relations of man to nature (subordinate, coordinate, superordinate); and the modality of striving (doing, becoming, being). Other dimensions come to mind: degree of consciousness or societal self-examination, mentioned earlier; cognitive styles (egocentric vs. sociocentric, field dependent vs. field independent) (Witkin, 1962); principles of justice (equity, parity, need) and sources of obligation (e.g., shame and guilt cultures); whether exchange is contractual or more loosely governed by the norm of reciprocity; and knowledge bases in science, magic, religion, or tradition.

Such selective inventories of the dimensions of culture and social structure do not give us an agenda for a structural approach to political behavior, but they should save us from excessive reliance on any particular list that may claim the imagination of a generation of scholars. The search for prime movers, for some irreducible dimension or ingredient, or for some single principle which, if only we grasped its essence, would permit us to account for behavior of all kinds will, no doubt, continue, but increasingly, it seems to me, some more modest systems theoretical approach, perhaps closer to ecology than to physics, with each element more or less contingent on other elements, offers greater promise. But that, too, is only an analogy. If we are to approach each nation, each policy, each practice, and also each theory about nations and policies and behavior as experiments from which we learn limited things to guide us in the next experiment, we will be on the right track. But of course we will be guided most profoundly by purpose: What would we like to find out? What would we like to see done?

The study of political behavior as a study of man in his social contexts is a contribution to that enterprise. By reporting, analyzing, and explaining the varieties of political behavior, and by relating these to their psychological and sociological parent disciplines, such a study tells us something about the human experiments that interest us. "If politics makes use of the other sciences, and also lays down what we should do and from what we should refrain, its end must include theirs; and this end must be the good for man" (Aristotle, 1976, p. 64). This *Handbook* does not tell us what we should do, but that question is better answered when we know something of what we do do, the immediate and long-term consequences of these doings, and their proximate and structural causes.

Robert E. Lane

Department of Political Science
Yale University
New Haven, Connecticut

References

Arendt, H. *The human condition*. Chicago: University of Chicago Press, 1958.

Aristotle. [*The nichomachean ethics*] (J. A. K. Thomson, trans.). Harmondsworth: Penguin, 1976.

Ayer, A. J. (Ed.). *Logical positivism*. Glencoe, Ill.: Free Press, 1959.

Bandura, A. Behavior theory and the models of man. *American Psychologist*, 1974, *29*, 859–869.

Battro, A. M. *Piaget: Dictionary of terms* (E. E. Rutschi-Herrmann & S. F. Campbell, Eds. and trans.). New York: Pergamon, 1973.

Becker, G. S. *The economic approach to human behavior*. Chicago: University of Chicago Press, 1976.

Blass, T. (Ed.). *Personality variables in social behavior*. New York: Halsted/Wiley, 1977.

Blau, P. M. *Exchange and power in social life*. New York: Wiley, 1964.

Breer, P. E., & Locke, E. A. *Task experience as a source of attitudes*. Homewood, Ill.: Dorsey, 1965.

Bruner, J. Psychology and the image of man. *Times Literary Supplement*, December 17, 1976.

Cassirer, E. *An essay on man*. New Haven: Yale University Press, 1944.

Coopersmith, S. *The antecedents of self-esteem*. San Francisco: Freeman, 1967.

Cutright, P. National Political Development: Measurement and analysis. *American Sociological Review*, 1963, *28*, 253–264.

Dye, T. R. *Politics, economics and the public: Policy outcomes in the American states*. Chicago: Rand McNally, 1966.

Ellul, J. [*The technological society*] (J. Wilkinson, trans.). London: Jonathan Cape, 1965. (Originally published, 1954.)

Entman, R. M. *The psychology of legislative behavior: Ideology, personality, power and policy*. Unpublished doctoral dissertation, Yale University, 1977.

Etheredge, L. S. *A world of men: The private sources of American foreign policy*. Cambridge, Mass.: M.I.T. Press, 1978.

Goldschmidt, W. Ethology, ecology, and ethnological realities. In G. V. Coelho, D. A. Hamburg, & J. E. Adams (Eds.), *Coping and adaptation*. New York: Basic Books, 1974.

Greenstein, F. I. *Personality and politics*. New York: Norton, 1975.

Hibbs, D., Jr. Political parties and macroeconomic policy. *American Political Science Review*, 1977, *71*, 1467–1487.

Hofferbert, R. I. Ecological development and policy change. *Midwest Journal of Political Science*, 1966, *10*. (Reprinted in I. Sharkansky [Ed.], *Policy analysis in political science*. Chicago: Markham, 1970.)

Homans, G. *Social behavior: Its elementary forms*. New York: Harcourt, Brace, & World, 1961.

Jackman, R. W. Political democracy and social equality: A comparative analysis. *American Sociological Review*, 1974, *39*, 29–45.

Key, V. O., Jr. *Politics, parties & pressure groups* (5th ed.). New York: Crowell, 1964.

Kluckhohn, F. R., & Strodtbeck, F. L. *Variations in value orientations*. Evanston, Ill.: Row, Peterson, 1961.

Lazarsfeld, P. F. The art of asking why. *National Marketing Review*, 1935, *1*, 26–38.

Lévi-Strauss, C. [*Structural anthropology*] (C. Jacobson & B. G. Schoepf, trans.). New York: Basic Books, 1963.

McGuire, W. J. Psychological factors influencing consumer choice. In R. Farber (Ed.), *Selected aspects of consumer behavior*. Washington, D.C.: Government Printing Office (National Science Foundation), 1977.

Mills, C. W. *The sociological imagination*. New York: Oxford University Press, 1959.

Mischel, W. Toward a cognitive social learning reconceptualization of personality. *Psychological Review*, 1973, *80*, 252–283.

Olson, M., Jr. *The logic of collective action*. New York: Schocken, 1969.

Parsons, T., & Shils, E. A. (Eds.). *Toward a general theory of action*. New York: Harper Torchbooks, 1962. (Originally published, 1951.)

Piaget, J. [*The moral judgment of the child*] (M. Gabain, trans.). New York: Free Press, 1965. (Originally published, 1932.)

Piaget, J. *The psychology of intelligence* (M. Piercy & D. E. Berlyne, trans.). Totowa, N.J.: Littlefield, Adams, 1960. (Originally published, 1947.)

Piaget, J., & Inhelder, B. [*The psychology of the child*] (H. Weaver, trans.). New York: Basic Books, 1968. (Originally published, 1966.)

Sawyer, J. Dimensions of nations: Size, wealth, and politics. *American Journal of Sociology*, 1967, *73*, 145–172.

Simon, H. *Models of man: Social and rational.* New York: Wiley, 1957.

Simon, H. The architecture of complexity. In L. von Bertalanffy & A. Rapoport (Eds.), *General systems* (Vol. 10). Ann Arbor, Mich.: Society for General Systems Research, 1965.

Smith, M. B. A map for the analysis of personality and politics. *Journal of Social Issues*, 1968, *24*, 15–28.

Strauss, L. *What is political philosophy?* Glenco, Ill.: Free Press, 1959.

Triandis, H. C. *The analysis of subjective culture.* New York: Wiley, 1972.

Walster, E., Berscheid, E., & Walster, G. W. New directions in equity research. *Journal of Personality and Social Psychology*, 1973, *25*, 151–176.

Weisskopf, V. F. The frontiers of science. *Bulletin of the American Academy of Arts and Sciences*, 1975, *28*, 15–18.

Wicklund, R. A. Objective self-awareness. In L. Berkowitz (Ed.), *Advances in experimental social psychology* (Vol. 8). New York: Academic Press, 1975.

Witkin, H. A. *Psychological differentiation.* New York: Wiley, 1962.

Wundt, W. [*Principles of physiological psychology*] (E. B. Titchner, trans.) (5th ed.). New York: Macmillan, 1904. (Originally published, 1874.)

Zajonc, R. B. Attitudinal effects of mere exposure. *Journal of Personality and social psychology*, 1968, *9*, 1–27. (Monograph Supplement).

1

SMALL GROUPS IN POLITICAL SCIENCE
Perspectives on Significance and Stuckness

ROBERT T. GOLEMBIEWSKI AND GERALD J. MILLER

Introduction

This chapter reflects a four-fold approach to the study of small groups as being significant as well as stuck. In turn, our attention will focus on three dimensions of the significance of the study of small groups; some basic orientations in the literature; a number of major dimensions that seem, at a minimum, required for differentiating small groups; and a few brief cases to show how small groups can be useful in comprehending the diverse subject matters of political science, whether the group phenomena merely emerge or are the result of planning and deliberate induction.

The fourth emphasis establishes that very real boundaries must constrain the up-beat quality of the preceding three perspectives. This emphasis provides an overview of how and why stuckness today complements the significance of the study of small groups. To a degree, this overview also sketches what will be necessary to transcend today's stuckness.

This may be an especially propitious time to draw attention to the significance and stuckness of the study of small groups, since, in fact, a recovery may be succeeding a fast fall from grace. Specifically, small-group analysis remained the hottest research area in several disciplines for a decade or more leading into the 1960s (Zander, 1979). But by middecade, the prestigious *Annual Review of Psychology* (Gerard & Miller, 1967) reported a definite downturn—not only had research energy diminished, but its tone

ROBERT T. GOLEMBIEWSKI • Department of Political Science, University of Georgia, Athens, Georgia 30601. **GERALD J. MILLER** • Department of Political Science, University of Kansas, Lawrence, Kansas 66045.

had become repetitious, its focus had narrowed (as in the emphasis on risky-shift or prisoner's dilemma studies), and its conclusions emphasized the familiar. Moreover, much of the remaining energy and excitement had been redirected to applied areas, especially those dealing with the use of groups to stimulate individual learning and organization change (Golembiewski & Blumberg, 1970, 1973, 1977).

What evidence suggests that this trend has recently been reversed? Several new small-group texts have appeared (Berkowitz, 1978; Hare, 1976; Raven & Rubin, 1976; Shaw, 1976; Wilson, 1978; Zander, 1977); the first flurry since the 1950s and 1960s; entire issues of two major journals have focused recently on small groups (Dies, 1978; Lakin, 1979); and a retrospective look at the impact of the small group on traditional concerns in political science also became available (Golembiewski, 1978).

Numerous other indications suggest a renewal of group-oriented work in the laboratory as well as in natural settings. "Interest in actual social interaction is increasing," conclude Davis, Laughlin, and Komorita (1976, p. 525). Why does this seem to be happening? We can only give voice to some prominent speculation. Steiner (1974), for example, gained notoriety in social psychology for arguing that interest in groups asserts itself during periods of economic turbulence only to recede during good times, with intervals of perhaps a decade between cycles. Similarly, three other social psychologists explain that today's growing interest in groups establishes that their colleagues "are responsive to the needs of . . . our times . . . the three E's—energy, economy, and environment—in a world of suddenly limited resources relative to increased population. This renews research interest in the collective behavior of individuals and fundamental questions about the individual's relationship to the collective" (J. H. Davis et al., 1976, pp. 524–525).

Four Basic Small-Group Orientations: Tracing the Literature's Major Themes

How far has small-group analysis progressed? Or, to put the query another way, where has it become stuck? The first step to puzzling through a workable answer to these questions involves an introduction to four orientations to suprapersonal phenomena. The focus below will be on facilitation, attraction, comparison, and control as perspectives on group life. This utilizes Smith's (1973) and Raven and Rubin's (1976) convenient and useful approaches.

Although the organization here must perforce be linear, two relational features deserve emphasis. First, the four themes should not be thought of as exclusive categories. Rather they shade and blend into one another in complex patterns. Second, the four themes should be thought of as the warp for the woof of numerous areas of application as broad as all social life. When convenient, the relevance of the four themes to political science phenomena will be sketched.

What motivates this approach, and what hopefully will come to motivate the reader? The normal considerations apply—to sketch basic orientations to viewing small-group phenomena, to introduce some of the literature, and to convey a flavor of how problems in the area are discovered, to be dealt with or neglected. Other considerations also apply, with even greater force. The dominant motive behind this approach, in fact, is the search for a definition-by-convergence of "small group." The more convenient approach would be divergent, focusing on some nominal definition of "small group" such as: a collection of individuals in more or less interdependent status and role relations, who can and do meet face-to-face and have a set of indigenous values or norms which regulate member behavior. This latter approach would be convenient, but it is false to reality in at least two senses. First, much of the literature deals with kaleidoscopic but imprecisely specified "social situations" and involves collectivities that range from momentary experimental encounters to long-lived groups in desperate straits. Second, the convenient approach also fails to capture the sense of the complex mappings from diverse perspectives that imply why and how the conceptual entity "small group" became the focus of so much attention—often diffuse attention, but attention that nonetheless converges and circumscribes an area of analytic significance.

In sum, "small group" represents a complex something to be worked toward, at this stage of analysis, not some definite reification to work from. In effect, the four perspectives immediately below quadrangulate that something.

Social Facilitation or Inhibition: Better or Worse Performance in Groups?

An early recognition of the effects of others focused on performance. This fixes a key issue, which has numerous practical and theoretical relevancies. Practically, differences in performance have a stereophonic relevance to much of life and represent a topic of relevance to many hosts or sponsors of research. Theoretically, effects on performance imply that some acting supraindividual "it" exists. Let us call a stimulating effect *social facilitation* and its opposite *social inhibition*.

Research Lessons Implicit in Early Research. Does the presence of others facilitate or inhibit performance? In ways characteristic of the natural-science approach, this key question proves both too much and too little for available research. How and why this occurred can be instructive to latter-day investigators of the small group, including political scientists.

The focus here will be historical and very selective, but conveniently available sources provide up-to-date detail and counterpoint (e.g., J. H. Davis *et al.*, 1976, esp. pp. 507–509).

Early research implied that the presence of others generated social facilitation. Triplett (1898) first drew attention to the general problem, as a spin-off of his observation that bicycle riders race faster against other riders than against a watch. Similarly, Triplett found in laboratory settings that children wound fishing reels faster when competing against another person than when working alone after being told to wind the reels as fast as they could.

Triplett's positive results attracted attention, as often happens, but typically, the literature soon also reflected contrary results. For example, F. H. Allport (1920) refined Triplett's experimental probe in two specific ways: he sought to minimize the effects of competition, as distinct from increments and decrements of performance attributed to coacting with others, and he provided subjects with a broad range of tasks to test the generalizability of the effects of others on performance. Allport at once confirmed and extended Triplett's findings. On some tasks (e.g., multiplication and word association) the presence of others facilitated performance; but on other tasks (e.g., disproving the arguments of ancient philosophers) quality diminished and performance was inhibited under the same condition.

In sum, Allport's research had one foot comfortably planted in Triplett's original work while the other dangled in unexplored and intimidating space. As later analysis will show, Allport's effects can be explained only by transcending the simple dichotomy of social facilitation or social inhibition. But let us be content here with the more modest extensions which Allport's results required. Clearly, and credibly, differences in *what* is being done seemed significant. So a taxonomy of tasks should become an item on an agenda of necessary research. In addition, it seems reasonable that *who* is present may be important. Hence, personality characteristics seem relevant in understanding the results of such research. And finally, but finally only on this very short list, *how* those present are related will be critical. Allport recognized this point by employing instructions to discourage competition, thereby seeking to isolate the effects of the simple presence of others from other modes of relationships. Far more broadly, even this early work implied that the only alternative to numerous deviant cases was a taxonomy of groupings and their properties.

Small-group analysis has accorded some attention to such desirables, but, in fact, their neglect buoyed the early interest in small-group analysis. In short, if early investigators really acknowledged the major difficulties involved, especially in laboratory experimentation with small groups, they might well not have even started preliminary work.

So the specification of conditions such as those sketched above never came easily, because of both their complexity and the comfort of simpler postures. Consider here only two task descriptors—collaborative effort on structured and unstructured tasks—that relate to facilitative effects of small groups. Structured tasks refer to those tasks whose successful completion can be verified independently, as in the case of a mathematical operation. Oppositely, performance of unstructured tasks often defies classification as correct or incorrect, at least immediately (e.g., Alcock & Mansell, 1977). Unstructured tasks might include corporate plans developed by top management groups, plans whose effects might not be known for years.

The relevant literature does not permit confident interpretation of the effects on performance deriving from differences in tasks. Although more clarity now exists about useful ways to distinguish tasks (e.g., Steiner, 1972), significant questions still abound. Consistent with Triplett's finding, Olson and Davis (1964) used structured arithmetic problems and found groups superior to individuals or to the pooled scores of individuals, a pseudo-group. But consider brainstorming, which is a technique development for working on unstructured tasks. Taylor, Berry, and Block (1958) found that brainstorming groups produced not only more ideas than individuals but also ideas of better quality and uniqueness. On its face, this would seem to deny the impact of task differences on performance in the presence of others. However, pseudogroups formed by pooling individual scores proved superior to both groups and lone individuals. Why? The question defies answer, at least within the context of social facilitation. Smith (1973) argues that the presence of others inhibited rather than facilitated creativity because of the character of the task. Others argue that the brainstorming groups provided integrated sets of ideas, performing an additional function beyond idea generation. Members unified their lists, possibly eliminating incompatible or irrelevant ideas. Thus, the group was more productive than the pseudogroup of pooled scores, some conclude (e.g., Collins & Geutzkow, 1964).

Risky Shift as a Multiple Finesse. The implied lessons for small-group analysis in this early experience with social facilitation did not go down easily, for reasons about which we can only speculate later. Perhaps relatedly, after a decade of intense concern with small-group properties based more or less on the model of the early research on social facilitation, tastes began to change in the 1960s.

We focus here on the risky-shift or choice-shift literature, one of those new research tastes all of which shared some major commonalities. Basically, they all involved explicit or implicit finesses of the research difficulties encountered in early analyses. The focus became individualistic rather than group centered—individual reactions to social situations rather than individuals in group membership roles got the lion's share of attention. Moreover, a few apparently simple tasks (the risky shift, prisoner's dilemma, and so on) with seemingly consistent effects provided the major stimuli. In the long run, such work also more or less duplicated the learning implicit in the early work on social facilitation: analysis of tasks was still critical; personality differences proved relevant even in short-lived groupings; and "social situations" had to be differentiated. Without such lines of sophisticated work, a distribution of findings and many unexplained deviant cases will remain.

Let us be somewhat more specific. The voluminous literature on the risky-shift phenomenon (J. H. Davis *et al.*, 1976; Dion, Baron, & Miller, 1970) at once recognizes the unresolved problems of focusing on performance in groups and succumbs to many of them. The risky-shift literature includes hundreds of studies, a number of them by political scientists (Kirkpatrick, Davis, & Robertson, 1976; Main & Walker, 1973; McWhirter, 1978; Semmel & Minix, 1978; T. G. Walker & Main, 1973). Not only is the stimulant a simple and generally reproducible one, but choice shift focuses on some key phenomena in social life. What happens to the choice processes of individuals exposed to groups such as committees, juries, and so on? The risky shift also no doubt attracted interest because, in sharp opposition to the usual view (e.g., Janis, 1972), its early formulations proposed that individuals do *not* become conservative in group contexts, that they do *not* somehow lose the qualities of self-determination and independence often associated with the ideal individual in much Western social commentary.

A few details will help here. According to Stoner's original experiments (1961), group decisions are significantly more risky than the average of individual decisions; members, it seems, risk more as a group. Most experiments take a similar path to explore that phenomenon. Individuals complete a questionnaire (Kogan & Wallach, 1964), which consists of 12 real-life situations for each of which individuals can opt for a safe decision or take a greater chance in the hopes of gaining a larger reward. Individuals first respond to the form and then meet in small groups to arrive at a consensus. After-choices tend to be riskier than before-choices.

The focus on the individual in social situations attracted much attention, via risky-shift experiments and the even more popular prisoner's dilemma variations, and over the longer run led to familiar conclusions. Thus, five emergent factors urge only tentative acceptance of the risky-shift hypothesis: experiments usually use *ad hoc*, leaderless groups, rather than established ones; the magnitude of the risky shift is usually small; not all subjects show the effect; the questionnaire usually used seems to encourage risk more often than caution; and, significantly, a conservative shift tends to occur on several items (Nordhoy, 1962), reflecting an effect that has been replicated many times but which is not understood. Relatedly, research with the prisoner's dilemma also highlights the fact that consistent results would depend on a complex interactive specificity about differences between individuals (e.g., Lindskold, McElwain, & Wayner, 1977), task properties (e.g., Bonacich, Shure, Kahan, & Meeker, 1976), and group characteristics (e.g., Hamburger, Guyer, & Fox, 1975).

In effect, a narrowing of focus from groups and performances to individual response to social situations does not avoid the older Triplett/Allport problems, as some investigators acknowledge (Kogan & Wallach, 1967). Indeed, in important senses, the risky shift compounds them. Note but one point. Some researchers (e.g., Kogan & Wallach, 1967) argue that the risky shift represents responsibility diffusion. That is, an individual entering a group opens self to influence and begins to share responsibility with others, thus diffusing the risk among several individuals. The influence process works toward both caution and risk in this explanation. But what can be made of the finding of Malamuth and Feshback (1972), verified by at least one other study (McWhirter, 1978), that the *expectation* of a group meeting can induce risky shift effects as marked as an actual meeting?

Social Attraction: How/Why Do I Love/Like You?

The research on facilitation has implications for many issues at the heart of social life. For example, if the mere expectation of the presence of others can affect performance significantly in brief periods, that suggests person-to-person attraction/repulsion constitutes a powerful force easily and quickly activated. And that, in turn, implies the even greater potency of "close affective relationships," which encompass at least three dimensions (Huston & Levinger, 1978, p. 115): favorable attitude toward another, behavioral involvement, and joint belongingness.

Hence "social attraction" reasonably came to be a robust arena for inquiry, "a crossroads for travel" by students with a diverse range of interests in phenomena involving at least a favorable attitude toward others (Huston & Levinger, 1978, p. 116). This minimal criterion encompasses quick impressions of others, actual encounters and contacts with them, and various degrees of relationships including friendships and marriages (Huston & Levinger, 1978, p. 116).

This important line of work has two basic implications for small-group analysis, one direct and the other indirect. Directly, the research suggests the incredible range of bonds that can tie individuals together, persons being viewed as affectively charged bundles variously affecting one another at multiple levels of meaning, in both brief encounters and extended relationships, in ways that at once bind together and differentiate people. The focus, then, is on heterogeneous vectors of attraction and repulsion, which constitute one of the vital sources of variance in social life. That should encourage small-group research. Indirectly, research on social attraction also implies the complexity and difficulty of researching social situations, even in "controlled" experimental conditions. Just as research more definitely established that numerous impactful vectors of attraction and repulsion operate even in brief encounters, so also have the practical and intellectual challenges facing small-group analysis burgeoned.

The trade-offs are difficult. Thus, some experimenters resort to "standard subjects," as via encounters of a single live subject with tape-recorded "others." This might limit interaction effects between subjects; but it also eliminates much that was vital in small-group analysis, as Borgotta (1954) and others sardonically note.

We will now provide some detail supporting these two significant implications of research on social attraction. Of the major sources of affectively charged reactions that individuals can have toward one another, covering the range from impressions to relationships, six factors seem especially central. They are reviewed here briefly, in no particular order of significance and with no pretense of exhaustiveness.

Physical Appearance. At once striking and banal is the mass of research that indicates how much the outward characteristics of people not only trigger affective responses but also influence choice processes. Thus, physical appearance influences not only how one feels about a potential marriage partner but also how children's transgressions should be treated (Dion, 1972) and even whether doctors in a county hospital emergency room will attempt to revive a patient "brought into the [hospital] with no registering heartbeat, respiration or pulse—the standard signs of death" (Sudnow, 1967). These examples do not represent loaded dice. Thus, Huston and Levinger conclude broadly that

> Good-looking individuals are given preferential treatment: they are seen as more responsible for good deeds . . . and less responsible for bad ones . . . their evaluations of others have more potent impact . . . their performances are upgraded . . . others are more socially responsive to them . . . more ready to provide them with help . . . more willing to work hard to please them. (Huston & Levinger, 1978, pp. 121–122)

Common Features and Mutual Identifications. Two classes of commonalities and mutualities stand out: identification with the same or a similar class or grouping (race, sex, religious affiliation, and so on) and a broad range of similar characteristics, beliefs, or attitudes.

That commonality and mutuality fuel social attraction can hardly be doubted, in general. Marriage partners tend to come from the same groups or classes (Blood & Wolfe, 1960; Schiller, 1932). Relatedly, when Laumann (1969) asked men to name their three best friends and describe them, respondents markedly tended to choose men similar to themselves in religion, race, political party, and socioeconomic status, as well as in education and age. Moreover, people tend to like others who agree with them. Newcomb (1943), for example, found that women who adopted the prevailing political and social attitudes of a college community were the most popular; and, consistently, opinional deviants tended to cluster. Similar findings have confirmed that similarities lead to attraction (e.g., Freedman & Doob, 1968; Schachter, 1951).

But the similarity-leads-to-liking hypothesis holds only in general. Huston and Levinger (1978, p. 126) urge "the importance of distinguishing among the various qualities and meanings of 'similarity' . . . We believe there is no singular 'similarity' effect, but a multiplicity of effects that depend on both content and context." Again, research establishes the complications of many variables being related to one another.

Common Threats and Shared Experiences. Common threats often provide powerful sources of attraction and repulsion, although a number of significant intervening variables seem appropriate even in those cases in which the relationship holds (Stein, 1976). Consider the work of researchers who investigated persons subjected to natural disasters (Raven & Rubin, 1976, pp. 124–125).

> Just after World War II, for example, some American visitors were shocked to hear Europeans say, in intimate moments, that they missed the war. This admission was usually followed by a significant qualification: "Well, I don't really miss it. It was a horrible time: fear, danger, death, hunger. But there was something there that we have not had since—a warm feeling for one another. We talked to each other during and after the raids. We helped one another. We cared for one another. This is something that I miss more than I can say."

Relatedly, the intense feelings that can arise from a common threat generate powerful exclusionary as well as in-group forces. Quarantelli and Dynes (1970) report that victims of serious disasters (such as floods, hurricanes, tornadoes, and earthquakes) tend to develop such strong in-group feelings that they sometimes resent the appearance of outside agencies such as government rescue teams. "It is their disaster, they seem to feel, and they dislike interference from outsiders who have not experienced their tragedy" (Raven & Rubin, 1976, p. 124).

A common threat can also override strong negative feelings and prejudices. In The Netherlands, a strong, individualistic, anticooperative tradition exists among the small shopkeepers, the butchers, greengrocers, bakers, and so on. Mulder and Stemerding (1963) induced a threat—that a supermarket chain was coming. This aroused high cohesiveness and mutual attraction among otherwise stand-offish shopkeepers.

Interpersonal Liking. As noted, people tend to like those who like them (e.g., Dickoff, 1961; Festinger, Schachter, & Back, 1950). The literature permits various fine tunings of this generalization, only one of which will be illustrated here. Specifically, Aronson and Linder (1965) experimented with the gain or loss of affection, using confederates or stooges of the experimenter. They found the pattern of variance more critical than consistency. The best liked confederate started by saying negative things about the subject, later becoming increasingly positive; the least-liked confederate was the one whose remarks were initially positive and then became increasingly negative (see Raven & Rubin, 1976).

Attraction as Exchange. Social relationships can be viewed as a social exchange centering around what must be surrendered and what can be achieved in a given relationship. Costs and benefits are weighed in a hoped-for relationship as well as past experiences.

Attraction as Familiarity. A growing body of research suggests that mere exposure to objects seem to increase their attractiveness, a conclusion that is assumed by advertisers, for example (see Raven & Rubin, 1976). Saegert, Swap, and Zajonc (1973) instructed female subjects to go into a number of booths, ostensibly to participate in a study of taste preferences. Each booth had a different test drink in it, and the subjects went from booth to booth in a prearranged order. The scheduling required two subjects to be in a booth tasting the same solution at a given time, but the number of times that each woman was in a booth with a specific other woman varied. Later, each subject completed a long questionnaire, including a question about how much she liked each of the other women who participated in the experiment. The results were quite clear—the greater the exposure, the greater the liking.

The results also seem generally stable, although everyone knows of cases in which greater familiarity bred heightened dislike or even contempt. In the experiment, for example, several alternative hypotheses were tested. Would subjects who tasted unpleasant, tart substances be as attracted to their pair as when the drink was pleasingly sweet? They were. Relatedly, field studies also indicate the significance of exposure. Festinger et al. (1950) found that within a residential community, people tend to like those with whom they have most contact, with that contact frequently depending on geographical location. Thus, a person whose apartment happens to be near the main stairway and entrance tends to have more friends in the building than the person who has a separate entrace to the street. In addition, an early study of desegregation in housing (Deutsch & Collins, 1951) indicated that racial prejudice can be reduced through such contact between whites and blacks. Note also that the effect seems to work at a mental and temporal distance. Recollection of past efforts often leads to increased attraction and so does anticipation of the future. If one knows that he or she will be working with someone for a considerable time, for example, that fact alone will tend to make the other person more attractive (Darley & Berscheid, 1967).

Attraction Impacts on Political Choice. These six brief summaries reflect powerful forces inherent in social situations, ranging from first impressions to lasting relationships, that can impact mightily on choice processes and behavior. The literature leaves no doubt about that general point, with a special emphasis on dating, mating, and separating.

Although seldom directly observed, such powerful forces reasonably should relate to political choices. And the popular wisdom certainly poses no major challenges to such a general view, as in the often reported association of family ties and electoral behavior, which is consistent with an attraction effect. More direct evidence derives from a speculative analysis of a political conversation among a small group of voters following an election (Hughes, 1975, pp. 150–163). The analyst concludes that much of the interaction seems related to the quest for social acceptance, even if it is often in oblique ways. He concludes that current political opinions consequently might stem less from personal predispositions, such as toward authoritarianism or powerlessness, and more from a kind of "infection of opinion" in the membership groups to which individuals are attracted and from which they seek acceptance.

Social Comparison: You're OK—How Am I?

The most influential orientation in the small-group literature regards others, and groups of others, as sources of information about physical and social reality. Thus, to meet an apparent need to hold "correct" opinions about the world and have an "accurate" sense of qualities and abilities, individuals compare themselves to others. Social-comparison theory at once rests on and extends the two orientations considered above. Most of the relevant literature focuses on the individual responding to "social situations," rather than on groups with specific properties. Clearly, however, small groups will be the prime loci for social comparison.

This introduction to social comparison is in four parts. First, the conceptual development of the notion will be traced. Then the value of the orientation in reconciling apparently opposed findings will be illustrated. The movement toward greater specificity will then be charted, with emphasis on the experimental elimination of rival views of social comparison. Finally, an estimate will be made of the usefulness of social comparison as an orientation to reality.

Conceptual Development. Social-comparison theory derives basically from the work of Leon Festinger (1954) and Stanley Schachter (1959), whose efforts are briefly summarized here. Note also that earlier work, such as that of Sherif (1935) with the autokinetic effect, also relates directly to social comparison.

Festinger (1954) proposes a simple explanation for one's use of others to define and create physical and social reality. He painted a picture of individuals whose need for information to reduce "cognitive dissonance" is great but whose objective, nonsocial means of appraisal are typically limited or not appropriate. Consider a person who wants information about his or her intelligence. Objective tests provide some data, but they are not sufficient, even in that limited case, because the attitudes of others about the person's intelligence may be even more important than the objectively determined estimates. In many other areas, perhaps in most of life, the individual stands in even greater need of others to provide data. Do you see me as powerful? Do you like me? Will you accept my view of how I see you? Here feelings, personal reactions, and preferences dominate. And others have a clear monopoly on this kind of information, which individuals will seek more or less based on the perceived similarities between the information seeker and the information holder.

Schachter (1959) extends Festinger's insight. For Festinger, comparison processes are centered around gaining information, but for Schachter, social comparison is the major way of reducing ambiguity and anxiety. The need for that reduction is the center of his psychology of affiliation. To put this crucial extension in another way, both Festinger and Schachter see comparison as arising from ambiguity. However, Schachter additionally posits that ambiguity results in anxiety and that comparison processes also serve to reduce anxiety. Information is always necessary to reduce anxiety, but it may not be sufficient.

Schachter's approach permits profoundly simple research. For example, consider this straightforward experiment concerning whether anxious subjects would prefer company. When being instructed about a purported experiment on the effects of electric shock, some subjects were told they would receive a mild shock and others were informed they should expect a severe and painful shock. The subjects could choose to pass the time after the introduction but before the start of the experiment either alone or with others. Of those subjects assigned to the painful-shock condition, almost two-thirds preferred waiting with others. Among subjects in the mild-shock group, only about one-third desired company.

Reconciling Divergent Findings. Even in its elemental parts, Schachter's seminal work has multiple implications. For example, it suggested ways out of conundra posed by earlier work in social facilitation; and it added impact and perspective to the burgeoning research on social attraction. Consider here only the early studies of Triplett and Allport that led to the imprecise conclusion that the presence of others can either facilitate or inhibit performance.

Zajonc's studies (1965) explained the double-edged effect of the presence of others in terms of social-comparison processes required by differences in tasks. On familiar tasks, the presence of others facilitates performance; on unfamiliar ones, social interaction may distract. Comparison involves a person's need for others so as to learn how to act in novel situations and to assess performance. On familiar tasks, Zajonc observed enhanced performance in groups. This poses no problem for social-comparison theory: "On a familiar task, the subject . . . is easily able to obtain what data he needs from others on how well he is working. The fruits will frequently be confirmatory, which will enhance his performance" (Smith, 1973, p. 67). In contrast, unfamiliar tasks require greater use of social comparison. Evaluation of success or failure is still necessary, but simply more difficult. The individual working on an unfamiliar task spends more time in gaining data, and performance consequently suffers.

But Schachter's insight encompasses a devilish complexity and a profound significance, in addition to providing conceptual tools of reconciliation of findings such as that attempted by Zajonc. The following two sections illustrate limited aspects of the complexity and significance, in turn.

Eliminating Alternative Explanations. Social comparison can be approached at two levels. Generally, its view of human behavior has this character: for ambiguous or novel events, social validation provides *the* cue to behavior; that is, when we do not know how to feel about something, or how to react to it, we look at others' reactions. According to Festinger, this comparison process places all data about ourselves in perspective and also provides limits for feelings and attitudes, inhibiting an overreaction or a reckless attitude. This seems credible at a general level.

Social comparison also requires more specific analysis, however. At least five alternatives can explain why the subjects in Schachter's original painful-shock condition wanted to spend time with others, and for many purposes one needs to determine which alternative is dominant. The possibilities include (Smith, 1973, pp. 14–17):

1. Escape or defense, in which case others could be useful and perhaps necessary
2. Clarification, in which case others could help explain any confusions about the experiment
3. Simply being with others, in which case comfort or possible empathy could reduce anxiety
4. Distraction, in which case the presence of others and/or communication with them could reduce anxiety by keeping the subjects' minds otherwise occupied
5. Uncertainty about how to react, in which case others could provide needed clues.

Ingeniously, Schachter conducted several experiments which eliminated some of these alternative hypotheses. He found that anxiety was reduced only if the subjects waited with others undergoing the same experiment, for example. Moreover, it did not matter whether the subjects talked or not. A number of experimental modifications also eliminated escape, clarification, and distraction as explanations. This left only direct anxiety reduction and comparing oneself to others.

Raising the Issue of Ubiquity. Such analytic considerations aside, how much of life can be accounted for in terms of social comparison? Conceding that social comparison provides a useful handhold on reality, how ubiquitous do the associated phenomena seem to be? Ubiquity would urge major attention to the small groupings in which social comparison processes often are worked through.

Opinions may differ on the degree, but social-comparison theory relates well to reality. Indeed, Smith (1973, pp. 18-19) sees ambiguity as universal, with major implications for the pervasiveness of group and interpersonal phenomena. He presents two kinds of data supporting his position, both from work contexts. First, at middle and senior managerial levels (Carlson, 1951; Horne & Lupton, 1965), individuals spend up to two-thirds of their time interacting with others as part of doing their job effectively; this includes gathering data about self-presentation and performance. Second, in the United States working population, substantial percentages of a representative sample surveyed by Kohn, Wolfe, Quinn, Snoek, and Rosenthal (1964) report deprivation of basically social sources of information sufficient to cause them distress. Their findings include:

- 35% of the respondents lacked clarity about the scope and responsibilities of their jobs
- 32% reported being under tension because they were unsure how their supervisors evaluated them and their performance
- 31% indicated distress because of a lack of information concerning possibilities for promotion
- 29% reported being bothered by uncertainty about what their peers expected of them.

Thus, we can reasonably posit, as does Smith, that the complexity of the social situation and the novelty of problem situations at work have two effects: they induce tension or distress and generate persistent efforts at social comparison. Ambiguity is widespread, making social comparison a constant process among managers as well as members of the workforce.

A long story can be concluded shortly then. Social-comparison effects can be expected to occur broadly in life—at work as well as elsewhere. As with the other broad orientations introduced thus far, this provides only a useful jumping-off point. What kinds of groups will have what specific effects for which individuals on what tasks? These are second-generation questions.

Social Control: How Are Individuals Tied into Broad Purposes?

Although the potency and ubiquity of small social groupings has long been manifest, as the three sections above should demonstrate, the basic role of the small group in social control apparently needs to be periodically relearned, or at least reinvigorated.

Recent Reminders of Small-Group Potency. In the last decade or two, several *causes célèbres* have emphasized the small group's role in social control. In fact, these cases may involve most of the major recent concerns of the behavioral sciences. Some of these cases follow:

- Reliance on, and concern about, the use of small learning collectivities, including "eastern National Training Laboratory (NTL) T-Groups," "marathon encounters," and so on, crested in the late 1960s. This motivated a massive literature, pro (Marrow, 1964), con (Steinbacker, 1971), and balanced (Golembiewski & Blumberg, 1970, 1973, 1977), that turned on the issues of the vulnerability of individuals to group pressures, as well as of the incidence and/or degree of associated psychological trauma.
- The use of small-group dynamics in "brainwashing" prisoners-of-war received substantial attention, especially in the aftermath of the Korean War (Biderman, 1963; Schein, 1956, 1961).
- The use of various forms of small-group pressures in breaking-down "recalcitrant" political attitudes received major attention over a period of 10–15 years in connection with native activist groups (SDS, Symbionese Liberation Army, etc.) as well as with the "permanent cultural revolution" in China (Whyte, 1974).
- The dramatic demonstrations of Milgram (1974) concerning the degree to which individuals respond to orders concerning objectionable acts implied to many the fragility of individual standards of conduct in the absence of social supports.
- Case studies from the highest levels of governance (Janis, 1972) describe how small groups could be so attractive as to inhibit even high-powered individuals from expressing views they thought were discordant but which were in fact more or less unanimously shared.

Powerful Groups, Needful/Vulnerable Individuals. The above illustrations imply important commonalities. In various forms, each of them involves some detachment from normal behavioral anchors; and they all involve the substitution of new behaviors mediated by group forces or (in Milgram's case) by the lack of group supports that could have helped individuals resist an authoritative person's objectionable orders. Generally speaking, all the examples relate to the same basic hope and/or fear: powerful groups can influence needful or vulnerable individuals, even overwhelm them.

The social control theme can be illustrated by the work of Milgram (1963, 1965, 1974). Milgram's work is widely known, of course, but a brief review here is useful because it has implications for powerful group effects even as it reflects the individualistic turn of psychological research in the 1960s. Overall, the focus of research about that time changed from groups to individuals and individual responses to social situations, both as targets (in Milgram's experimentation) and as targeters (e.g., Baumgartner, Buckley, & Burns, 1975).

In his experiments, Milgram instructed subjects to deliver electric shocks to other subjects in an experiment presented as a study of learning, the shocks constituting punishment for mistakes made by the "learner." The subjects administering the shocks used a "machine" marked by gradations from mild to severe shock. No shocks were actually given the "learner," but the realism was such that Milgram could study the conditions under which a subject obeyed an experimenter in an objectionable task. We can say "objectionable" for many reasons, not the least of which is that many compliant subjects had serious difficulty later in coming to terms with their obedience in light of their dislike of what they were doing while they were doing it. Subjects cooperated, in percentages and to degrees surprising to Milgram and most of his psychologist colleagues (Milgram, 1965). To get some sense of the cause for the surprise, Milgram reported his unsuccessful efforts to find a limit for obedience (1965, p. 74): "Cries from the victim were inserted; not good enough The victim claimed heart trouble; subjects still shocked him on command. The victim pleaded that he be let free, and his answers no longer registered on the signal box; subjects continued to shock him."

How do Milgram's studies illustrate the role of groups in social control? At least two aspects contribute to an explanation: the power of the authority figure and the lack of supports, including group-centered ones, for "normal" behavior.

The experimenter clearly dominated the subjects. Each subject was told to successively raise the severity of the shock to the "learner," finally reaching the maximum level. Of the 40 original subjects, 26 obeyed the experimenter's directions; they "went all the way."

Four major factors seemed to heighten the experimenter's potency. First, the subjects were paid $4.50 each before the experiment, so money may have motivated some subjects to obey. Second, the original experiment was associated with Yale University, perhaps adding the backing of a prestigious institution to the curious commands of the experimenter. In fact, when Milgram later moved the experiments to a decaying building and did not emphasize the backing of Yale, the number of subjects delivering the maximum shock decreased. Third, the victim was often remote, sometimes neither seen nor heard. In contrast, when the subjects were told to place the victims' hands directly on a shockplate, fewer subjects obeyed. Finally, the experimenter's presence was significant. When the experimenter was not present, but gave instructions by telephone, the percentage of subjects delivering the greatest level of shock decreased. Some subjects even lied about having given the highest voltages when they had in fact not done so.

By hypothesis, at least, the lack of group supports for potentially recalcitrant subjects augmented the experimenter's potency. Subjects usually worked singly with the experimenter. Thus, the unavailability of social comparison may help to explain the experimenter's social control. No guidance existed for behavior, and the task presented a novel dilemma; hence the subject often deferred to the experimenter. Viewed this way, the Milgram experiments imply how critically many individuals need social comparison and support, even in cases that seem not to pose very difficult choices. Numerous studies have shown that behavioral uniformity in groups is associated with such conditions as surveillance of the individual, unanimity of others present, and the ambiguous character of stimuli (Tyson & Kaplowitz, 1977). Conformity in the Milgram experiments, in effect, depended in some part on the absence of others who might have provided a source of social-comparison alternative to the prestigious experimenter. Subjects might have needed the social comparison to do what they actually preferred to do— desist from what they believed was painful shock giving.

Variations of the basic Milgram experiment suggest this hypothesis is not extravagant. In one variation, Milgram added two other subjects, actually experimenter's confederates. Three conditions were observed. Without the experimenter physically present, when the confederates urged higher shocks, the naive subject typically complied. With the experimenter present and the confederates remaining passive, the naive subjects continued to deliver high shocks as often as they had when alone. Finally, when the confederates role played a refusal to comply with instructions, naive subjects significantly increased their disobedience.

Some Small-Group Dimensions:
Toward Differentiating the Species

The four orientations to small groups just reviewed have some value, but far greater specificity is necessary. That is, while it is important to know that groups can provide significant contexts for social comparison, the key questions require a different level of complexity. The question of which kinds of groups, under what conditions, have what effects on members with definite personality characteristics remains. That question should be a familiar one by this time.

We now look at two approaches to this greater complexity and specificity. A sketch of a working model of small-group properties and effects receives attention first. Subsequently, five ways in which we commonly abuse what we know will be introduced.

A Primer on What We Know about Central Properties: Components of a Small-Group Model

It is both comforting and sad that a model proposed nearly 15 years ago (Golembiewski, 1965b) still suffices to sketch the essentials of what we know about key small-group variables, how they interact, and with what effects. It is comfort that the earlier work has proved serviceable and has not been easily set aside by subsequent work. The sadness comes from the unfulfilled expectation that "progress" should by now have carried us beyond that early synthesis, which was offered as tentative and certainly incomplete.

The suspicion lingers that the basic explanation for this continued serviceability resides less in the model's prescience than in two research trends. As already noted, research tastes in the 1960s deemphasized group properties and focused on the individual in social situations. Moreover, major attention in the last decade has been devoted to application of knowledge. In effect, the research breakthroughs of the previous two or three decades concerning the potency of small groups implied some sense of dynamics that would be useful for harnessing group power to specific purposes. Certainly the massive attention in the 1960s to small learning groups (sensitivity training, T-groups, or encounters) was focused on applications, and some observers like Rogers (1970, p. 11) see the development of that technology as the major event of the twentieth century. Originally approached as major research opportunities, such small-group applications soon became basically oriented toward individual learning and in many cases toward individual "peak experiences." The associated anticognitive orientation did not stop group research (Back, 1972). But that research was certainly inhibited or redirected into still other applications such as organization development (Golembiewski, 1979).

A Preliminary Concept/Operation Lexicon. For now, caution encourages us to eschew explanations of why small-group analysis went the way observers agree that it did (Lakin, 1979; Shepherd, 1978; Weick, 1978; and others), but we will present a limited but useful set of group properties. Table 1 outlines a few dimensions that can claim strong support for inclusion

Table 1. Selected Small-Group Concepts and Operations[a]

Designation	Conceptual definition	Operational definition
Leadership	A measure of general status, with at least three major dimensions: individual prominence, aiding group attainment, and sociability.	A two-fold operation is required: (a) determination of rank of group members on each of the three dimensions (by, e.g., responses to such questions as: Who stands out in your group?); and (b) determination of the congruence between group members' ranks on the three dimensions.
Role styles	A global measure of the style in which a group leader or a formal head behaves: "authoritarian" (directive) and "democratic" (permissive) are often used to distinguish two opposed styles.	An "authoritarian" style may be distinguished from a "democratic" one in terms of such factors as: (a) all determination of policy by leader or formal head; (b) dictation of work steps and coworkers; and (c) aloofness from groups, e.g., as in "personal" praise and criticism.
Atmosphere	A measure of the general tone of group interaction, which is often induced by the role style of the leader or the formal head.	Atmosphere differences may be measured via standard instruments such as Friedlander's Group Behavior Inventory or Likert's Profile of Organization Characteristics.
Personality	The "authoritarian syndrome" provides a useful approach to personality dimensions, high scorers being distinguished in terms of such factors as conventionalism, submission, aggression, and emphasis on strength and toughness.	This dimension may be approached via Forms 40 and 45 of the Adorno F-Scale. The FIRO Scales, which emphasize the degree to which various personality "mixes" imply high compatibility or low compatibility, could also be used.
Cohesiveness	A resultant measure of attraction to group, whose positive and negative vectors are based on factors such as prestige of group membership, prestige of task, and liking of group members.	The concept may be tapped by such resultant measures as answers to the question: How much do you want to remain a member of this group?
Norms	Reflections of social pressures which apply either to all group members or to performers of specific roles.	Asking group members to report on the norms influencing them in various situations, the consensus of group members on such reports being a crucial datum.

[a]Based on Golembiewski (1965b, pp. 89–90.)

in any set of properties convenient for observing and measuring group phenomena. Note that the material in Table 1 draws heavily on previously published materials (Golembiewski, 1965b, pp. 89–91), simplified for present purposes.

Due caution requires qualifying the phrase "strong support" in describing the properties listed in Table 1. What is important to observe in small groups and how such observations are to be measured certainly do not represent anyone's guess. But few firm limits constrain even the most exuberant soul, and the analyst of the literature faces the following problems:

1. The same concept defined in different operational terms in different studies
2. Similar concepts defined in similar operational terms in different studies
3. Similar concepts defined in different operational terms in different studies
4. Significantly different conceptualizations which purport to tap a similar phenomenal area and which are defined in different operational terms

It is no comfort for our present purposes that consistent results eventually indicate the concept–operation pairs appropriate at particular levels of comprehensiveness. Since Table 1 is based on the available research, it must recognize the diversity of concept–operation pairs; however, it also attempts to transcend that diversity, though without becoming deeply involved in the complicated and volatile details of either nominal or operational definition. The element of arbitrariness in Table 1 does not seem great, for detailed attention has been given these vexing problems elsewhere (Golembiewski, 1962a, 1962b).

A Simplified Map of Relations. The available literature permits a step beyond the simplified conceptual and operational lexicon of Table 1. Figure 1 diagrams a model of typical relations of the properties in a microsystem. In essence, the dimensions from Table 1 can be linked in four major ways, two types each being associated with high and low congruence of the functional roles of leadership. The solid lines connect the properties characterizing each of the four types. The number of variables has been limited deliberately, but only a little elaboration would be necessary to sketch the major variables that seem to link small groups into larger structures. Thus, the degree of "structural integration" (which relates to the rank of a formal head in a group's "internal leadership") would be relevant in such an elaboration. Specifying structural integration would also permit linking a number of outcome variables to Figure 1. For example, a highly cohesive small group that has low structural integration in some broader system could

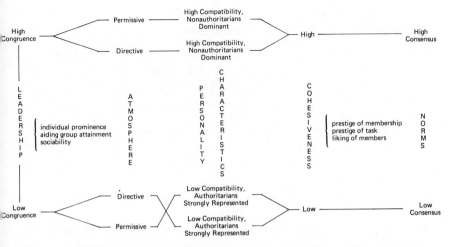

Figure 1. A simplified model of small-group properties: the small group as a microsystem. (From Golembiewski, 1965b, p. 91.)

derive satisfaction from being able to control its environment through low productivity (see Figure 2).

How do these considerations improve the four broad orientations introducing this chapter? Considering the issue of social facilitation, will a given group heighten or depress the performance of individuals, and how much will it do so? Neglecting differences in tasks for illustrative purposes, Figure 1 provides an unequivocal answer: it depends, among many other factors, on the group's degree of cohesiveness. The higher the cohesiveness, the greater is the probable control of member behavior. Hence, we would expect that highly cohesive groups would be associated with significantly increased performance of individual members in group conditions and decreased performance by members outside of the group context. That is, both very high and very low performance require high degrees of control of member behavior. Beyond this, knowledge of the major bases for cohesiveness not only enlarges understanding but opens the possibility of deliberate applied efforts to raise or lower cohesiveness. Figure 1 can be similarly applied to the other three basic orientations to small groups: social attraction, social comparison, and social control.

Figure 2

Five Particulars Disregarding What We Know:
Some Garden-Variety Misunderstandings

If Figure 1 serves as a reasonable model for representing what we know about small groups, impressive energies have also gone into disregarding what we know. Five particulars serve to illustrate more fully what Figure 1 implies, and what the common wisdom often neglects.

Groups Have Numerous Bases of Attraction. Despite the common and convenient assumption that a group is a group, the model in Figure 1 indicates that numerous bases of attraction and of cohesiveness have to be taken into account in defining a group. These bases derive from more or less permanent factors such as personality predispositions, as Figure 1 explicitly provides. The acknowledgment of authoritarian cohesiveness does not come easily to some; but it does seem to exist, and any resulting surprise implies the failure to recognize that groups can have bases of attraction other than positive affect (what some call "the warm fuzzies"). In addition, more complex analyses also could be built around Figure 1. For example, even low-authoritarian members might accord leadership to a high authoritarian and accept a directive or autocratic atmosphere, a basis of attraction that could derive from episodic factors such as a common threat. Figure 1 implies that such a situation would be unstable, most certainly so if the threat passed.

Neglect of the fact that groups have numerous bases of attraction is often expressed in raging debates over pseudoquestions. Are groups the engines of conformity in direct proportion to their cohesiveness? Or, following LeBon (1926), are groups the causes of virtually all mischief as they encourage otherwise heroic individuals into various fallacies and perversions? Or perhaps one prefers a pleasant alternative. Are not groups the vehicles for approaching unparalleled individual freedom based on heightened individual awareness and sensitivity, as seen by Carl Rogers (1970)?

The discussion thus far suggests a different tack, or at least a more specific one. Group situations can induce powerful forces on individuals for good or ill, especially under conditions which heighten individual needs for facilitation, affiliation, comparison, or control. Hence, potent group experiences often result in some unsettling from normal anchorages: meeting on a "cultural island," eliminating or reducing such individuators as status, and so on. This unsettling facilitates the development and acceptance of group norms or values, and depending on their character, groups can move in radically different directions. For example, witness the care taken to infuse appropriate values into T-groups (Golembiewski & Blumberg, 1977, pp. 175–255).

Cohesion Implies Degree, not Direction. Relatedly, it is apparent that one cannot stress often enough that a group's cohesiveness refers to the degree of the resultant of the forces attracting members into a group minus the forces encouraging them to leave. Often, however, observers awkwardly seek to attribute directionality to this degree of force. In a common formulation, for example, researchers associated high cohesiveness with high production in work contexts, only to be often disappointed by the results of empirical tests. Similarly, Unekis (1978) uses the degree to which members of a legislative committee vote together as an operational measure of cohesiveness in a study that generates mixed findings. Among other possibilities, one contaminant of findings in this research might be the notion that similarity of votes indicates cohesiveness. This often probably will be the case, but an alternative requires attention. A high-cohesive group could also provide a context within which even substantially dissimilar votes would lead neither to disunity nor other divisive consequences.

So, to make a central point again, high cohesiveness does presume a high degree of consensus about norms, but those norms can give diverse directionality to the degree of force (e.g., Janis, 1972). In the case of production levels, to illustrate the point, predictions should reflect the sense of high control of member behavior that could be expressed in different, even opposite, member behaviors. Thus high production (O'Kiefe, Kernoghan, & Rubenstein, 1975) and low production (Sakurai, 1975) can both be expected from high-cohesive groups.

Groups Have an "Inside" and an "Outside." Designations are often imprecise on the issue of a small group's boundaries, for reasons that are no less troublesome for being understandable. Perhaps the modal approach to the difficulties of drawing boundaries involves the assumption—whether implicit or explicit—that a group is a group. That is clearly not sufficient for most purposes. Various operational measures of cohesiveness, for example, require a clear specification of the "it"—the specific web of relationships involving definite individuals—whose forces of attraction and/or repulsion are being assessed (Golembiewski, 1962b, pp. 56–66). This matter is troublesome in temporary laboratory groupings, and it can especially bedevil natural-state research. Basically, the key issue is the differing degrees of interdependence that characterize different social situations. For example, being in a room with a tightly knit group, should, for many purposes, be distinguished from being in the same room with strangers or one's worst enemies.

What would be helpful on this point? Target identification will always be a problem, of course, until one can specify properties with substantial precision. And when detailed description becomes possible, designation is by definition no problem. Short of that precision, however, analysts should at least avoid reification, and there has been much of that. Some research strategies also might help. As Weick (1978, p. 485) proposes:

> I would not use large samples. . . . I am more favorable toward a clinical, idiographic, ethnographic, and sit-and-stare approach than I am toward

the accumulation of large amounts of data where minor statistical differences gain spurious significance.

Finally, efforts should be made to preserve qualitative differences or gradations in referring to specific "social situations." That, at least, expresses the intent underlying the model in Figure 1.

Operational Definitions Matter, and Gravely So. One of the unappreciated major contributions of small-group analysis has been the attention it directs to operational definitions, although that lesson seems difficult to learn and harder still to retain. Conceptual targets are typically associated with a range of effects—positive, negative, and piddling. Does this signal that the conceptual target is awkward? Perhaps. Alternatively, the conceptual target is often trapped by a range of operational definitions, variations in which can well account for the distribution of observed effects.

For reasons (beyond convenience) which are baffling, the variation in operational definitions has received only trifling attention. The most telling attention to what might be called "comparative operations analysis" relevant to the small group has been devoted to cohesiveness (e.g., see the summary in Golembiewski, 1962b, pp. 149–178) and to trust (Kegan & Rubenstein, 1972). The experience with such variables signals the crucial significance of differences in operational definitions. The point has not penetrated deeply into the consciousness of political scientists in general, although notable exceptions do exist (Dodd & Pierce, 1975; March, 1956).

A Theory of Groups Relevant to Politics Is Not "A Group Theory of Politics." The discussion above refers basically to a theory of groups relevant to politics, but historically the emphasis of research has been very broadly on "a group theory of politics," which has a reach as big as all nature but a tiny grasp. Hence, major critics like Odegard (1958) rightly felt obliged to excoriate (among other features) the neglect of value issues via such extravagant extrapolations as "might makes right." At other times, group theory has been seen as "interest group politics," which could be a comprehensive gestalt for careless users or could simply constitute that day's sacred cow toward which a ceremonial bow was given in "theoretical introductions" by political scientists who went on doing what they had done before.

So caution is most appropriate here, in at least four major senses, lest we be seen as contributing to a reprise of an unfortunate emphasis. First, "the group theory" occasioned major scholarly warfare beginning in the 1950s, but its raucous echoes still reverberate today (Garson, 1978). For the most part, the most exuberant domestic versions of "the group approach" were played out within a decade or so after the concept took center stage (Latham, 1952; Truman, 1951). As late as 1976, however, Odom felt it necessary to urge diluting "the group approach" to Soviet politics (as in Skilling & Griffiths, 1964), which he saw as having gained significant support in its bid to become the new dominant approach to interpretation in that area of interest.

Second, the historical puffery of "the group approach" cannot be dismissed, because it clearly happened and could reemerge. But that orientation can be put in some kind of perspective, which hopefully will also reduce the probability of reemergence. Briefly, "the group approach" was unwisely extrapolated into "a group theory of politics" because of incautious need, unmediated by the kind of natural science methodology that permits the summary in Figure 1 and that can also build on it. The correct observation

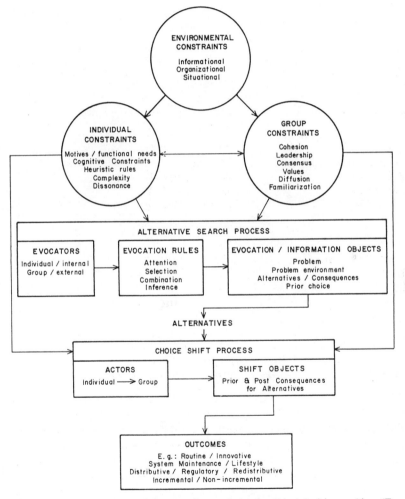

Figure 3. A theoretic framework for the microanalysis of political decision making. (From Kirkpatrick *et al.*, 1976, p. 52.)

of group, and especially small-group, influence was incautiously extended into these curious equivalents: small groups = organizations = categoric groups = pressure groups. And politics became simplified to a kind of pool game where "groups" of various sizes, momenta, and vectors collided within institutional contexts encompassing different games and different actors, with public policy resulting from these interacting forces.

Third, it is sometimes the case that propositions developed at one level of analysis are useful at other levels, but the burden of proof will be heavy. The documentation must be very careful, especially in the sense that findings at one level are always critically dependent on the operational definitions employed, and operational definitions appropriate at one level of analysis may be very deceiving at other levels (e.g., see Golembiewski, 1962b, pp. 56–66). Certainly, the homology will not be true because we assume it or find it convenient. For one approach to the generalizability of findings and hypotheses—from subgroups to organizations to larger social systems—consult Stavig and Barnett (1977).

Fourth, a theory of small groups may become part of "a theory of politics," but that will be the result of a very long line of development, not a jumping-off place for high-order generalizations. One's reach should not exceed one's grasp by too great a margin. "The group theory of politics" constituted a great leap beyond the early and nonspecific demonstration of group influence on individual behavior in diverse social settings.

What constitutes a useful if general map for appropriately viewing today's work toward a theory of small groups in politics? Tastes will differ, of course, and any choice would be highly conditional. Specifically, the next two sections urge a case-by-case approach to the usefulness of a small-group approach in numerous areas of traditional concern to political scientists. For those who prefer a more comprehensive effort toward putting small groups in their place, Figure 3 briefly outlines a theoretic framework relevant to some obvious microanalytic components of the process of political decision making (Kirkpatrick *et al.*, 1976).

Four Cases of Small Groups in Politics: Dynamics/Dimensions as Emergent/Contrived

Now we turn to the tasks of developing this more modest role for the study of the small group in political science and also establishing that the role has enough substance and value to lay a reasonable claim to the required resources. The approach here is straightforward. Four case studies serve to illustrate the kind and quality of political analysis that is possible with the small-group approach. The focus, in turn, will be on:

1. President Kennedy's executive team and how its attractiveness induced a crippling conformity among members that influenced major political decisions

2. Small groups that served as supports for voters whose electoral behavior deviated from the basic norms of their work place
3. President Nixon's "young team" and how its behavioral dynamics facilitated one-to-one control
4. The top policy and management levels of a mass-transit authority which sought to build into its operations specific truth-serving norms.

In sum, the first three of these case studies deal with natural-state situations which reflect the dynamics and dimensions of small groups as they often come to exist, without explicit and conscious intervention. The final case deals with a deliberate intervention in nature which was based on a knowledge of small-group dynamics and which sought to tailor an organization to order. The cases not only illustrate the value of small groups in political analysis, but they variously provide context and perspective for the extended discussion above.

Groups as Engines of Conformity: Groupthink on Kennedy's "Best and Brightest" Team

We focus on President Kennedy's team of the "Best and Brightest," borrowing David Halberstam's evocative usage, during a period of trouble and trial. Why go back in history, especially to a time so often remarked on and worked over? Janis's (1972) description of decision making by the Kennedy group in the Bay of Pigs fiasco serves two purposes. Examining the Kennedy group illustrates the utility of small-group analysis in a traditional area of inquiry—foreign-policy making. But even more, this case study focuses on the central group property of cohesiveness and the effect of that property on the group's activities and, in turn, on world politics.

Let us briefly recall the Bay of Pigs decision makers, those persons surrounding John F. Kennedy in the first months after his inauguration—Rusk at State, McNamara at Defense, Robert Kennedy at Justice, Bundy, Schlesinger, and Goodwin at the White House, Dulles and Bissell at the CIA and the Joint Chiefs of Staff. Most of them were new at their jobs, but all had sterling credentials; and most had bountiful experience in decision making under conditions of risk, in the public or private sectors.

The history of the Bay of Pigs is by now familiar. The group accepted a plan proposed by Bissell to invade Cuba with a few exiles. For the most part, the Kennedy team was uncritical of obvious faults in the plan which later would result in a fiasco. Janis explains the fiasco in terms of powerful group forces, seven of which arose from major factors in the team's environment. Reports of the participants provided Janis with his basic data.

The seven factors giving direction to the group's cohesiveness, and also deriving support from that cohesiveness, can be summarized briefly. First, the Kennedy group created the illusion of invulnerability—anything we do will succeed, if everyone agrees—during the period of euphoria following electoral victory and installation of the new government. The euphoria also led to impaired critical thinking, according to Janis, and a tendency to see rivals or outgroups (Castro and Cuba, in this case) in stereotypic terms—they are evil and weak and we are virtuous and strong. Second, the Kennedy group also fell prey to the illusion of unanimity. Given the respect among group members for each others' opinions, unanimous agreement seemed to validate the truth of any action or decision they took. The Kennedy group seems to have encouraged consensus and discouraged reality testing or critical thinking. Third, the illusion of unanimity may have led individual group members, Rusk and Schlesinger, for example, to suppress personal doubts about the CIA plan. Fourth, Robert Kennedy and Rusk may have acted as guardians of group consensus by overtly discouraging the expression of deviant opinions. Fifth, Kennedy's leadership also may have contributed to the dominance of pro-CIA opinions, as distinguished from independent and available assessments of the plan. Sixth, the group may also have evolved a norm against criticizing the CIA plan because the group members respected and wanted to protect the CIA members. Seventh, the group's esprit de corps and apparent unanimity discouraged questioning of the moral or ethical quality of decisions.

Janis's seven factors explain how a cohesive group of policymakers could develop norms which maintained esprit de corps but also permitted the group to accept massive risks based on questionable—even patently improbable—assumptions, with little if any dissent. This implies a risky-shift effect, of course. And one can easily envision the engines of social comparison and control, and perhaps even of social attraction, operating in the Kennedy team.

Janis's case study frontally assaults the unquestioned positive acceptance of group cohesion. Cohesion "cuts both ways," Janis notes (1972, pp. 2–13, 184–224), and he labels it negative manifestation "groupthink." Janis defines groupthink as members' acceptance of group consensus as the criterion of "good decisions," as contrasted with tough, critical analysis. High cohesiveness will incline a group toward groupthink, Janis concludes, but that effect is only probable, not inevitable.

Groups as Supports for Deviant Voting Behavior: The Case of Republican Auto Workers

Janis's caveat about cohesiveness cutting more than one way seems appropriate, as the following case of research on electoral behavior implies. Much research supports the hypothesis that group cohesion is reflected in uniformity of members' opinions and behavior, and this implies that cohesiveness should be a significant factor in perpetuating as well as in changing norms and values. The research reviewed here (Finifter, 1978) confirms conventional wisdom while extending it in a critical particular. That is, groups may also serve as havens for members whose opinions differ from those of their larger environment. This research demonstrates the need for caution in assuming linkages between the norms at two levels—membership group and categoric group. Moreover, Finifter also establishes that small groups can play a vital role in preventing political conformity by insulating individuals from the direct influence of other individuals and broader social contexts as well as by providing arenas for the development and expression of minority points of view (see also Kornhauser, 1959; Peterson, 1978).

Finifter's findings came as a surprise to her, the surprise deriving from the classic difficulty with defining the boundaries of "groups." Her research initially rested on the hypothesis that member integration in small, formal work groups would vary directly with the acceptance of the norms of the larger collectivities within which the primary work groups were found—a factory, a city, a locality, a state, and even a socioeconomic class. She found, oppositely, that high integration within the primary group tended to be associated with holding deviant political opinions. In general, members of the larger collectivity (a plant of auto workers) strongly tended to vote Democratic. But those employees most integrated into their smaller work groups tended to vote Republican. This implies two distinct patterns of political behavior and two sources of social control.

Let us look at the research design and findings. Finifter's data were collected through interviews with approximately 400 auto workers in the Detroit area. Each worker received a card listing all other members of his work group, that categoric group supervised by one particular foreman. Each worker was asked: "Of the people who worked under your foreman, which five would you say you are most friendly with?" Reciprocated friendship choices provided the operational measure of the individual's integration into the work group. Finifter also asked employees whether members discussed politics with others in their work group in the last campaign (1960) and whether individuals supported the presidential, gubernatorial, and senatorial candidates of the Democratic party, the favored party of the economic class and union to which work group members "belonged." Finifter found that the integration of work groups tended to vary directly with the frequency of political discussion but inversely with support for the Democratic party. That is, as integration into the work group increased, so did the amount of political discussion and the proportion of Republican voters.

Those findings contrast sharply with Finifter's original hypothesis, but we can hazard a reasonable explanation. Consider that most workers in the plants were Democratic partisans, as were most residents of the locality and the state. Rightly viewing themselves as political deviants, Republican workers may "have little political contact outside the work group and attempt to compensate for this by increasing work group friendships" (Finifter, 1978, pp. 138-139).

This reads like a clear case of the need for social comparison, but major questions are left open. For example, why did work groups become havens for those having deviant political opinions? Perhaps some social attraction processes were triggered after work groups were formed; or perhaps some complex self-selection occurred earlier. In any case, those few who voted Republican somehow clustered together and engaged powerful forces of social comparison which affected their votes and political discussion. Or perhaps many auto workers voted Democratic only because they lacked the social support to articulate their real convictions. More complicated still, did the predisposition to vote Republican predate membership in the work group? Or did group interaction somehow change voting preference?

These questions defy answer here, but they suggest the major potential for follow-up studies. Future work might well give more attention to Democratic auto workers, whose voting behavior one is tempted to explain in this straightforward but perhaps spurious way: individuals who have few worksite friendships tend to reflect dominant political attitudes and to participate less in politics.

Finifter's findings do not relate only to empirical issues, of course. What broader implications does she see? Finifter argues that legal processes may prove irrelevant "if basic social psychological processes act to discourage [opinional deviants] from holding or expressing [such] views" (Finifter, 1978, p. 156). Trends toward the atomization of individuals in society provoke concern because, as her research suggests, the small group may function as a defense against the extragroup environment, often providing the cohesion necessary to stand and fight rather than flee and disintegrate. More profoundly still, this view also implies an active role for deviants, who shape their responses rather than respond to their environment. Note that these dynamics also seem to characterize political loci quite removed from automobile plants, as the work of Janis (reviewed above) and Peterson's (1978) research on American courts make plain.

Finifter's conclusions should not be tied only to political deviance, however. The available research is slim, to be sure, but studies indicate that small-membership groups impact powerfully on voting. Thus, Burnstein (1956) provides data supporting two hypotheses about the relationship of social networks to party choice, using Israeli election surveys: measures of ties to social networks are more highly correlated with party choice than are standard background attributes such as class or ethnicity; and the impact of social networks is substantial even after controlling for individual background attributes. Patently, such findings receive massive reinforcement from the material reviewed above concerning the impact of small groups on behavior.

Groups and One-to-One Control: A Runaway Norm on Nixon's "Young Team"

Groups come in more varieties than Heinz's. Some are cohesive and supportive in the relatively warm and accepting terms implied in the two cases above. Other groups reflect harsher aspects, or at least different varieties of "social glue," as in the authoritarian cohesiveness sketched in Figure 1.

Consider a dramatic comparison of two major groups that influenced recent American politics. Kennedy's "Best and Brightness" team—which transmuted talent and standing into a dumb collective confidence that a handful of expatriates could successfully invade Cuba—has already been introduced. Consider now a brief summary of Raven's (1974) analysis of Nixon's "Young Team."

Both teams reflected groupthink symptoms, but beyond that, they differed in a profound way. Janis (1972) sees the Kennedy team as closely knit, with members sharing high esprit de corps and mutual respect. In contrast, Raven found two competing factions on Nixon's "Young Team," members of which held each other in disrespect if not dislike, although both factions were dependent on Nixon, who set the norms for both factions.

The "Young Team" was deliberately constructed, at least in one critical regard. It was Nixon's operating complement for his "Big Team," which included prominent people like Nelson Rockefeller and the basic role of which was to create an aura of credibility and respectability. Few people belonged to both teams. Not surprising, the "Young Team" became a strong in-group and often treated members of the "Big Team" condescendingly (Raven, 1974, p. 306), encouraged by Nixon's tendency to view many of the prominent members with contempt (White, 1973).

We can only speculate as to whether the factionalism within the "Young Team" was consciously designed to facilitate Nixon's control, but the evidence does suggest a pattern of authoritarian high cohesiveness like that shown in Figure 1. Some observers (e.g., Raven, 1974, pp. 310–311) report surprise at high cohesiveness without esprit de corps, but the sociometric diagram in Figure 4 shows how one-to-one control overrode deep factional division.

To provide some supporting details, Nixon's "Young Team" included two long-time loyalists—Haldeman and Mitchell—and the factionalism can be traced to their common history. Haldeman had worked for Nixon since 1956. Mitchell came on the scene during Nixon's years in political

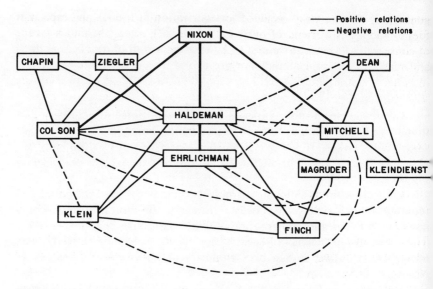

Figure 4. Sociometric choices on Nixon's "Young Team." President Nixon had positive relationships with nearly every one on the chart. Only the most significant of these are illustrated. (From Raven, 1974, p. 307.)

exile in New York following his 1962 gubernatorial election defeat in California. Mitchell and his wife Martha provided crucial support for Nixon at that time. Both Haldeman and Mitchell played major roles in Nixon's 1968 presidential race, at which time, Raven contends, a bitter rivalry developed between them. Almost all the other staff members freely associated with one but not both of the major figures. Raven argues, as the patterns of relationships in Figure 4 show, that Dean and Kleindienst associated with Mitchell; Ehrlichman and Colson sided with Haldeman. Only Magruder seems to have had relationships that spanned the two clusters.

The "Young Team" became intensely loyal to Nixon and both factions behaved similarly. These dynamics no doubt were significantly influenced by the fact that each member had attained his position only because of Nixon. The younger staff members—especially Dean, Colson, and Magruder—were dependent on Nixon for their sudden, high political standing; most had come from less-exalted or even lackluster positions; and they saw their new roles (in Magruder's words) as "a springboard to unlimited success." Moreover, in the terms of Figure 1, the "Young Team" had high norm consensus, but it was not based on the mutual respect and liking that characterized Kennedy's team. Despite their factionalism, yet in a sense because of it, Nixon's views of the world became the norms of the "Young Team." His political battles had clarified a distinct set of means to attain goals. This "Nixon way" included: categorization of friends and especially foes ("Nobody is a friend of ours. Let's face it."); retreat behind a facade of conservative American values, as by erecting a wall of decorum in dress and manner; and proclaiming warfare as *the* metaphor in life ("I believe in battle . . . continuing battle. . . . That's my way."). That members of the staff valued acceptance of the "way" is perhaps clearest in the case of Charles Colson's behavior and his understanding of the situation. Magruder (1974, p. 65) reports that Colson was "so effective in establishing himself through exaggerated loyalty to the chief, effective, driving, hard-hitting methods, and contempt for the president's enemies, [that] his position was secured."

In a very different way than on Kennedy's team, but to much the same effect, Raven proposes that the "Young Team" developed its own version of groupthink. Basically, loyalty to Nixon and perceived (manufactured?) external threats both overrode intragroup competition and intensified it. The group members sought to maintain or increase their favor with Nixon, so competition among them increased. Yet, cohesion was maintained by loyalty to Nixon and to his "way." These two factors probably enhanced the willingness among Nixon's staff members to take risks, to compete in the degree of zealotry about "the way." Raven (1974, pp. 311–313) develops this basic point by considering each of Janis's symptoms of groupthink. Here we illustrate only two:

1. *The illusion of unanimity.* Disagreements among members of the "Young Team" were recognized regarding specific details, but a general belief urged the importance of getting results by the most rapid and effective means available.
2. *Suppression of personal doubts.* If anyone considered a soft approach to moral or legal issues, these doubts had to be suppressed. They were "wrong" in terms of the ongoing social comparisons. No one wanted to be a millstone, or wishy-washy. Gradually, common suppression of personal doubts could lead all members to increase their acceptance of the basic philosophy of "the way."

This competition to take risks consistent with the "Nixon way" often got out of hand, Raven argues, suggesting to him a live case of risky-shift. Consider the dramatic occasion when Mitchell, Dean, and Magruder heard a plan—complete with six color charts—to employ prostitutes, kidnappings, blackmail, and burglaries to help destroy the Democrats. In retrospect, all expressed profound shock at the proposal. Mitchell said: "I not only should have thrown him out of the office; I should have thrown him out of the window." Yet at the time, no one said anything beyond suggesting that the plan was not exactly what they had in mind. Why not? No one can say for certain, but there is one answer that does not offend reason. A display of strong disapproval would have indicated weakness, implying that one was not a good team member and violating one of the basic norms of the "Young Team." One should not decry strong acts against the enemy—unless one wanted to be labeled as soft and could accept competitive disadvantage.

Groups and the Development of Truth-Seeking Norms: One Deliberate MARTA Intervention

With the possible exception of the last case, small-group phenomena so far seem to deal only with nature acting on people. This possible misperception needs to be corrected.

The major recent expressions of small-group analysis have been in applied technology—acting on nature to induce desired effects at individual, small-group, and large-organization levels (Golembiewski, 1979). This applied technology is usually referred to as the laboratory approach to organization development, or OD, and variously incorporates knowledge of small-group dynamics. Typically, such learning about small groups must be transferred into macro-organization contexts, which can be difficult.

The basic theoretical posture of interaction-oriented approaches to OD emphasizes the potency of small groups, in ways that Figure 1 will help express. Basically, OD seeks to energize high cohesive small groups, whose normative consensus applies this directionality to appropriate attitudes and behaviors: toward trust, interpersonal openness, and collaboration. "Family T-groups" and various "team-building" (Dyer, 1977) designs are employed most often, and they seek a supportive climate or atmosphere. Such a climate is compatible with the personality predispositions of most individuals, and is viewed as permitting more effective problem solving as well as greater sensitivity to personal needs. Feedback and disclosure processes can serve both needs, and relevant experience and skills are often provided by intact work teams. Typically, such designs seek to increase the degree of congruence between group leadership and formal roles, especially those of supervision. This may require major behavioral change by formal superiors, or it may be sufficient that open feedback and disclosure processes permit more effective vertical communication so that superior and subordinates can suitably adjust their behavior before macroadjustments become necessary.

Put another way, OD's reliance on groups reflects the four orientations to supraindividual phenomena discussed as an earlier point in this paper. Clearly, OD believes that groups with appropriate norms can facilitate performance. Moreover, social attraction and comparison processes facilitate the acceptance of appropriate norms in OD's small learning groups. As individuals find such processes rewarding, for themselves and the organization, so will social control relevant to the worksite become more probable. More broadly, OD as an applied technology serves the following purposes:

- Enriching the understanding of behavioral dynamics in natural-state organizations, especially at such critical times as start-up or when organization members experience unusual stress
- Generating learning designs that can help ameliorate some trauma experienced by individuals and groups in organizations
- Implying an internal logic that can reshape public administrative systems, as well as those in business organizations
- Requiring an explicit choice between alternative value sets, which provide a critical if often implicit foundation for all organizations, and which are vital in determining the quality of life generated by any organization

One application in the Metropolitan Atlanta Rapid Transit Authority (MARTA) illustrates the use of small-group technology in public agencies (Golembiewski, 1977, Part 2, pp. 1–42). This case deals with facilitating transitions between the several types of organizations MARTA would become over the agency's early life.

MARTA's key challenge involved developing multiple organizational personalities, as it were, in a very short time. From a small planning group in 1971, MARTA by 1981 was to design, construct, and then operate an integrated system of bus and rail transit. This would require "several MARTAs, whose development would be compressed in a brief time frame. The timeliness and smoothness of the unavoidable transitions would significantly influence the project's successful completion" (Golembiewski, 1977, Part 2, p. 10).

Dealing with these transitions required an open, proactive system oriented toward problem solving and timely change. The early preparation involved three key interventions, all learning designs based on the laboratory approach. First, the MARTA general manager and his senior staff began a team-building project. Second, the senior staff embarked on an interface experience with their subordinates. Third, the senior staff began an interface experience with the Authority's Board of Directors. Essentially, the operating goals involved increasing the cohesiveness of various small groupings within MARTA officialdom and integrating efforts within and between these groupings via acceptance of a common set of norms consistent with the collaboration–consensus system sketched in Table 2. The coercion–compromise model also described there outlines the more common managerial system which, it was proposed, would poorly suit the frequent transitions MARTA would have to make to succeed in its mission.

Team Building at the Top. Early on, MARTA's general manager (GM) and senior staff began a team-building experience which focused on

Table 2. Dominant Characteristics of Two Opposed Ideal Managerial Systems [a]

Coercion–compromise model	Collaboration–consensus model
• Superordinate power is used to control behavior reinforced by suitable rewards and punishments.	• Control is achieved through agreement on goals, reinforced by continuous feedback about results.
• Emphasis on leadership by authoritarian control of the compliant and weak, obeisance to the more powerful, and compromise when contenders are equal in power.	• Emphasis on leadership by direct confrontation of differences and working through of any conflicts.
• Disguising or suppressing real feelings or reactions, especially when they refer to powerful figures.	• Public sharing of real feelings and reactions.
• Obedience to the attempts of superiors to influence.	• Openness to the attempts to exert influence by those who have requisite competence or information.
• Authority and/or obedience is relied on to cement organization relationships.	• Mutual confidence and trust are used to cement organization relationships.
• Structure is power based and hierarchy oriented.	• Structure is task based and solution oriented.
• Individual responsibility.	• Shared responsibility.
• One-to-one relationships between superior and subordinates.	• Multiple-group members with peers, superiors, and subordinates.
• Structure is based on bureaucratic model and is intended to be stable over time.	• Structure emerges out of problems faced as well as out of developing consensus among members and is intended to be temporary or at least changeable.

[a]Based on H. Shepard (1965, pp. 1128–1131).

roles, relationships, and goals. Participants concentrated on confronting the GM and each other, for four basic purposes: to become more aware of one's own and others' reactions and feelings; to become more aware of stimuli inducing particular reactions and feelings in oneself and others; to accept and maintain norms that allow the expression of the full range of applicable information, reactions, and feelings; and to develop skills for sharing one's concerns in ways that encourage similar expression by other members. Based on a range of data, the GM and his staff began contracting with each other for starting, stopping, or continuing specific behaviors and attitudes. The two-step sequence—confronting and contracting—served to speed up psychological time in inducing heightened cohesiveness which, in turn, would facilitate the development of appropriate norms, roles, and relationships among MARTA's top managers. The sequence also provided experience with a process that could continue beyond MARTA's first years.

Multiple Interfaces Downward with Departments. Subsequently, senior staff began an interface exercise with the next lower tier in the hierarchy—the department directors. Two different formations were used: the entire directorate and staff (about 32 people); and each senior staff member with the cluster of directors reporting to him or her. The same type of confronting occurred, and contracting began on general personnel policies and procedures, as well as on issues among individual senior-staff members and their clusters of directors.

Interfacing Upward with the Board. As a final element in the early design, MARTA's senior staff and the Board of Directors met to work on their relationships. Active and motivated, Board members had only sporadic prior interaction with senior-staff members. The interface exercise directed energy to getting to know one another, to preventing conflicts due to incongruent views of responsibilities, and to continuing to work toward a collaboration–consensus model.

An In-Process Summary. These several interventions provided an infusion of data about how each of the four managerial elements in MARTA related to each other. Complex relationships became issues of public moment, and the processes extant between the major groupings were closely examined, sometimes uncomfortably so. The effort was aimed toward increasing cohesiveness among clusters of managers as well as among policymakers—integrating their efforts in pursuit of common norms while differentiating and clarifying their responsibilities. The early interventions provided an opportunity for process issues to receive close scrutiny before work and task issues captured the major attention of each group.

Attitudinal and anecdotal evidence suggests that the interventions succeeded. In addition, the data support the conclusion that progress was made toward the establishment of basic norms conducive to the development of an open, proactive, problem-solving, and adaptive climate.

Overview of Significance and Stuckness: The Condition of Small-Group Analysis Today

The aim of the remainder of this chapter is to induce political scientists to be more aggressive in small-group research and applications. The motivation for such study involves both a carrot that relates to significance, what an emphasis on small groups can do for political scientists, and a nonstick which suggests why stuckness came about and how it can be overcome.

Elaborating on Past, Present, and Future Significance: What the Small Group Can Do for Political Scientists

Five major points show how political scientists can benefit from the study of small groups, given both the ubiquity of small groups in relation to political phenomena and the usefulness of small-group perspectives in matters of moment, both conceptual and practical.

A Model for Sciencing. Although observers can, in good conscience and with substantial support of the facts, argue both sides of whether the "behavior revolution" has won the day in political science or whether its more extravagant pretensions have simply been exposed and sharply cut back to size (Eulau, 1963; Garson, 1978), improvement at sciencing the sciencable parts of the discipline still ranks high on the agenda of many political scientists. To the degree that such an agenda item exists, the emphasis on the small group can be most important from a methodological point of view.

The focus on the primary methodological value of small groups does not demean their substantive value to political science; rather, we seek to reflect an informed bias, as forcibly as possible, so as to put the matter in what we believe is a proper and useful perspective. One can easily oversell what the small group can deliver, and at what cost. This has happened in sociology and psychology, in fact. It was hoped that the small group would link the individual with the broadly social, the studies of which were threatening to split off and go in different directions. The small group would provide a common territory, many hoped, for working through some major issues in a general social theory which were too often lost in either a view that emphasized individuals to the neglect of structural issues or a view that emphasized structural aspects to the substantial exclusion of individuals. These expectations proved too lofty, so the approach here will be more modest. Substantively, small-group analysis provides no easy or quick fix. Methodologically, however, it does encourage development of skills and attitudes that will eventually facilitate major substantive progress in those areas of political science amenable to empirical analysis.

The more specific sense of the methodological value of small-group analysis can be sketched, relying substantially on materials published elsewhere (Golembiewski, 1978, pp. 16–17). Briefly, the study of small groups conveniently permits working in a natural-science mode (see Figure 5), largely because of the size of the research unit and the associated possibilities for experimental manipulation.

Perhaps the most useful simple metaphor for this mode is that of an expanding spiral that seeks to encompass more and more of reality. There will be resting orbits in this expanding spiral, and the spiral will sometimes collapse into itself toward some lower developmental level. But the game literally cannot be lost as long as the players are willing and able, since even gross failures can be helpful. Failure to verify predictions can be especially learningful, in fact. As such predictions are found variously wanting, the scientific subprocesses must recycle in complex ways. Thus, the failure may be remedied in various ways: by more extensive observation, by conceptualizations that are more nearly unidimensional, by operations that more validly and reliably measure variation of conceptual domains, and by more

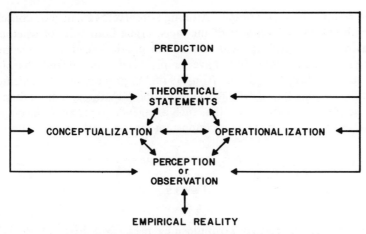

Figure 5.   A simplified model for empirical science.

sensitive theoretical statements. Success in verifying predictions might have less impact, and indeed can create an illusion that all is known that needs knowing. But nature typically cooperates in this regard, and even the theoretical statements in which we have the greatest confidence probably will have a short half-life.

This methodological advantage of small-group analysis well suits developmental needs in much of political science, where most approaches fit the natural-science mode poorly. Crudely, in fact, political science has been concept-rich and theory-glutted, but it has been weak in observation and poor in prediction. No small part of this record is due to the scarcity and difficulty of experimentation in the discipline which, in turn, derives from the fixation on the nation-state. This combination constitutes a potent duo—theoretical exuberance tends not to be tethered either by a convenient locus for analysis or by appropriate skills and attitudes. Hence, the half-life of a political theory will often be a long one, once it somehow catches hold.

Putting "Should" Theories in Their Proper Place.   Relatedly, small-group analysis will be helpful in separating what the case is, and what it ought to be. The need to be precise in this regard constitutes no new prescription: Bacon long ago applauded Machiavelli for making and respecting that distinction. But the distinction will not stay made simply because we say so. Eternal vigilance, as it were, remains the only defense, and it is a frail and fallible one at that.

The ideal represents no crude isolation of fact from value. Rather, the approach here envisions a complex interplay of the empirical and the normative, as shown by the simplified view of the interfaces in Figure 6. Again, the size and manipulability of the small group makes it a convenient unit

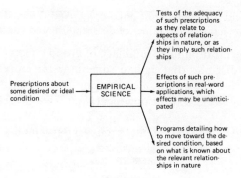

Figure 6

for respecting the related scrupulosities prescribed here, although one should not be lulled into believing this research will be easy. Small-group analysis can contribute to the development of political science in its concern with values and prescription as well as in its natural science description. The small group's thrust toward empirical science can also serve to define some limits for exuberant prescriptions, as well as to force fundamental questions about whether or not we should try to utilize some regularity that seems to exist in nature.

Political science has experienced much mischief in this central regard in an earlier flirtation with the "group approach." Good ideas were extended into conceptual grotesqueries, largely because students were not tethered by a natural-science model of empirical investigation, but also because it was convenient to neglect distributions between what is and what should be. Early insights about certain limited kinds of human groupings quickly became transmuted—via the key assumptions that a "group" is a "group," and that all political phenomena are "group"-dependent—into a diaphanous "group theory of politics." Moreover, this swiss-cheese-like theory not only passed muster as a descriptive "is," but was even extrapolated into a "should," that group pressure or might makes right.

Matters became complicated quickly, as political scientists variously seized on popular summaries of why and how groups can be significant (Truman, 1951), extending that correct but imprecise observation carelessly in unsuccessful attempts to deal with all their very much broader concerns. Thus, one careful observer (Garson, 1978, p. 71) sketched this range of overexuberances:

> Group theory served the intellectual purpose of aiding in the redefinition of democracy to avoid the seemingly unrealistic assumptions about individual rationality and motivation. It served the ideological purpose of defending contemporary democratic practice against the

surge of fascist and communist philosophy. And it served the cultural purpose of revitalizing the values of decentralism and consensus.

The author of the most popular summary of group effects had tried to warn both critics and disciples that he had something far more modest in mind (Truman, 1960). But the group interpretation for a short while became too good to let go, by proponent or opponent, and the scholarly fur often flew. Thus, Dowling (1969, p. 953) did not let Truman's caveats stand, and excoriated the latter's "faith" in the group interpretation which Dowling concluded "has been, if I am not mistaken, almost wholly evil."

Exploring Numerous Areas of Traditional Concern. As far as group analysis in the last decade or so is concerned, one may summarize the history as having two themes. Time has been rough on "the group theory of politics," and justly so. As Garson (1978, p. 191) concludes of this gross extrapolation: "the disintegration of the group approach to political science [came] in the 1970s."

At the same time, work by political scientists focusing on small groups in a natural science mode has continued at a steady if not spectacular pace. The research on small groups survives and prospers as an orientation to practically all traditional areas of research concern in political science. And applications of the small-group orientation might also be applied to areas of professional development and teaching. The conclusions below derive from two sources: the last published survey of small-group research in political science (Golembiewski, 1978) and an intensive search of the periodic literature since that survey.[1]

We offer here only three perspectives on the actual and possible diffusion of small-group perspectives throughout political science. First, several research uses of the small group will be sketched. Second, several dominant features of those research uses will be outlined. Third, some professional uses of small-group perspectives will be indicated.

Twenty Research Uses. Even as Garson sees "the group approach" in political science as dead or dying, no less than a score of pathways for dif-

---

[1] This survey extended to 31 periodicals: Administration and Society, Administrative Science Quarterly, American Behavioral Scientist, American Journal of Political Science, American Political Science Review, Annals of the American Academy of Social and Political Science, British Journal of Political Science, Comparative Political Studies, Comparative Politics, Contemporary Sociology, European Journal of Political Research, Experimental Study of Politics, Foreign Affairs, Human Relations, Journal of Conflict Resolution, Journal of Political Science, Journal of Politics, Policy Studies, Political Methodology, Political Methods, Political Science Reviewer, Polity, Public Administration Review, Public Opinion Quarterly, Public Policy, Review of Political Science, Small Group Behavior, Social Forces, Social Science Quarterly, Western Political Quarterly, and World Politics. In addition, major small-group researchers in political science have been contacted about work that may be still in progress or unpublished.

fusion of the small-group approach have been taken. These multiple pathways can be sketched in outline form; they aspire to represent comprehensively what has happened to the small group in political science.

1. Two efforts by political scientists, both of which originated in
   doctoral studies, sought to comprehend large bodies of group research and to identify their relevance to traditional concerns in
   political science (Golembiewski, 1962b; Verba, 1961).
2. A retrospective review of group-oriented research and application over the two decades anchored by the mid-1970s has been
   published (Golembiewski, 1978), with emphasis on the work of
   about two dozen political scientists dealing with natural groupings, as well as with experiments and simulations.
3. Political scientists increasingly come to the conclusion that apparent behavioral or attitudinal incongruities between individuals
   at aggregate levels of analysis in categoric groups may in fact con-
   ceal a more basic consistency with the norms of smaller groups
   within some large collectivity (e.g., Finifter, 1978; Kirkpatrick &
   McLemore, 1977). In this sense, the small group becomes an important locus for systematically explaining behavior that may
   seem deviant from some broader perspective and avoids assuming
   some homology between different levels.
4. Relatedly, political theorists have become increasingly aware of
   the "missing middle" in their theories, paralleling but post dating
   a similar awareness among social psychological theorists (e.g.,
   Shils, 1951). The historic focus emphasizes the individual on the
   one hand and macroaggregates like the "state" or "society" on
   the other. For example, Halebsky (1976) criticizes two aspects of
   theories of "mass society." First, descriptively, they inadequately
   provide for intermediate groups, including various small groupings. Thus, he explains: "The bases and means of maintaining
   ties, involvements, meaning, and personal satisfaction may be
   much more various than suggested by most theorists. There is
   little warrant to suggest a widespread existence of the isolated
   individual, therefore, at least in a fashion creating political availability" (1976, p. 83). Second, mass theory undervalues the mobilizing effects of various intermediate groups which may "suggest
   new reform policies . . . serve to revitalize political and social society and overcome the often [strong] elements of rigidity and con-
   straint of the existing system" (1976, p. 88).
5. Important applications have been made to the judiciary. Thus,
   the justices of the Supreme Court were analyzed as an interacting

group. (Danelski, 1974; Murphy, 1966; E. Snyder, 1958; Ulmer, 1965, 1971).

Similarly, aspects of judicial leadership and decision-making have been explored (e.g., Danelski, 1974; T. G. Walker, 1976a, 1976b; T. G. Walker & Main, 1973).

6. Group-level constructs have been used to describe and explain the behavior of legislators and legislatures (Dodd, 1972; Fenno, 1962; Francis, 1972; Hebert & McLemore, 1973; Hinckley, 1975; Manley, 1965; Perkins, 1978; Unekis, 1978).

7. Small-group methods and perspectives have been used to analyze public decision-making groups, at both high governmental levels (de Rivera, 1968; Janis, 1972) and low levels (Blanchard, 1975; Golembiewski, 1962a; Gordenker, 1959).

8. Sometimes dramatically, the power of small groups in shaping political attitudes has been demonstrated, both in the natural state (Burnstein, 1976; Hughes, 1975) and by deliberate manipulation in the natural state (e.g., Schein, 1961) and in experimental settings (Golembiewski, 1978).

9. New and more sophisticated attention has been given to the family, a ubiquitous grouping, as an agency of socialization in the development of political attitudes and behaviors (Maccoby, Matthews, & Morton, 1954; McClosky & Dahlgren, 1959; Siegel, 1965).

10. Impacts of small groups on voting and electoral behavior have been studied (Finifter, 1978; Hughes, 1975; McClosky & Dahlgren, 1959).

11. The impact of small work groups on political behavior has been documented (Elden, 1976, 1977; Finifter, 1978; Torbert & Rogers, 1972; Walker, 1976a), directing attention to a range of intriguing covariants: political deviance, alienation, anomie, voting behavior, sense of political efficacy, and so on.

12. Group level constructs have enriched the analysis of politically relevant decision making in both experimental (Barber, 1966; Bloomfield & Padelford, 1959; Dyson, Godwin, & Hazlewood, 1978; March, 1956; Snyder, 1955) and natural state contexts (Allison, 1971; de Rivera, 1968; Gore, 1956; Janis, 1972; Shils, 1951).

13. The value of group-level analysis has been demonstrated for a range of administrative issues and situations historically dealt with by political scientists, such as public administration (Blau, 1955; Golembiewski, 1962a, 1977; Golembiewski & Eddy, 1978) and international relations (Galtung, 1968; Gordenker, 1959; Ruge, 1978; Semmel & Minix, 1978; Toma, 1968).

14. Two increasingly popular kinds of research in political science—simulation and experimentation—typically generate and require group-level analysis (Guetzkow, Alger, Brody, Noel, & Snyder, 1963; LaPonce & Smoker, 1972; Ruge, 1978). Note also that a journal for conveniently showcasing such work, *Experimental Study of Politics*, has begun publication.

15. Groups have been shown to be major, apparently massive, determinants of such critical political processes as climates for decision making (Lewin, Lippitt, & White, 1939), patterns of forming consensus and/or conflict (Deutsch, 1949; Sherif & Sherif, 1953), the formation of opinions deviant from group standards or norms (Finifter, 1978; Scioli, 1971), and the broader processes of developing opinions (Baur, 1960; D. F. Davis, 1978).

16. Group analysis has been extended to such politically central areas as jury behavior (Grofman, 1979; Strodtbeck, James, & Hawkins, 1957).

17. Political scientists have become conversant with the techniques of group analysis and have even innovated such techniques (Madron, 1969; Walcott & Hoppmann, 1978).

18. Attempts have been made to build into political science (Madron, 1969) and into public administration (Golembiewski, 1977; Golembiewski & Eddy, 1978) methodological concerns and lessons derived from empirical research on small groups.

19. Group-oriented methods and theory have been used in an "applied science" approach to induce appropriate social systems in public agencies (Golembiewski, 1977, 1979; Golembiewski & Eddy, 1978).

20. Small-group pathologies of great relevance in various areas of political science have been isolated and explored, both in the natural state (Janis, 1972) and in experimental and other settings (McWhirter, 1978).

Dominant Features of Research Uses.   We cannot detail each of these multiple pathways for research, but we will examine three general aspects of them.

First, numerous convenient opportunities exist for integrating small-group perspectives with traditional concerns. Consider political decision-making processes, for example. T. G. Walker (1976b) concludes that, from a microanalytic perspective, social psychology and political science have made many of the most important contributions to understanding political decision making. Yet the two literatures remain substantially independent of one another. That inadequacy can be remedied in numerous particulars with no great difficulty, however, given sufficient ingenuity. Consider the leader-selection process for the small groups of judges sitting as the courts of last resort in 34 states during 1961–1967. Two kinds of selection processes existed, essentially: those based on arbitrary criteria such as seniority or rotation; and those variously based on merit, even if loosely defined. Figure 1 suggests that these two selection processes would have significantly different consequences on the leadership role, as in increasing the probability that merit-selected judges would score higher on the congruence of functional roles of leadership. Merit selection might not relate at all to the functional role "sociability," but clear connections seem to exist to "individual prominence" and "aiding group attainment." And as Figure 1 also implies, high congruence on the functional roles of leadership implies high cohesiveness and high consensus about norms. In an unobtrusive design using only publicly available data, T. G. Walker (1976a) confirmed the impact of selection style on performance in one significant particular. Merit-choice courts had lower rates of dissent than those whose chief judge was chosen by arbitrary methods.

Second, most uses of the small group in political science can be characterized as particularistic and *a posteriori*, utilizing extensions of available research that relate more to the spirit than to the substance of small groups. As the study excerpted above suggests, uses tend to focus on one or a few variables, even when they seek to test hypotheses or to track relationships; in contrast to common usage, Figure 1 presents quite a comprehensive map of variables in their relationships. In even more cases, the reliance on small-group variables is both speculative and *a posteriori*, as well as particularistic, as in retrospective interpretations that seek credible explanations of action sequences by employing novel concepts and highlighting different relationships (e.g., Golembiewski, 1962a; Janis, 1972).

This bias is both understandable and reasonable, but care is appropriate lest extensions and extrapolations become too robust. For example, small-group analysis has emphasized the centrality of norms in the control of member behavior. Understandably, then, political scientists like Hebert and McLemore (1972) search for norms in the Iowa legislature, rooting the concept in a small group context, and defining legislative norms as "widely shared sets of beliefs regarding appropriate behavior for legislators as legislators where these beliefs are not only shared but believed to be shared by legislators and are supported by social mechanisms encouraging conformity" (pp. 507–508). This may seem unobjectionable, but caution is appropriate. For example, we do not know whether these are "aggregate norms" whose incidence reflects that each legislative house is the behaviorally relevant and norm-sending unit, or whether they are "accidental norms" reflecting only a similarity between the norms of numerous and smaller behavioral identifications within, or even transcending, the legislature. For many purposes, that is a critical distinction, particularly in the design of operational definitions to test specific patterns of relations, as between cohesiveness and norm consensus. In the case of "fortuitous similarity," to illustrate, high cohesiveness (as measured by resultant attraction to some macrounit such as "the House") would have no predictable association with the norm consensus scores of individual members.

Third, many areas of common concern in political science are amenable to a fuller scale exploitation of small-group variables and relationships. Consider Danelski's (1974) work concerning the leadership exercised by chief justices of the United States Supreme Court. Danelski focused on the functional roles of leadership as they impact on cohesiveness and on three outcome variables—degree of conflict, personal satisfaction, and productivity. Basically, Danelski isolated four types of role constellations that chief justices might fit (see Figure 7). Following Bales (1958)—and, in effect, paralleling Figure 1—Danelski postulated (for example) that role constellation I would be associated with high cohesiveness, low conflict, and high satisfaction and productivity. He retrospectively reviewed the records of several chief justices to test the general applicability of his analytical approach.

We eschew details here, for the purpose is to illustrate applicability rather than to make an application. Note only that similar applications in organization contexts would do well to distinguish behavioral from categorical groups. The Supreme Court is a small group only in categoric terms— it might in fact encompass several more or less mutually exclusive sets of "group boundaries," whose distinction would be critical for most predictive purposes and many explanatory ones. For example, in such a case, some or all of the encompassed small groups might be highly cohesive while the cohesiveness of the entire Supreme Court qua collectivity could be low, with much resulting mischief for Danelski's predictions. Sociometric charts like that used to illustrate Nixon's "Young Team" can help isolate such behavioral anchorages with formal collectivities. And the specification of functional role constellations also helps, especially in the case of great men, whose existence presumes that mutually exclusive small groups do not dominate in some categoric collectivity. The focus on behavioral versus

	TASK LEADERSHIP	SOCIAL LEADERSHIP
I. Great Man	+	
II. Socioemotional Specialist	−	+
III. Task Specialist	+	+
IV. Follower	−	−

Figure 7

categoric anchorages also encourages thinking of (for example) Nixon as a great man in two groups rather than on one "Young Team." This distinction concerning target units is most crucial when designing operational definitions.

Professional and Teaching Applications. Two other important applications of small groups are possible: in professional development and in teaching. Useful models for various professional activities (e.g., curriculum building and departmental governance) have been developed (Gaff, 1975; Sikes, Schlesinger, & Seashore, 1974). Given the significant problems within political science (e.g., J. L. Walker, 1978), these models might well have a substantial use.

Applications of small-group principles related to teaching seem even more obvious, and major contributions toward a new technology for teaching have been made in areas such as organization behavior. Breakthroughs have been made in providing appropriate teaching materials (e.g., Kolb, Rubin, & McIntyre, 1971, 1974, 1979) for what is often called "experiential learning." This approach makes full use of group properties, both in the design of learning packages and in heightening interest and motivating performance. These themes characterize *Exchange*, a journal of an active interest group which focuses on the teaching and learning of organization behavior.

Political scientists lag behind in such applications of group dynamics to teaching. To be sure, there has been a long-standing if limited recognition of the value of engaging small-group forces to heighten the classroom experience for learners, as in the cases of Inter-Nation Simulation (Alger, 1963, pp. 178–179), or SIMSOC (Gamson, 1978). But few teaching materials in political science have explicitly sought to exploit this potential. The few exceptions to this generalization, for example, Public Broadcasting Laboratory (Rabin, Hildreth, & Miller, 1981), cluster in public administration, and many rely on simulation formats or the use of case studies as stimuli for role playing and other learning designs. Moreover, few political scientists seem to focus on group phenomena in the classroom; nor are they encouraged to do so by their training or (as is implied above) by available teaching materials.

Researching the Linkages of Individuals to Political Systems. As several points above suggest, and as the concept itself implies, small groups mediate the linkages of individuals to broader systems. That simple fact explains why small-group perspectives apply so ubiquitously. This section looks in some detail at the implied opportunities for research in political science. In turn, the focus will be on political participation generally and then more specifically on the impact of differences in working places on political performance.

Small Groups as Training Grounds for Political Participation. Verba

(1961, pp. 17–60) has summarized the general senses in which various small groups can powerfully influence the ways in which individuals come to be socialized in attitudes, values, and behaviors that have politically relevant consequences, both immediate and delayed. To simplify, small groups provide training grounds whose products will appear in political behavior. Thus, a child's first and perhaps primary experience with crucial elements in life—with leadership, role differentiation, conformity, participation, and so on—will be gained in such primary groups as the family. Hence, Verba concludes that the political scientist is ill-advised to focus only on organizations and individual personalities as they impact on political affairs. He adds:

> a significant level lies between that of the organization and of the individual personality: the level of the face-to-face group. These groups— families, committees, juries, informal discussion groups, face-to-face groups of all sorts—are basic units of the political system. Analysis of the many roles they play in the political process should further our understanding of that process. (Verba, 1961, p. 17)

Given this general view of small groups as training grounds for political performance, the following brief list suggests a much fuller catalog of analytic targets which seem particularly attractive. Consider only these five foci for research:

1. Performance of small-group roles at least provides experience for broader political roles, and the one may be antecedent to the other, in such common arenas as leadership and followership, alienation, deviance, and so on.

2. Small groups seem critical in the formation of attitudes relevant to politics, not only in specific topical senses but more significantly in connection with pervasive processes or mind sets (e.g., how to assert authority and respond to it, how to react to deviant opinions, what to share and how in communicating with others).

3. Small groups can variously conflict or be congruent with political norms or systems, and that balance can be critical not only in determining individual responses but also in shaping the major parameters of broad political systems. For example, reaction to deviance in small groups will trigger not only individual reactions, but in the aggregate it can also exert a telling pressure on responses to deviance in broader political systems.

4. Small groups can be used consciously to create identifications with a broader political system, albeit with serious practical and ethical consequences. For example, the use of "group decision making" to encourage homemakers to change food habits during wartime (Shils, 1951, pp. 56–57) seems unobjectionable, but far more care

seems appropriate concerning the use of "group confessions" to reveal political deviance and to convert deviants. Many other examples between these two could be cited, raising more difficult questions.

5. The interaction of personality predispositions and "climates" or "atmospheres" in small group settings encompass major foci for inquiry (e.g., Ruge, 1978). Consider the "authoritarian personality," a sufficient incidence of which would imply serious consequences for a republican or democratic form of government. Are such predispositions learned in small groups? Can the "rough edges" of such predispositions be "smoothed" by small-group experiences, as seems to be the case (Harrison, 1965)? These research questions relating to crucial political issues typify those suggested by the crucial interaction of personality and group climate or atmosphere.

Differences in Worksites and Political Performance. The more specific senses in which small-group experiences determine the character and quality of an individual's linkages to political systems still constitute major agenda items for the future, but some promising beginnings have been made. Perhaps the most promising work today is that which seeks to relate experiences at work to political attitudes and performance.

We provide some brief background. Many commentators have noted a central paradox in the Western experience: representative government exists in various forms in the political arena, but our basic organizational forms have been and remain authoritarian, if not autocratic, in public and business sectors. In relatively recent years—here and there, in the Scandinavian countries and in both "mature" and "developing" economies—ideology and some practice have sought a closer balance between work and governance. Moreover, this movement stands matters on their head in a significant manner. Democratic forms of political governance do not suffice; the emphasis has shifted to creating authority structures at work (and later elsewhere) that will permit people to develop resources for participative politics. This, Elden (1977, p. 5) notes, "inverts the popular radical cry." Industrial democracy's common aversion—traditional organization forms—is some self-fulfilling cycle typified (Elden, 1977, p. 3) by Figure 8.

Alternatives to the common approach to organizing work have been sought with increasing vigor, especially over the last two decades, for two basic reasons. First, increasing numbers of influential people have become concerned with incongruence beween the political and work arenas. The second, and probably the primary, impetus derives from accumulating evidence (e.g., Golembiewski, 1965a) that associates major awkward motivational and economic outcomes with the traditional approach to organizing

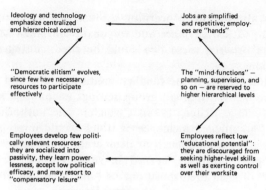

Figure 8

work, at least beyond early stages of organization growth. These awkward effects include: low satisfaction, low output, high absenteeism, and so on.

Several alternatives for organizing work have been developed—job enrichment (e.g., Ford, 1969), autonomous teams (e.g., Walton, 1977), sociotechnical variants (e.g., Thorsrud, 1976), organizing around flows-of-work versus functions (e.g., Golembiewski, 1965a)—and they all tend toward a definite ideal type. Relying on Elden (1977, p. 9), this ideal type would have properties, among others too numerous to mention here, such as those shown in Table 3. Basically, these alternative models rest on two fundamental tenets. First, they imply that individuals have a kind of internal gyroscope—some set of basic needs or preferences toward which people tend, at least when they have a reasonable opportunity for doing so and sometimes when that opportunity is limited or even hazardous. Generally, the gyroscope is oriented to moving toward greater competence and com-

Table 3. A Comparison of Two Types of Organization Structure

| | Alternative authority structures | |
	Hierarchical/elitist	Self-managed/democratic
Basic unit for organizing work	One man, one job	Aggregate related tasks for group work
Flow of control and relevant information	Basically vertical	Up, down, or across the organization, as the situation requires
Work routines	Fragmented and simplified; little learning possible	Integrated into "whole" tasks with variety, learning possibilities, and intrinsic rewards
Locus for handling variances	Next highest organizational level above level where variance occurs	Team as a whole: little variance is "exported" upward in the hierarchy

prehensiveness, toward growth. Second, the alternative models imply the powerful effects of small groups—in meeting individual needs for intimacy, acceptance, and security as well as for setting and maintaining norms that legitimize certain ranges of behavior while proscribing others. Hence, alternative models tend to organize around groups.

Mountains of research have been devoted to the mixed effects of the traditional model for organizing work, which in effect denies the two fundamentals of the alternative models. Thus, the traditional model tends to neglect individual predispositions for growth and comprehensiveness, especially at lower organizational levels. By hypothesis, this need deprivation is frustrating and results in low satisfaction and/or productivity, which seem to be common abreactions to frustration. In some few cases, to sketch an interesting deviant outcome, frustrated individuals can direct their aggression inward and work harder. In addition, the traditional model at least neglects groups, and even seeks to undercut them so as to (one supposes) make individuals more dependent on authority figures by denying them opportunities for social comparison and control. For example, that model emphasizes vertical and one-to-one relationships. By hypothesis, one of two effects will occur. The formation of groups may be inhibited, in which case most individuals will suffer need deprivation under most circumstances, and low satisfaction and/or productivity will often result. Note that highly dependent employees or high authoritarians may prefer this vertical, one-to-one pattern, but they usually constitute a minority of employees. Alternatively, underground groups may develop and persist, despite the contrary thrust of the traditional model and its underlying philosophy. In such cases, which probably constitute a distinct minority, groups often will be highly cohesive and have antimanagement norms. Thus, satisfaction may be high because, for example, such groups control their worksite and management, but productivity typically will be low.

The key questions concerning the broader political effects of such alternative approaches to organizing work have seldom been embodied in conscious research design, but the available evidence provides ample motivation for additional study. Consider one case (McWhinney, 1972; also Elden, 1976, 1977) which asked one of the key questions: If a worksite were set up to reflect the self-managed/democratic alternative for organizing work, would favorable consequences on broader political attitudes and behavior be observed? The research focused on three sets of consequences: those affecting the work unit, those impacting on work, and those affecting personal, political, and social outcomes beyond the worksite. In regard to consequences with political effects beyond the worksite, questionnaire items focused on *personal potency*, or the degree to which one feels powerless and controlled by fate or luck, *political efficacy*, which measures one's attitude to being able to influence government and seems to covary with the degree of political participation by individuals, and *social participation*, which relates to the degree that individuals involve themselves in various discretionary time organizations (i.e., those oriented to community, service, and so on).

What were the major covariants of the self-managed/democratic alternative for organizing work? A complete answer to this question would overwhelm the present review, involving as it does complex statistical (McQuitty, 1957) and interpretive (Elden, 1976, especially Chap. 4) issues. So we will refer here only to Elden's (1977, p. 18) summary conclusion:

> democratized authority structures are likely to benefit individual workers (more work satisfaction, personnel development and skills acquisition); their organization (increased identification and contribution as reflected for example in better quality, less absenteeism, and turnover); and their social class or society as a whole (increased political resources more widely diffused and decreased alienation).

Elden drives home his basic conclusion in italics. "In other words," he notes (1977, p. 18), having "some power over one's work co-varies with one's attitudes toward taking up participative opportunities. . . . Empirically there appears to be a *political dimension to everyday worklife.*"

Such conclusions still should be couched in tentative terms, but they have encouraged further work which has, if anything, only added further attractiveness and urgency to this line of study. Convenient summaries of such related work exist (Elden, 1976, especially Chap. 6); and the more specialized reader can usefully consult some of the specific research (Bernstein, 1975; Sheppard, 1976; Sheppard & Herrick, 1973; Torbert & Rogers, 1972).

Providing an Applied Component in Political Science. Political scientists can scarcely disregard the major import of lines of research like that just reviewed. Much the same conclusion would apply to a variety of other group-oriented research (e.g., studies of which conditions of political socialization tend to lead to which effects, or studies concerning the ways and means of inducing democratic versus autocratic styles of leadership.)

It is obvious that as we develop substantial confidence about covariants in nature, to that degree it becomes sensible (even imperative) to develop energetic "applied" uses of such knowledge to approach desired conditions. This building on knowledge of empirical regularities, but moving beyond them, constitutes the obvious promise of Elden's work which has just been reviewed.

There is a loss of leverage inherent in the general disregard of such applied work by political science. And general disregard it has been, without a doubt. The recent work with organization development in public agencies constitutes the major exception to the rule, and that work has only begun and still has numerous developmental problems (Golembiewski, 1977, 1978,

1979). At least three points show why applied work in political science could be very useful.

First, applied work constitutes a major check on the adequacy of existing theoretical work. If certain phenomena are really understood, it should be possible, in general, to induce them. And if some phenomena can be regularly induced, that also implies substantial understanding, as well as a foundation for increasingly complete comprehension in the future. Lewin was so correct when he noted that there is nothing as practical as a good theory.

Second, since political science has an important prescriptive component, a viable applied capability has an especial urgency. Given a condition that we value, the basic question involves approaching that value in practice. How that approach can be made, with what probability, and with what range of side effects—these constitute critical issues, even *the* critical issues. They can only be approached via applied work that has a growing sense of what is to be preferred, as well as an increasingly comprehensive sense of what variables covary in nature. The latter competency, in sum, makes us more effective in achieving our prescriptive goals—a just state, a beneficent commonwealth, and so on. Avoiding this classical issue can only impoverish political science.

Third, applied work constitutes a powerful kind of outreach which seems related not only to service to hosts but also to a sense of personal self-esteem. Consider the political scientist (Foss, 1973, p. 69) who worried about why he and his colleagues were so seldom impactful in decisions about policy. Suddenly, he knew. Political scientists talk about things basically of concern only to other political scientists. Effective applied work requires the broadening of who talks to whom about what, as well as of who derives benefit from work in political science.

Understanding and Escaping Contemporary Stuckness: Whatever Happened to Small-Group Research?

The five areas of significance above must be balanced by the present stuckness of small-group analysis. Generally, political science has much catching up to do, so some would argue that confronting the stuckness can be delayed without cost. Sooner or later, however, it must occur. And the view here is that the sooner this happens, the better. Underdeveloped areas of empirical research have a major advantage. With skill and some luck, they can either avoid or at least better anticipate the analytical cul-de-sacs experienced by more-developed areas.

So the goal here is to learn from past experience to avoid being forced to relive it. A broad range of relevant advice in this regard is available elsewhere, reflecting the views of representatives of sociology (Shepherd, 1978) and psychology (Weick, 1978). The focus here, in contrast, is macroscopic, and stresses six points. The initial three points sketch central assumptions of small-group research, and detail their increasingly awkward consequences. A fourth point provides some perspective on why research became stuck—why these assumptions were not discarded after their cost/benefit ratios had turned unfavorable, after their early convenience had been far outweighed by the mischief to which the assumptions led. The two concluding points focus on moving beyond the stuckness, on what needs to be done and how.

A Person ≠ A Person. Small-group analysis reflects the awkward assumption, both early and late, that a person is not a person. On the whole, research fails to differentiate characteristics of group members. Group-oriented research in political science (e.g., Guetzkow *et al.*, 1963) also followed this tradition, understandably.

Numerous factors no doubt encourage this common "white rat" assumption. It is convenient, in a kaleidoscopic sense. Specifying individual differences is variously untidy: some subjects might have to be rejected; batches of experimental subjects would have to be much larger to accommodate any subclassifications by personality differences; and so on. And while some no doubt noted that the taxonomy for differentiating individuals was nowhere to be found, others hoped that "random assignment" or experimental treatments would wash out or overwhelm any individual effects.

There seems no doubt that the assumption has been mischievous, on balance, however understandable it may be. "Subject effects" can be as profound as "treatment effects." Studies of the covariance of a and b may show a more-or-less definite tendency but, typically, replications will show that a and b covary in diverse ways: a little, or a lot, or not at all. Some may see such dispersion of effects as reflecting the chaotic nature of the subject matter; others may lament that the research is just more complicated than they hoped; and we would guess that personality variations often contribute significantly to the differences, and sometimes we have even successfully tested to document such effects (Golembiewski & Hilles, 1979, pp. 225–241 and 243–267).

A Group ≠ A Group. Much small-group analysis rests on another assumption, which often escapes notice although it certainly looks strange when set down in black and white. A kind of homogeneity hypothesis characterized much early research (Golembiewski, 1962b, pp. 26–32). Despite notable exceptions, the tradition remains. Consider the numerous studies on the risky shift, in which differences between groups and/or their members are rarely specified. This leaves open serious questions. For example, do group properties account for cases in which a shift to risk does not occur? If so, which properties induce that effect? Even more globally, can consistent differences in risky shift be associated with differences in groups, or individuals?

Evidence convincing to us establishes that a group is not a group and also suggests a way out of the present impasse. Consider the work of Bowers and Hausser (1977), who utilized complex statistical procedures to manipulate the following five major classes of data from members of over 500 small work groups:

1. *Organization climate*, which relates to decision-making practices, communication flow, and so on
2. *Supervisory leadership*, which deals with supervisor-to-member relations via such factors as support, facilitation of work, and so on
3. *Peer leadership*, which refers to member-to-member relationships
4. *Group process*, which deals with group-level phenomena such as coordination
5. *Satisfaction* which involves several facets, such as satisfaction with pay

Statistical procedures indicated that 17 profiles, or patterns of scores, were sufficient to classify nearly 95% of the 500 groups in Bowers' research population.

Bowers posed a significant question about these 17 profiles and had a positive if necessarily tentative answer. Bowers essentially asked whether five specific classes of ameliorative organizational interventions seem to be differentially applicable to groups with different profiles. Even with 500 groups, Bowers's matrix of 17 profiles by 5 alternative interventions often had cells with few or no cases. Nonetheless, major differential affinities did show up in the data—some kinds of interventions seemed effective in groups with certain profiles, while other designs in the same kinds of groups proved to be duds or even counterproductive. Bowers and his coauthor are encouraged to conclude (1977, p. 94) that "Even in its present crude form the [approach] provides a guide for intervention choice." But the existing data set has numerous empty cells; and the distinctions between interventions are fuzzy enough to urge caution about overinterpreting their findings.

The counterarguments to differentiating groups do not impress us, although we acknowledge them. For example, much small-group research utilizes batches of short-lived experimental collectivities, and it has sometimes been argued, but more often implied, that distinctive styles, atmospheres, and norms are therefore unlikely to develop. That might often be true, but we are more impressed with three other points. First, those distinctive elements represent precisely what is significant about the small group, and such differences thus constitute the essence for analysis rather than experimental contaminants. Put otherwise, a theory of laboratory small groups would be of only sharply restricted interest. Moreover, compelling evidence—from the earliest research (Lewin *et al.*, 1939) onward—implies that many newly assembled collectivities quickly develop distinctive features. Absent a confident classification of groups, reported effects defy easy interpretation, and "deviant effects" will abound, at least attenuating if not actually obscuring central tendencies in nature. Finally, voluminous research on social attraction implies that a broad range of individual features can quickly and substantially influence even short-term interaction.

Operationalization$_1$ $\neq$ Operationalization$_2$. An additional assumption further bedevils small-group analysis. Typically, operational measures of even the same conceptual domain will differ, often with profound effects on the results of individual studies. Despite exceptions that are sensitive to this problem (Eisman, 1959; March, 1956); all too often its implications are not given sufficient attention in interpretations of results. In the case of one magnum opus, in fact, distinctions between operations were entirely neglected. Studies were surveyed, and all studies of, for example, "cohesiveness" were similarly coded, and their effects on productivity, satisfaction, and so on were coded and punched on Hollerith cards. A countersorter run then would indicate to researchers what the literature "said" about specific "relationships." But the literature used speaks with multiple tongues, as it were, and the failure to take into account specific differences in operational definitions assumes far too much.

Distinguishing operational definitions makes analysis far more difficult, but that difficulty seems unavoidable. Failure to do so will have numerous ill effects, perhaps the major one of which relates to the boom-and-bust character of many areas of small-group research. Thus, a study using operational definition A of a concept will isolate some statistically significant covariations or correlations with variables of interest, each with its own operational definition. And for a time there will be a boom, as replication follows replication. But many of these replications—with the same nominal targets for analysis—will employ different operational definitions. Very robust relationships can overcome this untidiness. Far more often than not, however, and usually sooner rather than later, a dispersion of findings will result. Some studies will find strong relationships between the target variables; other studies will find weak relationships, or none at all; and some studies will find inverse relationships. This pattern characterized early research on cohesiveness, for example (see Golembiewski, 1962b, pp. 149–170). In that case, inconsistent results led to conceptual and operational refocusing. Far more often, however, malaise sets in, as investigators begin to doubt that the relationship is at all robust. Such doubts may be real, but shifting operational definitions can obscure even dominant relationships.

Perspectives on Analyticus Interruptus. Why were the above assumptions, which encouraged early research by simplifying the perceived major challenges but later proved increasingly troublesome, not discarded?

That question has no easy answer although, in general, the early success of small-group analysis proved in several senses the basic stimulus for its decline. However, four elements of small-group analysis constitute major parts of a more specific answer to the question:

1. The dominant research style was characterized by small-scale studies using only a few variables in small batches of usually undifferentiated groups, which made replication chancy (Mullins, 1973).

2. Research in specific areas had a boom-and-bust quality: one or a few studies would isolate significant relationships; then replications, often using different operational definitions, would generate a spectrum of findings and researchers would tend to move on.

3. No comprehensive theoretical framework and no intellectual leader evolved (Mullins, 1973) to go beyond the central but limited finding that small groups can have profound behavioral outcomes and deal with such key questions as which kinds of groups under what specific conditions will generate which specific effects (Bednar & Kaul, 1979).

4. Small-group analysis has been oversold, and major unanticipated difficulties have discouraged research in the longer run.

This list could be extended easily, but only to the same or similar end. The overall picture implies a kind of *analyticus interruptus* that is not complete but is significant.

Suddenly, in the early 1960s, two major shifts occurred. First, research tended to neglect group properties, rapidly becoming fixated on individual responses to social situations. As Davis *et al.* (1976, p. 501) note:

> many of the phenomena of social interaction gradually have been removed from their natural habitat, the small group, to situations permitting greater experimental control and convenience in observation and measurement. For example, conformity, attraction, attitude change, and social influence are typically studied with a single individual as the unit of analysis.

In this sense, the desire for methodological purity, to control for the diverse effects that occurred in even brief and temporary experimental collectivities, contributed to substantive sterility as far as group properties were concerned (Back, 1974, p. 380). Some researchers tried to control all stimuli, as via simulations using "one-person groups." Others noted that this process could easily be extended too far, in effect "controlling" the specific variance that was at the heart of the small group. Borgotta (1954) clearly belongs in the latter camp. He sardonically looked forward to no-person groups, where "every-one" is simulated.

The second major shift in the early 1960s was the development of two more or less dominant emphases: application and research. Without doubt, application-oriented work with small groups literally exploded. Emphasis shifted to *applied concerns and issues* as well as to *practical techniques*, paralleling theory development and testing. There had been antecedent group-oriented applications (Back, 1974, pp. 368–371), but of modest proportions. In temporal order, this explosion emphasized (Back, 1974, p. 367):

- The application of specific properties of group interaction to produce a relatively specific range of intended effects, as in group psychotherapy, T-groups or sensitivity training, and encounter groups
- The use of small groups as strategic loci for changing individual behavior or for beginning to solve organizational problems, as via organization development

With greater qualifications, it can also be said that research and application tended to grow estranged in the 1960s. Back (1974, p. 371) makes this latter point in describing the fates of the theoretical or academic orientation to the small group and the orientation concerned with intervention techniques. He notes that these orientations at first remained "strongly allied, encompassing a field known as group dynamics," but adds that "these two wings separated . . . although many of those in the field have retained overlapping interest in the two fields."

These two major shifts were massively reinforced for some time. Perhaps the most powerful stimulus derived from a double-barreled euphoria: not only did small groups marshal massive forces, but one could economically engage those forces in deliberate ways. Thus, Back (1974, p. 374) emphasizes the "surprising amount of agreement about general principles" among those interested in application. For example, they nearly universally agreed that: "The only effective ways of changing a person are either to change the whole [old] group or to unfreeze the person who wants to change by abolishing the forces which anchored him in the [old] group and making him choose a new group as anchor."

No doubt the intensity of this general agreement goes a long way toward explaining a significant point, that applications tended to rest on a model of group properties more rudimentary than even that reflected in Figure 1. This critical point deserves some elaboration. Consider four ways of viewing the small group:

1. As a social system capable of powerfully influencing member behavior
2. As a target of research concerning basic properties and processes
3. As a target for change, as when group norms are changed to influence levels of productivity
4. As the basic agent of change, as in a T-group when the group con-

text provides support and nurturance for individual learning, consistent with norms of the laboratory approach

Roughly, attention quickly slipped to levels 3 and 4, based on the nonspecific if significant insight at level 1 and perhaps a decade of more rigorous work at level 2. Moreover, as the several lines of application took on aspects of successful movements, even less attention was accorded to group properties. In fact, most applications rested essentially on a level 1 view of the small group. Argyris (1979, p. 297), for example, correctly articulates the theory underlying T-groups or sensitivity training in these revealing terms:

> The cohesive groups that produce closeness, warmth, and trust, [proponents argue] are the key vehicles for learning. Such groups can encourage participants to become more candid, to take more risks, and hence to produce more valid information. Once people are helped to express the inexpressible and to discuss the hitherto undiscussable, the difficulties created by the personal and societal censorship endemic to modern life can be greatly reduced.

Argyris goes on to emphasize the simplicity of this and other assumptions underlying T-group applications, especially in organization settings.

Much research certainly occurred at levels 3 and 4 above, but the character of this research tended to shift in complex but definite ways. Earlier, for example, research focused on basic group properties and their interactions; later, the focus might have shifted to the degree of change induced in individual behavior in contexts like T-groups, whose specific properties as groups often received secondary attention (e.g., Bunker & Knowles, 1967). Back is hard on this tendency. Indeed, for our tastes, he is too hard, although we do not dispute the central tendency to which he refers. Back concludes (1974, p. 381):

> The question in all research is not whether anything occurs at all, but under what conditions it occurs and how it can be controlled. From the point of view of research it is more important to show how the production of even a small effect occurs than it is to demonstrate changes in some people without knowing what caused them and what kind of people they are. Of course, in order to publicize the programs and to impress people that something is happening, the former approach is significant, but it can hardly be considered what is conveniently called research.

The sudden switches described above—away from research on group properties and toward group-oriented applications—occurred for multiple reasons, no doubt, the speculative catalog of which could be lengthy. We provide here only illustrations rather than voluminous chapter and verse. The stridency about "relevance" in the 1960s no doubt played a major role in these changes, perhaps even the dominant role. Moreover, and especially given the several urgencies of the 1960s, the undeniable potency of small groups encouraged efforts to exploit their power for various educational and therapeutic purposes. In addition, after the early blushes of overenthusiasm, small-group analysis came to be seen as implying greater practical and methodological problems than anticipated. These unexpected difficulties no doubt also discouraged research, since they pointed to more complex and larger-scale efforts than prevailing tastes and styles tolerated. Finally, the rapid emergence of legions of practitioners—T-group trainers, process facilitators, group therapists, organization development intervenors, and the like—many of them with little research interest, also had a profound impact. Finally, application-oriented effort was also very rewarding in many ways. These and other forces encouraged a switch in research interests away from groups and toward individuals, as well as a shift away from research and toward application.

In a few words, then, these two changes in emphasis resulted in stuckness that affected both research and application, sooner rather than later. Let us develop this critical point in some detail, lest it be underappreciated. Here, we will add three related perspectives on stuckness. First, a kind of intraprofession stuckness needs to be acknowledged. Despite the fact that some individuals function as practitioner *and* researcher, the two roles tend to split, with important consequences. Bednar and Kaul (1979, p. 316) refer to the matter in these concerned terms:

> the species researcher and the species practitioner are failing to cross-breed and on the verge of divorce. . . . It suggests a dramatic shift in focus. We are no longer very interested in the problem of whatever happened to group research (we have already concluded not very much), and much more interested in what can become of it. [Can] group practitioners and group researchers . . . learn to communicate; can they still crossbreed with each other? Can they establish some synchronous relationship which would enhance the adaptive evolution of both?

Second, and relatedly, the failure to isolate and theoretically relate group properties can be consequential for both researcher and practitioner. Kaul and Bednar reviewed over 100 studies of groups, and they provided only a conditional conclusion. Thus, they observed (Bednar & Kaul, 1978, p. 792) that "although it may not be the best question to ask, there is a large body of research that indicates that group treatments 'work.'" But causal statements of greater specificity still elude our theoretic grasp, they note elsewhere (Bednar & Kaul, 1979, p. 314):

> The reports tell us little or nothing about groups, *qua* groups. We cannot say, in general, what it is about the group treatments that makes

them effective. We know a little about the characteristics of effective group leaders, something about feedback, practically nothing about group composition factors, and least of all about the effects of the unique roles of group members in group treatments. In short, we know essentially nothing about the characteristics of groups which supposedly make them unique forms of psychological intervention. We know only that they worked in some instances.

Third, both practitioners and researchers, not to mention their clients, experience with special force the deficit of knowledge concerning group properties when treatments fail, as they have in group therapy (Bednar & Lawlis, 1971), T-groups or sensitivity training groups (Lieberman, Yalom, & Miles, 1973; Smith, 1975), and encounter groups (Hartley, Roback, & Abramowitz, 1976). Small groups can be impactful, as it were, for good or ill. Dies concludes (1979, p. 364–365):

> there is evidence that group interventions can precipitate deterioration effects among a certain small percentage of group participants. The casualty rates vary and the hypothesized antecedents to these negative outcomes are not fully understood, but there is widespread concern over their existence.

In such cases, patently, knowledge of which group properties have specific effects on what kinds of individuals is of the highest importance.

So how bad is the stuckness, the *analyticus interruptus*? To begin to answer this question, we would observe that the stuckness applies to second- or third-generation research and does not undercut the seminal observation of the significance of small groupings. Moreover, the stuckness can hardly be called complete. Progress has always continued, and even the severe critic Back (1974, pp. 832–883) counts among the new trends an increasing attention to group properties. For example, the assumptions and beliefs associated with an intervention have been related to group properties (Boderman, Freed, & Kinnucan, 1972) and the efficacy of specific interventions for 17 kinds of small groups has been tested (Bowers & Hausser, 1977). As Dies (1979, p. 366–367) observes with specific reference to group psychotherapy:

> researchers are clearly moving toward greater specification of group parameters. The question is no longer "Does group therapy work?" but rather "What particular aspects of group functioning contribute to specific therapeutic outcomes?" Both the process and outcome dimensions are becoming progressively clarified as researchers become more sophisticated and the data base continues to accumulate. Even more significant is the beginning recognition that group methods may contribute uniquely to therapeutic outcome. . . . [Two researchers] identify participation in a developing social microcosm, interpersonal feedback,

consensual validation, and reciprocal functioning as unique to group treatments, and they suggest that certain outcome criteria can be linked to these specific sources of influence.

In addition, what happened in small-group analysis is understandable and reasonable. Researchers intially saw it as the easy link between the individual and society, but their expectations wilted before unexpected complexity. And practitioners saw enormous ameliorative potential for individuals in the undoubted potency of small groups and so pushed applications more energetically than wisely in some cases.

This early innocence clearly now must be left behind. Consequently, moving beyond stuckness represents today's major challenge, and the concluding two points of this section address this matter in an introductory but hopefully useful way.

Two Ways out of Stuckness. Forceful rejection of the three assumptions described earlier in this section can come in one of two basic ways, each of which constitutes distasteful medicine in its own way. First, investigators can emphasize clinical studies, often with a single unit and especially in the natural state. This approach is often reflected in case studies which seek to utilize a range of behavioral concepts or perspectives to more specifically describe situations than is possible with commonplace concepts (e.g., Allison, 1971; Golembiewski, 1962a). As the citations above suggest, political science presents numerous analytical targets for such work. Reality reinforces convenience in this case. Basically, political scientists in many areas could contribute to this clinical, descriptive focus.

Such clinical work has some good points, and some bad. At its best, such work provides a test of more rigorous and multiunit research; and it can familiarize users and readers with appropriate concepts and models. These consequences should not be denigrated, but overvaluation should be guarded against. Without common and similar concepts, and without similar classification of similar cases, single-unit research can defy generalization and generate analytical mazes (witness the major effort in public administration to "test the participation hypothesis" via analysis of a number of case studies of reorganization [Mosher, 1967]).

Second, investigators can turn to large-batch studies such as laboratory or survey designs. Vast projects would be necessary, not only to map theoretical territories but especially to choose among the many available alternative operational definitions of the numerous, possibly relevant concepts. Such large-scale research will provide relational mappings showing, for example, under what conditions, and how, productivity is related to satisfaction. Of course, we presently have some notions about such territory, albeit mostly from small-scale studies that explore only narrow ranges of contingencies. Simultaneously, this large-scale research will also deal with such questions as: Of the numerous ways of measuring "satisfaction," does the JDI really enjoy the major advantages that it seems to? What constitute useful profiles of group properties? We have very little knowledge of such direct comparisons (Eisman, 1959; March, 1956), vital though they are, in large part because they are very tentative in the small-batch, few-variable research that has been characteristic of small-group analysis. Too many things can vary, perhaps wildly, in between-batch comparisons.

This vital knowledge will be costly, and the magnitudes will be unparalleled in social research. Note that Bowers and Hausser (1977) utilized 500 groups in their study, whereas 5,000 or so would have been more like what they needed to provide even a minimal number of cases in the outermost cells of their 17 × 5 matrix. Political science is not prepared to carry much of the burden of this macroresearch. In a somewhat whimsical moment, the senior author of this chapter called for a Manhattan Project of the social sciences as the only viable approach to the massive job of "comparative operational analysis." The interest group that explored some details of such an approach took on a revealing name—The Committee of $N = 500,000$.

Such a focus on larger scale studies constitutes the only way out rather than an easy way out. Basically, very much larger data batches than usual seem necessary to choose between multiple operational definitions; and this Manhattan Project approach implies other major changes in the ways of doing behavioral research. It will not be easy to get over the problems, either to develop the social organization necessary for the initial large-scale study of small-group dimensions and operationalizations or to return to the small-scale, clinical research necessary for fine tuning.

Overcoming Stuckness and Paradigmatic Change. Looked at from a perspective which political scientists can fully appreciate, either of the two ways out of stuckness sketched above will be difficult because they require a change in basic mind set. "We [students or groups], and social psychology generally," reports one eminent researcher (Mills, 1979, p. 407), "have undergone a crisis, not simply of confidence . . . but, more profoundly, of paradigm, of our general form of thought. It was as though the life-giving substance in the air we breathed became insufficient."

What paradigmatic gods have failed? Mills (1979) discusses five elements, which can be listed briefly. First, the vision of the small group as the analog for all levels of social organizations remains, but it has proved chimerical. The attractive vision of "the small group becoming to sociology what the fruit-fly has been to genetics" has been dashed. And severe constraints are necessary to restrain the exuberance of designing precise experiments that would generate a general theory of action. Second, the "experimenter effect" shook researchers, and there seemed no easy way to neutralize critical interactions that impacted on, if not fundamentally determined, "the findings." Thus, experimenters tended to find what they sought, and subjects often cleverly learned what the experimenter wanted and supplied it (Rosenthal, 1966). Third, analysts discovered—to use Geertz's (1973) revealing terminology—that group process was *thick* rather than *thin*, containing profound quantities of data or messages. The challenge had seemed more manageable earlier, perhaps even trivial (to judge from the exuberantly simple early systems for coding interaction). Fourth, investigators became more impressed with the *reflexivity* of small-group research. That is, humans can learn, and this raises the issue of whether we need a second theory to account for behavior when group members become aware of a first theory. Fifth, it was both humbling and learningful to become more conscious of the exclusion in much small-group research of the very variables that accounted for much of the long-run variance in group development and performance. Mills (1979) drives this point home, hard. The less constrained a group—as in self-analytic or sensitivity training groups—"the more clearly emerged the ancient issues that had preoccupied humans since primordial times: power and authority, abandonment and loneliness, love and attachment, sex and aggression, the taboos, the profane and the sacred."

Listing these paradigmatic anomalies does not resolve them, of course, but the catalog does serve two purposes. It adds perspective on why small-group analysis became stuck. And it adds urgency to the two basic, apparently divergent, but actually reinforcing ways suggested for escaping stuckness: to inaugurate a massive winnowing process to isolate some manageable number of concepts and operations and to focus increasingly on small-batch studies, especially in the natural state, to test the adequacy of prevailing theoretical maps, at once testing the results of the larger winnowing process and contributing to its comprehensiveness.

References

Alcock, J. E., & Mansell, D. Predisposition and behavior in a collective dilemma. *Journal of Conflict Resolution*, 1977, *21*, 443–457.

Alger, C. F. Use of the inter-nation simulation in undergraduate teaching. In H. Guetzkow (Ed.), *Simulation in social science*. Englewood Cliffs, N.J.: Prentice-Hall, 1963.

Allison, G. T. *Essence of decision: Explaining the Cuban Missile Crisis*. Boston: Little, Brown, 1971.

Allport, F. H. The influence of the group upon association and thought. *Journal of Experimental Psychology*, 1920, *3*, 159–182.

Argyris, C. Reflecting on laboratory education from a theory of action perspective. *Journal of Applied Behavioral Science*, 1979, *15*, 296–310.

Aronson, E., & Linder, D. Gain and loss of esteem as determinants of interpersonal attractiveness. *Journal of Experimental Social Psychology*, 1965, *1*, 156–171.

Back, K. W. *Beyond words*. New York: Russell Sage Foundation, 1972.

Back, K. W. Intervention techniques: Small groups. *Annual Review of Psychology*, 1974, *25*, 367–387.

Bales, R. F. Task roles and social roles in problem-solving groups. In E. E. Maccoby, T. M. Newcomb, & E. L. Hartley (Eds.), *Readings in social psychology* (3d ed.). New York: Holt, Rinehart, and Winston, 1958.

Barber, J. C. *Power in committees*. Chicago: Rand-McNally, 1966.

Baumgartner, T., Buckley, W., & Burns, T. Relational control: The human structuring of cooperation and conflict. *Journal of Conflict Resolution*, 1975, *19*, 417–440.

Baur, E. J. Public opinion and the primary group. *American Sociological Review*, 1960, *25*, 208–218.

Bednar, R. L., & Kaul, T. J. Experimental group research: Current perspectives. In S. L. Garfield & A. E. Bergin (Eds.), *Handbook of psychotherapy and behavior change: An empirical analysis* (2d ed.). New York: Wiley, 1978.

Bednar, R. L., & Kaul, T. J. Experimental group research: What never happened. *Journal of Applied Behavioral Science*, 1979, *15*, 311–319.

Bednar, R. L., & Lawlis, G. G. Empirical research in group psychotherapy. In A. E. Bergin & S. L. Garfield (Eds.), *Handbook of psychotherapy and behavior change*. New York: Wiley, 1971.

Berkowitz, L. (Ed.). *Group processes*. New York: Academic Press, 1978.

Bernstein, P. *Workplace democratization*. Unpublished doctoral dissertation, Stanford University, 1975.

Biderman, A. D. *March to calumny*. New York: Macmillan, 1963.

Blanchard, P. D. Small group analysis and the study of school board conflict: An interdisciplinary approach. *Small Group Behavior*, 1975, *6*, 229–237.

Blau, P. M. *The dynamics of bureaucracy*. Chicago: University of Chicago Press, 1955.

Blood, R. O., Jr., & Wolfe, D. M. *Husbands and wives: The dynamics of married living*. New York: Free Press, 1960.

Bloomfield, L. P., & Padelford, N. J. Three experiments in political gaming. *American Political Science Review*, 1959, *53*, 1105–1115.

Boderman, A., Freed, D. W., & Kinnucan, M. T. "Touch me, like me": Testing an encounter group assumption. *Journal of Applied Behavioral Science*, 1972, *8*, 527–533.

Bonacich, P., Shure, G. H., Kahan, J. P., & Meeker, R. J. Cooperation and group size in the N-person prisoners' dilemma. *Journal of Conflict Resolution*, 1976, *20*, 687–706.

Borgotta, E. F. Sidesteps toward a nonspecial theory. *Psychological Review*, 1954, *61*, 343–352.

Bowers, D. G., & Hausser, D. L. Work group types and intervention effects in organizational development. *Administrative Science Quarterly*, 1977, *22*, 76–94.

Bunker, D. R., & Knowles, E. S. Comparison of behavioral changes resulting from human relations training laboratories of different lengths. *Journal of Applied Behavioral Science*, 1967, *3*, 505–523.

Burnstein, P. Social networks and voting: Some Israeli data. *Social Forces*, 1976, *54*, 833–847.

Carlson, S. *Executive behavior*. Stockholm: Stromberg, 1951.

Collins, B. E., & Guetzkow, H. *A social psychology of group processes for decision-making*. New York: Wiley, 1964.

Danelski, D. J. The influence of the chief justice in the decisional process. In W. F. Murphy & C. H. Pritchett (Eds.), *Courts, judges and politics* (2d ed.). New York: Random House, 1974.

Darley, J. M., & Berscheid, E. Increased liking as a result of the anticipation of personal contact. *Human Relations*, 1967, *20*, 29–40.

Davis, D. F. Search behavior of small decision-making groups. In R. T. Golembiewski (Ed.), *The small group in political science*. Athens, Ga.: University of Georgia Press, 1978.

Davis, J. H., Laughlin, P. R., & Komorita, S. S. The social psychology of small groups. *Annual Review of Psychology*, 1976, *27*, 501–541.

de Rivera, J. *The psychological dimension of foreign policy.* Columbus, Ohio: Charles P. Merrill, 1968.

Deutsch, M. A theory of cooperation and competition. *Human Relations,* 1949, *2,* 129–152, 199–231.

Deutsch, M., & Collins, M. E. *Interracial housing: A psychological evaluation of a social experiment.* Minneapolis: University of Minnesota Press, 1951.

Dickoff, H. *Reactions to evaluations by another person as a function of self-evaluation and the interaction context.* Unpublished doctoral dissertation, Duke University, 1961.

Dies, R. R. (Ed.). Symposium on therapy and encounter group research: Issues and answers. *Small Group Behavior,* 1978, *9,* 163–304.

Dies, R. R. Group psychotherapy: Reflections on three decades of research. *Journal of Applied Behavioral Science,* 1979, *15,* 361–373.

Dion, K. K. Physical attractiveness and evaluation of children's transgressions. *Journal of Personality and Social Psychology,* 1972, *24,* 207–213.

Dion, K. K., Baron, R. S., & Miller, N. Why do groups make riskier decisions than individuals? In L. Berkowitz (Ed.), *Advances in experimental social psychology* (Vol. 5). New York: Academic Press, 1970.

Dodd, L. C. Committee integration in the Senate. *Journal of Politics,* 1972, *34,* 1135–1171.

Dodd, L. C., & Pierce, J. C. Roll call measurement of committee integration: The impact of alternative methods. *Polity,* 1975, *7,* 386–401.

Dowling, R. E. Pressure group theory: Its methodological range. *American Political Science Review,* 1969, *54,* 944–954.

Dyer, W. G. *Team building.* Reading, Mass.: Addison-Wesley, 1977.

Dyson, J. W., Godwin, P. H. B., & Hazlewood, L. A. Political discussions and decision-making in experimental small groups. In R. T. Golembiewski (Ed.), *The small group in political science.* Athens: University of Georgia Press, 1978.

Eisman, B. Some operational measures of cohesiveness and their interrelations. *Human Relations,* 1959, *12,* 183–189.

Elden, M. *Democracy at work for more participatory politics.* Unpublished doctoral dissertation, University of California at Los Angeles, 1976.

Elden, M. *Political efficacy at work.* Paper prepared for the Seminar on Social Change and Organization Development, Inter-University Center for Graduate Studies, Dubrovnik, Yugoslavia, 1977.

Eulau, H. *The behavioral persuasion in politics.* New York: Random House, 1963.

Fenno, R. F. The House Appropriations Committee as a political system: The problem of integration. *American Political Science Review,* 1962, *56,* 953–960.

Festinger, L. A theory of social comparison processes. *Human Relations,* 1954, *7,* 117–140.

Festinger, L., Schachter, S., & Back, K. *Social pressures in informal groups: A study of human factors in housing.* New York: Harper, 1950.

Finifter, A. The friendship group as a protective environment for political deviants. In R. T. Golembiewski (Ed.), *The small group in political science.* Athens: University of Georgia Press, 1978.

Ford, R. N. *Motivation through the work itself.* New York: American Management Association, 1969.

Foss, P. O. Policy analysis and the political science profession. *Policy Studies Journal,* 1973, *2,* 67–71.

Francis, W. L. Influence and interaction in a state legislative body. *American Political Science Review,* 1962, *56,* 953–960.

Freedman, J. L., & Doob, A. N. *Deviancy.* New York: Academic Press, 1968.

Gaff, J. D. *Toward faculty renewal.* San Francisco: Jossey-Bass, 1975.

Galtung, J. Small group theory and the theory of international relations. In M. A. Kaplan (Ed.), *New approaches in international relations.* New York: St. Martins Press, 1968.

Gamson, W. A. (Ed.). SIMSOC (Simulated Society) (3rd ed.). New York: Free Press, 1978.

Garson, G. D. *Group theories of politics.* Beverly Hills: Sage, 1978.

Geertz, C. *The interpretation of cultures.* New York: Basic Books, 1973.

Gerard, H., & Miller, N. Group dynamics. *Annual Review of Psychology,* 1967, *18,* 287–332.

Golembiewski, R. T. *Behavior and organization.* Chicago: Rand-McNally, 1962. (a)

Golembiewski, R. T. *The small group.* Chicago: University of Chicago Press, 1962. (b)

Golembiewski, R. T. *Men, management, and morality.* New York: McGraw-Hill, 1965. (a)

Golembiewski, R. T. Small groups and large organizations. In J. G. March (Ed.), *Handbook of organizations.* Chicago: Rand-McNally, 1965. (b)

Golembiewski, R. T. *Public administration as a developing discipline* (2 parts). New York: Dekker, 1977.

Golembiewski, R. T. (Ed.). *The small group in political science.* Athens: University of Georgia Press, 1978.

Golembiewski, R. T. *Approaches to planned change* (2 parts). New York: Dekker, 1979.

Golembiewski, R. T., & Blumberg, A. (Eds.). *Sensitivity training and the laboratory approach.* Itasca, Ill.: F. E. Peacock, 1970, 1973, 1977.

Golembiewski, R. T., & Eddy, W. B. (Eds.). *Organization development in public administration* (2 parts). New York: Dekker, 1978.

Golembiewski, R. T., & Hilles, R. *Toward the responsive organization.* Salt Lake City: Brighton, 1979.

Gordenker, L. *The United Nations and the peaceful unification of Korea: The politics of field operations.* The Hague: M. Nijhoff, 1959.

Gore, W. J. Decision-making in a federal field office. *Public Administration Review,* 1956, *16,* 281–291.

Grofman, B. Research note: A pilot study of individual behavior as mediated by the group context: Three and five-member mode juries. *Experimental Study of Politics,* 1979, *7,* 41–54.

Guetzkow, H., Alger, C. F., Brody, R. A., Noel, R. C., & Snyder, R. C. *Simulation in international relations.* Englewood Cliffs, N.J.: Prentice-Hall, 1963.

Halebsky, S. *Mass society and political conflict.* Cambridge, England: Cambridge University Press, 1976.

Hamburger, H., Guyer, M., & Fox, J. Group size and cooperation. *Journal of Conflict Resolution,* 1975, *19,* 503–531.

Hare, A. P. *Handbook of small group research* (2nd ed.). New York: Free Press, 1976.

Harrison, R. Group composition models for laboratory design. *Journal of Applied Behavioral Science,* 1965, *1,* 409–432.

Hartley, D., Roback, H. B., & Abramowitz, S. I. Deterioration effects in encounter groups. *American Psychologist,* 1976, *31,* 247–255.

Hebert, F. T., & McLemore, L. E. Character and structure of legislative norms: Operationalizing the norm concept in the legislative setting. *American Journal of Political Science,* 1973, *17,* 506–527.

Hinckley, B. Policy content, committee membership, and behavior. *American Journal of Political Science,* 1975, *19,* 543–557.

Horne, J. H., & Lupton, T. The work activities of "middle" managers. *Journal of Management Studies,* 1965, *1,* 14–33.

Hughes, A. *Psychology and the political experience.* Cambridge, England: Cambridge University Press, 1975.

Huston, T. L., & Levinger, G. Interpersonal attraction and relationships. *Annual Review of Psychology,* 1978, *29,* 115–156.

Janis, I. *Victims of groupthink.* Boston: Houghton Mifflin, 1972.

Kahn, R. L., Wolfe, D. M., Quinn, R. P., Snoek, J. D., & Rosenthal, R. A. *Organizational stress: Studies in role conflict and ambiguity.* New York: Wiley, 1964.

Kaul, T., & Bednar, R. L. Conceptualizing group research: A preliminary analysis. *Small Group Behavior*, 1978, *9*, 173–191.

Kegan, D. L., & Rubenstein, A. H. Measures of trust and openness. *Comparative Group Studies*, 1972, *3*, 179–200.

Kirkpatrick, S. A., & McLemore, L. Perceptual and affective components of legislative norms. *Journal of Politics*, 1977, *39*, 685–709.

Kirkpatrick, S. A., Davis, D. F., & Robertson, R. D. The process of political decision-making in groups. *American Behavioral Scientist*, 1976, *20*, 33–64.

Kogan, N., & Wallach, M. A. *Risk-taking: A study of cognition and personality*. New York: Holt, Rinehart and Winston, 1964.

Kogan, N., & Wallach, M. A. Risk-taking as a function of the situation, the person, and the group. In G. Mandler, P. Mussen, N. Kogan, & M.A. Wallach (Eds.), *New directions in psychology* (Vol. III). New York: Holt, Rinehart and Winston, 1967.

Kolb, D. A., Rubin, I. M., & McIntyre, J. M. *Organizational psychology*. Englewood Cliffs, N.J.: Prentice-Hall, 1971, 1974, 1979.

Kornhauser, W. *The politics of mass society*. New York: Free Press, 1959.

Lakin, M. (Ed.). Special issue: What's happened to small group research. *Journal of Applied Behavioral Science*, 1979, *5*, 257–440.

LaPonce, J. & Smoker, P. (Eds.). *Simulation and experimentation in political science*. Vancouver: University of Vancouver Press, 1972.

Latham, E. *The group basis of politics*. Ithaca: Cornell University Press, 1952.

Laumann, E. O. Friends of urban men: An assessment of accuracy in reporting their socio-economic attributes, mutual choice, and attitude agreement. *Sociometry*, 1969, *32*, 54–70.

LeBon, G. *The crowd*. London: T. F. Unwin, 1926.

Lewin, K., Lippitt, R., & White, R. K. Patterns of aggressive behavior in experimentally created "social climates." *Journal of Social Psychology*, 1939, *10*, 271–299.

Lieberman, M. A., Yalom, K. D., & Miles, M. B. *Encounter groups: First facts*. New York: Basic Books, 1973.

Lindskold, S., McElwain, D. C., & Wayner, M. Cooperation and the use of coercion by groups and individuals. *Journal of Conflict Resolution*, 1977, *21*, 531–550.

Maccoby, E. E., Matthews, R. E., & Morton, A. S. Youth and political change. *Public Opinion Quarterly*, 1954, *18*, 23–39.

Madron, T. *Small group methods and the study of politics*. Evanston: Northwestern University Press, 1969.

Magruder, J. S. *An American life: One man's road to Watergate*. New York: Atheneum, 1974.

Main, E. C., & Walker, T. G. Choice shifts and extreme behavior. *Journal of Social Psychology*, 1973, *91*, 215–221.

Malamuth, N. M., & Feshback, S. Risky shift in a naturalistic setting. *Journal of Personality*, 1972, *40*, 38–49.

Manley, J. F. The House Committee on Ways and Means. *American Political Science Review*, 1965, *59*, 927–939.

March, J. G. Influence measurement in experimental and semi-experimental groups. *Sociometry*, 1956, *19*, 260–271.

Marrow, A. *Behind the executive mask*. New York: American Management Association, 1964.

McClosky, H., & Dahlgren, H. E. Primary group influence on party loyalty. *American Political Science Review*, 1959, *53*, 757–776.

McQuitty, L. L. Elementary linkage analysis for isolating orthogonal and oblique types and typal relevancies. *Education and Psychological Measurement*, 1957, *17*, 207–229.

McWhinney, W. *Open systems—traditional hierarchies*. Paper presented at Quality of Working Life Conference, Arden House, 1972.

McWhirter, D. A. Testing for groupthink: The effect of anticipated group membership on individual decision making. In R. T. Golembiewski (Ed.), *The small group in political science.* Athens: University of Georgia Press, 1978.

Milgram, S. Behavioral study of obedience. *Journal of Abnormal and Social Psychology,* 1963, *67,* 371–378.

Milgram, S. Some conditions of obedience and disobedience to authority. *Human Relations,* 1965, *18,* 57–76.

Milgram, S. *Obedience to authority.* New York: Harper & Row, 1974.

Mills, T. M. Changing paradigms for studying human groups. *Journal of Applied Behavioral Science,* 1979, *15,* 407–423.

Mosher, F. C. *Governmental reorganizations: Cases and commentary.* Indianapolis: Bobbs Merrill, 1967.

Mulder, M., & Stemerding, A. Threat, attraction to group, and need for strong leadership. *Human Relations,* 1963, *16,* 317–334.

Mullins, N. C. *Theories and theory groups in contemporary American sociology.* New York: Harper & Row, 1973.

Murphy, W. F. Courts as small groups. *Harvard Law Review,* 1966, *79,* 1565–1572.

Newcomb, T. M. *Personality and social change.* New York: Dryden, 1943.

Nordhoy, F. *Group interaction in decision-making under risk.* Unpublished masters thesis, Sloan School of Industrial Management, Massachusetts Institute of Technology, 1962.

Odegard, P. H. A group basis of politics: A new name for an ancient myth. *Western Political Quarterly,* 1958, *3,* 689–702.

Odom, W. E. A dissenting view on the group approach to Soviet politics. *World Politics,* 1976, *28,* 542–567.

O'Kiefe, R. D., Kernoghan, J. A., & Rubenstein, A. H. Group cohesiveness: A factor in the adoption of innovation among scientific work groups. *Small Group Behavior,* 1975, *6,* 282–292.

Olson, P., & Davis, J. H. Divisible tasks and pooling performance in groups. *Psychological Reports,* 1964, *15,* 511–517.

Perkins, L. P. *Member goals and committee behavior: The House Judiciary Committee.* Paper delivered at the Annual Meeting of the Southern Political Science Association, Atlanta, 1978.

Peterson, S. A. *Dissent in American courts.* Paper presented at the Annual Meeting of the Southern Political Science Association, Atlanta, 1978.

Quarantelli, E. L., & Dynes, R. R. Organizational and group behaviors in disasters. *American Behavioral Scientist,* 1970, *13,* 325–426.

Rabin, J., Hildreth, W. B., & Miller, G. J. *Public budgeting laboratory.* Athens: Institute of Government, University of Georgia, 1981.

Raven, B. H. The Nixon group. *Journal of Social Issues,* 1974, *29,* 297–320.

Raven, B. H., & Rubin, J. Z. *Social psychology: People in groups.* New York: Wiley, 1976.

Rogers, C. R. *Carl Rogers on encounter groups.* New York: Harper & Row, 1970.

Rosenthal, R. *Experimenter effects in behavioral research.* New York: Appleton-Century-Crofts, 1966.

Ruge, M. H. Image and reality in simulated international systems. In R. T. Golembiewski (Ed.), *The small group in political science.* Athens: University of Georgia Press, 1978.

Saegert, S. Swap, W., & Zajonc, R. B. Exposure, context, and interpersonal attraction. *Journal of Personality and Social Psychology,* 1973, *25,* 234–242.

Sakurai, M. M. Small group cohesiveness and detrimental conformity. *Sociometry,* 1975, *38,* 340–357.

Schachter, S. Deviation, rejection, and communication. *Journal of Abnormal and Social Psychology,* 1951, *46,* 190–207.

Schachter, S. *The psychology of affiliation: Experimental studies of the sources of gregariousness.* Stanford: Stanford University Press, 1959.

Schein, E. H. The Chinese indoctrination program for prisoners of war. *Psychiatry,* 1956, *19,* 149–172.

Schein, E. H. *Coercive persuasion.* New York: W. W. Norton, 1961.

Schiller, B. A quantitative analysis of marriage selection in a small group. *Journal of Social Psychology,* 1932, *3,* 297–319.

Scioli, F. P., Jr. Conformity in small groups: The relationship between political attitude and overt behavior. *Comparative Group Studies,* 1971, *2,* 53–64.

Semmel, A. K., & Minix, D. Group dynamics and risk-taking. *Experimental Study of Politics,* 1978, *6,* 1–33.

Shaw, M. E. *Group dynamics.* New York: McGraw-Hill, 1976.

Shepherd, C. Some challenges for future group research: Reflections on the experience in sociology. In R. T. Golembiewski (Ed.), *The small group in political science.* Athens: University of Georgia Press, 1978.

Sheppard, H. *The humanization of work.* Paper presented at the Conference on Social Planning, Humanization of Work and Organization, Warsaw, Poland, 1976.

Sheppard, H., & Herrick, N. *Where have all the robots gone?* New York: Free Press, 1972.

Sherif, M. A study of some social factors in perception. *Archives of Psychology,* 1935, *27,* No. 187.

Sherif, M., & Sherif, C. *Groups in harmony and tension.* New York: Harper & Row, 1953.

Shils, E. A. The study of the primary group. In D. Lerner & H. D. Lasswell (Eds.), *The policy sciences.* Stanford: Stanford University Press, 1951.

Siegel, R. *Political socialization: Role in the political process.* Philadelphia: American Academy of Political Science, 1965.

Sikes, W. W., Schlesinger, L. E., & Seashore, C. W. *Renewing higher education from within.* San Francisco: Jossey-Bass, 1974.

Skilling, H. G., & Griffiths, F. (Eds.). *Interest groups in Soviet politics.* Princeton: Princeton University Press, 1964.

Smith, P. B. *Groups within organizations.* New York: Harper & Row, 1973.

Snyder, E. The Supreme Court as a small group. *Social Forces,* 1958, *36,* 232–238.

Snyder, R. C. Game theory and the analysis of political behavior. In R. C. Snyder (Ed.), *Research frontiers in politics and government.* Washington, D.C.: Brookings, 1955.

Stavig, G. R., & Barnett, L. D. Group size and societal conflict. *Human Relations,* 1977, *30,* 761–765.

Stein, A. A. Conflict and cohesion: A review of the literature. *Journal of Conflict Resolution,* 1976, *20,* 143–172.

Steinbacker, J. *The child seducers.* Fullerton, Calif.: Educator Publications, 1971.

Steiner, I. D. *Group process and productivity.* New York: Academic Press, 1972.

Steiner, I. D. Whatever happens to the group in social psychology? *Journal of Experimental and Social Psychology,* 1974, *10,* 94–108.

Stoner, J. F. *A comparison of individual and group decisions involving risk.* Unpublished masters thesis, Sloan School of Industrial Management, Massachusetts Institute of Technology, 1961.

Strodtbeck, F. L., James, R. J., & Hawkins, C. Social status in jury deliberations. *American Sociological Review,* 1957, *22,* 713–719.

Sudnow, D. Dead on arrival. *Trans-action,* 1967, *5,* 36–44.

Taylor, D., Berry, P. C., & Block, C. H. Does group participation when using brainstorming facilitate or inhibit creative thinking? *Administrative Science Quarterly,* 1958, *3,* 23–47.

Thorsrud, E. *Model for socio-technical systems.* Oslo: Work Research Institutes, 1976.

Toma, P. A. Sociometric measurements of the Sino-Soviet conflict: Peaceful and nonpeaceful revolutions. *Journal of Politics,* 1968, *30,* 732–748.

Torbert, W. C., & Rogers, M. *Being for the most part puppets.* Cambridge, Mass.: Schenkman, 1972.

Triplett, N. The dynamogenic factors in peacemaking and competition. *American Journal of Psychology,* 1898, *9,* 507–533.

Truman, D. *The governmental process.* New York: Knopf, 1951.

Truman, D. On the invention of systems. *American Political Science Review,* 1960, *54,* 494–495.

Tyson, H. L., Jr., & Kaplowitz, S. A. Attitudinal conformity and anonymity. *Public Opinion Quarterly,* 1977, *41,* 226–234.

Ulmer, S. S. Toward a theory of sub-group formation in the United States Supreme Court. *Journal of Politics,* 1965, *27,* 132–152.

Ulmer, S. S. *Courts as small and not so small groups.* New York: Learning Press, 1971.

Unekis, J. K. *The impact of Congressional reform on decision-making in the standing committees of the House of Representatives.* Paper presented at the Annual Meeting of the Southern Political Science Association, Atlanta, 1978.

Verba, S. *Small groups and political behavior.* Princeton: Princeton University Press, 1961.

Walcott, C., & Hoppmann, P. T. Interaction analysis and bargaining behavior. In R. T. Golembiewski (Ed.), *The small group in political science.* Athens: University of Georgia Press, 1978.

Walker, J. L. Challenges of professional development for political science in the next decade and beyond. *PS,* 1978, *11,* 251–262.

Walker, T. G. Leader selection and behavior in small political groups. *Small Group Behavior,* 1976, *7,* 363–368. (a)

Walker, T. G. Microanalytic approaches to political decision-making. *American Behavioral Scientist,* 1976, *20,* 93–110. (b)

Walker, T. G., & Main, E. C. Choice shifts in political decision-making. *Journal of Applied Social Psychology,* 1973, *3,* 39–48.

Walton, R. E. Work innovations at Topeka. *Journal of Applied Behavioral Science,* 1977, *13,* 422–433.

Weick, K. E. Some challenges for future group research: Reflections on the experience in psychology. In R. T. Golembiewski (Ed.), *The small group in political science.* Athens: University of Georgia Press, 1978.

White, T. H. *The making of the president—1972.* New York: Bantam Books, 1973.

Whyte, M. K. *Small groups and political rituals in China.* Berkeley: University of California Press, 1974.

Wilson, S. *Informal groups.* Englewood Cliffs, N.J.: Prentice-Hall, 1978.

Zajonc, R. B. Social facilitation. *Science,* 1965, *149,* 269–274.

Zander, A. *Groups at work.* San Francisco: Jossey-Bass, 1977.

Zander, A. The study of group behavior during four decades. *Journal of Applied Behavioral Science,* 1979, *15,* 272–282.

2

GOVERNMENT LEARNING
An Overview

LLOYD S. ETHEREDGE

Does the executive branch of government learn from experience in the long run? If it does, what are the processes? If not, what are the barriers? And what can be done to make government policy more intelligent and effective?

Government learning is a new interdisciplinary field of social science inquiry. With only three books addressing the problem generally (Argyris & Schon, 1978; Schon, 1971; Wilensky, 1967); and a handful of related conceptual discussions (Deutsch, 1963; Dror, 1971; Lasswell, 1971; March, 1965), much of this chapter will be primarily an original overview of how the field looks to one practitioner. While there are important comparative dimensions, I will take as my illustrative focus the American executive branch.

Introduction

The concern to promote intelligent government invites attention for reasons beyond simple efficiency or effective governance in a changing world. The modern, high-technology state gives political leaders the capability to destroy most human life with ease; it also gives them the resources (and often puts them under pressure) for legitimate, extensive intervention in and even management or regulatory control of society to effect resolutions of problems as defined by different groups (Lowi, 1978; J. Q. Wilson,

LLOYD S. ETHEREDGE • Department of Political Science, Massachusetts Institute of Technology, Cambridge, Massachusetts 02139.

1975). In poorer countries, simple humanitarian concerns (15 million annual deaths from starvation, mean life expectancies in the low 40s), as well as agendas for economic growth and political stability or reform might be better addressed by greater government intelligence. Both fear of what governments might do wrong and hope for what governments might eventually learn to do right are incentives to analyze existing practices and to create constructive alternatives.

Beyond being a direct study and drawing on relevant concepts and theories from the behavioral sciences, the analysis of executive-branch learning processes is also a self-reflective study for the professional social scientist in three ways. First, as it is about adult learning, it poses a personal question: How do any of us, as adults, learn about ourselves, and about life? How well do we do it? To the extent that we are good at it, we may have important insights about how people in the executive branch of government can learn well. And to the extent we do not learn well, and can explain why, there may also be useful and transferable diagnostic insights.

A second question involves how competent and well organized social scientists are at the job of rapidly and efficiently answering important questions about political life (including the problem of executive-branch learning). To the extent that we are competent, individually and collectively, at our jobs as social scientists, we probably have additional important insight into how the executive branch could proceed.

Third, as professional teachers and scholars, university-based social scientists have additional personal experience from which to draw. In principle, universities and academic disciplines hold a special role and responsibility as the institutional memories of society, charged with the codification of human experience and charged as well to effectively develop skills and accumulated knowledge and wisdom in students who, in their turn, will govern and apply (if anyone does) the hopefully increasing intelligence of the human race about the conduct of its public affairs. But how adequate and successful are current curricula and teaching methods? One test for a medical faculty is whether, when they become ill, faculty members would trust their well-being to a randomly selected graduate certified by their program. A similar test for the quality of the burgeoning public policy programs for undergraduates and graduate students in America is whether the faculty would trust the assessment of reality and selection of foreign and domestic policy to randomly selected graduates. To the extent that we have already devised or can devise effective and fully satisfactory curriculum contents and educational theories, we have a useful set of ideas about what people in government should know and how to increase the traction of their learning processes.

A Model for Theory Development: Medical Diagnosis Capability

This chapter proposes a general orchestration of issues and literatures; its aim is not to advocate one simple, general theory. Medicine is, I think, an appropriate model for theories in the social sciences, and my goal is to orchestrate intellectual frameworks and midrange theories as a first step in developing a competence at differential diagnosis, analogous to the capacity for differentiated diagnosis acquired by a skilled physician. For example, when a patient presents the general symptom of low energy, a good physician knows the evidence must be evaluated anew for each case; there could be any one (or several) of thousands of causes which produce this symptom. The good physician has available his own knowledge of the particular patient's history, his sensitivity and skill in observation, direct examination, and interviewing, and both an extensive body of well-differentiated theory and a diverse repertoire of empirical laboratory tests to use as aids in diagnosis.

Although systems with strong norms can simplify and reduce the variance of behavior, there seems little reason, in principle, to expect that processes of individual and collective behavior are simpler than those of a single human body or as simple as the first generation of public-policy case studies would have us believe (see Ross, 1977). In the case of a malfunction in executive-branch learning, the ideal would be for well-trained social scientists to be able to approach each case with personal sensitivity and skill, a knowledge of the relevant history, background training in a field providing a rich body of well-researched theories about alternative problem origins and effective interventions, and a repertoire of empirical diagnostic tests. For example, one case of failure in organizational learning might arise because of failures in leadership and motivation, perhaps the absence of anyone articulating a persuasive vision to integrate an image of a better world with a long-range research and learning agenda for the agency. Another program's difficulty might arise from an excess of ideological motivation, for example, a strong activist, emotional commitment that blocks heterodoxy or self-critical reflection (Etheredge, 1979c). In a third case, a program might be so bureaucratized by red tape that gifted personnel have left and the remaining staff are so demoralized they have become only burned-out time servers. At another agency, at another time and place, the problem might be a simple absence of people whose formal jobs give them time, resources, and responsibility to learn. A fifth case could be explained by the absence of any pressure or incentive for learning from the political environment, while at the agency down the block the problem may involve so much political pressure for performance that no one can risk self-critical evaluations that might turn up problems. A seventh agency might have acquired or produced timid bureaucrats who are afraid to "get off the reservation" (i.e., who have "individuation anxiety") and think boldly and independently. And of course, all of these problems, and many more, could be present within a single agency—or indeed, in different ways, within the same individual (Etheredge, 1976a, pp. 29–30).

Overview and a Preliminary Caution

There is a lot that will be discussed in the following pages. I feel obliged to caution the reader that we are not yet at a stage where it can be said how everything fits together. There have been enough search-lights lit by researchers to see key problems, but not enough to see the full landscape clearly. Moreover, at the present state of knowledge, the vocabularies of applicable research traditions differ (the familiar "paradigm incommensurability" problem). The reader who prefers bold and authoritative theses and tightly integrated arguments will be disturbed—hopefully constructively (see p. 107)—and is invited to join the search.

In the sections that follow I will first define a conception of learning and then address briefly normative issues and the descriptive problem of assessing trends. I will then review issues of causation as they interpenetrate across the contexts of individuals, organizations, the Washington political environment, and society and the world. Next, I will address the problem of learning rates as a function of problem types, and finally, I will propose a brief review of diagnostic alternatives and offer some concluding reflections.

Defining Learning

There are two basic ways to define learning. The usual descriptive definition is to say that learning has occurred whenever there is a change in behavior or belief. For example, Hilgard and Bower (1975, p. 17), in the standard advanced text in educational psychology, propose that "Learning refers to the change in a subject's behavior to a given situation brought about by his repeated experiences of that situation, provided that the behavior change cannot be explained on the basis of native response tendencies, maturation, or temporary states of the subject (e.g. fatigue, drugs, etc.)." (Note that in some cases this conception can be tricky—if you do it right the first time and then simply persist, learning has occurred even though there is no change; learning in this case must be indexed not as change within a situation but as a nonrandom deviation from the organism's baseline behavior or search patterns.)

A second, analytical definition, which I propose to use in this review, is that "true" learning should be assessed not by behavior change or attitude change but by the dual criteria of increased *intelligence and sophistication of thought* and increased *effectiveness of behavior*.[1] To take the first criteria, various people who previously opposed the SALT II treaty could become favorable to it, yet very different internal processes might be involved (e.g., either simple instinctive, amoeboid reaction to possible electoral defeat or thoughtful and detailed study of the issues). An intelligent analyst will want to know which process is involved to decide if the individual is thinking and understanding with greater intelligence and sophistication.

Changes in intelligence and sophistication can be assessed, as they are in teaching, by expert judgment of those who possess these qualities. But three useful indices can be drawn from Heinz Werner's (Werner, 1948; Werner & Kaplan, 1963) application of Herbert Spencer's earlier view that intellectual development always involves processes of both *increased differentiation* (recognition and articulation) and *increased levels of hierarchical integration*. To apply these criteria, we would first assess how many new and different relevant arguments and considerations a person thought about when considering the SALT II problem; and we would further assess the depth and degree of differentiation of thought within each argument (if the person holds views about Soviet motivation, is the Soviet Union seen only as a unitary actor or is the issue differentiated as a problem of internal Soviet politics with discussion of the different actors and processes involved)? Werner also believed that intellectual development involves increased capacity for the *differentiation of the self from its symbols and first-order thought processes*, so a second assessment

---

[1] I will leave unaddressed the issue of the alternative goals and values in relation to which effectiveness can be assessed. There are many, and it would require a major essay to codify the alternatives systematically. I will list just a few criteria different observers or different decision makers currently do (or could) employ: (a) achieving official program goals; (b) democratic responsiveness; (c) political stability; (d) impact (net or minimizing downside risk) on swing voters in congressional and presidential elections; (e) advancing the personal career of the decision maker; (f) serving presidential interests; (g) maintaining or developing credits with key members of Congress to increase overall executive effectiveness; (h) military deterrence capability based on realistic-encounter scenario performance; (i) military deterrence capability based on symbolic political assumptions; (j) efficiency; (k) rational consistency; (l) equity; (m) symbolization of a collective myth of hope and efforts for progress; and so on.

Greater effectiveness is probably, in part, a function of both increasingly accurate factual knowledge and the usefulness of increased intelligence and sophistication (see Lindblom & Cohen, 1979) as well as other sources (e.g., greater power) discussed in the text. "Knowledgeable" is a term which can be used to refer to the marriage of intelligence and sophistication with accurate information content.

would be how much perspective, insight, and self-reflective capacity (see Hofstadter, 1979; Natsoulas, 1978) an individual showed about his or her own assumptions, models, and inference processes (an inquiry that would also assess whether the subject is deeply self-reflective or only developing better rationalizations; see Etheredge, 1978; Lane, 1969; Searles, 1972/1979). Finally, we would assess the hierarchical integration of the thought processes: Does our subject coherently pull together and systematically organize all the complexity, relate parts of the problem to each other, relate parts to wholes, to evidence and inference? (On methods of assessment see Goldstein & Blackman, 1978, pp. 136–173; Miller & Wilson, 1979.)

These indices can be used to generate a quick preliminary diagnosis of the intelligence and sophistication attained by a government official about a policy area. For example, someone who speaks only of "the poor," shows less intelligence about the problem than someone who talks sensibly about different categories of poor people. Thirty years ago, people spoke of "underachieving children"; today, a sophisticated government expert can discuss types of underachievers produced by different processes (reading problems of differentiated types; nutritional deficiencies; subcultural disadvantage; subcultural, community, and school norms; school phobias; etc.) and point to different programs and current research about each of these. Or in national-defense debates, one can compare the "big bangs for a buck" sophistication in political-elite discussions of the 1950s with the current differentiated concepts of first-strike, second-strike, counterforce, and other types of strategic-weapon systems.

Being able to talk and think with more intelligence and sophistication does not, however, mean government can be more successful in translating available resources into effective problem solutions. Mental patients can have brilliantly elaborated and integrated beliefs and yet be out of touch with reality; social scientists may only invent new—but unhelpful —ways to talk about the same old things or develop a sophisticated capacity to reject old answers more rapidly than their capacity to find better ones. And even brilliant individuals can be ineffective in organizational surroundings.

However, increased effectiveness cannot, by itself, index increased learning. Increased effectiveness can result from perseverance more money, more power, changed public receptivities, and many other causes. Nor does decreased effectiveness necessarily warrant the inference of poor learning. For example, if relevant societal processes change (as in the success of American macroeconomic policy in the early 1960s compared with stagflation of the 1970s), government's effective intelligence, growing less rapidly than the phenomenon changes, may still decline. And not everyone in America or the world cheers for the success of Washington; conflicting individuals, corporations, or other countries may themselves become more intelligent over time and thus decrease government effectiveness (some economic policy tools, for example, may have become less effective because of investor game plans that now take account of the government's plans for them; see Andersen, 1977). And there is the problem of quagmire public policy, as incremental changes to increase effectiveness in the short term (e.g., escalations of the Vietnam War) lead to even larger problems in the long term. It is also possible that the nature of individuals (Bass & Brown, 1973; Hurlbert, 1979) or of social processes (including successful implementation of government policy) will turn out to be stochastic, so complete knowledge can provide only limited control and effectiveness.

Finally, it is important to be self-reflective—and empirical—about the hope that better learning will yield solutions to social problems, a hope which is currently strong in America and has also captured people's imaginations at other times throughout history (Frankena, 1973, pp. 79–80). First, you may learn that you cannot solve some problems. Second, you may find that solutions are not politically or practically feasible in an America with a limited government. For example, we already know, in principle, how to reduce violent crime by 90% (turn America into Japan). We already know how to solve poverty (massive transfer payments). Often, the call in American politics to "learn about" how to solve problems is not a call for good ideas but a call for practical solutions—that is, incremental rather than radical, and involving bureaucratic programs, appropriations, and management rather than leadership or strengthened norms.

Types of Individual Learning

With this initial overview, I now want to develop a more differentiated view of learning by discussing five distinct types of individual learning (scientific-method learning, intuitive understanding, creativity, skill, and wisdom), within which the criteria for differentiated recognition and articulation, hierarchical integration, and perspective (i.e., for appropriate selection among alternatives) can be applied.

Scientific Learning. The best developed image of a formal learning process is the well-known scientific positivist vision. The type of learning requires clarity and explicitness for all key terms and procedures, and explicit codification of the degree of confidence in conclusions.

An individual can be said to have increased scientific intelligence to the extent that his or her ways of thinking about the world exhibit use of

- Explicit models, theories, and hypotheses
- Key terms within such formulations which are translated into operational definitions that point clearly to the phenomena in the external world being discussed—that is, good (valid, reliable) referential indexing for all terms

- Inferences of causation based on explicit evidence which is further subscripted in the individual's mind by explicit reference to the following: (1) the degree of reliability and validity of all measures employed; (2) the sample characteristics and the validity of such samples for drawing broader conclusions; (3) the inferential criteria (probabilistic inferential logic) supporting the causal hypothesis; and (4) the alternative hypotheses or additional relevant variables that still remain untested or uncontrolled

Here, and for the other four types of learning, it seems useful as well to consider two further second-order characteristics to index good learning within different modes:

- *Speed and completeness of knowledge scanning and summary*— how quickly and comprehensively an individual can scan, retrieve, and combine pieces of relevant scientific information from memory to reach conclusions both about what is known and what is not known
- *Efficiency of processing*—judging not just speed and completeness but efficiency (effortlessness); going through all the steps with less effort and less wasted motion (by analogy, the better athlete runs a mile in 6 minutes using 45% of capacity compared with someone who can do the same using 85% of capacity); a person can be said to know something better when processing, storing, and combination of information are virtually effortless and automatic (a beginning driver may shift gears and steer at the same speed as an experienced driver, but for the experienced driver the task is second-nature, whereas the beginner has to concentrate all his attention and capacity on what he is doing) (see Brown, 1962; Moray, 1979; Reason, 1977)

Intuitive Capacity.   Intuition refers to the capacity to sense or grasp, with incomplete objective data, the nature, qualities, or operating principles of physical objects, people, or situations. The relevant data and rules of inference in intuition may, as Polanyi (1958, 1966) has argued, not be amenable to explicit codification.

Scientific knowledge refers to learning about causes. Intuitive knowledge can refer to this and more—for example, to grasping "what is going on here," the essential dynamic, in a given situation, to understanding meaning (Bernstein, 1978), to sizing up people, to viscerally "knowing" what to say to put people at ease or the timing of when to be firm in a negotiation.

A promising theory is that intuition is a function of empathy, of identification, and hence a function of insight—the capacity of access to the self and its own actual or potential experiences as a resource for being sensitive to what is happening in the world (Gauss, 1973; Maslow, 1969; Royce, Coward, Egan, Kessel, & Mos, 1978; Stotland, Mathews, Sherman, Hansson, & Richardson, 1978; Westcott, 1968). It is important to emphasize, I think, that intuition is a *capacity*. Although some positivists have proposed that intuition is merely prescientific, it is probably more useful to note the psychometric evidence for at least two forms of mental functioning, the analytic (scientific) and the verbal (intuitive), based on the two brain hemispheres (Ornstein, 1972; Jaynes, 1976), and to respect the possibilities that both modes can be usefully developed. Weimer (1974), however, makes an argument that almost all knowledge is tacit and intuitive and that investigation, use, and refinement of this mode ought therefore to take precedence over the formally scientific mode.

Creativity.   Creativity refers to the activity of generating novel ideas, conceptions, or perspectives which others find to have value. It is especially important to governmental effectiveness in times of change or increased responsibilities where older theories, methods, or concepts based on previous experience prove ill-suited to new conditions. The problem of creativity has been studied primarily at the individual level and secondarily at the small-group level (e.g., Bion, 1977; Brenman-Gibson, 1976, 1978; D. T. Campbell, 1960, 1974; Ducey, 1976; Gruber, 1974; Kohut, 1976/1978; Mitroff, 1974; Stein, 1974). There is also increasing work on creation of "smart organizations" in research and development management which I will discuss in a later section. There is yet to be a systematic integration of this literature into the study of political or public-policy behavior.

Skill.   Skill refers to the capacity, given adequate technologies and resources, to translate intentions into successful outcomes. It is engineering knowledge, applied practical knowledge of how to make things happen. It may be the skills of drafting a good briefing paper or an effective State of the Union address. It may involve applying current intellectual technologies to analyze the costs and benefits of a neutron bomb. It may be the skills necessary to set political agendas, to maneuver a Panama Canal or SALT II treaty through Congress or to pass a windfall profits tax through the mastery of standard techniques of psychodrama and symbolic politics, salesmanship, and coalition building, or the skill to implement a program once it is enacted (Bardach, 1972).

Skills obviously draw on scientific knowledge, intuition, and creativity, but their core involves the know-how to combine these efficiently and with grace (effortlessness and economy of effort) and with appropriate linkage of ends to means to translate intentions into desired consequences while avoiding or minimizing undesired or unknown outcomes.

Wisdom and Good Judgment.   A fifth type of learning one would want of individuals in the executive branch is wisdom. We can decompose the concept of wisdom into three related components: a sense of values and goal hierarchies, a sense of perspective, and a mature integrative capacity to draw efficiently on scientific knowledge, intuition, creativity, and skill. Together, these qualities produce people who can be depended on for good judgment about important issues (Plato, *The Republic*, 4, 428a).

Aristotle held that the development of moral learning was, basically, learning to love and praise what one ought to love and praise and learning to reject and condemn what one ought to reject and condemn. But major approaches to the study of values seem only partly suited to measure a government employee's learning by Aristotle's agenda: Rokeach's value inventory (1973) allows self-reports of what people value positively, but it omits some values important in the political process, such as pragmatic compromise, genuine belief in democratic processes, or a favorable press image, and it does not assess what people condemn or how strongly they condemn it. Kohlberg's (1969, 1971) approach to the study of developing moral reasoning (toward a rationalist Kantian universalism) is well structured to assess distributions of different approaches traditional to political philosophy, although there have been continuing methodological and conceptual problems (Gilligan, 1977; Kurtines & Grief, 1974). But here again, the relevant question is not whether someone can think like Kant in a paper-and-pencil dilemma whose content is quite different from his job. What is of greater importance is whether there are many issues in Washington defined solely as moral issues distinct from confounding or supervening role responsibilities (including the belief that moral judgments are not one's appropriate job), political costs and benefits, and personal risk (Minsky, 1975; Neisser, 1976; Schank & Abelson, 1977).

Values and qualities of moral reasoning are a part of wisdom about politics and public policy, especially in forming a public philosophy, but it is more important to assess the sense of perspective—whether, beyond short-term pragmatism, there is a well-developed sense of what is valuable and what goals are more important for the long run (the knowledge of where one wants to go). Such perspective, rather than being solely moralistic, might also include a sense of perspective on morality itself—when a highly moral solution or a more pragmatic one is called for (Machiavelli, 1935). And it might include, too, a perspective on the appropriate restraint of American government power.

Organizational Learning

Organizational learning can be indexed similarly to individual learning, by primary reference to the intelligence and sophistication of thought which informs decisions, policies, and programs and to external efficacy, and by secondary reference to speed, completeness of relevant knowledge scan, and efficiency of thought and action. And we can look to the scientific learning base, the intuitive understanding, creativity, skill, and wisdom and good judgment embodied in (and summed across) the actions of individuals in their official capacities.

Organizational learning, however, has several likely requirements which transcend the case of individuals, even though there may be analogies at the personal level. The first of these, the intelligence embodied in standard operating, staff analysis, and decision-making procedures, reflects the fact that what one individual within an organization knows can be qualitatively different from what other individuals in the organization know. For example, in a special sense most federal officials above about the GS-12 level are increasingly out of touch with specific details about concrete reality. That is, the specialists who know technical details and technologies about coal gasification or who understand problems of running the public service jobs program in Chicago are at lower levels. It is one of the responsibilities of senior officials to design such a specialized division of labor and then to establish reporting, monitoring, and analysis systems so they will learn what they need to know, when they need to know it, and without being distracted by more information than they need (Wohlstetter, 1962). Without good internal learning systems, an organization's manifest policy decisions may be less intelligent than the intelligence located in its constituent parts. In the ideal case, of course, such decisions can actually be more intelligent when a good analysis staff uses an internal process to structure, clarify, and debate issues or initiate proactive learning activities so that new perspectives and understandings are generated.

Internal role networks and operating procedures within organizations thus crucially affect the intellectual quality of the overall policy direction senior officials can provide. But a second dimension is that of the consultative and adversarial procedures involving people outside government employment—agencies can be "open" systems (Katz & Kahn, 1978) with much learning from critics, lobbyists, consulting firms, public regulatory hearings, political constituencies, academic specialists, the professional and mass public news media, congressmen and senators and their staffs, and so forth. Weick (1979) reports few organizations change fundamentally from their own internal resources, and an agency which listens only to itself, however efficiently, is unlikely to learn well. (In a later section I will argue that major government learning often occurs as a dependent variable, only after people outside of government become more intelligent or more knowledgeable, or at least more vocal.)

A third factor in organizational learning is adequate organizational memory, potentially a crucial problem because of the high rate of job turnover at political, and often bureaucratic, levels (with high turnover rates being official policy in the foreign service and military).

Finally, organizational learning involves the embodiment of new understandings or revised policies in the action and understanding of people throughout the organization. In this sense, policy is a matter of executive decision only as a first step; coherent and effective policy, crucially, is a matter of attitude change, of creating common objectives and capturing imaginations, of a social movement (see Berman, 1974, for a case study of highly effective implementation) and an action mood, perhaps of change in organizational identity and culture, of getting people rounded up, coordinated, and moving in the same direction—and in Washington, civilian bureaucratic cooperation and enthusiasm is partly voluntary, not produced only by orders (Neustadt, 1960).

Learning Agendas

It may be useful to think of seven agendas for learning by individuals and/or organizations: the individual, a specific job, interpersonal and organizational relationships, external problem conceptualization, external substantive policy issues, the political environment, and intra- and inter-organization functioning. It is in these functional areas that we can look to assess shortfalls in learning.

The Individual.   Each of the five types of learning can be examined by using oneself as an agenda for understanding: How much systematic data collection, appraisal, and self-reflection is there in a scientific mode? How much intuitive feel and rapport is there with one's own feelings and internal processes? How much creativity is there in synthesizing and inventing new concepts or capacities for thought, feeling, behavior? How much self-reliant skill is there at science, at problem-solving using a creative interplay of preconscious and conscious processes? How much wisdom does one have about one's own life decisions? How well does one learn about oneself? (See Duval & Wicklund, 1972; Fingarette, 1969; Kleinke, 1978.) Such assessments may be particularly important for individuals with key positions for independent decision making.

The Specific Job.   Most people spend most of their time on the job doing their job. Usually this is not an enterprise of "big think" contemplation but of traditional management and routine work responsibilities. Most people at career levels probably do learn how to do what is expected of them. But a critical issue here concerns those more self-defined jobs at senior and White House levels which require special initiative, vision, good judgment in novel situations, and taking the leadership to deal with or effect change. In such positions, effectiveness cannot be acquired by asking a superior who can be counted on to know the answer.

Interpersonal Relations.   Most learning in Washington is probably created not from reading but through interpersonal relationships: living, sharing, talking with, going to meetings with, and gossiping about other people. Much of the learning about how to do things in Washington is personalistic, learning how to work well with these people. It is important how well people learn from (or about) each other (Adams-Webber, 1979; Thomas & Harri-Augstein, 1977). It is also important to question how much these discussions yield accurate and sophisticated learning or simply become the creation and uncritical acceptance of a "conventional wisdom" of (contrary to Katz & Kahn's, 1978, view of "open systems") a peculiarly ineffective and out-of-touch Washington-based view of the world?

External Problem Conception. A fourth learning agenda is iterative clarification and reformulation of what a problem is and of what one is trying to do. "What business are you really in?" is a standard question management consultants find many clients cannot readily answer. (See also footnote on p. 77). For example, one might think of the problem of better education as a problem of better teachers and thus charge off to upgrade credentials and increase salaries to attract better teachers. If, however, one slightly alters the problem to terms of better learning, one might devote more efforts to other arenas—for example, the problem of norm creation in schools (see also pp. 137, 140). Perhaps the crucial agenda and contribution of academic social science lies in this area of generating better problem conceptions (Cohen & Garet, 1975; Etheredge, 1976a; Rein & White, 1977).

External Substantive Policies and Programs. Program design, implementation, and evaluation in "high policy" decisions to solve major problems with major, multibillion-dollar programs is perhaps the most visible and important agenda of inquiry. Fifteen years after the Great Society, executive-branch agencies have not codified their organizational memories to learn how to implement programs or how to design programs that can be implemented. Why not? In 30 years of foreign aid and 80 years of hemispheric (and then global) military interventions, what has been learned?

Political Processes. Working within the political environment is probably also a useful area to differentiate; learning in this area may take special sensitivities, and it is conventional wisdom that "some people," who may be very apt at scientific method learning, "just will never understand politics." Learning to deal with the political environment, in this conception, would include not only learning to work with specific people and committees on Capitol Hill, the media, and the constituency groups of substantive programs, but also, in part, learning how to cooperate usefully with (or gameplan) other agencies, the Office of Management and Budget, and the president and White House staff members (see, e.g., Halperin, Clapp, & Kanter, 1974; Wildavsky, 1964).

Intra- and Interorganizational Functioning. A final agenda for learning is intra- and interorganizational functioning. This might include management (or bureaucratic politics), or simply organizing (or gameplanning) subordinates, superiors, and processes. It might include learning how to run a good committee meeting with different people and different issues, allegedly a rare ability everywhere (see Meehl's, 1977, likely classic essay on "feckless vocalizing" and other annoyances). But the broad issue is learning about the optimal design and efficient operation of massive organizations employing tens or hundreds of thousands of people and annual expenditures of tens or hundreds of billions of dollars (see Cherns, 1977; Cohen, March, & Olsen, 1972) and how to interface and coordinate in a federalist system (see Evan, 1978; Fesler, 1978; Yin, 1979). Indeed, one study of 30 policymakers found that the major problems they consistently voiced were organizational and specific interpersonal issues rather than policy content issues (Lindblom & Cohen, 1979, p. 55).

Normative Issues

There is a normative dimension to government learning which deserves thoughtful attention: What should government learn and what should government not learn? First, a government should learn how to do its legally prescribed jobs efficiently. But the scope we want may be broader than government efficiency, so a second example might be that presidents should learn to lead and govern wisely. Let me indicate several additional prescriptive issues in setting a learning agenda for government.

A third issue is the support of knowledge as a public good. The economic theory of market failure includes the argument from public-goods theory that an appropriate role of government is to supplement the functioning of the market by direct funding (as with the National Institutes of Health) or indirect funding (as with the National Science Foundation) of some types of knowledge activities. How much government should invest can be a tricky question to resolve, especially because the problem is not limited to uncaptured advantages to the current population: knowledge can accumulate and pay off, like an investment, to future generations and is thus a public good to them as well.

Moreover, the traditional policy of allowing the demand for research as a public good to be determined primarily by the demand for universities is (or should be) now in serious question. With an "oversupply" of Ph.D.s, there is a substantial and growing underutilized capacity for increased intelligence which could be funded. Also, the accelerating rate of global knowledge accumulation (doubling every 10 years, Price, 1963) will increasingly overload the fixed American supply of academic researchers who must perform the jobs of codifying experience with intelligence and sophistication, keeping track of all relevant literature, and remembering where they have filed things.

A fourth way to think about government's larger agenda for learning is with the aid of democratic theory. For example, one might use the guiding injunction that government should acquire and disseminate information that increases the informed decision making of individuals both in their capacities as citizens supporting (or opposing) government and in their private lives (see, for example, Goldschmid, 1979).

In the public arena, recent legal or presidential requirements have increased government learning by mandating research in the form of impact statements (e.g., environmental, economic, community, regulatory analyses) that are publicly available documents and can enter into public decision-making processes. Such research, although probably often done after a decision has been made, has become the basis for political, legislative, and legal activities on the part of affected groups, often in opposition to executive-branch preference. Recent developments in the legal doctrine of "standing to sue" promise to increase such litigation (Zacharia, 1978). The Freedom of Information Act has further disseminated to the public what government has learned, albeit with occasional kicking, screaming, and damage containment games and strategies by affected agencies (see, e.g., Committee on House Administration, 1979, on recent legislation).

Beyond information on what it is doing and learning, and publishing research estimates forewarning of the impacts of what it plans to do, government also acquires and makes available information and assessments on a wide range of aspects of American life. The Census Bureau is a basic supplier of information to many users; economic time series data and forecasting supported by the federal government are ingredients in many business decisions. Government monitoring of American society and reflection of these data in publicly available statistical reports already cover an enormous range.

A wide range of information that is, in principle, useful to individuals in their private lives is also available, including estimates of the gasoline mileage for new cars, guides to cost-effective decisions on home insulation, tens of thousands of books and guides published by the Government Printing Office indicating how to repair cars, build log cabins, treat diseased plants in a backyard vegetable garden, and so on.

The other side of the question stated at the beginning of this section is what government should not learn? It is certainly naive to trust government totally. Arguably, in many political systems, the most effective guarantee of the freedom of the people has been the inability of the government to learn about much of what is going on. Knowledge can be the basis of political intervention, especially in a pluralist society where the activities of any one group may be different from, or in conflict with, the values of some politically effective coalition that can be roused to action by better information. Further, constitutional limitations on the search powers of government, and legal guarantees on privacy of official records of individuals, express the belief that there are some things government should not learn about people (see, for example, the journal *Information Privacy*); and HEW guidelines restrict domestic learning activities in government-sponsored research to methods deemed ethical.

The only substantive area of research explicitly banned by a president has been offensive biochemical-warfare technology. But it would not be difficult to think of other areas which a cautious citizenry would bar from its government's knowledge, or, once acquired, would restrict to only some users.

Trends

Hard data on trends in government learning, differentiated by the five types and seven agendas discussed earlier, are not available. But let me report several observations beyond those embedded elsewhere in the text. First, there seems to be an increased capacity for differentiated discussion of substantive domestic problems among some career specialists, who typically assert that they do understand the world better today than they did 20 years ago. What is less clear is whether they have differentiated and sophisticated maps of differences across the state and local political systems within which they seek to implement programs and "torque" responsiveness (e.g., to the poor, to health cost control concerns), whether there has been much progress in foreign policy, whether there is an overall intellectual integration in either the foreign or domestic area, whether the organizations "know" what the best specialists know, or where ("we've been learning what doesn't work") there is increased effectiveness.

A growing descriptive base for scientific causal analysis of American social and economic processes is reflected in the massive growth of statistical time series tabulated and published regularly by the federal government and in the social indicators movement (see the journal *Social Indicators*). The number of basic federal economic and census time series on computer was about 100,000 in 1979; DRI, a consulting firm with government contracts had about 5,000,000 (the reliability of some of these numbers is a matter of dispute, see, e.g., House & Williams, 1978.) There are important gaps, probably attributable to fear that accurate knowledge could either undercut desirable or motivate unwanted political action—there are, for example, no reliable data on the effective income of poor people (counting welfare benefits, transfer payments, public services) (Ginzberg, 1979, p. 32), no reliable data on the number of Americans without any health insurance, and no reliable current data on the distribution of wealth.

The most important development in the political arena has probably been the wide adoption of public-opinion polling to aid electoral and policy decisions. It is unclear how much such polls affect decisions or how accurate they are as guides to public-opinion processes. It is also unclear whether, if they do have an effect, they increase genuine democratic responsiveness, shift concern away from substance and genuine leadership toward an image, public-relations approach, or in different ways, achieve both of the above.

In foreign policy, the trends in accurate factual knowledge are often cloaked in national-security secrecy. Defense policy informants, however, are virtually unanimous in attributing major increases in factual knowledge of Soviet weapons development, troop movements, and agriculture to observation satellites and other advanced technology aids.

It is probably true that many elites and the press discuss most issues in more sophisticated terms today. But whether this also reflects a growth of accurate sophistication about how the world really works or is something other than more sophisticated rationalizations is unclear.

It is common, as of this writing, to attribute deficient political intuitions, psychodrama skills, creativity, and vision to the Carter Administration and to tentatively assert that there is a new sensitivity to moral and ethical issues in the aftermath of Vietnam, the CIA revelations, and the Watergate and Koreagate scandals. But is is not clear that substantive competence is lower than under Nixon or Ford (on increasing situational constraints see Wildavsky, 1975). Also uncertain is whether there is a new, genuine, and enduring height of moral sensitivity or only an episodic and superficial moralism adopted for pragmatic and imagery concerns.

The long-term story of government innovations lacks a systematic list (analogous to that of Deutsch, Platt, & Senghaas, 1971) of what would count as genuine creativity, although clearly there have been enduring innovations in programs (e.g., the Great Society), technological aids to decisions (see M. M. Gray, 1979), weapons, political phrases and imagery (Safire, 1978), campaign techniques (Hess, 1978), institutions (e.g., Corporation for Public Broadcasting, Congressional Budget Office, Department of Energy, Senior Executive Service), and analytical tools (e.g., cost/benefit, PERT, PPBS, systems analysis, MBO, ZBB; but see Hyde & Shafritz, 1978, and Sapolsky, 1972, for skeptical accounts of impact). There is also the beginning of sophisticated studies on the origins and diffusion paths of public-policy innovations (Aaron, 1978; Berman, 1978; G. D. Brewer, 1973; Garet, 1979; C. O. Jones, 1975).

Whether government does its job more wisely today than 25 years ago must be left to the reader to judge.

One notable gap is the absence of knowledge of the actual learning agendas for individuals and agencies. Some agencies seem to be alive with people explicitly trying to learn (e.g., Department of Energy), others to be routinized into standard operating procedures without any urgent collective feeling that qualitative increases can be made (Department of State), still others to constrain learning within single paradigms (Council of Economic Advisers).

I should also report that a significant number of people in Washington think they understand the world quite well and believe no fundamental increase in intelligence is necessary or (since they believe we are there already) even possible. This confidence seems especially high in self-attributed understanding of American political processes. These self-reports run counter to Braybrooke and Lindblom's belief that "Decisions . . . not guided by a high level of understanding . . . are the decisions typical of ordinary political life" (C. O. Jones, 1975, p. 316).

Motivation and Cognition—Individual Bases

Three Images of Individual Learning

In this section, I will review three images which organize different bodies of research about processes of individual learning. The first image is that people never learn or change very much. The second image is that people are psychologically embedded within their immediate context and learn passively and reactively in response to reward and punishment. The third image is that people in Washington are active learners, striving continually to clarify, organize, gain perspective on, and solve the problems they confront. Following this overview I will turn to a review of several selected issues.

Fixed Behavior and Thought Patterns.   The first view of individual learning is that human beings are fixed, either at conception by genetic determinants or by early childhood experience. As adults, people do not change very much, they are creatures of habit, terrible reality testers, basically inflexible. If their genetic endowments and early emotional patterning fit later requirements or opportunities in the world they encounter as adults, they have productive, successful lives. But if there is a mismatch, or if they confront changing worlds, they seldom adapt successfully; they become unhappy and demoralized, feel lost, their competence slips relative to the new tasks they confront, and in the extreme they have nervous breakdowns. At best, they only "learn" better rationalizations to excuse their failures.

Fixed Emotional Drives.   A classic view, still very much alive, holds that, fundamentally, inherited emotional drives and instincts produce human behavior. From this point of view, one never needs to postulate very much intelligent behavior to understand the unchanging story of political life. Nothing about politics or the follies of humanity has changed from the beginning of time; people have more technology today, but, from culture to culture, from primitive tribes to "modern" societies, across historical epochs, the story of politics is the same—people seek and do the same things, face the same issues, repeat the same dismal idiocies, and they always will.

One example of an instinct explanation of politics is Freud's theory of aggressive drives, for which he claimed support from study of his patients; everyone is seeking to dominate and run the lives of everyone else (Freud, 1933/1973; Nelson, 1974). This drive could be as obvious as warfare or as sublimated as philosophy or social science, but the ultimate goal is to be above others, control their lives, destroy their independence.

By this theory we would expect the main story of politics in Washington to be empire building; regardless of intellectual facade and rationalization, everyone will be trying for more power, more money. Washington bureaucrats will try to expand the federal government into every nook and cranny of American life—and American power into every nook and cranny of the world—unless checked by budget or legal limits or by countervailing forces. At the margin, they will perhaps learn modestly about strategy and tactics for accomplishing this successfully. But, as for the main story of Washington's "war against all," intelligence will have as little autonomous or fundamental a role as it does in the primitive tropisms of the amoeba that expands to engulf whatever food is in its vicinity.

In recent years, work in sociobiology has proposed an entirely different theory of basic human motivation, still allegedly determined by innate animal nature—the preponderance of altruistic motivation, of self-sacrifice and dedication for the good of the whole (D. T. Campbell, 1978; E. O. Wilson, 1975; Wispé, 1978). By one interpretation of this image, the major story of politics in Washington will not be clashes of egotistical greed, vanity, and selfishness, but rather cooperation or conflict generated by deeply felt, albeit different, visions of collective ideals to be achieved. People will not necessarily be intelligent in what they do, but their hearts are in the right place, and if you can show them better ways they may try to learn them, although perhaps what they will not accept are limits of power, a wisdom sometimes to leave well enough alone.

Limited and Fixed Abilities and Intelligence. A second body of literature implying that fixed elements of human nature are central to behavior raises the possibility that different people are naturally good, and not good, at different things. Moreover, there will be strict upper limits, determined by natural endowments, to how well a person can learn (Block & Dworkin, 1976). To the extent that these theories of a fixed genetic base are true, we should not expect much qualitative increase in government performance; indeed human beings might not even be bright enough, as Camus and Herbert Simon have argued (March, 1978), to become rational. There may be room for marginal improvement by better matching of people to jobs, better coordination, and so forth (French, 1974; Pervin, 1968), but we are stuck with each other pretty much as we are, according to this theory.

Fixed Personality Structure and Dynamics. The major body of theory maintaining early personality crystallization is Freud's psychoanalytic perspective. Freud felt that human nature was implicit in the behavior of babies and young children: a primacy of strong emotions ranging from angelic joy and bliss to dark rage; selfishness; biting; playing with imaginary companions; irrationality; instinctive reactions and the absence of any tendency to think. People have to be molded, through both love and discipline, not to be childish (although, in Freud's view, adult childishness is never deeply transformed but merely goes underground where it continues as the deep structure beneath the rationalized surface forms).

In Freud's psychoanalytic theory, the main emphasis is on the *id* and its fate. The id is the deep source of energy, passions, fears, and both irrationality and (when accessible under conscious control in rare individuals) creativity. But individuals exhibit *libidinal inertia*, maintaining the forms and channels of their energies in their behavior and in their emotionally expressive thought; that is, they do not like to change, preferring even to court disaster or retain only marginal competence with the comfortable old ways, a conservatism of perpetual repetition compulsions (Freud, 1920/ 1973).

Let me extract from Freud some further predictions, beyond his libidinal inertia hypothesis of perpetual repetition compulsions.

Freud claimed that his investigations demonstrated, beneath a veneer of civilization, the *primacy of selfishness and greed* in human behavior. Indeed, in his later years he dismissed the injunction to love one's neighbor as oneself on the ground that it showed Pollyannish naiveté about human nature; most people, Freud said, were too low quality, unworthy of being loved (Freud, 1930/1973).

If Freud is right about this, one prediction is that there should be few genuinely warm, generous, and altruistic people in the executive branch, few will be found striving with all their energy to learn to make a better world as an expression of a deep love and compassion for the rest of us. Rather, their main preoccupations will be the same old habits (libidinal inertia) of acquiring power, status, money, and the sexual prerogatives and charismatic sexual attraction some psychoanalysts hypothesize people associate with career success and high political office. People in Washington will be found to care about themselves and their careers, but not much about the issues.

It is this view of human nature in American government institutions which is, for example, advanced by David Mayhew (1974) in his research on Congress. Selfishness, greed, egotism, and self-interested shrewdness are, he thinks, the rule: "there are few saints." Vaillant (1977) also seems to hold this view of American life in his study of the careers of men from the Harvard Class of 1937, many of whom attained (and still hold) high offices in American government and society; few, he says, can be classified as altruistic.

A corollary of the theory of the primacy of self-interest is *opportunism* and *intellectual superficiality*. That is, while their deeper ambition remains unchanged, people will be as intellectually opportunistic and changeable as chameleons. If program evaluation studies win points, there will be endorsement of program evaluation studies, at least by younger people aspiring to high office. If one is in an agency (e.g., HEW) in which social activism is de rigueur, then one will become an activist. But, just as attitude theorists tell us there is only a modest component of careful independent thought and systematic analysis behind what most people believe and say (Abelson, Aronson, McGuire, Newcomb, Rosenberg, & Tannenbaum, 1968; Kiesler, Collins, & Miller, 1969; Lane, 1969; Smith, 1968), so there will be little depth and self-reflection behind all the talk and surface sophistication in Washington.

A second corollary of Freud's view of selfish preoccupations is that people in Washington will have remarkably little curiosity about the world. People may advocate program evaluation or more research (if that is a way to achieve advancement within Washington), but even the research programs actually started by the government will not flow primarily from a deep curiosity or drive to know about people and the world.

To take another view, research in psychology analyzing the relation of personality to belief systems (e.g., Elms, 1976; Etheredge, 1978; Lane, 1969; Lasswell, 1930; Stone, 1974; Warr, 1970) shows both policy attitudes and beliefs about the nature of other people to be partly an expression of *emotional predisposition*. Apparently people often rely on an intuitive "feel" about the way the world works and they use the strength of this subjective feeling to calibrate whether they are right. The result, this research tradition would predict (and often shows), is that people in Washington (and many other places) "underexperience" and badly miscalculate the true level of their ignorance and display bold, macho, authoritative styles exceeding that to which they would be entitled based on a true understanding of the world (although, of course, the stylistic requirements of politics and public leadership may require, and train people to, a bold self-presentation; see Geertz, 1964).

Direct documentation of this naturally occurring overconfidence in Washington has recently become available, and it apparently flows from personal emotional dynamics (Etheredge, 1978), from common cognitive mechanisms, and from socialization patterns. To take an example, the CIA has developed a test in which its political analysts answer simple questions whose answers they may not know with complete confidence (e.g., Do herpetologists study snakes or viruses? Which is larger, Australia or Greenland?);

they also estimate their subjective confidence in their answers. Data volunteered from several hundred professional political analysts show that almost all systematically and massively overestimate their true degree of knowledge—when the typical intelligence community political analyst gives a "90% confident" rating, the actual hit rate is only slightly above chance. Curiously, some groups (e.g., professional meteorologists) are quite accurate in estimating the confidence of their knowledge of these items (Cambridge & Shreckengost, 1978). This "boldness shift" phenomenon, appearing in factual tests without political content, argues against Allison's (1971, p. 178) more reassuring "51-49" explanation of overconfidence (that people in Washington know their level of ignorance but, once the balance of argument has tilted, argue boldly in public as a tactic). (See also Einhorn & Hogarth, 1978, Janis & Mann, 1977, Jervis, 1976, and Ross, 1977, for further discussion of overconfidence processes.)

General Observations. Let me make several additional observations by way of guidance to literature relevant to this first model. First, so far as genetic bases of drives or aptitudes are concerned, no one has yet isolated the genes allegedly involved. Until that happens, the more empirical members of the scientific community will probably remain skeptical. Still, there is a large body of evidence from animal studies for possible major genetic effects; for example, different breeds of dogs differ substantially in temperament (either nervous and yippy or soporific), intelligence, social responsiveness, and acquisition of self-restraint (Freedman, 1958). It is quite widely accepted, on the basis of studies with twins and other methods, that there is a genetic component to IQ (Block & Dworkin, 1976) and a genetic predisposition to schizophrenia. J. A. Gray (1973, 1975) has argued for a genetic predisposition to neurosis and for (among others) a greater genetic role in the sensitivity of some people's feelings (nervous systems) to criticism, a susceptibility which could produce conflict, inhibition, and withdrawal in a pluralist society where any feeling or behavior can be imagined as potentially criticizable by someone. A corollary (assuming political success often comes from boldness and perseverance) is that people whose behavior tends not to be extinguished by criticism because their nervous systems make them less reactive to it may have a genetically based advantage in politics. Eaves and Eysenck (1974) have published suggestive evidence of a genetic predisposition to conservative preferences among people whose nervous system structure makes novel stimulation unpleasant.

Efforts to test Freud's various theories rigorously have yielded very mixed results, suggesting (albeit with many measurement problems) that his specific hypotheses are, at best, true only to some degree and only of some people (i.e., the theories are better than random) but are not true of everyone or complete (Fisher & Greenberg, 1977a). A major failure has been the inability to make broad, reliable predictions of adult personality (measured, however, only by overt behavior) from early childhood behavior or from allegedly key psychosexual traumas, although the absence of a mother or a substitute special relationship with a caretaker in early infancy has serious long-term effects (Hunt, 1979). There may, however, be continuities of subjective outlook that might be traced, in complex ways that differ for different people, to early childhood.

Adult personality studies suggest that, rather than strict continuity, people probably do change in some ways as they grow older, becoming (from the late teenage years through their sixties) more emotionally stable, less prone to feel guilty, insecure, or threatened, and gaining greater ego strength (Buss & Poley, 1976, pp. 142–146); their concerns sometimes also change (e.g., toward generativity) (D. Levinson, Darrow, Klein, Levinson, & McKee 1978). Test results suggesting broad declines in intellectual ability after middle age now seem to have been premature and to have partly reflected a decrease in physical energy, speed, and perhaps lack of interest in restructuring, rather than in ability *per se*. But with increasing age, there is some evidence for fading of long-term memory abilities and an apparent decline in giving full attention (at least to psychologists giving tests). With the raising of the federal retirement age to 70, such changes may have increased significance (Carroll & Maxwell, 1979).

It also seems clear that there are some issues which many adults "outgrow," or at least rarely rethink in fundamental ways. Argyle (1964) reports, for example, that there is a sharp rise in concern for such questions as the existence of God during teenage years but that after their early 20s, few people seem to worry about the problem, apparently either having resolved it and put it behind them or lost interest. Etheredge (1978) reports indirect evidence that, among foreign-service officers, tendencies to advocate or oppose the use of force consistently reflected personality predispositions in scenarios spanning at least a decade; earlier experience did not call into question the basic personal predispositions to advocate or oppose the use of military force.

In sum, then, there is little direct data for or against most of these hypotheses as far as adults in Washington are concerned. But it is probable that there are significant genetic predispositions, overconfident miscalibration of ignorance levels, and some personality-based predispositions not usually subject to rethinking.

Passive Reactive Models of Human Learning.   Social-learning theory, in advancing an essentially passive, reactive image of learning processes, specifies five characteristics of learning: (1) *sensationism*, the belief that people derive knowledge solely from experience; (2) *reductionism*, the belief that all complex ideas are built from basic, simple ideas; (3) *reactive mechanism*, the belief that the mind has no mysteries and operates in reaction to environmental stimuli with passive copying using simple additive rules; (4) *associationism*, the belief that learning occurs through linkages formed between ideas that reflect their contiguity in experience; and (5) *hedonism*, the belief that people's sole motivation is to obtain pleasure and avoid pain.

The operating mechanism here, the so-called law of association (4), has been claimed as the basis of learning for centuries, most notably by such British philosophers as Thomas Hobbes, John Locke, David Hume, James Mill, and John Stuart Mill. The theoretical apparatus of this social-learning theory has been impressively developed by such researchers as Thorndike, Pavlov, Guthrie, Tolman, Hull, Skinner, and Bandura.

This is not the place for a detailed discussion of social-learning theory, which has become extraordinarily complex since such classic experiments as Pavlov conditioning his dogs. In Albert Bandura's (1977a, 1977b) formulation, the theory now aspires to a broad, differentiated, and unified account of behavior with sophisticated attention to such issues as attentional processes, retention processes, motor reproduction processes, motivational processes (vicarious reinforcements and self-reinforcements in addition to external reinforcements), and cognitive controls. Here, however, I will abstract some key mechanisms and predictions of social learning—and other passive and reactive approaches—to illustrate both the plausibility and the potential value to be gleaned from these traditions.

The Theory of Context Embeddedness. A hypothesis common to many theorists—beginning at least with Plato's allegory of humans as cave dwellers in *The Republic*—is that most people are subjectively embedded within, and hence do not experience with perspective, the immediate context of the conventional rewards, punishments, roles, and aspirations of their society. They are dependent variables of their time and place, endogenous to the system.

One way to formulate this theory, and test it, is to express it as a hypothesis about spatial imagery encoding. For example, do people experience American government as a powerful presence above their sense of themselves? Does a 6'3" bureaucrat imaginatively encode a 5'9" Jimmy Carter or department secretary as taller than, above, his sense of himself? (This is context-embedded metaphysics, not physics.) Are goals (such as getting more money or some different job) experienced secularly and realistically, or are they primarily encoded magically and imaginatively as self-charismatic moves "upward"?

The current state of imagery-encoding theory as an approach to socialization and internalized power relationships in American life postulates nine alternative relations between the self and superior images (i.e., those images encoded as above the sense of the self), varying by the degree and quality of animistic power embedded within the higher image (hostile, benevolent, or neutral) and the degree and mode of control of the self for protection from potential hostility or to secure potential indulgence. The important point, for present purposes, is that some people apparently do not imaginatively encode political and social realities in this hierarchical way and appear to be more autonomous, more mature and subjectively grown-*up* (literally, i.e., without a sense of subjective subordination), to think with more perspective and freedom from stimulus–response embeddedness (Etheredge, 1979a, 1979c).

"Will This Be on an Exam?" Social-learning theory tells us that people learn what will bring them rewards or will avoid punishment. Thus, a familiar "will this be on an exam?" psychology may be central in Washington—if the boss, or Congress, or the president wants people in bureaucracies to learn *x*, and holds them accountable, they will be more likely to learn it. And, if the incentive systems (Clark & Wilson, 1961) are hostile to learning about *x*, it probably will not happen. This is not to say, however, that simply saying, "we think you should learn *x*" will accomplish the goal, just as my putting a book on a list of assigned or recommended reading scarcely guarantees that it will be read or thoughtfully considered by students; bureaucrats (and departmental secretaries) have to know that, for example, they will be in serious trouble with the Congress at the next appropriations hearings if they have not done good evaluation studies. And they probably need to know that the work will be evaluated by tough standards (see Aberbach, 1979, on congressional oversight trends).

The Necessity for Leadership. Social-learning theorists hold that people are solely reactive. Freud also thought most people he observed were dependent: "Only very few civilized people are capable . . . of coming to an independent opinion. You cannot exaggerate the intensity of people's inner lack of resolution and craving for authority" (Freud, 1910/1973, p. 146).

If left alone, many people will just sit, anomic and unhappy. They do not have an inner sense of direction. They need leadership to create a context of carrots and sticks, an agenda of problems to solve or goals to be achieved (Selznick, 1957). Those incentive systems and contexts for action need not be based on monetary incentives; in fact, ideals may often be more effective as the person is continually self-motivated by the sense of the wonderfully rewarding experience when the ideal is achieved.

Imitation of High-Status People. The belief that people tend to fixate on and imitate others of high status is an old one; the classic belief of aristocrats that they set the standards for the rest of society does appear, on the basis of research evidence, to be more than just a self-absorbed delusion of aristocrats themselves (Rosenthal & Zimmerman, 1978). Thus, we would expect to find that one of the major determinants of learning will be not the explicit reward structures of a bureaucracy, but the personal example and tone set by the top people. If they are dedicated, hard-working, and care about the issues, everyone else will learn. If they are selfish and just in it for the money or to have their ticket punched for a better job when they return to the private sector, their subordinates will go through the motions cynically and without enthusiasm (Fallows, 1979a, 1979b). Organizational psychologists have yet to give major attention to this theory.

Avoiding Unpleasantness. There seems to be a tendency for potential pain and unpleasantness to loom larger and more vividly in the imagination than potential rewards. Social-learning theorists say the avoidance gradients of human beings are often steeper than approach gradients. Economists say most people are risk aversive. Possibly there is an inherited survival instinct at work; the mind is programmed so that the sight of a beautiful wildflower close at hand is less instantly arousing and motivating than the sound, three hills away, that might be a tiger.

Many observed dysfunctions of bureaucracy, including problems of organizational nonlearning, may follow from this apparent fact that it is easier to scare people than to reassure them (Kline, 1977, p. 77), that the human nervous system is calibrated to react more vividly to potential pain than to potential reward. For example, Argyris and Schon's (1978) work on pathologies of organizational learning can be interpreted to reflect this basic mechanism—most people nervously avoid telling unpleasant truths to superiors, they self-protectively distort upward communication, and they prefer to avoid unpleasant confrontations and troubling issues. Research may show the imagination of many people in bureaucracies to be more actively fixated on all the tigers that might get them if they are not careful or make the wrong move than it is on what might be gained through boldness and forthrightness.

Two corollaries follow from this theory:

First, we can conceive, in principle, that people would be absolutely fascinated by the unknown, even have to be held back in their eagerness to rush off and explore it—that they might be adventuresome, experimental, inquisitive, excited about the potential for adventure, new competencies, new rewards, new discoveries. But, in fact, this may not be basically true of life in Washington. On the contrary, out of a *fear of the unknown and of change*, people may more typically prefer the safety of routine and worry more about being hurt than expect to be pleasantly surprised.

The second corollary is that people in Washington either will be slow to notice or *will not learn unpleasant truths* (see Erdelyi, 1974; McGuire, 1968). Such a proposition sets the mind in motion: What might these unpleasant, unsettling truths be? HEW liberals may continually overestimate government capacity to regulate many facets of American life wisely. The Nuclear Regulatory Commission may not learn that there are unsolvable problems with safe storage of nuclear wastes. Conservatives may not learn about or fully appreciate the extent of suffering that continues because of the absence of new government programs. Presidents may not learn that their instincts and interpersonal styles are sometimes inappropriate guides in foreign-policy decisions. The list could go on. A related prediction is that such blockages will follow from a personal-taste criterion for truth: "if an idea makes me feel uncomfortable, it is wrong."

Cross Reward System Interference. It is a key assumption of social-learning theory (and many other theories in psychology) that what appears to be unintelligent or dysfunctional behavior from one point of view is always quite intelligent from another, just as psychoanalytic theory also postulates that a symptom or problem at one level is always an attempted (albeit implicit) solution to another problem at a deeper level. In a pluralist, nontotalitarian society, the multiple incentive systems of life can similarly interfere with each other so that official rewards are not the most salient. For example, most administrations probably receive more highly salient rewards (e.g., election victories) from good press relations than from time spent designing intelligent, long-range learning programs that will pay off far in the future. And most cabinet officers are probably more immediately rewarded (and avoid more grief) by behaving reactively to what the president and their interest group and congressional constituencies want than by becoming specialists on substantive issues and trying to convince these constituents what they should want. So presidents will learn primarily to spend resources on press relations and cabinet secretaries on placating their constituencies.

Probably the most important set of alternative reward systems relevant to learning in Washington are those of private life. Many people might find that they prefer time with their wives, children, and friends or working in a garden to taking home briefcases at night, working on weekends, and expending the energy (and encountering the frustrations) necessary to do their jobs beyond a routinely acceptable level. The evidence is sparse, but it appears one likely determinant of whether rewards are sought mainly from jobs or from private life might be early career experience, especially a good relationship with a mentor in the late 20s or early 30s (Levinson *et al.*, 1978).

General Observations. Let me add several general observations by way of guidance to the literature. There is something to be said for the conditioning approach to learning, perhaps much, but it must be said carefully. First, there is no strong evidence supporting the old theories of simple, direct, automatic conditioning processes in adults, at least not without very inventive and complex *post hoc* explanation. This is not to say that humans are unaffected by reward and punishment contingencies, but it is to say that experiments of direct stimulus–response conditioning of the nervous system, especially after about age 5 and even in the simplest eyeblink conditioning and finger withdrawal experiments, produce results whose deviations from predictions are best accounted for by assuming that higher cognitive controls can readily supervene. (For example, if you condition eyeblink responses with a buzzer followed by the flash of a bright light, the extinction of eyeblink reflex following the buzzer sound [i.e., when it is no longer followed by the flash] stops almost immediately if you simply tell people when you have disconnected the light; and such extinction via cognitive controls occurs more rapidly than extinction based on the experience of multiple runs without a light flash, Brewer, 1974.) Moreover even "simple" behavior in "simple" animals reveals complex genetic bases and environmental and genetic interactions—for example, a review of current mouse attack theory concludes: "strain and species differences also abound . . . making it next to impossible to integrate experiments using different strains and species" (Powell & Buchanan, 1978, p. 703). Few psychologists today believe that general variations in single reinforcement schedules in the classroom or on the job can have *automatic* major effects on behavior (Estes, 1970, p. 87; Locke, 1977). For example, real income of government employees has more than doubled since WWII, but no one contends that the amount of physical or mental energy called forth (or the commitment to work) has similarly increased. One likely explanation is that, as economists would predict, there is diminishing marginal utility to income, and thus to income as a reinforcer, an explanation paralleling Helson's theory (1959; see also Appley, 1971) of an adaptation level to reinforcers and akin also to Maslow's (1954) notion that lower motivations (like earning money to ensure survival) fall off and are replaced by higher motives (like finding challenging work) when lower need satisfaction is taken for granted.

While not assuming direct and invariant nervous system conditioning, a model of "rational" response to reward–punishment contexts has been the major one in industrial and organizational psychology. This "expectancy–instrumentality–valance" tradition analyzes work effort (not necessarily learning) as a function of the expectation that effort will lead to task accomplishment, the instrumentality of task accomplishment for attaining or avoiding task contingent outcomes, and the valance or attractiveness of the outcomes. However, about 35 published studies show that the model so far explains only, at best, 10% of the variance in both field and laboratory experiments, and more often about 6% (J. P. Campbell & Pritchard, 1976, pp. 91–92). But let me offer four observations. First, this theory may work best only to explain major differences, whereas the present range of subject variation has been limited—usually subjects are those currently employed, and thus performing within satisfactory bounds—and the range of tasks has also been limited. Adding a large number of impossible tasks or tasks with painful consequences would undoubtedly raise R^2 for this theory, although without being much help for explaining variations in normal job behavior. Second, effort spent on a task is probably more a function of the time and effort necessary to do the task to acceptable standards (Stein-

bruner, 1974) and is not necessarily correlated with expected outcomes—
a $100 million decision might be made in 5 minutes, but a complex or con-
troversial $10 million decision might take much longer. Third, the time and
energy available may be relatively fixed so that, especially at top levels, the
(originally piecework) industrial-psychology theory that a man will work a
lot harder if more highly motivated may not apply at these upper bounds.
Fourth, tough-minded, systematic, rational planning about jobs and work
may be an individual difference variable: Etheredge (1978) found that while
a majority of military officers reported long-range rational calculation
in their careers, a majority of civilian analysts at the Office of Management
and Budget reported a tendency to muddle through and to "satisfice"—
to find a job that looked interesting and work at that. (A discussion of other
problems with VIE theory, including poor agreement among effort measures, may be found in J. P. Campbell & Pritchard [1976, p. 95].)

The theory that most people already know exactly what they want in
life and rationally and consistently apportion their energies to do what is
necessary to get it seems not to work very well (see Ajzen & Fishbein, 1977,
for a related review). There may be some personality basis involved in learning—perhaps some people have more energy and by nature are workaholics,
or are good at learning and thus feel satisfaction from it, or (as in McClelland's theory) are driven by high need to achieve or fear of failure (J. P.
Campbell & Pritchard, 1976). Medawar (1979, p. 45) proposes that there is
an "obsessional single-mindedness required by almost any human endeavor
that is to be well done." Although research on the effect of personality and
motivational predisposition in school achievement typically gives low
correlations for any one trait (Entwistle, 1972), the mean level of boredom
in public schools is probably fairly high; personal factors may be highly
predictive in situations where there is a special fit between a person and a
personally engaging learning agenda.

One of the major debates in psychology over the past decade has been
whether differences between individuals in fixed personality traits explain
most of the variation in behavior across situations. The present conclusion
is that they do not—both sociology (situational characteristics) and social
psychology (complex interactions of predisposition and situation) usually
explain more (Bowers, 1973; Magnusson & Endler, 1977; Pervin, 1968;
Sarason, Smith, & Diener, 1975). Of the several approaches to emphasize
social induction of motivation, one is Ralph Linton's theory of boredom
avoidance: "it seems possible that the human capacity for being bored,
rather than man's social or natural needs, lies at the roots of man's cultural
advance" and Bertrand Russell's assertion that "at least half the sins of
mankind are caused" by fears of boredom (cited by Gannett, 1979, pp.
1–2). That is, people hate it when nothing is happening and might be easily
induced to work on a wide variety of problems that are intrinsically inter-

esting (Deci, 1975) or challenge their abilities and offer increased competence (De Charms, 1968) and may unconsciously create foul-ups if there is
nothing else interesting to do. Goal-setting theory is in this tradition, and
the evidence is that the higher the goal that is set, the higher the performance,
assuming the goal is accepted (Mitchell, 1979, pp. 255–258; see also Kerr
& Jermier, 1978). A high level of aspiration of the work group also seems to
increase individual effort (Hare, 1976; Starbuck, 1963). A related idea (discussed earlier) is Selznick's (1957) theory that effective leaders motivate
workers by articulating a conceptual canopy which integrates their particular task within a vision of the ultimate importance of the work (e.g., "You
may be a file clerk, but what you're really doing is helping to win the war").
Other vocabulary terms to emphasize the cognitive context that makes
work meaningful have been Minsky's "frame" (1975), Goffman's (1974)
use of the same term, and Kuhn's (1970) theory of a paradigm which gives
assurance of contributing to worthwhile progress; the traditional terms have
been "myth" (Murray, 1968; Nimmo, 1974), "legitimation system" (Berger
& Luckmann, 1967), and "definition of the situation" (Ball, 1972).

These theories all suggest that meaningful work on worthwhile problems (Klinger, 1977) is partly a social construction (Berger & Luckmann,
1967; Kaufman, 1960). The opportunity to make progress on such problems does seem to capture the imagination and to be highly motivating
(among groups that seem highly motivated these days are people working
on energy problems, biologists getting started on recombinant DNA research, people at the Center for Disease Control working on worldwide
inoculation programs with technology they know can dramatically increase world public health, and so forth.) These theories suggest further
(excuse the lack of cynicism) that many people hate to be selfish and that
altruism, an understanding of their work as having a positive impact on
other people, will call forth a commitment. Altruism theories have not been
tested in business settings and are complex, but one ingredient seems to be
a sense of personal responsibility and a belief that the individual can make
a recognized contribution that is unique and hence will not be achieved if
he is uninvolved (Wispé, 1978). The feeling of doing socially recognized
work that is needed and has a positive impact on other people has been reported as a major predictor of physical health (Palmore, 1969).

Active Learning—Developmental Theories.   Developmental theorists sometimes agree that learning theories based on either fixed behavior
or conditioning can be useful to understand some people at lower levels of
development. But they see people as fundamentally seeking, and often
achieving, further qualitative personal growth or development, the achievement of which is partly facilitated or blocked by their environment. This
developmental, so-called rationalist, tradition holds an active, construc-
tionist view of learning, believes there are innate capacities and predispo-

sitions of the mind to make independent sense out of the world, capacities for active internal processing, self-reflection, and qualitative transformation of understanding and competence independent of external hedonistic incentive systems. The tradition of rationalist philosophers (e.g., Descartes, Leibniz, Kant) has continued in the diverse work of such theorists as Piaget, Werner, and Chomsky, within formally designated learning-theory literature, and in such affective-cognitive research as the ego and moral development research of Loevinger and Kohlberg, recent work in psychoanalytic theory (Erikson, 1959; Gedo, 1979; Gedo & Goldberg, 1973; Kohut, 1971, 1977; Levinson *et al.*, 1978), the humanistic growth psychologies of Carl Rogers and Abraham Maslow, and the cognitive development work of the Harvey group (Miller, 1978).

I will summarize briefly key elements in the theories of Werner, Maslow, Loevinger, and Elliott Jaques, a psychoanalyst associated with the Tavistock Institute who has worked in field settings specifically to develop an understanding of personal growth and bureaucracy.

Heinz Werner's model (Werner, 1948; Werner & Kaplan, 1963; see also Langer, 1970) has been described briefly above: increased differentiation by the knower both within the objects of knowledge and in the sensitivity and perspective on the symbols and models used as tools to construct and think about self and the world; instead of only confusion and complexity, there is eventually a movement toward coherence using hierarchical levels of integration. There is also greater perspective and psychological distance, a differentiation of the self from its objects of knowledge, and hence, greater autonomy and capability for rationality:

> Increasing subject-object differentiation involves the corollary that the organism becomes increasingly less dominated by the immediate concrete situation; the person is less stimulus bound and less impelled by his own affective states. A consequence of this freedom is the clearer understanding of goals, the possibility of employing substitutive means and alternative ends. There is, hence, a greater capacity for delay and planned action. . . . In short, he can manipulate the environment rather than respond passively to the environment. (Werner, 1957, p. 127)

Although there may be some transfer of developmental stages, there need not be similar levels in all systems of thought and action within an individual: a brilliant mathematician may be totally bewildered and confused about processes of economic development in the Third World without a period of separate study.

Abraham Maslow's (1954) theory of motivation imagines people to have a series of preoccupations, pursuing the satisfaction of lower needs (e.g., security, safety), until these are satisfied, then becoming concerned about other needs and deficiencies (esteem and respect, affection), and finally, if deficiencies are met, being motivated to develop and express all of his or her latent talents and higher capacities (self-actualization, needs for beauty, truth, etc.). One useful example might be to think of the theory as applied to the typical academic career: concerns with safety and survival (getting a doctorate and tenure), then a shift to respect needs and desire for genuine prominence and status in the field, only then having more time for family and friends, and finally a less driven and more relaxed concern to develop and express all those abilities, capacities, generativities, and interests that have earlier been pushed aside or left unattended in the pursuit of a career. Maslow is explicit in proposing that mentally healthy self-actualized people are "better knowers"; writing in *The Psychology of Science* (1969), he proposes that some people have a higher capacity for "taoistic knowing"—a natural, receptive, undistorted attunement with processes in the world.

Jane Loevinger's work on ego development (Loevinger, 1976; see also Hauser, 1976) is concerned with the principles or organization of the mind, especially the changing relations among emotional dynamics and internal structure. Her evidence supports a view of six qualitatively different stages involving a move from essentially egocentric, asocial selfishness (the childish psychology of Freud's id) to a social integration and context embeddedness responsive to authority and social conformity, to an outgrowing of authority and conformity in individuation, maturity, and autonomy. Both Loevinger and Maslow agree that their highest stages are attained by almost no one.

Jaques (1976) has explored the development of work capacity in organizations and sought to explain the endurance of social and political hierarchy as a consequence of the distribution of seven qualitatively different mental capacities to deal with abstractions and to work comfortably with far-reaching concerns.

Jaques's first level, *perceptual-motor concrete*, refers to projects which are accomplished with physical examples of the desired output and require no independent judgment—for example, a clerk-typist who does straight manuscript typing, a card-punch operator, a supermarket cashier, an army private.

The second level, *imaginal concrete*, involves tasks in which there is no physical model to copy and the worker must grasp an abstract idea of an ideal result. What must be achieved, however, is always action keyed concretely to specific people. Examples would include a head nurse allocating personnel among different functions and time schedules and a social worker who must diagnose needs and check eligibilities of clients and route them to the appropriate agencies.

At the third level, *imaginal scanning*, it becomes physically impossible to oversee or imagine all at once the work task, thus, success depends on a "feel" for multiple aspects of the job, each of which must be scanned separately in somewhat abstract forms (see also Etzioni, 1968, pp. 282–309; Hilgard, 1976, 1977). For example, the owner of a small business with 150 employees would need to be able to deal separately with accounting functions, inventory levels, sales activities, production scheduling, and so forth, typically using abstract summary input (balance sheets, cost-effectiveness ratios, productivity indices, etc.) rather than direct physical perception of activity. Level three is characteristic of work involving responsibility for roughly 50 to 350 people where there is at least some mutual recognition of who the people are.

At level four, *conceptual modeling*, there is a profound increase in work capacity—a capacity to work with multilevel abstractions using only occasional reference to physical things or specific people. At this level, the individual must become self-starting rather than relying on orders or a well-specified structure since neither the output nor the way to proceed can be foreseen or known concretely in advance. For example, an assistant departmental secretary whose job is "welfare reform" or "reducing health costs" or the head of a policy-planning staff at the State Department need to generate their own original, long-range, integrated work plans and be able to process multilevel intuitive feels for behaviors of entire systems composed largely of people they have never met.

Jaques believes that few people reach his fifth (*intuitive theory*), sixth (*institution creating*), and seventh (unlabeled) levels, but these all involve (a) increased capacities for perspective, autonomy, and intelligent innovation and leadership with (b) an increasingly accurate intuitive sensibility about the behavior, trends, and needs within massively complex and far-flung arenas of responsibility, including entire societies and the world, and (c) an increasing capacity for taking and working effectively within longer time perspectives.

Jaques's theory of developing work capacity fits well, I think, some common-sense observations about the world. To give a personal example, I remember how shocked I was in junior high school to be assigned to write a five-page paper. Five pages! I could not imagine how anyone could ever write a paper that long! By senior year in college, most schools routinely expect a 20-page capacity, usually on single topics and with planning and work capacity levels of several months. By early graduate school, 40-page papers synthesizing and appraising diverse models or literatures are expected. By the doctoral stage we expect conceptual modeling, independent work, and multiyear planning on a "normal science" (i.e., single paradigm) project. The contributors to this volume probably evidence substantial further evolution to Jaques's fourth level or above in the perspective and capacity to orchestrate, have a differentiated intuitive feel for, critically appraise, and suggest innovations for, entire multiparadigm fields of inquiry.

Jaques's theory is not well tested as yet, but it goes beyond (and differs from) the work of Werner in several respects. For example, it implicitly argues that formally rigorous cognitive development (categories, rules, models) is less important than the development of personal sensibilities and intuitive "feels" for behavior of people and qualities of institutions (in this sense it is closer to Maslow's notion of taoistic understanding as the highest level). Second, Jaques believes there are upper bounds to any individual's potential for developing these capacities—people need challenging work geared just above their level of easy work capacity (over their heads, they become lost or paralyzed; too low, they become bored) to develop their potential, but the ability to do high-level work is not common.

Developmental theories are diverse, and the selected hypotheses below will use several ideas (especially from psychotherapy; see Garfield & Bergin, 1978) not present in the above brief overview.

The Prediction of Semiconfused Thinking. Most development theorists propose a series of high-level stages that they believe only a few people out of a hundred ever reach. At these stages, people are often described as wise, with an integrated sense of themselves, a sense of perspective on life and on their own assumptions and thinking processes, a sense of vision, a humane, rationally based ethics, and a deep love of beauty and truth; they are described as altruistic and generative—caring deeply about mankind and future generations. They have attained a natural intuitive understanding of the behavior of people and institutions. They think more clearly and with more differentiation, flexibility, and creativity than ordinary people; they have good judgment. In their personal relationships they are solid, trustworthy, capable of a deep love for their friends and for mankind.

Perhaps the central prediction to be derived from such theorists is that most people in Washington have not reached these stages. Thus, research should show most people there to be semiconfused about what they are doing and why they are doing it, somewhat vague about their assumptions and supporting evidence, and with only modest differentiation, integration, and perspective in their thinking about the functioning of American society and the world (see Lindblom, 1959). They should turn out, in reality, also to be semiconfused in their thinking about issues in political and public philosophy and to lack a coherent, thoughtful, explicit, and systematically integrated vision for either domestic or foreign policy. Many will have lurking and deep suspicions and confusions, often not conscious, that they do not clearly understand what they are doing, the meaning and purpose of life, or where everything is or should be going. Even those who are bold and active will be bold simply because they have a bold style rather than because they have first dealt thoughtfully, clearly, and fully with these issues —underneath, they too will turn out to be semiconfused.

The Prediction of Massively Underutilized Capacity. Almost all developmental researchers believe few people ever achieve the higher levels of understanding or the full use of their capabilities, a shortfall usually attributed to the poor design of society. In this perspective, a major source of the shortfall in government learning will be the inhibiting, stultifying things bureaucratic life does to the mind and spirit (see pp. 111–113 for a discussion of dysfunctions of bureaucracy).

The Need for Optimum Conflict. Most developmental theorists hold that the creation of appropriate problems, conflicts, and mystery is one key to growth. Hirschman (1958), for example, recommends a strategy of "optimal disorder," the creation of bottlenecks and problems; and there is a nascent theory of "readiness" and sequencing of issues in psychotherapy. As teachers, I think we often make such a calculation implicitly, structuring a course to begin with simple problems, then moving to more complex problems when the capacity to handle the simpler ones is developed, structuring a flow from basic courses to more advanced courses that assume automatization of basic distinctions and skills and a Werner- or Jaques-like progression in capabilities. The best guess of how to do problem sequencing is still a metaphor, with conflict and complexity introduced so mastery is "one stage" beyond current levels. For example, attitude change theorists (social-judgment theory) posit there is a range of differences from an individual's own views that can be challenged effectively and lead to change, to viewpoints that are so different that they are simply rejected (Kiesler *et al.*, 1969). Lieberman (1978) maintains that optimal problem structure and sequencing in therapy requires a problem to be neither too easy nor too hard for the mastery ability latent in a patient at a given time. It also seems to be useful to introduce conflict within a progressive "frame," a conception that the task is one of mastery or learning or economic development rather than, for example, a debate between opposing orthodoxies or a demand from authority where some vital core of the individual would be felt to be potentially overwhelmed or under attack (Frank, Hoehn-Saric, Imber, Liberman, & Stone, 1978). This may be aided by new linguistic theories specifying symbolic formulations that can be deployed and sequenced with reference to the individual's existing, context-embedded, cognitive structure (Bandler & Grinder, 1975a, 1975b; Haley, 1973; Watzlawick, 1978). (On the role of criticism generally, see Lakatos & Musgrave, 1970 and Radnitsky, 1973.)

The Need for Outside Perspectives. One of the central processes in psychotherapy is empathetic mirroring; that is, the simple process of someone else understanding what a person is feeling or doing and verbalizing it to make the perspective readily available (Kohut, 1977; Rogers, 1961). This capacity of the outsider to understand and explicate what is implicit, to put the self in perspective, has also been held to be crucial for advance in the social sciences (Berlin, 1962, p. 19). The usual assumption that knowledge is something one acquires from the outside is replaced by these theorists with the hypothesis that it is how individuals implicitly think—and also how they do not think—that is the key barrier to greater intelligence (see Laing, 1972).

To some extent, good reporters and columnists help to provide this perspective. Humor (such as the comic strip *Doonesbury* or the columnist Art Buchwald) probably also helps to develop perspective. But one crucial research issue is whether there are enough good people with enough resources, who are psychologically independent from current policy.

Usable Memory as a Basis for Autonomy. One of the problems which psychotherapy addresses is that many people *are* only their histories, a congeries of their memories and past behavioral patterns. That is, they continue patterns of behavior, perception, thought, and emotional reaction developed in the past rather than developing a perspective which allows them a selective use of their experience. By analogy, the executive branch may be deficient in two respects. First, it may have little effective memory (extending, at best, back only to the early 1960s in the lifetimes of people still there, but made worse because people today have different jobs than they held then, leaving new occupants to make the same old mistakes). Second, the onrush of history, with alleged rapid change, may not leave time to think about what could have been learned. (See Deutsch, 1953, 1963.)

General Observations. Developmental theories have yet to be carefully tested in application to the executive branch. Perhaps the most hopeful approach is Loevinger's. Her measurement instrument has been developed with great care and psychometric rigor, and it is one of the great achievements in both validated theory and psychological instrumentation in recent years. Kohlberg's manual is still changing and has traditionally been difficult for coders to learn to use. Maslow's theory has produced mixed results, probably because of different interpretations of his predictions, problems of scale construction (the most successful effort is Alderfer, 1972), and perhaps faults of the theory itself (Campbell & Pritchard, 1976). Werner's theory has not been tested with adults, and Jaques has yet to develop a measurement instrument.

Developmental theorists pose three issues directly. The first is the fear-security debate. Those theorists writing from therapeutic traditions often believe fear is poisonous to growth, a view which is a radical challenge to theorists such as Freud, who proposed it as one of the keys to inducing people to stay civilized and pursue higher order values.

The second issue is the conflict–nurturance controversy between Maslow and most other developmental theorists. Maslow implies that an environment providing security, respect, and love will lead to growth. Most other theorists believe conflict is also necessary. An associated (but not completely correlated) difference is between theorists who believe there is a growth instinct, a driving feeling in people that there is something missing in their lives, and those theorists who posit a state of equilibrium which must be disturbed by conflict to produce growth and who further believe (along with Plato) that the process can be extraordinarily painful, especially in dealing with separation anxiety issues (Bowlby, 1977a, 1977b) provoked by outgrowing authority structures, context embeddedness, and imagery encodings of trusting dependency on hierarchy. (On the suffering theory of growth, see also Suzuki from the Zen tradition in Barrett, 1958, p. 83; Odajnyk, 1973, p. 146 on Jung; and E. Wilson, 1972, p. 403.)

A third issue is whether the capacities for higher-order growth are universal or whether (Maslow, Jaques) some people lack the strength or native ability to develop that far. This is an empirical issue with potentially far-reaching political implications for normative democratic theory.

Selected Additional Issues

The above three images of individual learning—unchanging nature, passive-reactive conditioning, and active engagement and autonomous development—although in many ways logically contradictory, are all in good repute among at least some members of the scientific community and among different people in Washington (Wolfsfeld, 1979); both Sagan (1977) and MacLean (1973) imply (correctly, I think) that all three images will be useful as the "triune" human brain operates, at different levels, by these three different processes simultaneously and partly independently. In this section, I want to set forth briefly additional bodies of specialized theory in five categories. First, I will discuss induced barriers to learning: stress, aversive motivation, burnout, and freezing following public commitment. Next I will deal with the two general emotional issues of unconscious dynamics and action moods in the collective identity of organizations or the polity. Third, I will discuss cognitive process models designed to describe learning from experience and the trends in artificial intelligence models. Fourth, I will discuss briefly two emerging fields in the physiology of knowledge and intelligence: body state encodings of qualitative knowledge and brain physiology processes. Finally, I will discuss the issues of recruitment and socialization.

Induced Blockages and Aversions

Stress. The concept of a generalized stress syndrome is widely accepted and has been diagnosed as a major inhibitor of government learning and rational decision making, especially in international-relations crises, both in its individual (George, 1974; Holsti, 1972; Janis & Mann, 1977) and small-group (Janis, 1972) effects. While there are major differences between individuals in the predisposition to feel stress and in response syndromes (Horowitz, 1976), there seems to be general agreement that stress syndromes are triggered by situations of perceived threats to survival in which effective control is uncertain—which may include physical threats, threats to the psychological well-being of the individual (being fired, failure, criticism, loss of respect or love from others or loss of esteem for oneself, and identity changes, which for some people include an aversion to success), and threats to the well-being of people or causes the individual cares about. Stress syndromes are, at their base, physiological changes in functioning of the central nervous system and include increases in arousal and systematic physiological changes in blood and brain chemistry.

Characteristics of this shift to survival-mode functioning are probably familiar in academic settings ("final exam" syndrome). Major features (see Hermann, 1979) include (a) reduced capacity to focus and concentrate (e.g., staring at a book or rereading sections several times without anything registering); (b) chronic low-level fatigue; (c) alterations in sleep patterns (inabilities to sleep or to have restful sleep, or great increases in the need for sleep); (d) reduced sense of humor and increased irritability; (e) rigidity and "freezing up" (being stuck and unable to respond flexibly, innovate, or change behavior); (f) reduced time horizon (inability to think in long-range perspective); (g) fear of impending catastrophe (a fear that the world has the potential to come apart or collapse, with a complete loss of control); (h) frenetic hyperactivity (trying to do everything at once, usually accompanied by a flooding of thoughts about everything that must be done or that might go wrong); (i) emotional withdrawal (reduced depth of emotional involvements and reduced range of normal activities as these are "shed" to divert energies to the survival issues).

Associated physiological changes often include greater susceptibility to illness and disturbances in eating patterns and digestion. Restorative and self-therapeutic efforts can include increased search for emotional support (with reduction in critical thinking and interpersonal conflict) (Janis, 1972), increased use of alcohol to unwind, and a hyperactive sex life used primarily to reduce and manage tension levels (a general review is Monat and Lazarus, 1977).

It is widely believed that performance is an inverted U-shaped function of stress—that is, either no stress or high stress leads to rapid deterioration of performance. As well, a second feature of this Yerkes–Dodson Law (of the relation between physiological arousal and performance) is that the more complex the task, the lower the threshold at which stress begins its deteriorating effect (Kahneman, 1973, pp. 33–37). A major related hypothesis from research on the audience effect suggests that physiological arousal levels increase in the physical presence of other people and perhaps when (as in government) there is imagined a potentially critical audience. As with well-trained athletes who typically set their best records in public, such arousal can improve performance of well-rehearsed behaviors by providing an optimum level of arousal for their performance; but it can also freeze up executive-branch cognitive restructuring, block flexibility, and undercut long-range thinking once an administration is in office and in the political spotlight (Zajonc, 1965).

We do not have data on typical stress levels in the executive branch, although Lasswell (1971) believed they were very high for senior officials and were primarily induced by the unconscious knowledge of inadequacy to handle complexity or control significant outcomes successfully. If present, such stress levels in political life, higher than the Yerkes–Dodson optimum for learning, would have serious implications: for priority research on amelioration of stress proneness through psychological or physiological intervention; for planning that major thinking and new learning will have to occur away from government and the front lines, in quieter settings; and quite possibly for a shift of responsibility away from the overloaded federal arena.

I would like to make two further observations. It is possible that one effect of stress is a kind of adrenaline "high," and there is also a possibility that it may be mildly addictive for some people. It should finally be noted that some informants in Washington are deeply skeptical that anyone there is under much stress.

Aversive Motivations. Mainstream organizational psychology literature seems to assume the legitimacy of hierarchy and managerial aims, but there is a secondary literature which argues that there is a disquieting, turbulent psychology of subordination which has dysfunctional effects for both the individual and the organization.

First, it is alleged, there is a conflict between personal ambition and the reality of pyramidal structure (most people will not be fully successful if they want top jobs), and it has been proposed that there are routine processes of "cooling out" employees (e.g., through incremental demoralization of employees while maneuvering them to accept the outcome as legitimate, B. R. Clark, 1970). Second, as a part of this process Janis and Mann (1977) postulate an unacknowledged climate of frequent bad faith (or at least game playing and a lack of candor) on the part of many higher officials who, without actually lying, nevertheless mislead subordinates about their chances of career advancement. One study of this phenomenon, in the Department of State, showed that 600 career foreign service officers privately believed they had at least a "good" chance of eventually being promoted to one of only 85 ambassadorships (Harr, discussed in Etheredge, 1978, p. 140).

Third, the empirical work of Zaleznick and De Vries (1975) reports an undercurrent of envy, fear, and hostility on the part of the typical subordinate. In their view, hierarchies and contingent and uncertain rewards make people feel insecure, powerless, vulnerable, and dependent; they fear being a potential victim of authority. As one Department of Commerce employee put it: "They look at you and smile and seem supportive, but they have a loaded revolver sitting on the table. And they're going to use it, they'll fire you, if they get unhappy. You have to play along like there really is no revolver because they also get angry if you question whether they are nice people." Freud's central prediction, over a half-century ago, was that males have an instinctive fear of aggression from older males in positions of authority; it is probably timely to test this idea.

Fourth, a substantial amount of bureaucratic life is held to produce covert rebellion, growing both from resentment of dependency and fear and from depersonalization. This rebellion is manifested in pervasive lack of enthusiasm, boredom, low productivity, red tape, and officious compensatory behavior to achieve recognition and respect. In the case of depersonalization, it is alleged that people in bureaucratic positions experience themselves to be there as functionaries, to do their job, and that beyond this no one in authority cares very much about them, that they do not get the respect they deserve (see also the theory of ressentiment [sic] of Nordstrom, Friedenberg, & Gold, 1967).

Such theories of fear, resistance, and covert rebellion, as well as theories of psychological reactance to a lack of power and of vulnerability to others who are powerful (Brehm, 1972; Lefcourt, 1976; Sennett & Cobb, 1973) are not well studied in government. But insightful work by Argyris (1967), at the Department of State, and by Argyris and Schon (1978) suggests that the official norms and talk of candor and mutual aid in problem solving are often belied by real games and maneuvers to stay out of trouble, norms that undercut bases for open communication, effective top-level monitoring, and organizational learning. "Cover your ass," "don't make waves," and "keep your skirts clean" are apparently taken by many people to be good maxims—although organizational psychologists have not yet tested the obvious prediction that such well-known maxims have Darwinian survival value in some organizations.

A final theme in this realist tradition is that top managers themselves profess innocence about how subordinates perceive them and react to their messages, apparently having an invariantly virtuous self-image and attributing the causes of fear, avoidance, timidity, and caution to the employees themselves rather than to their vulnerability, powerlessness, and lower respect vis-à-vis management. A familiar analogy is the classroom where professors seem universally to profess that students should feel free to disagree with them and not be deferential—and believe that it is safe for students to do so—but where some students feel the realities are quite different and, in fact, speak only to score points, and if they are confused, unsure of themselves, feel inadequate, or in trouble, tend to maintain a bold front, avoid teachers, and thus (to their mind) avoid a bad reputation or doubts about their ability. (Professors, too, probably attribute this to student immaturity.) Which reality—trustworthy or mistrusting—is more realistic is an open question.

What these theories also imply, however, is that employees do not simply have fixed motives for which they seek satisfaction, as the economists would have it. Instead, they become part of organizations which induce motivational preoccupations and reactions, often through real deprivation or fear of potential deprivations produced within the system itself. One motivation for upward mobility, then, is to increase or regain a secure autonomy and respect of which one is deprived as a condition of employment and to finally achieve a position where one does not have to take orders and be at risk from the potential capriciousness of multiple layers of supervisors or where, simply and poignantly, one can achieve the recognition and agreement that one exists as a worthwhile person symbolized by a private office.

Burnout. Another phenomenon is "burnout"—that bureaucracies are often frustrating places to work and can wear people down (Seligman, 1975). The American political system is so pluralistic, with so many veto points, that even enormous effort can often prove unrewarding. And if one wants to influence "high" policy, a typical government job may not give any greater advantage than working for an interest group, a consulting firm (perhaps at higher pay—one reason, in addition to politically inspired personnel "ceilings"—that there has been a massive shift to contract consultants), or a university. One theory is that young, idealistic, energetic people may "last" 5–7 years; unless they have a chance to make genuine contributions, they begin to adjust, stop working weekends, and lower their levels of hope and aspiration.

Resistances to Rethinking after Personal and Public Commitment. Although there are some dissenters (e.g., Leonard, 1969), many writers have proposed that learning is uncomfortable or even painful, perhaps especially when a person already has views or ways of thinking and the implication of learning is that those views were wrong and that the person was not in as much intellectual control as imagined (Langs, 1978). The problem here is that top-level political appointees often make public commitments which could make it even more painful (personally as well as politically) to rethink and change (Abelson *et al.*, 1968; Festinger, Riecken, & Schachter, 1956; R. A. Jones, 1977; March & Olsen, 1976, p. 79). And although American politicians may be especially pragmatic and nonideological (Payne & Woshinksy, 1972), earlier public commitments may become embodied as major elements of personal identities for people recruited to staff required agencies and implement older policies (Arrow, 1974, p. 29; Searles, 1961). Unfortunately, public policy today is like medicine was for most of history:

practitioners are accountable to produce results without a validated theory of how to do it. Thus, there is good reason to think they ought to learn and change. But meanwhile it is also traditional American political practice to scream and yell and browbeat an administration for its failure to solve all the problems of the world—and for not doing it quickly enough. If clinical theorists are right that people only learn, fundamentally "unfreeze," in situations of trust and unconditional positive regard, the likelihood of new directions is probably lower after many people are personally and publicly committed to old ones.

General Emotional Issues

Unconscious Motivation. The theories of major unconscious motivation in Washington are largely untested, as indeed they are in the case of political life generally (see De Board, 1979; Brown, 1981; Brown and Ellithorp, 1970). Solving the problem (if one exists) is perhaps relevant especially to clarify the problem of what people in Washington are doing other than learning. Harold Searles (1979) has made an impressive beginning by differentiating over two dozen unconscious contributors to apathy in the face of the environmental crisis, and imagery-encoding theory (discussed above, pp. 96–97) may offer promising avenues by providing a structural translation of psychoanalytic work.

Let me list 18 basic areas of unconscious motivation relevant to executive government (see also pp. 117–118): (1) narcissistic ambition and hardball politics (Etheredge, 1979b; Kael, 1974/1977); (2) machismo and other overconfidence syndromes (Etheredge, 1978 and above, pp. 93–94); (3) the elements of transference and hyperactivity–despair bipolar organization engaged with the imagery encoding of liberal activists (Etheredge, 1979c); (4) Oedipal syndromes (e.g., male envy, jealousy, anger, and fear in relations with older and more powerful adults); (5) Erik Erikson's theory of a pervasive Laius syndrome (older male adults enforcing subordination and identity engulfment on younger males, jealously guarding their power and prerogatives, being fearful of or hostile toward those who are bright, creative and independent; generation and sustaining of institutions that demoralize young people and mold them into second-rate, conformist sycophants) (Erikson & Newton, 1973, pp. 117–118); (6) unconscious guilt over inadequacy (Lasswell, 1971); (7) countertransferences (Searles, 1979) to the American public or client groups (e.g., as children); (8) Washington, agency, political, age cohort, interest group, professional, or individual ethnocentrisms (LeVine & Campbell, 1972); (9) obsessive syndromes in the quest for intellectual or political control; (10) fears of obtaining knowledge and of competence in problem solving (Maslow, 1968); (11) avoidance of feelings of loss and depression in resistance to change (Marris, 1974); (12) conscious or unconscious fears and extrapolations of loss of control (e.g., domino scenarios) stirred up by change (Jaques, 1955); (13) inhibiting and distorting effects of control ambitions (Maslow, 1969); (14) hypnotic effects of power hierarchies and subordination (Etheredge, 1976b; Freud, 1921/1955); (15) resistance to influence from "strong" thinkers (Bloom, 1973; Kohut, 1979); (16) alleged unconscious anal sources of impersonal, controlling approaches to problems and subordinates (N. O. Brown, 1959, Part 5); (17) restricted learning agendas and specializations as a defensive maneuver to preserve a coherent and manageable identity (Snyder, 1973).

Perhaps the key contribution, from depth psychology, will be an elaboration of (18) dependency theories of bureaucratic life. Dependent people tend to be fearful of, and to resist, change (Searles, 1955/1965, esp. pp. 118, 131, and 1961/1965). They may have a greater need for leaders to define reality, lead, and think for them (Etheredge, 1979c; Freud, 1921/1955), be more prone to stress, complain without being constructive, avoid responsibility, and tend to wait for other people to solve problems. They may also be prone to symbolic politics rather than substantive problem solving. It is important to emphasize, however, that dependency can be induced and sustained by bureaucracies and need not be solely a personality trait (Etheredge, 1976b; Fenichel, 1945, pp. 491–492). A key marker of psychological dependency appears to be a structure of spatial imagery encoding (see pp. 96–97) of reality in which, for example, a departmental secretary or president is experienced as located subjectively above the individual (Etheredge, 1977, 1979a).

Action Mood Theory. Motivation theories often postulate that learning follows only after a prior emotional consensus, the crystallization of an individual, organizational, or national "action mood" experienced subjectively as a decision to "move" (see muscle innervation theories of thinking in below, pp. 117–118) in a "direction." At the individual level, kindergarten teachers speak of "reading readiness" (meaning both cognitive and emotional developmental stages) and psychiatrists often speak of the "readiness" of individuals to face and deal with certain issues. At the political level, the phenomenon was portrayed by a researcher at NIMH who spoke about developing special physiological tests and using national random samples to monitor stress levels in American society and use these results to design better federal public health programs. But, he commented wistfully, "it will probably be 20 years before we are ready for this"—not primarily because of technical barriers, but because people are not ready to move in this direction and support learning how to do it.

It is asserted by various writers that the phenomenon of action moods exists and that they are crucial to public-policy directions: ideas whose time has come (which, allegedly, nothing is more powerful than) and which capture imaginations. Schon (1971) refers to "ideas in good currency," Burnham

(1970) to "critical elections" when the American electorate reformulates emotional consensus, and Downs (1972) to "issue cycles." J. Q. Wilson (1966) asserts that a sense of crisis increases innovation.

Cognitive Process Modeling

Learning from Experience. It is sometimes argued that experience can be a defect, that it reduces learning rates because it sustains old habits and previously formed views, and that only young beginners can see the world fresh and without encumbrance of the codified error embedded within the legitimacy of the establishment (creativity rates often drop by the mid-20s in mathematics, by 40 in the social sciences). Nonetheless, it is possible that some people learn substantially from experiences, and I will concentrate here on the theory that it can be a good teacher (see Muir, 1977, Chaps. 10–12, on the effects of holding power on personal development).

What is it that makes people better at learning from experience? One likely theory is that *varied* experience is a key. It takes at least 15 years of hard work for even the most talented individuals to become world class chess masters; what they seem to learn is a repertoire for recognizing types of situations and scripts (Schank & Abelson, 1977) or intuitive sensibilities and understanding about how these situations will likely unfold. Simon (1978) estimates a differential repertoire of 50,000 situation recognitions at the world class level in chess. (There are not yet any comparable estimates for politicians and areas of political life.) There is also some increase in overall long-range strategic-planning ability—beginners typically are hard pressed to think beyond one move, whereas world class players often think three, or sometimes five, moves ahead in calculating alternative reactions of their opponents.

Evidence from Axelrod (1973, 1976), Hart (1976), Etheredge (1978), Reychler (1978), and Holsti (1976, 1977), implies (although it may be a method artifact) that national-security elites tend to see only one move at a time in reactive patterns, without perspective on feedback loops or their own thought processes; a growing perspective on arms race dynamics, however, suggests a two-move perspective capability may be developing. Bloomfield's (1978) study of elite foreign-policy planners also suggests that a one-move capacity theory might be too low for some top-level planners, as does Lefberg's (1978) study of a Supreme Court justice.

Data from experienced and highly successful chess players, poker players, and tennis players suggest the theory that one further kind of learning from experience is the capacity not just to diagnose specific game situations but to model ("psych-out") different opponents (Findler, 1978). It is also likely that experienced players have developed more efficient scanning, with the ability to discard unnecessary information and arrive at a general, intuitive sense of where to devote attention; for example, the inefficiency of computer chess programs is that they have to do too much analysis of unproductive possibilities to arrive at good moves (on the use of superior memory rather than superior heuristics in medical diagnosis expertise, see Elstein, Schulman, & Sprafka, 1978; Szolovits & Pauker, 1978).

Artificial Intelligence and Cognitive Processes. The work to develop artifical-intelligence models in social science has been spurred in part by visions of moving beyond the simple, fixed coefficient equation models of first-generation social science to formally recognize and explicitly integrate richer, more differentiated, and more psychologically complete accounts of perceptual, interpretive, emotional, and decision-making processes—including formal representation of the capacity for self-reflection (e.g., using new mathematical functions which take themselves as arguments). (See, for example, Alker, 1979; Lachman, Lachman, & Butterfield, 1979; Simon, 1979). The trend in basic research is likely to accelerate both from the Sloan Foundation decision to fund centers for cognitive studies at several major universities and from exponential increases in low-cost computer power. At the moment, however, federal models of the economy (and far more detailed energy models of several thousand equations designed to model each oil field and energy source and estimate demand by fuel type and congressional district through 2020) do not have within themselves the formal capacity to learn; nor do they model any of us as having a capacity to learn or change qualitatively beyond simple reactions to prices. As well, good, integrated models of American or world social processes (other than economic) have yet to be developed in Washington and lag far behind existing sophistication (Etzioni, 1968) about the processes and likely cross-sector and cross-level impacts that should be included.

Physiology of Knowledge and Learning

Body State Encoding. One hypothesis implied by psychoanalytic writers is that thinking involves physical energy and sensations and that knowledge and blockages to knowledge are encoded as body states (see, e.g., Ferenczi, 1953; Freud, 1895/1966; Klinger, Gregoire, & Barta, 1973; Lichtenberg, 1979; Schachtel, 1966). These physical bases can range from subvocalization of words in writing, reading, and some forms of thinking, to the body state encoding of intuitive "feels" for problems. For example, learning psychotherapy skills can involve processes of emotional (hence physical, body encoded) discomfort and pain in acquiring knowledge (Langs, 1978, p. 6); it is not uncommon for some political-science students to report physical discomfort when studying statistics; and creative individuals are said typically to experience almost unbearable tension states when working on a problem (Kohut, 1978, pp. 818–819), probably because of their deployment and restructuring of personal identity fragments when encoding problems and during the creative process (Brenman-Gibson, 1978).

Work to develop a differentiated theory of body state encoding, while involved in some of the new psychotherapies (Geller, 1978), has only recently begun (Fisher, 1970; Fisher & Greenberg, 1977b). The central therapeutic and educational hypothesis is that awareness of ("being in touch with") such body state encoding increases effective intelligence, especially in the intuitive mode. Work on field dependence (with over 3,000 studies to date) has produced strong evidence that differences in body boundary sensations are linked to major cognitive-style differences and sensitivities to other people (see Bennett, 1981; Witkin, Moore, Goodenough, & Cox, 1977).

Brain Physiology. Work on the base of learning in brain physiology, especially chemical and neuronal storage and retrieval of memory, is increasing rapidly. Research mapping the processes of stress effects is also increasing (see pp. 109–111, above). There is growing research on pertinent drug-aided learning, which is already relevant because people in Washington now make routine and heavy use of one chemical (caffeine) to augment learning rates, attention, and memory functioning (Nash, 1962; see also Sitaram, Werngartner, & Gellen, 1978). Other chemicals (alcohol and to some extent marijuana) are also used routinely in Washington, in part to cope with stress. Assuming the validity of extrapolation from national rates, about 12% of the men and 20% of the women in the executive branch also use the "minor" tranquilizers (e.g., Valium) regularly (Harvard Medical School Health Letter, 1978, pp. 3–4). Reviews of current research on brain processes are available widely—for example, in the new journal *The Behavioral and Brain Sciences*, Luria (179), Hyden (179), Gazzaniga (1978), and, in more popular forms, Restak (1979). For further implications see below, p. 140.

Recruitment and Socialization Patterns. The capacity to attract, to Washington jobs, first-rate, intellectually restless people, who are highly motivated, self-starting, and willing to take personal responsibility for solving important problems rather than just doing an acceptable 9-5 job, is probably crucial to effective learning and probably depends on historical circumstances as well as agency characteristics. To a significant extent, first-rate people are probably attracted by what, in their times, are considered important, challenging problems where there is opportunity for significant movement. Meehl (1977) gives theology as an example of a field which over the past century has seldom attracted first-rate minds. And in Washington there is active informal discussion among first-rate people about job opportunities, where the action is, and who is good to work for. In an informal poll of policy analysts, the United States Office of Education had a reputation as a hopeless quagmire, a place where no one should go, and the Department of Commerce was considered boring; the Social Security Administration, Council of Economic Advisers, and Food and Drug Administration had high marks.

For current reviews of socialization theories about work careers see Van Maanen (1977), Van Maanen and Schein (1979) and McCall and Simmons (1978).

Distinct attractions of political life or public-service careers may produce recruitment patterns which simplify both motivational analyses and the design of different incentive systems for different people. Meltsner (1976), for example, finds Washington policy analysts can be reliably categorized as either substantively problem oriented or political-process oriented (and, rarely, as both). (See Winter, 1981, for further research.)

From a comparative perspective, one of the key important processes may be recruitment from university public-policy programs which seek to develop professional identities in their students and which have "in-and-outers" who return to universities and make current inside information and top-level perspectives available to young people. Policymaking in most other countries is often more elitist and closed than it is in the United States, with consequent deprivations of students (see, e.g., Sundquist, 1978a).

Organizational Structure and Dynamics

It is useful in a somewhat abbreviated context here to outline several relevant issues in organizational analysis. I will first discuss two general classes of literature, "smart" organization theory and organizational memory. I will then propose a cautionary perspective in a section of potential qualitative differences of public bureaucracies. Following this cautionary perspective are several specific sections on intelligence and decision-making processes in bureaucracies. For a recent general collection of relevant articles and bibliography, see Technology Review (1979).

"Smart" Organization Theory

Research on how to build, staff, and operate "smart" organizations has been growing in the managerial and organizational literature (R & D management, organizational development). There are 19 theories in this area which seem especially useful to the study of government learning and decision making. They are arranged below under people theories; organizational-process theories, and culture formation theories.

People Theories. Theories which postulate greater organizational intelligence as a function of people in the organization and how they relate to each other include: (1) *creative individual theory*—the theory there are a small number of innovative individuals who can make and stimulate major policy or product breakthroughs and that the problem is to find and hire them (Chandler, 1962, Chap. 6); (2) *interpersonal chemistry theory*—the hypothesis that organizational efficiency and/or effectiveness comes because specific people just mesh and work well together as a team (McGregor, 1966); (3) *new blood theory*—the idea that resources are needed to continually hire skilled new people who bring fresh ideas or first-hand knowledge of what other people are doing (this is perhaps especially important in areas of rapid policy or product change); (4) *role constellation theories*—the argument that a mix of skills and age, that is, good administrators, good midcareer researchers, good support staff, and bold young researchers, are all needed for unsolved (and heretofore "unsolvable") problems, along with "gray heads" (experience) to provide a sense of memory, perspective, and advice. Sundquist's (1978b) proposal for boundary-spanning roles and skills (e.g., salesmanship) to maintain an "open," innovative system also receives strong agreement in the literature (Roberts, 1968, 1977); (5) *peer competition theories*—contrary to the strict interpretation of Taylorism, designing redundant work units with peer competition may increase motivation and reduce error (Landau, 1969/1978); (6) *impact opportunity theory*—the hypothesis that the best new people gravitate to important problems "where the action is," so being concerned with such problems should lead organization to attracting people who will help; (7) *leadership theory*—the belief that when top leadership is no longer "satisficed" with the status quo and promotes search for innovation, it is more likely to occur (March & Simon, 1958, Zaltman, Duncan, & Holbek, 1973 pp. 153–186).

Organizational-Process Theories. Theories which relate intraorganizational functioning to the policy or product innovation process include: (8) *critical mass theory*—organizations need enough people working together on a problem to be intellectually self-stimulating and self-sustaining (the number is unclear) (H. Levinson, 1972); (9) *heterodoxy theory*—belief that a diversity of viewpoints, backgrounds, and skills in research increases creativity and enhances the probability of organizational success; (10) *environmental competition theory*—the hypothesis that learning occurs more rapidly in highly competitive fields by changing processes internal to organizations (e.g., Niskanen, 1979); (11) *communication flow theories*—a diverse body of literature that proposes innovation rates are increased by particular patterns of communication and by networks of institutions and intrainstitutional structures that create and support them; as well, there is an argument that much innovation (as well as intelligence and sophistication in the sense defined in this chapter) is embedded within the changing quality of communication (Allen, 1977; Tushman, 1979; Westin, 1971); (12) *specialized group process technology theories*—the alleged advantage to those groups which use brainstorming, Delphi, synectics, etc. (e.g., Stein, 1974, Vol. 2); (13) *administrative structure theories*—the alleged advantage of standard organizational units to handle R & D responsibilities; (14) *rational technology and analytic-decision theories*—organizations which commit heavily to advanced rational analyses (systems modeling, operations research, PPB, evaluation studies, etc.) are said to learn more rapidly; (15) *money theory*—the more money and other resources the better.

Culture Formation Theories. These theories can be seen as extending what Barnard (1938) originally discussed as the integration of formal and informal organizational behaviors (and relevant environmental characteristics) in the molding of a particular set of bureaucratic routines, values, understandings, identities, and worldviews (Kaufman, 1960; Packenham, 1973) to create and sustain organizational cultures and subcultures (Fine & Kleinman, 1979). The study of organizational culture and norms is not well developed, but it is perhaps crucial to understanding bureaucratic learning if the findings of Argyris (1967), Argyris and Schon (1978), and the report of Coleman, Campbell, Hobson, McPortland, Mood, Weinfeld, & York (1966) generalize across federal agencies. Culture theories include (16) *optimum norm theory*—the belief that certain organizations create cultures and climates especially conducive to research; these are typically thought (in America) to be open, egalitarian, problem-oriented rather than status or career centered, and achievement cultures rather than ascriptive cultures; (17) *newcomer theory*—the hypothesis that major innovations come from new, fresh, typically small firms; (18) *technology theory*—the view that technology creates culture, for example, that new technologies drive R & D processes and change organizations in their wake (see below, pp. 123–124) and create professionalism which increases innovation; (19) *synergistic harmony theories*—the extent to which organizational design practices align individual risks and incentives with those of the organization (Argyris & Schon, 1978; Cherns, 1977; Mohr, 1973; Wildavsky, 1978).

Organizational Memory

Apart from literatures seeking to describe "smart" organizations, another key aspect of learning is usable memory (Deutsch, 1963). Many informants suggest that poor organizational memory is the critical problem in Washington. "Bureaucracies aren't designed to learn, just to solve problems in the in-basket. There are too many transitions and too few personnel with long-term experience, and those who remain don't really care about acquiring what you call organizational memory." Certain features of Washington life reduce concern for memory, among them: (a) the belief of new political elites (and perhaps of younger people) that world problems continue only because they have not yet been in power (Etheredge, 1978; Heclo, 1977); (b) subjective overconfidence of those in power (see above, pp. 93–94); (c) short-term time horizons; and (d) activist (as opposed to contemplative) orientations (better to spend time and use power in activism and learning from experience than to waste time studying the past). Perhaps the most crucial of these is the overconfidence and ignorance calibration problem, the difficulty people have in assessing what they might learn from better memory.

The typical practice follows the "gray head" theory. Many agencies deliberately make efforts to keep people whose personal memories of top-level issues extend back 20 years or more. Historical offices, even if they exist and are more than archival, are not designed to codify experience by useful analytic categories (crisis decision behavior, negotiating with the Russians, implementation). In foreign policy, the British Foreign Office once made it routine practice to consult historians in policy deliberations, but this has not been an American practice.

The central opportunity here is institutional—designing long-term, usable, retrievable systems for executive departments. The potential benefit is there, since generic problems will probably be around a long time: in forty years, we will likely still be negotiating SALT (VIII), worrying about economic development, inflation, poverty, energy, food policy, health costs (still "out of control"), crime prevention, and so on. The key intellectual challenges are conceptual. The first is selecting the problems; since not everything can be studied, priorities must be set. The second problem is how to codify experience to learn useful lessons; this will be especially challenging because, in a sense, developing intelligence and sophistication involves learning later what you should have noticed originally. That is, we may already have sufficient experience in human history to learn everything we want to know about human behavior—if we only knew how to read our experience. But we need not lament inadequate records for the last 2,000 years. Today there are thousands of large organizations with good or poor learning records (including state and local governments), thousands of people who are passing through government public schools, crime rehabilitation, alcoholism, and drug programs, and so on. If we could simply figure out how to understand everything going on now, we could specify completely the conceptual requirements for a first-rate bureaucratic memory encoding and retrieval system. We have not yet created this intelligence, so the best frame is probably to think of the memory design program as itself a learning agenda (see May, 1973, on current memory inadequacy; see also Berninger & Adkinson, 1978; Cermak & Craik, 1979; Krippendorff, 1975).

Qualitative Differences of Public Bureaucracies

Shifting our emphasis slightly, the following discussion is much in the spirit of a cautionary note. Almost all organizational and industrial psychology (in the United States) has been derived from the private, profit-making business sector. Certainly almost all the empirical validation work has been done here. There are some signs of change—M. D. Cohen and J. G. March (1974) have completed a study on college presidents, there have been some macrolevel investigations of managerial structure in federal bureaucracies (e.g., Beyer & Trice, 1979), and of job satisfaction and other variables in the military (e.g., Berger & Cummings, 1979; Fiedler, 1967)—but the conventional mode is still the analysis of the profit-making firm (Cyert & March, 1963; Likert, 1961; March & Simon, 1958). One of the major ideas in organization theory, beginning with the work of the Yale Technology Project and the Tavistock Institute study of the British coal industry, is the neo-Marxist analysis that the mode of production, the technology employed by an organization (broadly defined), determines its internal structure, the way people treat each other, and much else (e.g., Gillespie & Mileti, 1977). How might the "mode of production" of the executive branch be different in ways that could make for qualitative differences in applicable theory? It is an empirical question, but some likely candidate variables are the following:

A. Frequent turnover of high-level political personnel, specialized recruitment patterns for these positions, and the potential for shortfalls of personnel preparation and poorly orchestrated transition processes (Heclo, 1977)

B. Budget funding and program decisions determined by political processes involving multiple constituencies rather than the market

C. Multiple, sometimes poorly specified, sometimes conflicting internal and external goals in the executive branch (Halperin et al., 1974), and the (perhaps necessarily) frequent symbolic or psychodrama nature of activity (Edelman, 1964; Mohr, 1973)

D. The scope and magnitude of congressionally mandated department responsibilities (agencies far larger and more diverse than most private businesses)

E. The absence of a market system for performance feedback

F. The monopolistic or oligopolistic character of the federal government and hence the absence, in many areas, of competition (Sapolsky, 1968)

G. Special professional codes, loyalties, and norms among public servants (Miles, 1978; Mosher, 1968)

H. The legitimate role of ideology for prescription and evaluation

I. In foreign policy, the considerable absence of formal legal restraint in policy choice

J. The capacity to use regulation and law as policy tools

K. The important place of the news media in monitoring performance and setting agendas

L. The use by interest groups of the magnitude of expenditure rather than efficiency as a criterion for evaluation, and the liberal view that efficiency concerns are niggardly antihumanitarian

M. The special concerns of government to effect major change in thought, feeling and behavior of both individuals (e.g., crime, poverty, education) and political and organizational systems (e.g., economic development, state welfare systems, nuclear deterrence of Russia) rather than simply providing a product or service

N. Special legal restraints and political processes characteristic of relationships with public-employee unions

O. Right of public access, under the Freedom of Information Act, to most internal documents

P. The special salience of political news stories and the high profitability of books revealing inside detail, especially that of a controversial nature

Q. Conflict of interest regulations

R. Special legal restrictions on individual initiative and flexibility, on processes of Civil Service hiring, firing, and promotion, and on contracting, that make public bureaucracies more akin to true bureaucracies in Weber's sense

S. Special motivational attractions to certain areas of federal employment (Etheredge, 1978; Meltsner, 1976)

T. The low margin of victory typical in American electoral politics, giving special salience to small, highly mobilized groups (i.e., the power of "special interests")

U. The special power of key congressional committees and key individuals on Capitol Hill

For other lists of variables, consult Drucker (1978), Rapp (1978), and Fuchs (1968).

Intelligence Functions and Decision-Making Processes

There is not yet a theory of policy formation and learning which predicts more (or less) intelligent and effective outcomes. Indeed, George

(1972) is almost alone in proposing a normative model for multiple-advocacy decision processes (see also Destler, 1972; Kling, 1978; Thibaut & Walker, 1975, 1978). There is a substantial, though largely descriptive, literature on presidential advisory systems, chiefly analyzing foreign policy (see George, 1980; Greenstein, Berman, Felzenberg, & Lidtke, 1977; Hess, 1976; Pious, 1979). Overviews of the issues are provided by Lasswell (1971, 1975) and Dror (1971).

In considering organizational intelligence and decision-making processes, I will briefly focus here on four issues: institution creation strategies, the use of social science research in aiding the analysis of organizational behavior and substantive problems, professionalization and its possible impact on organizational culture and decisions, and contract evaluation research and the puzzle of its unrealized capacity as a feedback device.

Institution Creation Strategies.   A common approach to minimizing error and increasing intelligence in policy formation is the design of bureaucratic structures or routines which are seen as inherently superior to the old. This is usually termed reorganization or organizational development (Beer, 1976; Harmon, 1975; Warwick, 1975). The central idea is the rearrangement of how things get done (formally or informally).

In major federal agencies, the last fifteen years have seen the establishment of assistant secretaries for planning and evaluation (or their equivalents) in almost all agencies. They have not been systematically studied and evaluated. Examples of learning routines (or at least work and political routines) include Administrative Procedures Act notices and hearings, impact statements, circulation of draft proposals within government (usually including, for major issues, congressional, press, and legal specialists), varied policy information provided to interest groups (either directly or through news leaks), the annual OMB budget analysis and review (supplemented by *ad hoc* task forces and the deployment of special assistants to cover high-salience issues), and informal networks idiosyncratic to agency personnel. As well, there are agencies or programs whose primary job is information (e.g., CIA, DIA, NSA, Census Bureau).

Beyond these standard institutions and practices for "in-house" thinking, the federal government has developed seven additional institutional designs to aid learning; (1) standing interagency working groups; (2) high-level layerings in specialized councils and staffs within the executive office of the president (the Council of Economic Advisers has traditionally had a major role, OSTP has grown in importance, and the National Security Council staff has now evolved into a miniature State Department); (3) federally run research institutes (e.g., for health, education, energy, and nuclear weapons); (4) endowed think tanks with contract research supplements (e.g., Rand Corporation in its early years); (5) scientific, peer review grant programs (e.g., National Science Foundation); (6) contract research with consulting firms; and (7) advisory councils and commissions, sometimes with mandated participation for various groups (see Lipsky & Olson, 1977). The relative effectiveness of these alternatives has not yet been assessed.

Use of Social Science. The use of social-science research in policy formation is the subject of a growing analytic literature (e.g., Andersen, 1977; G. D. Brewer, 1973; Greenberger, Crenson, & Crissey, 1976; Lynn, 1978; National Research Council, 1978–1979). Efforts to provide a general theory and estimate usage rates are at a preliminary stage (Caplan, 1979). If the definition of use is decisive policy impact from single studies, then estimates of low usage common in the literature are probably correct. But it would be hard to conceive of policy discussion or decision making in Washington without modern social-science concepts and research methods; they are simply taken for granted, dramatically so in the case of economic theories and concepts. Questions more relevant than current usage rates are: What important studies that should have an impact are not used? What specific capacities for policy-relevant knowledge from social science are underutilized?

Professionalization Trends. Existing research suggests that increased professionalization leads to a more "cosmopolitan" organizational identity, to the use of more extensive and varied sources of information, to greater interest in and receptiveness to new ideas, to less suppression of negative or troubling information, and to higher rates of innovation in firms with higher proportions of professionals (e.g., Greenwood, 1966; Wilensky, 1967; J. Q. Wilson, 1966). Becoming a professional probably involves being socialized into a learning "frame" and legitimation system (Berger & Luckmann, 1967) locating the individual within an historical progression (from less competence in the past to the promise of increasing competence in the future), and a commitment to learning and to adopting new potentials for increased competence (Colvard, 1961; Krause, 1971; Moore, 1970). Professionalization of government service (Mosher, 1968) may include advanced training in research skills, a critical attitude toward received authority, legitimation of an identity as an investigator, a sense of craft, a sense of ethics (Grundstein, 1962), and a preference for scientific rational problem solving over symbolic politics or moralism. It might also create a sense of security, not only in peer support, but also because professional certification may increase job mobility and because one aspect of professionalization is expert agreement and support against "unreasonable" performance standards (if the economy goes into recession the economic adviser is not personally discredited if his colleagues do not know the answer either).

Undoubtedly there will turn out to be other professionalization effects as well: stubborn autonomy, independent political power, occasional resistance (probably often healthy) to political control or subservience, in-group ethnocentrisms, trained incapacities so some professionals will not recognize truths until they are officially recognized within their literature and expressed in its specialized jargon, and so forth.

Not all professional training is the same: the classic British aristo-cratic model of learning Latin and Greek, the common-law heritage from Blackstone, Bentham, and Mill, and the role models of Plutarch (how men with high character and noble virtues made wise judgments and benefited their people while men of dissolute personal morals or overweaning hubris brought defeat) have given way to cost–benefit analysis and pragmatic dis-cussions of why sunshine laws, PPB, or ZBB will not work. The techno-cratic, managerial version of civil-service preparation is increasingly the American alternative, although with what trade-offs is not clear.

Performance of Contract Evaluation Research.   Federal agencies have in the last decade attempted to monitor more closely the impacts of policy decisions (see E. Katz & B. Danet, 1973). Various technologies of analysis have been developed and applied, but there is apparent consensus that program evaluation studies conducted through contract research are typically abysmal and useless. Knowing why would be fruitful. The fol-lowing fourteen theories appear in good repute: (1) competitive bidding reduces quality, especially because lower salaried (or at least lower com-petence) people do the work (G. D. Brewer, 1973); (2) lack of high pro-fessional standards, integrity, and competence by consultants; (3) covert pressure from agencies which dilutes critical findings in the interest of main-taining good relations; (4) lack of evaluation criteria specified by Congress in legislation; (5) the belief that evaluation studies are not significant in the political process and hence, no one cares or pays much attention; (6) explicit agency decisions that studies are solely adversarial weapons (that is, that evaluations can only hurt them politically and not help them), de-liberate decisions to undercut the process; also the intentional commis-sioning of studies to discredit programs or embarrass a competitor; (7) inadequate overview competence by agency contact monitors; (8) under-supply of social scientists able to do first-rate research; (9) pressures for fast turnaround from agencies and the political process ("You want it bad, you get it bad"); (10) inadequate critical scrutiny of evaluation studies by Congress; (11) low salience of evaluation in activist organizations like HEW; (12) low salience of evaluation research at the presidential level; (13) lack of routine competition (evaluations of evaluations) by competi-tive contract consultants; (14) the belief that evaluation studies are "cap-tured" by the agency being evaluated, through selective distortion of in-formation or other techniques.

There are two further problems with evaluation studies. First, they are not integrated and cumulative. Government programs fall into some

obvious categories: demonstration projects; federally mandated procedures, citizen participation requirements (Denk, 1979) and formula match
grants with various reimbursement rates to "torque" state and local systems; use of supply interventions versus demand interventions (building
public housing directly or providing vouchers to individuals, running public school systems or providing vouchers); use of regulations versus economic incentives; behavioral change programs aimed at foreign governments; personal change programs aimed at individuals; and so forth.
Unfortunately for analytical and learning purposes, this type of cross-
agency grouping does not occur in designing a long-run research strategy
to develop theories of program effectiveness. Second, evaluation studies
are not yet behavioral (Etheredge, 1976a). That is, they are not designed
to provide a high yield of information or to explain why programs do not
work for some people or some cases, and thus are likely to be resisted because they have a low probability of being constructive (i.e., agencies feel
they are doing the best they can, are acutely aware of their vulnerability
to criticism, and see little gain from this first generation of evaluation
studies).

The Washington Political Environment

Most of the other chapters in this handbook refer to theories of political behavior and are relevant here at least to the problem of why people
spend their time on other things than thinking and learning. All other variables in this chapter are linked with the political environment—the structure of incentive and risk systems, money, cognitive abilities of elites,
action moods, presidential leadership and goals, stress, recruitment patterns, top level inexperience, bureaucratic design, and much else. I will
leave these implicit and, in the interest of an efficient use of space, select
only four specific issues. These will include the impact of time structures,
lobbying, accountability processes and possible trade-offs between learning and legitimacy, and the adequacy of information channels. I will then
structure a discussion of two general problems in the explanation of political behavior: the case for behavioral theories unique to political life and
the metaissue of the politics of politics.

The Structure of Time in Washington

To an investigator who adopts an anthropologist's sensibility, political and bureaucratic life is strikingly rhythmic and cyclical: the diurnal
and workweek cycles, the budget and congressional-year cycles, summer
vacations, the two- and four-year electoral accountability cycles, and
press deadlines. Also striking are the periodic ceremonies and rites (not
always successful) to achieve transitions in action moods, identities, and

leadership directions through annual executive-branch budget prepara-
tions, the State of the Union Address, and congressional hearings for each
agency. Most of the activity at middle and higher levels in Washington is
orchestrated to respond to such deadlines, and the risk is that everyone
concentrates only on the short term, with superficial thought and the norm
of quick turnaround. In all likelihood, one simple reason that there is little
concern for long-range learning is that there are no scheduled final exams
to create, within the executive branch, cycles of agenda creation and review of long-range learning activities in preparation for public scrutiny.

Lobbying

Both Congress and the executive branch depend heavily on lobbying-
group representatives for proposals, criticism, and information on substantive programs and for learning the likely political reactions of different
constituencies. In addition to private enterprise and professional and trade
associations, most states and large cities have opened offices in Washington to facilitate lobbying communication (see Haider, 1974). Between elections, policy formation is largely intra-Washington politics. A research
program might: (a) address what groups or interests, from the standpoint
of democratic theory, are not represented effectively or are overrepresented, and (b) develop a theory of the most effective selling points, to
different actors, of how to be represented effectively (see Bacheller, 1977).

Accountability and Review Systems: Legitimacy Trade-Offs

Washington life is often an adversarial process; initiators specialize
in presenting the merits of their proposal and others act as critics (Wildavsky, 1964). And it is a standard human tendency to be sympathetic to those
with whom one deals (Edelman, 1964). However, the standard "monitoring agent" theory of how to design intellectual integrity into collective
processes that recognize these individual tendencies and compensate for
them is not universally applied. To be sure, the presence of OMB helps keep
agencies honest (and gives department leadership the breathing space to
please internal constituents and pass along more dubious requests knowing that rejection will probably occur and be blamed on someone else). But,
like having outside examiners in the academic world, or the structures of
appeal courts for review in the judicial world, or independent auditing in
the business world, the executive branch could probably become more
honest and effective in its learning processes by a system of independent
critics who, though increasing headaches in the short run, could reduce
them in the long run. The bases for such monitoring are present—the staffs
of congressional committees have increased markedly in recent decades,
both in number and formal academic credentials. Members of Congress

have traditionally developed expertise in selected areas, and the General Accounting Office and Legislative Reference Service of the Library of Congress have been expanding their roles. Brookings Institution has always played an important role, and the American Enterprise Institute may become similarly important. Foundation studies have often been crucial. But even allowing for such capacity and change as has occurred, there may not be enough heterodoxy and independence among the people who are now funded; J. Coleman (1978, pp. 701–702), for example, reports evidence from a review of 38 cases of policy research that government contract research (as opposed to independent agent research) produced interpretations of results substantially less critical of the policymaker and less sensitive to the interests of people affected by programs.

Perhaps the bottom-line problem in the political fate of learning agendas is the potential trade-off between legitimacy and learning. Admitting that you have something to learn implies your competence cannot be completely trusted now.

News Media Effects

Although they can use many channels in their areas of responsibility, most people in Washington generally rely on only a few sources of information (even for knowing what the government is doing): *The Washington Post, The New York Times, Newsweek,* and *CBS Evening News.* A crucial and unresolved issue is what is missed or received in distorted form (*Editor and Publisher,* 1979; Gans, 1979) and especially whether the causal explanations received are accurate. Another issue is the degree to which the level of intelligence and sophistication in these channels probably affects the general quality of elite thinking.

"Media fear" is probably one of the central psychological facts in political life; to survive, officials must automatically ask how their actions and words might appear in the press. Thus, good, sophisticated reporters probably help to keep government responsive, but their breathless tendency to sensationalize and their love for symbolic politics may keep many critical studies from being done. As well, some editorials, some columnists, and humor (e.g., *Doonesbury* and Art Buchwald's columns) probably contribute significantly to perspective and, occasionally, to a public philosophy (e.g., George Will, David Broder) and to greater compassion (e.g., Tom Wicker).

Uniqueness and Self-Transforming Capacity

The Uniqueness of Political Behavior. One implicit issue in the analysis of political behavior is the extent to which political behavior is qualitatively different from behavior in other arenas. For example, if you want to explain what people are doing in some competitive sport, the main outlines of behavior (and good understanding and accurate predictions) fall into place through simply knowing the rules, rationales, and standard plays developed in the history of the game; football is not baseball or golf. Nor does explaining the behavior of short-order cooks (if that is what most politicians are) require a doctorate in biochemistry.

The issue is simply whether people behave in qualitatively different —and especially in highly sociologically constrained—ways in political life. If the answer is yes, although we can point to these differences using a social science vocabulary ("there are different roles, norms, and motives engaged there"), political scientists are alone to chart a unique and well-bounded field of inquiry and also have a warrant for considering much theoretical and empirical work in other disciplines to be irrelevant. But to the extent that there is nothing unique or constrained about "the ecology of games" (Bardach, 1977) and other features of American political life, political scientists are also *de facto* psychologists and sociologists who need to integrate—and can aid their understanding by doing so—the developing intelligence of these disciplines.

I do not intend here to resolve the issue of the extent to which all the theories and concepts in this chapter can or should substitute for, expand, deepen, and/or place in context a *sui generis* understanding of the game of politics. I simply want to illustrate the issue with respect to two traditions: "hardball politics" analysis and group-level analysis.

Hardball Politics Assumptions. One well-honored tradition of political analysis sees the game of Washington politics as solely that of tough-minded, Machiavellian players, striving and maneuvering—behind a public facade of idealism and altruistic concern—primarily to achieve well-defined self-interests for power, money, and status. There has been a "sociology of knowledge" in sectors of political science so that this interpretation of the political game is taken *prima facie* as the mark of being a realistic political analyst. But the diverse theories and concepts considered in this chapter call into question the adequacy of such a tradition. Hardball politics is only one syndrome of behavior, cognition, and motivation (Etheredge, 1979b), and although it is clear that some political actors are of this stripe (and perhaps that people with such concerns are especially drawn to Washington politics) there is a growing view that a wide variety of motivations exist in elite American politics and often within individuals (Barber, 1965, 1972; Etheredge, 1978; Meltsner, 1976; Payne & Woshinsky, 1972; Winter, 1981), and that politicians act not solely for themselves but also from ambivalences and sympathetic identifications with other actors (Edelman, 1964; Searles, 1979, on symbiosis and ambivalence in countertransference). Thus we have the paradox that realpolitik analyses may be a bit naive. Even if political actors want to be successfully selfish, however, it has been proposed that on most issues, the majority of them find themselves quite unsure and confused about where their true self-interest (selfish or enlightened) lies (Bauer, Pool, & Dexter, 1972).

In raising these issues of whether everyone in political life is selfishly "political" in the hardball, realpolitik sense, I must of course anticipate scorn for being "naive" from those who already "know" that this is why people do things. Still, the predictive value of the traditional hardball selfishness model as the unique nature of Washington political games can be tested rigorously.

When is Group Sociology a Complete Explanation? The second issue raised implicitly by this review is whether political actors in Washington are organized into groups by strong sociological constraints which limit players to certain roles in distinctive units with well-specified rule-like relations; Banfield (1964), Altshuler (1977), and many others have proposed that organized groups are the central determinants in our political life. But an increasing number of political analysts are arguing that such constraints, if once present, might be dissolving (Gergen, 1973). They suggest that American politics is more chaotic than it seemed, that group loyalties are weak, that social class explains less and less, that individual entrepreneurship is central in Congress, that both bureaucracies and the executive branch itself are often "loosely coupled" congeries of individuals, that alliances are *ad hoc* and shifting, that the concept of individual networks of contacts and influence may be more useful (Pool & Kochen, 1978/1979), that norms of party discipline are largely nonexistent, and that it is the unique personality traits and operational codes of individual decision makers that are decisive in policy formation across a wide range of politically feasible options (Barber, 1972; Bauer *et al.*, 1972; Etheredge, 1978; Heclo, 1977; Mayhew, 1974; Wyden, 1979). Thus, the argument that analysis of American political life is almost exclusively that of a well-defined and predictable minuet of group conflict and accommodation is probably in trouble, and adequate political analysis may often (although not always) require more than the traditional explanatory repertoire if it is to keep up with the intelligence and sophistication of behavioral science.

Self-Transformation Capability. A final issue for political analysis is "the politics of politics." Or, as one reformer put it, "Is American politics an explanation or an excuse?" Thus, to the extent that politics is governed by norms, these norms themselves might be transformed through the political process. And, for example, if "muddling through" incremental adjustment (Lindblom, 1959) actually arises partly from characteristics of actors (e.g., the context embeddedness of Jaques's lower level cognitive capacities, which now preclude synoptic understanding and statesmanlike vision), these too might be changed. At the moment, however, behavioral research on politics has yet to clarify whether there is a major potential for qualitative transformation—in the present case, the potential for giving greater collective priority to statesmanlike long-range learning. It may be (see pp. 102–106) that most of our theories and estimated coefficients for explaining political life will turn out, in retrospect, to be mere "place-holders," that is, answers to the question "how did people and organizations behave before they became smarter and wiser?"

Societal, World, and Historical Contexts

It is unlikely that we are naturally brighter than people of 1,000 years ago. We just have a lot more to work with: the potential perspective on past successes and failures, the intellectual and physical technologies stored and transmitted in educational systems (including the formal scientific method and statistical tools), the economic resources (beyond subsistence) to allow for specialized careers and for the first one-third of many people's lives spent outside the production system in formal education, and the doubling of individual longevity since the American Revolution. Whether we truly are increasing "our" knowledge ever faster today, accelerating up the logarithmic curve postulated by some theorists, is not clear; natural science *publications* increase at this rate. But natural science learning is a special case—people can use computers or a new drug without being scientists. In the humanities or social sciences (outside of economics), diffusion of knowledge poses special problems because people cannot just naively use physical embodiments.

It should be noted, however, that societies can also forget. Some knowledge and skills have clearly been lost to most people (e.g., farming), and there are always the issues of whether the quality of American elites has declined since the time of the founding fathers, whether people are becoming more cranky, dependent, and anomic, and whether "the intelligence we once had" is dissipating as Western civilization progresses by declining.

I will have little to say about international networks or about society or history in general (see Gouldner, 1979; Lane, 1978; Naroll, Benjamin, Fohl, Fried, Hildreth, & Shaefer, 1971). I want instead to focus on two theories (truth norms and secularization), and one hypothesis (that government learning may be a dependent variable.)

Truth Theory

One theory of an effective learning environment is that it is simply one in which people tell the truth to each other. A substantial part of psychotherapy proceeds first by establishing a relationship where this is possible; therapy is in part a healing through simple truth-telling. Some people maintain that an essential quality of being a good teacher is to be truthful enough to admit a lack of knowledge; sociologists of science say the norm of truth-telling is crucial to advance (Ben-David, 1971). A veteran Washington lawyer, asked how to make the world work better, told me the key was to "get all the liars to tell the truth." If so, one theory is that America is in good shape in this regard: Rokeach (1973) reports that Americans rank honesty as more important than a comfortable life, wealth, or peace of mind—indeed honor it and want it more than all other values. However, the opposite conclusion is advanced by Edelman (1964), who records a substantial amount of evidence that, in political life, both the public and politicians prefer strategic dissembling, psychodrama, and illusion.

Secularization and Orthodoxy Theories

A standard theory among sociologists has been that secularization of society increases learning activity and, more generally, that any prescribed orthodoxy can restrict learning. Thus, one research issue is the extent to which implicit or explicit orthodoxies in America are sufficiently strong to restrict free speech and investigation (Habermas, 1970; McCarthy, 1976). A related issue is whether secularization has produced a loss of intelligence and hard-won understanding about life. Vonnegut (1970/1976, pp. 165–167), for example, suggests that the best that social scientists can do is to spend their lifetimes hacking their way through open doors with wretchedly complicated methodologies to rediscover old truths about the normative basis of a good society:

> It has been said many times that man's knowledge of himself has been left far behind by his understanding of technology, and that we can have peace and plenty and justice only when man's knowledge of himself catches up. This is not true. Some people hope for great discoveries in the social sciences, social equivalents of $F = ma$ and $E = mc^2$ and so on . . . . We don't need more information. . . . All that is required is that we become less selfish than we are.
>
> We already have plenty of sound suggestions as to how we are to act if things are to become better on earth. For instance: Do unto others as you would have them do unto you. About seven hundred years ago, Thomas Aquinas had some other recommendations as to what people might do with their lives, and I do not find these made ridiculous by computers and trips to the moon and television sets. He praises the Seven Spiritual Works of Mercy, which are these:
>
> To teach the ignorant, to counsel the doubtful, to console the sad, to reprove the sinner, to forgive the offender, to bear with the oppressive and troublesome, and to pray for us all.

He also admires the Seven Corporal Works of Mercy, which are these:

To feed the hungry, to give drink to the thirsty, to clothe the naked, to shelter the homeless, to visit the sick and prisoners, to ransom captives, and to bury the dead.

A great swindle of our time is the assumption that science has made religion obsolete. All science has damaged is the story of Adam and Eve and the story of Jonah and the whale. Everything else holds up pretty well, particularly the lessons about fairness and gentleness. . . .

Science has nothing to do with it, friends.

Government Learning: A Dependent Variable?

Because it puts in a broader perspective the internal-process perspective in the classic works of Deutsch (1963) (government as principal investigator), Argyris and Schon (1978), and even the "open-systems" model of Katz and Kahn (1978), one hypothesis I want to emphasize again is that government learning is often the dependent variable. It is dependent on what universities teach, on what the voters want or can be sold, on what lobbying groups say, on the agendas the news media set, on the standards and quality of critics, on the action mood of the times, on conceptual and methodological innovations from university research, on whether people have enough genuine trust to tell the truth, and on much else. It is probably also true that learning by government is often a function of current, active political conflict and the public adversary processes by which opponents of established policy do the research that ultimately makes government more intelligent (see Lawrence & Lorsch, 1967; Starbuck, 1976). Research may even show that presidents and the executive bureaucracy have seldom originated qualitative increases in their own intelligence and that almost all conceptual and program innovations have had to be imported (Deutsch et al., 1971).

Problem Types

Government learning rates depend crucially on the types of problems to be solved. They also depend (in ways that are still somewhat unclear) on who is trying to solve them. Ackoff (1978) notes, and we have seen earlier, that implicit constraints in the cognitive and intuitive processes of the knower, as well as his or her level of motivation, characteristics of identity, and perceived norms, resources, constraints, and risks in the social and political location (and so forth) need to be included in the model. As a beginning to the problem of differentiation, I will briefly sketch 14 problem types that may generically be more or less difficult for government to solve.

No Problem

The first type of problem, for which there will be little progress, occurs when the agendas and incentive systems of jobs and the beliefs held by other people in the organization (Berger & Luckmann, 1967) create the understanding that there is no problem. That is, one condition which applies to many people in many jobs in Washington is that they see no important problems to solve or learn about. The job is routine, the individual feels his or her sole responsibility and appropriate role is just to do the job. The surrounding organizational identity, culture, and norms legitimate the status quo; the interest groups, Congress, and bureaucratic superiors are either satisfied with, or indifferent to, the work. Thus, even if the individual is not context embedded (see pp. 96–97, above) and feels a personal drive for better solutions, and even if he or she attributes to learning the potential of providing a better solution, there are no resources or support to make headway. And the individual will likely anticipate (probably realistically) that even if he or she made personal headway there is no receptive action mood that can be used to move the organization.

Technology-Dependent Problems

It is likely that most people do not try to learn about how to solve problems if the current technologies (intellectual, data generation, and manipulation) seem unlikely to provide an answer. On the other hand, there can be a miniature stampede when an important new technology makes progress possible. In the social sciences, the development of statistical time series has been the basis for most of the work in economics, with important impacts also on government learning. Another example is from psychology, where one of the major spurs to learning is when someone conceptualizes a new and interesting variable (i.e., discovers variance or articulates an aspect of reality in Werner's sense) and develops a good measurement instrument. This usually sets into motion a flurry of research (e.g., on authoritarianism, Machiavellianism, locus of control, fear of success, field dependence). One of the metaproblems of government and social-science learning is what new technologies would be useful to increase learning rates.

Resource-Dependent Problems

A third class of problems are those which can be answered in principle but where there are inadequate resources allocated to learning activities. For example, if the executive branch wanted to give serious national priority to learning about voting behavior, it could probably increase learning rates substantially by funding separate centers to compete with the Survey Research Center at the University of Michigan and providing each with the money necessary to do long-range planning and conduct national probability studies.

Similarly, many theories, measurement techniques, and training instruments are available for research on how to improve crisis decision-making processes at the political level in foreign-policy or nuclear (e.g., Three Mile Island) crises, or to diagnose and potentially ameliorate the "groupthink" syndrome outlined by Janis (1972). These problems could probably be solved with enough resources. In these and many other cases, continued government ignorance does not seem to depend on the absence of good ideas or technologies but rather reflects low or nonexistent action moods, levels of aspiration, and thus, commitment of resources.

Known-Answer Problems

A fourth type of problem is that where answers are known by someone, but the people who need to know them do not. If it is a *known expert* type of problem, learning is easy—call up or hire the expert to tell you the answer. If it is a *fragmented and elusive expertise* type of problem, where many people have pieces of the puzzle or relevant knowledge and viewpoints, then the answer will be more difficult and require sophisticated management, multiple channels (Landau, 1969/1978), and alertness to the risk of being gameplanned by one set of experts. Neustadt and Fineberg's (1978) study of the Ford Administration swine flu decision is a recent case study of top government decision makers who could easily have learned more than they did if they had accurately diagnosed their needs and the functioning of their own organizations.

Unproductively Conceptualized Problems

A fifth type of problem is that which can be described in a general way, but where what is lacking is a useful specification of the processes involved which could render the symptoms within a treatable framework (Etheredge, 1976a). For example, to say that government does not learn because bureaucrats are "under-motivated, deferential, conservative, unimaginative, won't accept responsibility, and have no curiosity" could imply that the people involved, and the recruitment practices, are the problem—and that little can be done. Alternative definitions, however, might conceptualize these behaviors as intervening variables with the real nature of the problem being, among others, fear of authority, poor job design, poor leadership, learned helplessness and withdrawal in bureaucratic environments, high stress, low stress, inadequate competition, and so on. Conceptualizing the nature of the problem in these terms may be a better alternative because it could allow one to do something effective.

Thus, another metaproblem of government learning is to identify when the true problem is a current way of thinking about the nature of the problem.

Problems Amenable to Full Scientific Method

Some problems (e.g., in chemistry, physics, engineering, or plant biology) can be investigated with the full power of the scientific method; that is, rigorous experimental conditions and controls applied to phenomena whose natures can be exactly specified and precisely measured, multiple experimental trials can be done at low cost, and constant coefficients can be expected. Since the scientific method appears to be absolutely reliable in ascertaining causation (at least where there are good and careful researchers), government learning rates should be highest when resources are devoted to these types of problems, as in the impressive growth in weapons technology or putting a man on the moon.

Strong-Norm-System Problems

A type of problem which is relatively easy to learn about is behavior in social systems with strong norms (i.e., where the answer is obvious because the legitimacy of the norms, their salience, and the costs of deviance override other variables and idiosyncratic variance). In the army, for example, if you want to learn why people shine their shoes regularly, you probably need to look no further to find an answer than the norms of the system. Shoe shining in civilian life, however, is probably devilishly complicated to predict.

Another example of strong-norm systems is economic-rationality systems where profit or utility maximization is a strong norm, the major benefits and costs are normatively specified and fully monetized to allow the actors to apply the norms. Here, at least in principle, government can learn the reasons for behavior by analyzing variations of a (relatively!) small number of variables and can specify, in principle, the appropriate policy changes. (I do not mean to imply that the American economy is the full economic-rationality system of the textbooks—norm changes away from profit maximization to satisficing, or from monetary rewards to leisure activities, for example, may be at work, and so forth.)

Pluralist, Low-Norm-Salience or Rapid-Change Problems

An eighth type of problem, common in the human behavior area of government activity in pluralist societies like America, is opposite from the preceding type—freedom, or absence of strong totalitarian control and thus of simple invariant norms, can multiply enormously the number of variables that can be relevant (perhaps in different ways for different people, Etheredge, 1976a) among people whose behavior constitutes the problem. At one time you could predict the likelihood that a marriage would end in divorce (it wouldn't) because almost everyone agreed that marriage vows should be binding. Today, learning how to predict or solve the problem of divorce can be much more complicated, especially in a country like the United States where limited government reduces the capacity to produce authoritative norms (see Emery & Trist, 1965; Trist, 1976, on the "causal texture" of environments; see also La Porte, 1975; Sproull, Weiner, & Wolf, 1978).

Forecasting with Uncertain Precedents

A ninth type of problem is forecasting (Ascher, 1978; Choucri & Robinson, 1978; Kahn, 1975), especially forecasting effects of nonincremental change or novel innovations. To the extent that this is a qualitatively changing world, government may not be able to forecast accurately. Thus, learning will always lag, even in the ideal case where all previous experience is codified and retrievable, until new experience accumulates.

Problems Unanswerable or Unposable from Brain Constraints

A tenth type of problem may be that which, because of the problem's essential structure, the human mind is incapable of understanding. Chomsky, for example, has argued that an explanation of the functioning of the brain may fall outside the domain of theories we are able to understand (cited in Restak, 1979, pp. 323–326). Permuting Chomsky's idea, it is also possible that there are useful questions government officials are incapable of even posing. These would be of two types: those that cannot be thought of but which we could answer, and those that cannot be thought of and could not be answered in ways the human brain could comprehend.

Secrecy Penetration Problems

Foreign-policy decisions often present special problems of gaining access to secret information. Secrecy-blocked learning situations not only affect current American planning but, perhaps more seriously, turn the inference process into a partial projective test (Etheredge, 1978) with resulting overconfidence and added difficulty in interpreting feedback from past experience (May, 1973) to learn in the long run.

Different People and Different Cultures Problems

People usually have a strong edge in intuitive understanding of others who are like themselves (Cronbach, 1955, 1958; Wrightsman, 1977, pp.

104–112). Presumably then, government will lag more seriously in learning to understanding people or countries whose personalities or cultures are qualitatively different.

Time-Constraint Problems

Learning seems to require calendar time, not just hard-work time, possibly because of natural upper bounds to the speed of physiological processes of DNA memory-protein resynthesis and neuron path rewirings (analogous to the calendar time which, even under the best of conditions, is necessary to develop physical fitness). If some sectors of the world change more rapidly than people can rethink, there will be a growing shortfall in the growth of intelligence that can be translated into effective policy.

Incoherent-Policy Problems

It is presumably easier to learn from experience when you know what you are doing and why you are doing it. If goals, theories, and overall logical structure of government programs are incoherent, people should find it difficult to know what is succeeding or failing, in what ways, and why (Richardson, 1975; Sproull et al., 1978).

Diagnostic Repertoires

Overview

A major theme of this review is that, at least by my reckoning, social scientists have an impressive collective capacity to think with intelligence and sophistication about the problem of government learning rates. This does not mean that anyone knows in advance which conceptions and theories apply to different individuals or agencies any more than a physician can diagnose in advance the causes of the problems of the next patient to be seen. Nor does it mean that all diagnoses can yet be linked to effective remedies. But it is a respectable beginning.

Illustrative Individual Diagnoses

In Table 1, I give a list of some major diagnostic alternatives of shortfalls in individual learning; space limitations necessitate deferring a full listing to another place. Undoubtedly, the reviewers who address this field in future years will be able to add more alert differentiation, tighter integration, some empirical weights of more likely diagnoses, codify procedures for taking relevant details of a patient's history, and offer suggestions

Table 1. Illustrative Diagnoses of Individual Learning

Theoretical perspective	"Your problem is that you . . ."
Fixed nature	
Motivational and emotional	Do other things Don't want to learn Love routine Don't use your unconscious effectively Think you're right already Are too old to change
Ability	Don't have the ability Aren't suited to this job
Passive-reactive	Don't think for yourself Just want to have a good time Need a good leader Need some ideals Follow the course of least resistance Need an interesting problem Are too realistic about what you can accomplish Need to think of yourself as a professional Need a better identity
Developmental	Have to keep working at it Are underchallenged or over your head Aren't getting the respect and appreciation you feel entitled to Need better critics Need a sense of perspective Don't like responsibility Are scared to grow up because you would feel lost, confused, alone, and vulnerable Need incentives to grow up and take charge Are too deferential and too intimidated by authority
Stress	Have too much stress Are trying to do too much Have too little stress Feel complexity or change threatens your sense of control
Aversive motivation	Resent being a subordinate Are scared you're a potential victim Are too realistic about how much your superiors care about you Need psychotherapy Work in a bad organization Are afraid to admit you don't know the answer already

for multistage empirical examinations of organizations that are equivalent to the standard "general-physical" screening exam and the use of indicated laboratory tests. In the left column of Table 1, I make general reference to the high-level theory or issue involved. In the right column I have grounded the theories by less formal language; social science is not in another world but, usually, only codifies in perspective what Clifford Geertz (1973) called "the hard surfaces" of daily (there isn't any other kind) life, in the schedules, appointments, meetings, and deadlines in bureaucratic and political jobs.

Concluding Reflections

As I suggested above, the capacity to think intelligently about issues in adult and organizational learning seems to have accelerated impressively since Wilensky's (1967) review of the field 13 years ago. Perhaps the field, at least as indexed by increasingly differentiated diagnoses and partially integrated appraisals of all the elements and processes involved, is accelerating up the "takeoff" path of the logarithmic "S" curve beloved to some developmental theorists. However, the criterion for full integration remains unmet (and may require further self-reflection—a formal integration on the model of a Bach fugue may be inappropriate if political life in America actually has the character of a Bartok composition, a Thelonious Monk jazz ensemble, or even [shudder!] the "modern" music of John Cage). Moreover, the second criterion for learning I have proposed—greater effectiveness produced from using such a wealth of theories—has still to be demonstrated.

Researchers in this field will have their own agendas, but I want to flag seven problems where it seems the issues are clear enough, the basic research technologies available, and the likely impact from good research and creative thought sufficiently strong to warrant special attention.

The Design of Institutional-Memory Capabilities

The fact must now be faced, I am afraid, that academic social science in the United States, since it is tied to student enrollment, has peaked and is unlikely to increase for the next several generations. And there is just too much unknown for academic social science to take the responsibility on itself for codifying and learning from all relevant experience of all government agencies. The key will be to help design the codification and retrieval systems that agencies themselves can implement and to train the generation of researchers who will staff them and build greater analytic behavioral theory.

Increasing Effective Transitions and Competence of Political Appointees

It is widely agreed in Washington that it takes one to two years for most political appointees to learn their jobs, except perhaps in the foreign-policy area where the Council on Foreign Relations provides upcoming elites with prior exposure and experience. A variety of institutional innovations are possible, although they probably need to be initiated independently of government (such as, e.g., Johnson Foundation Health Staff Seminars) and could probably be aided by more knowledge of how well shadow cabinet systems operate to provide effective transitions.

Quality of Watchdog and Critic Systems

If I had to place a bet on the validity of only one policy-relevant theory of learning, it would be "Will this be on an exam?" Until there are institutions and practices to hold the executive branch accountable for its long-term learning, performance will fall short of capacity. And the bottom line is that if you have anything new to learn that will help you become more effective, you won't learn it from people who already think you're completely right. Expanded congressional staffs, and especially increased critical capabilities by the General Accounting Office, are improving the intelligence of criticism, but probably a useful innovation would be to require regular reports to Congress on long-run learning agendas and on results in selected programs or problems that would be subjects of public hearings. For example, reports by the Secretary of Health, Education, and Welfare every three years on what HEW has been learning about program implementation or education achievement, or from the Justice Department on criminal rehabilitation, or from the State Department on terrorism, could be instituted as routine. It is also possible that a three-year evaluation plan, developed in consultation between committee staff and agency officials and subject to a full-dress congressional hearing, could be a routine requirement for every program (see Aberbach, 1979).

A related problem is developing accountability for the intelligence, sophistication, and long-term learning agendas of the news media, particularly of the key 500 to 1,000 top journalists in the country. One problem is whether they have adequate funding for independent research and evaluation to sharpen their own explanatory and diagnostic capabilities.

Dependency Theory of Motivational Blockage

A critical issue is the development and testing of dependency theory approaches to life in hierarchical bureaucracies (see above). Merton's (1952) classic attack on the Weberian theory that large hierarchical organizations make people rational and responsible seems capable of being pressed much further, especially on dissociation of personal responsibility, restricted personal identity, increased inertia and fear of change, ritualization and other symptoms of primary process shifts, dependent complaining, reactivity, hierarchical imagery context embeddedness, and so forth. As well, there is the issue of whether "free-ridering," dependency, and dependent complaining strategies are rational and effective (Hirschman, 1970; Olson, 1965; Schelling, 1978).

Good Judgment

Plato's concern (see above, pp. 81–82) to facilitate the development of people who can be trusted to have good judgment on important issues remains alive today. It is likely that in any field there are people with reputations for particularly sound advice and perspective, but within the wide array of decision-making studies, injunctions, and technical analytical aids, the problem of who makes good decisions has yet to be addressed.

Overload and How to Cope

There is a simple mathematics of overload: if 50 scientists in a field each publish one paper a year, each scientist has only to read 49 papers to stay current and continue working. If there are 1,000 scientists in a field and each publishes one paper a year, the system can start to overload, self-absorb, self-dampen, and reduce individual productivity because each individual now faces 999 relevant papers to read. (People cope in various ways, but it has been alleged that even now the typical academic social scientist has time to read thoughtfully only about 20% of the books in his or her office.) Government officials face a similar time and capacity problem: there is a simple mathematics of a growing bureaucracy or government overloading and self-absorbing itself merely in maintenance and survival functions. By the end of the 1980s, if current practices continue, there will still be the same limited number of top-level people in the executive branch and Congress, most of them newcomers to their jobs, trying to manage massive agencies, survive, and accomplish something within a partially chaotic domestic and international political process. And, to be sure, their environment will not always be filled with mutual support and good will. They will be held responsible to solve and set policy directions on (literally) every important problem in the world. Perhaps some may even want to do a responsible job of planning and overseeing over $1 trillion in annual outlays, spending 25% of our GNP (and with an extremely important role in some areas, such as health care, defense, and education, much more than this 25% average). There is probably considerable knowledge about how to help people run these processes successfully that needs to be made available, and thinking about the research agendas to produce it would have high potential yield (with such annual outlays, a 1% increase in effectiveness or efficiency would yield $10 billion in the first year alone, and that means a massive benefit/cost ratio that could justify extraordinary increases in research funding).

The Critique of Ideology and Overconfidence

Ideology still plays a significant role in decisions and, to the extent that the relevant assumptions can be explicated and tested and the empirical results diffused, there is probably a major potential to increase realistic problem solving (Edelman, 1977; Etheredge, 1976a). (To take one minor example, research on welfare recipients seems to have reduced, over the past 25 years, the harshness of conservative virulence about bums, cheats, and rip-off artists by simply differentiating and counting types of people, such as mothers with small children, who apply.) And the development of a professional and medical diagnostic capability for social problems will probably also be increased by related efforts to more reliably calibrate ignorance levels given the direct evidence (cited earlier) that many people in Washington overestimate how much they already know and mistake simple intuitive plausibility for true understanding.

ACKNOWLEDGMENTS

I have found that many of the variables in this chapter apply to my own work, and this leaves me with debts too numerous to acknowledge fully. The National Science Foundation's support, through grant SOC 77-27470, was crucial. My research assistant, James Short, has been a valued critic; Lynn Etheredge will recognize the benefits of his ideas and criticisms throughout. Barbara Noble and Kathy Fanning handled secretarial tasks and Chuck Lockman handled computer word-processing responsibilities with high professionalism and good cheer. Peter Brecke, Lewis Gannett, Pat Hanratty, and Frank Lerman have provided research assistance which is partly expressed here.

The memories and intelligence of institutions and societies are only partly in libraries; they live as well in the qualities of mind developed by scholars and passed by their personal example to their students—to the extent that there is, at times, alert and discerning intelligence in these pages, the reader will be detecting the effects not only of works cited in the bibliography, but also the touch of Robert Lane and the late Harold Lasswell.

To many others, including colleagues and interview subjects in Washington, I extend my thanks.

References

Aaron, H. J. *Politics and the professors: The Great Society in perspective*. Washington: Brookings, 1978.

Abelson, R., Aronson, E., McGuire, W., Newcomb, T., Rosenberg, M., & Tannenbaum, P. *Theories of cognitive consistency: A sourcebook*. Chicago: Rand-McNally, 1968.

Aberbach, J. D. Changes in congressional oversight. *American Behavioral Scientist*, 1979, *22*, 493–515.

Ackoff, R. L. *The art of problem solving: Accompanied by Ackoff's fables*. New York: Wiley, 1978.

Adams-Webber, J. R. *Personal construct theory: Concepts and application*. New York: Wiley, 1979.

Ajzen, I., & Fishbein, M. Attitude-behavior relations: A theoretical analysis and review of empirical research. *Psychological Bulletin*, 1977, *84*(5), 888–918.

Alderfer, C. *Existence, relatedness, and growth: Human needs in organizational settings*. New York: Free Press, 1972.

Alker, H. R., Jr. *From political cybernetics to global modeling*. Unpublished paper, Massachusetts Institute of Technology, 1979.

Allen, T. J. *Managing the flow of technology*. Cambridge: M.I.T. Press, 1977.

Allison, G. *Essence of decision: Explaining the Cuban missile crisis*. Boston: Little, Brown, 1971.

Altshuler, A. The study of American public administration. In A. A. Altshuler & N. C. Thomas (Eds.), *The politics of the federal bureaucracy* (2nd ed.). New York: Harper & Row, 1977.

Andersen, D. F. *Mathematical models and decision making in bureaucracies: A case story told from three points of view*. Unpublished doctoral thesis, M.I.T. Sloan School, 1977.

Appley, M. H. (Ed.). *Adaptation-level theory*. New York: Academic Press, 1971.

Argyle, M. Seven psychological roots of religion. *Theology*, 1964, *67*(530), 1–7.

Argyris, C. *Some causes of organizational ineffectiveness within the Department of State*. Washington: State Department, 1967. Occasional Paper #2 of the Center for International Systems Research.

Argyris, C., & Schon, D. *Organization learning: A theory of action perspective*. Reading, Mass.: Addison-Wesley, 1978.

Arrow, K. *The limits of organization*. New York: Norton, 1974.

Ascher, W. *Forecasting:An appraisal for policymakers and planners*. Baltimore: Johns Hopkins University Press, 1978.

Axelrod, R. M. Schema theory: An information processing model of perception and cognition. *American Political Science Review*, 1973, *67*, 1248–1266.

Axelrod, R. (Ed.). *Structure of decision: The cognitive maps of political elites*. Princeton: Princeton University Press, 1976.

Bacheller, J. M. Lobbyists and the legislative process: The impact of environmental constraints. *American Political Science Review*, 1977, *71*(1), 252–263.

Ball, D. W. 'The definition of situation': Some theoretical and methodological consequences of taking W. I. Thomas seriously. *Journal for the Theory of Social Behavior*, 1972, *2*, 61–82.

Bandler, R., & Grinder, J. *Patterns of hypnotic techniques of Milton H. Erickson*. Cupertino, Calif.: Meta Publications, 1975. (a)

Bandler, R., & Grinder, J. *The structure of magic* (2 vols.). Palo Alto: Science and Behavior Books, 1975. (b)

Bandura, A. Self-efficacy: Toward a unifying theory of behavioral change. *Psychological Review*, 1977, *84*(2), 191–215. (a)

Bandura, A. *Social learning theory*. Englewood Cliffs, N.J.: Prentice-Hall, 1977. (b)

Banfield, E. C. Politics. In J. Gould & W. L. Kolb (Eds.), *A dictionary of the social sciences.* Glencoe: Free Press, 1964.

Barber, J. D. *The lawmakers.* New Haven: Yale University Press, 1965.

Barber, J. D. *The presidential character.* Englewood Cliffs, N.J.: Prentice-Hall, 1972.

Bardach, E. *The skill factor in politics.* Berkeley: University of California Press, 1972.

Bardach, E. *The implementation game.* Cambridge: M.I.T. Press, 1977.

Barnard, C. *The functions of the executive.* Cambridge: Harvard University Press, 1938.

Barrett, W. (Ed.) *Zen Buddhism: Selected writings of D. T. Suzuki.* New York: Doubleday, 1958.

Bass, L. R., & Brown, S. R. Generating rules for intensive analysis: The study of transformations. *Psychiatry,* 1973, *36,* 172–183.

Bauer, R. A., Pool, I. D. S., & Dexter, L. *American business and public policy: The politics of foreign trade* (2nd ed.). Chicago: Aldine, Atherton, 1972.

Beer, M. The technology of organization development. In M. D. Dunnette (Ed.), *Handbook of industrial and organizational psychology.* Chicago: Rand-McNally, 1976.

Ben-David, J. *The scientist's role in society.* Englewood Cliffs, N.J.: Prentice-Hall, 1971.

Bennett, W. L. Perception and cognition: An information-processing framework for politics. *Handbook of political behavior* (Vol. 1). New York: Plenum Press, 1981.

Berger, C. J., & Cummings, L. L. Organizational structure, attitudes, and behaviors. In B. M. Staw (Ed.), *Research in organizational behavior* (Vol. 1). Greenwich, Conn.: JAI Press, 1979.

Berger, P., & Luckmann, T. *The social construction of reality.* Garden City, N.Y.: Doubleday, 1967.

Berlin, I. Does political theory still exist? In P. Laslett & W. G. Runciman (Eds.), *Philosophy, politics and society* (2nd series). Oxford: Basil Blackwell, 1962.

Berman, P. *Revolutionary organization: Institution-building within the People's Liberation Armed Forces.* Lexington, Mass.: Lexington Books, 1974.

Berman, P. *Designing implementation to match policy situation: A contingency analysis of programmed and adaptive implementation.* Paper presented at the annual meeting of the American Political Science Association, September 1978. (Rand Paper P-6211)

Berninger, D. E., & Adkinson, B. W. Interaction between the public and private sectors in national information programs. In M. E. Williams (Ed.), *Annual review of information science and technology* (Vol. 13). White Plains, N.Y.: Knowledge Industry Publications, 1978.

Bernstein, R. J. *The restructuring of social and political theory.* Philadelphia: University of Pennsylvania Press, 1978.

Beyer, J. M., & Trice, H. M. A reexamination of the relations between size and various components of organizational complexity. *Administrative Science Quarterly,* 1979, *24,* 48–64.

Bion, W. R. Learning from experience. In W. R. Bion, *Seven servants: Four works by Wilfred R. Bion.* New York: Jason Aronson, 1977.

Block, N.J., & Dworkin, G. (Eds.). *The I.Q. controversy: Critical readings.* New York: Pantheon, 1976.

Bloom, H. *The anxiety of influence: A theory of poetry.* New York: Oxford University Press, 1973.

Bloomfield, L. P. Planning foreign policy. *Political Science Quarterly,* 1978, *93*(3), 369–391.

Bowers, K. S. Situationism in psychology: An analysis and a critique. *Psychological Review,* 1973, *80,* 307–336.

Bowlby, J. The making and breaking of affectional bonds: I. Aetiology and psychopathology in the light of attachment theory. *British Journal of Psychiatry,* 1977, *130,* 201–210. (a)

Bowlby, J. The making and breaking of affectional bonds: II. Some principles of psychotherapy. *British Journal of Psychiatry,* 1977, *130,* 421–431. (b)

Brehm, J. W. *Responses to loss of freedom: A theory of psychological reactance*. Morristown, N.J.: General Learning Press, 1972.

Brenman-Gibson, M. Notes on the study of the creative process. In M. M. Gill & P. S. Holzman (Eds.), *Psychology versus metapsychology: Psychoanalytic essays in memory of George Klein*. New York: International Universities Press, 1976.

Brenman-Gibson, M. The creation of plays: With a specimen analysis. In A. Roland (Ed.), *Psychoanalysis, creativity, and literature*. New York: Columbia University Press, 1978.

Brewer, G. D. *Politicians, bureaucrats, and the consultant*. New York: Basic Books, 1973.

Brewer, W. F. There is no convincing evidence for operant or classic conditioning in adult humans. In W. B. Weimer & D. S. Palermo (Eds.), *Cognition and the symbolic processes*. Hillsdale, N.J.: Erlbaum, 1974.

Brown, I. D. Measuring the "spare mental capacity" of car drivers by a subsidiary auditory task. *Ergonomics*, 1962, *5*, 247.

Brown, N. O. *Life against death: The psychoanalytic meaning of history*. Middletown, Conn.: Wesleyan University Press, 1959.

Brown, S. *Psychoanalysis and political analysis*. Unpublished manuscript, 1981.

Brown, S., & Ellithorp, J. Emotional experiences in political groups: The case of the McCarthy phenomenon. *American Political Science Review*, 1970, *64*(2), 349–366.

Burnham, W. D. *Critical elections and the mainsprings of American politics*. New York: W. W. Norton, 1970.

Buss, A. R., & Poley, W. *Individual differences: Traits and factors*. New York: Gardner Press, 1976.

Cambridge, R. M., & Shreckengost, R. C. *Are you sure? The subjective probability assessment test*. Washington, D.C.: Central Intelligence Agency, 1978.

Campbell, D. T. Blind variation and selective retention in creative thought as in other knowledge processes. *Psychological Review*, 1960, *67*, 380–400.

Campbell, D. T. Evolutionary epistemology. In P. A. Schilp (Ed.), *The philosophy of Karl Popper* (Vol. 14-I). LaSalle, Ill.: Open Court Publishing, 1974.

Campbell, D. T. On the genetics of altruism and the counterhedonic components in human culture. In L. Wispé (Ed.), *Altruism, sympathy, and helping: Psychological and sociological principles*. New York: Academic Press, 1978.

Campbell, J. P., & Pritchard, R. D. Motivation theory in industrial and organizational psychology. In M. Dunnette (Ed.), *Handbook of industrial and organizational psychology*. Chicago: Rand-McNally, 1976.

Caplan, N. The two-communities theory and knowledge utilization. *American Behavioral Scientist*, 1979, *22*(3), 459–470.

Carroll, J. B., & Maxwell, S. E. Individual differences in cognitive abilities. In M. Rosenzweig & L. Porter (Eds.), *Annual review of psychology* (Vol. 30). Palo Alto: Annual Reviews, 1979.

Cermak, L. S., & Craik, F. I. M. (Eds.). *Levels of processing in human memory*. New York: Halsted Press, 1979.

Chandler, A. D., Jr. *Strategy and structure*. Cambridge, Mass.: M.I.T. Press, 1962.

Cherns, A. B. Can behavioral science help design organizations? *Organizational Dynamics*, 1977, *6*, 44–64.

Choucri, N., & Robinson, T. W. (Eds.). *Forecasting in international relations: Theory, methods, problems, prospects*. San Francisco: W. H. Freeman, 1978.

Clark, B. R. The "cooling-out" function in higher education. In O. Gursky & G. A. Miller (Eds.), *The sociology of organizations: Basic studies*. New York: Free Press, 1970.

Clark, P. H., & Wilson, J. Q. Incentive systems: A theory of organizations. *Administrative Science Quarterly*, 1961, *6*, 129–166.

Cohen, D. K., & Garet, M. S. Reforming educational policy with applied research. *Harvard Educational Review*, 1975, *45*(1), 17–43.

Cohen, M. D., & March, J. G. *Leadership and ambiguity: The American college president.* New York: McGraw-Hill, 1974.

Cohen, M. D., March, J. G., & Olsen, J. P. A garbage can model of organizational choice. *Administrative Science Quarterly*, 1972, *17*(1), 1–25.

Coleman, J. Sociological analysis and social policy. In T. Bottomore & R. Nisbet (Eds.), *A history of sociological analysis.* New York: Basic Books, 1978.

Coleman, J. S., Campbell, E., Hobson, C., McPortland, J., Mood, A., Weinfeld, F., & York, R. *Equality of educational opportunity.* Washington, D.C.: Department of Health, Education, and Welfare, 1966.

Colvard, R. Foundations and professions: The organizational defense of autonomy. *Administrative Science Quarterly*, 1961 (September), *6*, 167–184.

Committee on House Administration. *Information policy: Public laws from the 95th Congress.* Washington, D.C.: Government Printing Office, 1979.

Cronbach, L. J. Processes affecting scores on "understanding others" and "assumed similarity." *Psychological Bulletin*, 1955, *52*, 177–193.

Cronbach, L. J. Proposals leading to analytic treatment of social perception scores. In R. Taguiri & L. Petrullo (Eds.), *Person perception and interpersonal behavior.* Stanford: Stanford University Press, 1958.

Cyert, R. M., & March, J. G. *A behavioral theory of the firm.* Englewood Cliffs, N.J.: Prentice-Hall, 1963.

De Board R. *The psychoanalysis of organizations.* London: Tavistock Publications, 1979.

De Charms, R. *Personal causation: The internal affective determinants of behavior.* New York: Academic Press, 1968.

Deci, E. L. *Intrinsic motivation.* New York: Plenum Press, 1975.

Denk, C. E. *The Massachusetts Growth Policy Development Act: Structuring situations for learning by local officials.* Unpublished honors thesis, Massachusetts Institute of Technology, 1979.

Destler, I. M. Comment. Multiple advocacy: Some limits and costs. *American Political Science Review*, 1972, *66*, 786–790.

Deutsch, K. W. Communication in self-governing organizations: Notes on autonomy, freedom, and authority in the growth of social groups. In L. Bryson, L. Finkelstein, R. MacIver, & R. McKeen (Eds.), *Freedom and authority in our time: Twelfth symposium of the conference on science, philosophy, and religion.* New York: Harper & Brothers, 1953.

Deutsch, K. *The nerves of government: Models of communication and control.* New York: Free Press, 1963.

Deutsch, K., Platt, J., & Senghaas, D. Conditions favoring major advances in social science. *Science*, 1971, *171*, 450–459

Diesing, P. *Reason in society.* Urbana: University of Illinois Press, 1962.

Downs, A. Up and down with ecology—The "issue-attention cycle." *The Public Interest*, 1972, *28*, 38–50.

Dror, Y. *Design for policy sciences.* New York: American Elsevier, 1971.

Drucker, P. F. Managing the public service institution. In F. S. Lane (Ed.), *Current issues in public administration.* New York: St. Martin's Press, 1978.

Ducey, C. The life history and creative psychopathology of the shaman: Ethno-psychoanalytic perspectives. In W. Muensterberger & A. Esman (Eds.), *The psychoanalytic study of society* (Vol. 7). New Haven: Yale University Press, 1976.

Duval, S., & Wicklund, R. A. *A theory of objective self awareness.* New York: Academic Press, 1972.

Eaves, L. J., & Eysenck, H. J. Genetics and the development of social attitudes. *Nature*, 1974, *249*(5454), 288–289.

Edelman, M. *The symbolic uses of politics.* Urbana: University of Illinois Press, 1964.

Edelman, M. *Political language: Words that succeed and policies that fail.* New York: Academic Press, 1977.

Editor and Publisher. "10 best censored stories" picked by panel of judges. *Editor and Publisher*, June 2, 1979, 16, 18.

Einhorn, H. J., & Hogarth, R. M. Confidence in judgment: Persistence of the illusion of validity. *Psychological Review*, 1978, *85*(5), 395–416.

Elms, A. C. *Personality in politics.* New York: Harcourt, Brace, Jovanovich, 1976.

Elstein, A., Shulman, L., & Sprafka, S. *Medical problem solving: An analysis of clinical reasoning.* Cambridge: Harvard University Press, 1978.

Emery, F. E., & Trist, E. L. The causal texture of organizational environments. *Human Relations*, 1965, *18*(1), 21–32.

Entwistle, N. J. Personality and academic attainment. *British Journal of Educational Psychology*, 1972, *42*, 137.

Erdelyi, M. H. A new look at the new look: Perceptual defense and vigilance. *Psychological Review*, 1974, *81*, 1–25.

Erikson, E. H. Identity and the life cycle. *Psychological Issues*, 1959, 1–171.

Erikson, E., & Newton, H. P. *In search of common ground: Conversations with Erik H. Erikson and Huey P. Newton.* New York: W. W. Norton, 1973.

Estes, W. K. *Learning theory and mental development.* New York: Academic Press, 1970.

Etheredge, L. *The case of the unreturned cafeteria trays.* Washington, D.C.: American Political Science Association, 1976. (a)

Etheredge, L. S. The hypnosis model of power. *Psychoanalysis and Contemporary Thought*, 1976. (b)

Etheredge, L. S. Optimal federalism: A model of psychological dependence. *Policy Sciences*, 1977, *8*, 161–171.

Etheredge, L. S. *A world of men: The private sources of American foreign policy.* Cambridge: M.I.T. Press, 1978.

Etheredge, L. S. *Context embeddedness: A spatial imagery encoding model of power and response in society.* Unpublished manuscript, 1979. (a)

Etheredge, L. S. Hardball politics: A model. *Political Psychology*, 1979, *1*(1), 3–26. (b)

Etheredge, L. S. *The liberal activist in hierarchical contexts.* Unpublished manuscript, 1979. (c)

Etzioni, A. *The active society.* New York: Free Press, 1968.

Evan, W. M. (Ed.). *Inter-organizational relations.* Philadelphia: University of Pennsylvania Press, 1978.

Fallows, J. The passionless presidency. *Atlantic*, 1979 (May), *243*, 33–46.

Fallows, J. The passionless presidency, part II. *Atlantic*, 1979 (June), *243*, 75–81. (b)

Fenichel, O. *The psychoanalytic theory of neurosis.* New York: W. W. Norton, 1945.

Ferenczi, S. Thinking and muscle innervation. In S. Ferenczi, *Further contributions to the theory and technique of psychoanalysis.* New York: Basic Books, 1953.

Fesler, J. W. The basic theoretical question: How to relate area and function. In F. S. Lane (Ed.), *Current issues in public administration.* New York: St. Martin's Press, 1978.

Festinger, L., Riecken, H. W., & Schachter, S. *When prophecy fails.* Minneapolis: University of Minnesota Press, 1956.

Fiedler, F. E. *A theory of leadership effectiveness.* New York: McGraw-Hill, 1967.

Findler, N. V. Computer poker. *Scientific American*, 1978 (July), *241*, 144–151.

Fine, G. A., & Kleinman, S. Rethinking subculture: An interactionist analysis. *American Journal of Sociology*, 1979, *85*(1), 1–20.

Fingarette, H. *Self-deception.* London: Routledge & Kegan Paul, 1969.

Fisher, S. *Body experience in fantasy and behavior.* New York: Appleton-Century-Crofts, 1970.

Fisher, S., & Greenberg, R. P. *The scientific credibility of Freud's theories and therapy.* New York: Basic Books, 1977. (a)

Fisher, S., & Greenberg, R. Stomach symptoms and up-down metaphors and gradients. *Psychosomatic Medicine*, 1977, *39*(2), 93–101. (b)

Frank, J., Hoehn-Saric, R. Imber, S., Liberman, B., & Stone, A. *Effective ingredients of successful psychotherapy*. New York: Brunner/Mazel, 1978.

Frank, S. J. Just imagine how I feel: How to improve empathy through training in imagination. In J. L. Singer & K. S. Pope (Eds.), *The power of human imagination: New methods in psychotherapy*. New York: Plenum Press, 1978.

Frankena, W. K. Education. In P. P. Wiener (Ed.), *Dictionary of the history of ideas: Studies in selected pivotal ideas* (Vol. 2). New York: Scribner's, 1973.

Freedman, D. G. Constitutional and environmental interactions in rearing of four breeds of dogs. *Science*, 1958, *127*, 585–586.

French, J. R. P., Jr. Person-role fit. In A. McLean (Ed.), *Occupational stress*. Springfield, Ill.: Charles C Thomas, 1974.

Freud, S. *Project for a scientific psychology*. In *The complete psychological works of Sigmund Freud* (Vol. 1). London: Hogarth Press, 1966. (Originally published, 1895.)

Freud, S. *The future prospects of psycho-analytic therapy*. In *The complete psychological works of Sigmund Freud* (Vol. 11). London: Hogarth Press, 1957. (Originally published, 1910.)

Freud, S. *Beyond the pleasure principle*. In *The complete psychological works of Sigmund Freud* (Vol. 18). London: Hogarth Press, 1955. (Originally published, 1920.)

Freud, S. *Group psychology and the analysis of the ego*. In *The complete psychological works of Sigmund Freud*. (Vol. 18). London: Hogarth Press, 1955. (Originally published, 1921).

Freud, S. *Civilization and its discontents*. In *The complete psychological works of Sigmund Freud* (Vol. 21). Longon: Hogarth Press, 1973. (Originally published, 1930.)

Freud, S. *Why war?* In *The complete psychological works of Sigmund Freud* (Vol. 22.) London: Hogarth Press, 1973. (Originally published, 1933.)

Fuchs, V. R. *The service economy*. New York: National Bureau of Economic Research, 1968.

Gannett, L. *Boredom and hierarchicality*. Unpublished manuscript, Massachusetts Institute of Technology, 1979.

Gans, H. J. *Deciding what's news: A study of CBS Evening News, NBC Nightly News, Newsweek and Time*. New York: Pantheon, 1979.

Garet, M. *The implementation of social policy: An assessment of organizational capability*. Unpublished doctoral dissertation, Massachusetts Institute of Technology, 1979.

Garfield, S. L., & Bergin, A. E. (Eds.). *Handbook of psychotherapy and behavior change: An empirical analysis* (2nd ed.). New York: Wiley, 1978.

Gauss, C. E. Empathy. In P. P. Wiener (Ed.), *Dictionary of the history of ideas: Studies in selected pivotal ideas*. (Vol. 2). New York: Scribner's, 1973.

Gazzaniga, M. S. (Ed.). *Neuropsychology: Handbook of behavioral neurobiology* (Vol. 2). New York: Plenum Press, 1978.

Gedo, J. E. *Beyond interpretation: Toward a revised theory for psychoanalysis*. New York: International Universities Press, 1979.

Gedo, J. E., & Goldberg, A. *Models of the mind: A psychoanalytic theory*. Chicago: University of Chicago Press, 1973.

Geertz, C. Ideology as a cultural system. In D. Apter (Ed.), *Ideology and discontent*. Glencoe: Free Press, 1964.

Geertz, C. *The interpretation of cultures: Selected essays by Clifford Geertz*. New York: Basic Books, 1973.

Geller, J. E. The body, expressive movement, and physical contact in psychotherapy. In J. L. Singer & K. S. Pope (Eds.), *The power of human imagination: New methods in psychotherapy*. New York: Plenum Press, 1978.

George, A. L. The case for multiple advocacy in making foreign policy. *American Political Science Review*, 1972, *67*(3), 751–785.

George, A. L. Adaptation to stress in political decision making: The individual, small group, and organization contexts. In G. V. Coelho, D. A. Hamburg, R. Moos, & P. Randolph (Eds.), *Coping and adaptation*. New York: Basic Books, 1974.

George, A. L. *Presidential decisionmaking in foreign policy: The effective use of information and advice*. Boulder, Colo.: Westview Press, 1980.

Gergen, K. Social psychology as history. *Journal of Personality and Social Psychology*, 1973, *26*, 309–320.

Gillespie, D. F., & Mileti, D. S. Technology and the study of organizations: An overview and appraisal. *Academy of Management Review*, 1977, *2*(1), 7–16.

Gilligan, C. In a different voice: Women's conception of the self and of morality. *Harvard Educational Review*, 1977, *47*(4), 481–517.

Ginzberg, E. Planning full employment. In I. L. Horowitz (Ed.), *Constructing policy: Dialogues with social scientists in the national policy arena*. New York: Praeger, 1979.

Goffman, E. *Frame analysis*. Cambridge: Harvard University Press, 1974.

Goldschmid, H. J. (Ed.). *Business disclosure: Government's need to know*. New York: McGraw-Hill, 1979.

Goldstein, K. M., & Blackman, S. *Cognitive style: Five approaches and relevant research*. New York: Wiley-Interscience, 1978.

Gouldner, A. W. *The future of intellectuals and the rise of the new class*. New York: Seabury Press, 1979.

Gray, J. A. Casual theories of personality and how to test them. In J. R. Royce (Ed.), *Multivariate analysis and psychological theory*. New York: Academic Press, 1973.

Gray, J. A. *Elements of a two-process theory of learning*. New York: Academic Press, 1975.

Gray, M. M. *Computer science and technology: Computers in the federal government: A compilation of statistics—1978* (Special publication 500-46). Washington, D.C.: National Bureau of Standards, 1979.

Greenberger, M., Crenson, M., & Crissey, B. *Models in the policy process: Public decision making in the computer era*. New York: Russell Sage, 1973.

Greenstein, F., Berman, L., Felzenberg, A., with Lidtke, D. *Evolution of the modern presidency: A bibliographic survey*. Washington, D.C.: American Enterprise Institute, 1977.

Greenwood, E. Attributes of a profession. In H. M. Vollmer & D. L. Mills (Eds.), *Professionalization*. Englewood Cliffs, N.J.: Prentice-Hall, 1966.

Gruber, H. *Darwin on man: A psychological study of scientific creativity*. London: Wildwood House, 1974.

Grundstein, N. D. Prolegomena to ethics for administrators. In H. Cleveland & H. D. Lasswell (Eds.), *Ethics and bigness: Scientific, academic, religious, political, and military*. New York: Harper & Brothers, 1962.

Habermas, J. Towards a theory of communicative competence. *Inquiry*, 1970, *13*, 360–375.

Haider, D. H. *When governments come to Washington: Governors, mayors, and intergovernmental lobbying*. Chicago: Aldine, 1974.

Haley, J. *Uncommon therapy: The psychiatric techniques of Milton H. Erickson*. New York: W. W. Norton, 1973.

Halperin, M. H. Clapp, P., & Kanter, A. *Bureaucratic politics and foreign policy*. Washington, D.C.: Brookings Institution, 1974.

Hare, A. P. *Handbook of small group research* (2nd ed.). New York: Free Press, 1976.

Harmon, M. H. Organization development in the State Department: A case study of the ACORD Program. In *Appendices* of (Murphy) Commission on the Organization of the Government for the Conduct of Foreign Policy (Vol. 6). Washington, D.C.: Government Printing Office, 1975.

Hart, T. G. *The cognitive world of Swedish security elites.* Stockholm: Swedish Institute of International Affairs, 1976.

Harvard Medical School Health Letter. The "minor tranquilizers"—Use or abuse. *3*(6), April 1978, 3–4.

Hauser, S. T. Loevinger's model and measure of ego development: A critical review. *Psychological Bulletin*, 1976, *83*(5), 928–955.

Heclo, H. *A government of strangers: Executive politics in Washington.* Washington: Brookings Institution, 1977.

Helson, H. Adaptation level theory. In S. Koch (Ed.), *Psychology: A study of a science* (Vol. 1). New York: McGraw-Hill, 1959.

Hermann, M. Indicators of stress in policymakers during foreign policy crises. *Political Psychology*, 1979, *1*(1), 27–46.

Hess, S. *Organizing the presidency.* Washington, D.C.: Brookings Institution, 1976.

Hess, S. *The presidential campaign.* Washington, D. C.: Brookings Institution, 1978.

Hilgard, E. R. Neodissociation theory of multiple cognitive controls. In G. E. Schwartz & D. Shapiro (Eds.), *Consciousness and self-regulation: Advances in research* (Vol. 1). New York: Plenum Press, 1976.

Hilgard, E. R. *Divided consciousness: Multiple controls in human thought and action.* New York: Wiley-Interscience, 1977.

Hilgard, E., & Bower, G. *Theories of learning* (4th ed.). Englewood Cliffs, N.Y.: Prentice-Hall, 1975.

Hirschman, A. *The strategy of economic development.* New Haven: Yale University Press, 1958.

Hirschman, A. O. *Exit, voice and loyalty.* Cambridge: Harvard University Press, 1970.

Hofstadter, D. R. *Gödel, Escher, Bach: An eternal golden braid.* New York: Basic Books, 1979.

Holsti, O. R. Time, alternatives, and communications: The 1914 and Cuban Missile Crises. In C. F. Hermann (Ed.), *International crisis: Insights from behavioral research.* New York: Free Press, 1972.

Holsti, O. Foreign policy formation viewed cognitively. In R. M. Axelrod (Ed.), *Structure of decision: The cognitive maps of political elites.* Princeton: Princeton University Press, 1976.

Holsti, O. *The "Operational Code" as an approach to the analysis of belief systems: Final report to the national science foundation.* Mimeograph, Duke University, 1977.

Horowitz, M. J. *Stress response syndromes.* New York: Jason Aronson, 1976.

House, P. W., & Williams, E. R. Data inconsistencies and federal policymaking. *Policy Analysis*, 1978, *4*(2), 205–225.

Hunt, J. M. Psychological development: Early experience. In M. R. Rosenzweig & L. Porter (Eds.), *Annual review of psychology* (Vol. 30). Palo Alto: Annual Reviews, 1979.

Hurlbert, R. T. Random sampling of cognitions and behavior. *Journal of Research in Personality*, 1979, *13*, 103–111.

Hyde, A. C., & Shafritz, J. M. (Eds.), *Government budgeting: Theory, process, politics.* Oak Park, Ill.: Moore Publishing, 1978.

Hyden, H. Learning as differentiation of brain cell protein. In L. G. Nilsson (Ed.), *Perspectives on memory research: Essays in honor of Uppsala University's 500th anniversary.* Hillsdale, N.J.: Erlbaum, 179.

Janis, I. *Victims of groupthink.* Boston: Houghton Mifflin, 1972.

Janis, I. L., & Mann, L. *Decision making: A psychological analysis of conflict, choice, and commitment.* New York: Free Press, 1977.

Jaques, E. Social systems as a defense against persecutory and depressive anxiety. In M. Klein, P. Heimann, & R. E. Money-Kyrle (Eds.), *New directions in psychoanalysis: The significance of infant conflict in the pattern of adult behavior.* New York: Basic Books, 1955.

Jaques, E. *A general theory of bureaucracy.* New York: Halsted Press, 1976.

Jaynes, J. *The origin of consciousness in the breakdown of the bicameral mind.* Boston: Houghton Mifflin, 1976.

Jervis, R. *Perception and misperception in international relations.* Princeton: Princeton University Press, 1976.

Jones, C. O. *Clean air: The policies and politics of pollution control.* Pittsburgh: University of Pittsburgh Press, 1975.

Jones, R. A. *Self-fulfilling prophecies: Social psychological and physiological effects of expectancies.* New York: Wiley, 1977.

Kael, P. On the future of movies (1974). In P. Kael, *Reeling.* New York: Warner, 1977.

Kahn, H. On studying the future. In F. Greenstein & N. Polsby (Eds.), *Handbook of political science* (Vol. 7), *Strategies of inquiry.* Reading, Mass.: Addison-Wesley, 1975.

Kahneman, D. *Attention and effort.* Englewood Cliffs, N.J.: Prentice-Hall, 1973.

Katz, D., & Kahn, R. L. *The social psychology of organizations* (2nd ed.). New York: Wiley, 1978.

Katz, E., & Danet, B. (Eds.). *Bureaucracy and the public: A reader in official-client relations.* New York: Basic Books, 1973.

Kaufman, H. *The forest ranger.* Baltimore: Johns Hopkins Press, 1960.

Kerr, S., & Jermier, J. M. Substitutes for leadership: Their meaning and measurement. *Organizational Behavior and Human Performance,* 1978, *22,* 375–403.

Kiesler, C., Collins, B., & Miller, N. *Attitude change: A critical analysis of theoretical approaches.* New York: Wiley, 1969.

Kleinke, C. L. *Self-perception: The psychology of personal awareness.* San Francisco: W. H. Freeman, 1978.

Kline, P. Personality and learning. In M. J. A. Howe (Ed.), *Adult learning: Psychological research and applications.* New York: Wiley, 1977, 63–83.

Kling, R. Information systems in policymaking: Computer technology and organizational arrangements. *Telecommunications Policy,* 1978, *2*(1), 3–12.

Klinger, E. *Meaning and void: Inner experience and the incentives in people's lives.* Minneapolis: University of Minnesota Press, 1977.

Klinger, E., Gregoire, K., & Barta, S. Physiological correlates of mental activity: Eye movements, alpha, and heart rate during imagining, suppressing, search, concentration, and choice. *Psychophysiology,* 1973, *10,* 471–477.

Kohlberg, L. Stage and sequence: The cognitive-developmental approach to socialization. In D. A. Goslin (Ed.), *Handbook of socialization theory and research.* Chicago: Rand-McNally, 1969.

Kohlberg, L. From is to ought: How to commit the naturalistic fallacy and get away with it in the study of moral development. In T. Mischel (Ed.), *Cognitive development and epistemology.* New York: Academic Press, 1971.

J. Gedo & G. Pollock (Eds.), Freud: The fusion of science and humanism, *Psychological Issues,* Monograph 34/35. New York: International Universities Press, 1976.

Kohut, H. *The analysis of the self.* New York: International Universities Press, 1971.

Kohut, H. *The restoration of the self.* New York: International Universities Press, 1977.

Kohut, H. Creativeness, charisma, group psychology: Reflections on the self-analysis of Freud. In P. H. Ornstein (Ed.), *The search for the self: Selected writings of Heinz Kohut: 1950–1978* (Vol. 2). New York: International Universities Press, 1978. [Originally published in J. Gedo & G. Pollock (Eds.), Freud: The fusion of science and humanism, *Psychological Issues,* Monograph 34/35. New York: International Universities Press, 1976.]

Kohut, H. The two analyses of Mr. Z. *International Journal of Psychoanalysis,* 1979, *60*(1), 3–27.

Krause, E. A. *The sociology of occupations.* Boston: Little, Brown, 1971.

Krippendorff, K. Some principles of information storage and retrieval in society. *General Systems*, 1975, *20*, 15–35.

Kuhn, T. S. *The structure of scientific revolutions* (2nd ed.). Chicago: University of Chicago Press, 1970.

Kurtines, W., & Grief, E. B. The development of moral thought: Review and evaluation of Kohlberg's approach. *Psychological Bulletin*, 1974, *81*, 453–470.

Lachman, R., Lachman, J., & Butterfield, E. *Cognitive psychology and information processing: An introduction.* New York: Halsted Press, 1979.

Laing, R. D. *The politics of the family and other essays.* New York: Vintage Books, 1972.

Lakatos, I., & Musgrave, A. (Eds.). *Criticism and the growth of knowledge.* London: Cambridge University Press, 1970.

Landau, M. Redundancy, rationality, and the problem of duplication and overlap. In F. S. Lane (Ed.), *Current issues in public administration,* New York: St. Martin's Press, 1978. (Reprinted from *Public Administration Review,* 1969 [July/August], *29.*)

Lane, R. E. *Political thinking and consciousness: The private life of the political mind.* Chicago: Markham, 1969.

Lane, R. E. Autonomy, felicity, futility: The effects of the market economy on political personality. *Journal of Politics,* 1978, *40,* 2–24.

Langer, J. Werner's comparative organismic theory. In P. H. Mussen (Ed.), *Carmichael's manual of child psychology* (3rd ed.). New York: Wiley, 1970.

Langs, R. *The listening process.* New York: Jason Aronson, 1978.

La Porte, T. R. (Ed.). *Organized social complexity: Challenges to politics and society.* Princeton: Princeton University Press, 1975.

Lasswell, H. D. *Psychopathology and politics.* Chicago: University of Chicago Press, 1930.

Lasswell, H. D. *A pre-view of policy sciences.* New York: Elsevier, 1971.

Lasswell, H. D. Research in policy analysis: The intelligence and appraisal functions. In F. Greenstein & N. Polsby, *Handbook of political science* (Vol. 6). Reading, Mass.: Addison-Wesley, 1975.

Lawrence, P. R., & Lorsch, J. W. *Organization and environment.* Cambridge: Harvard Graduate School of Business Administration, 1967.

Lefberg, I. *Analyzing judicial change: The uses of "systematic biography" in anticipating the court and shaping its future policy.* Unpublished doctoral thesis, Massachusetts Institute of Technology, 1978.

Lefcourt, H. M. *Locus of control: Current trends in theory and research.* New York: Halsted, 1976.

Leonard, G. *Education and ecstasy.* New York: Dell, 1969.

LeVine, R. A., & Campbell, D. T. *Ethnocentrism: Theories of conflict, ethnic attitudes, and group behavior.* New York: Wiley, 1972.

Levinson, D., Darrow, C. N., Klein, E. B., Levinson, M. H., McKee, B. *The seasons of a man's life.* New York: Ballantine, 1978.

Levinson, H. *Organizational diagnosis.* Cambridge: Harvard University Press, 1972.

Lichtenberg, J. The testing of reality from the standpoint of the body self. *Journal of the American Psychoanalytic Association,* 1979, *26*(2), 357–385.

Lieberman, B. L. The role of mastery in psychotherapy: Maintenance of improvement and prescriptive change. In J. Frank, R. Hohen-Saric, S. D. Imber, B. L. Liberman, & A. R. Stone (Eds.), *Effective ingredients of successful psychotherapy.* New York: Bruner/Mazel, 1978.

Likert, R. *New patterns of management.* New York: McGraw-Hill, 1961.

Lindblom, C. E. The science of "muddling through." *Public Administration Review,* 1959, *19,* 79–88.

Lindblom, C. E., & Cohen, D. K. *Usable knowledge: Social science and social problem-solving.* New Haven: Yale University Press, 1979.

Lipsky, M., & Olson, D. J. *Commission politics: The processing of racial crisis in America.* New Brunswick, N.J.: Transaction Books, 1977.

Locke, E. A. The myths of behavior mod in organizations. *Academy of Management Review,* 1977, *1,* 543–552.

Loevinger, J., with A. Blasi. *Ego development.* San Francisco: Jossey-Bass, 1976.

Lowi, T. Europeanization of America? From United States to united state. In T. J. Lowi & A. Stone (Eds.), *Nationalizing government: Public policies in America.* Beverly Hills: Sage, 1978.

Luria, A. R. Neuropsychology of complex forms of human memory. In L. G. Nilsson (Ed.), *Perspectives on memory research: Essays in honor of Uppsala University's 500th anniversary.* Hillsdale, N.J.: Erlbaum, 1979.

Lynn, L., Jr. (Ed.). Knowledge and policy: The uncertain connection. *Study project on social research and development* (National Research Council, National Academy of Sciences). Washington, D.C.: National Academy of Sciences, 1978.

Machiavelli, N. *The prince* (L. Ricci, trans.; rev. E. R. P. Vincent). London: Oxford University Press, 1935.

MacLean, P. D. *A triune concept of the brain and behavior.* Toronto: University of Toronto Press, 1973.

Magnusson, D., & Endler, N. S. (Eds.). *Personality at the crossroads: Current issues in interactional psychology.* Hillsdale, N.J.: Erlbaum 1977.

March, J. E. (Ed.). *Handbook of organizations.* Chicago: Rand-McNally, 1965.

March, J. G. Bounded rationality, ambiguity, and the engineering of choice. *Bell Journal of Economics,* 1978, *9*(2), 587–608.

March, J. G., & Olsen, J. P. *Ambiguity and choice in organizations.* Bergen, Norway: Universitetsforlaget, 1976.

March, J. G., & Simon, H. A. *Organizations.* New York: Wiley, 1958.

Marris, P. *Loss and change.* New York: Pantheon, 1974.

Maslow, A. H. *Motivation and personality.* New York: Harper & Row, 1954.

Maslow, A. H. The need to know and the fear of knowing. In A. H. Maslow, *Toward a psychology of being* (2nd ed.). New York: Van Nostrand, 1968.

Maslow, A. H. *The psychology of science: A reconnaissance.* Chicago: Regnery, 1969.

May, E. R. *"Lessons" of the past: The use and misuse of history in American foreign policy.* New York: Oxford University Press, 1973.

Mayhew, D. *Congress: The electoral connection.* New Haven: Yale University Press, 1974.

McCall, G. J., & Simons, J. L. *Identities and interactions: An examination of associations in everyday life* (rev. ed.). New York: Free Press, 1978.

McCarthy, T. A. A theory of communicative competence. In P. Connerton (Ed.), *Critical sociology: Selected readings.* New York: Penguin, 1976.

McGregor, D. *Leadership and motivation.* Cambridge: M.I.T. Press, 1966.

McGuire, W. J. Selective exposure: A summing up. In R. P. Abelson, E. Aronson, W. J. McGuire, T. M. Newcomb, M. J. Rosenberg, P. H. Tannenbaum (Eds.), *Theories of cognitive consistency: A sourcebook.* Chicago: Rand-McNally, 1968.

Medawar, P. B. Advice to a young scientist. *Harper's,* 1979 (September), *256,* 39–46.

Meehl, P. (Ed.) *Psychodiagnosis: Selected papers.* New York: W. W. Norton, 1977.

Meltsner, A. J. *Policy analysts in the bureaucracy.* Berkeley: University of California Press, 1976.

Merton, R. K. Bureaucratic structure and personality. In R. K. Merton, A. Gray, B. Hockey, & H. Selvin (Eds.), *Reader in bureaucracy.* New York: Free Press, 1952.

Miles, R. E., Jr. Non-subservient civil servants. In F. S. Lane (Ed.), *Current issues in public administration.* New York: St. Martin's Press, 1978.

Miller, A. Conceptual systems theory: A critical review. *Genetic Psychology Monographs,* 1978, *97,* 77–126.

Miller, A., & Wilson, P. Cognitive differentiation and integration: A conceptual analysis. *Genetic Psychology Monographs,* 1979, *99,* 3–40.

Minsky, M. A framework for representing knowledge. In P. H. Winston (Ed.), *The psychology of computer vision.* New York: McGraw-Hill, 1975.

Mitchell, T. R. Organizational behavior. In M. Rosenzweig & L. Porter (Eds.), *Annual review of psychology* (Vol. 30). Palo Alto: Annual Reviews, 1979.

Mitroff, I. *The subjective side of science: A philosophical inquiry into the psychology of Apollo moon scientists.* New York: American Elsevier, 1974.

Mohr, L. The concept of organizational goal. *American Political Science Review,* 1973, *67*(2), 470–481.

Moore, W. E. *The professions: Roles and rules.* New York: Russell Sage Foundation, 1970.

Moray, N. (Ed.). *Mental workload: Its theory and measurement.* New York: Plenum Press, 1979.

Mosher, F. *Democracy and the public service.* New York: Oxford University Press, 1968.

Muir, W. *Police: Streetcorner politicians.* Chicago: University of Chicago Press, 1977.

Murray, H. A. (Ed.). *Myth and mythmaking.* Boston: Beacon Press, 1968.

Naroll, R., Benjamin, E., Fohl, F., Fried, M., Hildreth, R., & Schafer, J. Creativity: A cross-historical pilot study. *Journal of Cross-Cultural Psychology.* 1971, *2,* 181–188.

Nash, H. *Alcohol and caffeine.* Springfield, Ill.: Charles C Thomas, 1962.

National Research Council, National Academy of Sciences. *Study project on social research and development* (Vols. 1–6). Washington, D.C.: National Academy of Sciences, 1979.

Natsoulas, T. Consciousness. *American Psychologist,* 1978, *33,* 906–914.

Neisser, U. *Cognition and reality: Principles and implications of cognitive psychology.* San Francisco: W. H. Freeman, 1976.

Nelson, S. Nature/nurture revisited II: A review of the biological bases of conflict. *Journal of Conflict Resolution,* 1974, *18,* 285–335.

Neustadt, R. *Presidential power: The politics of leadership.* New York: Wiley, 1960.

Neustadt, R. E., & Fineberg, H. V. *The swine flu affair: Decision making on a slippery disease.* Washington, D.C.: Department of Health, Education, and Welfare, 1978.

Nimmo, D. *Popular images of politics: A taxonomy.* Englewood Cliffs, N.J.: Prentice-Hall, 1974.

Niskanen, W. A. Competition among government bureaus. *American Behavioral Scientist,* 1979, *22,* 517–524.

Nordstrom, C., Friedenberg, E. Z., & Gold, H. A. *Society's children: A study of ressentiment in secondary school education.* New York: Random House, 1967.

Odajnyk, W. The political ideas of C. J. Jung. *American Political Science Review,* 1973, *67,* 142–152.

Olson, M. *The logic of collective action.* Cambridge: Harvard University Press, 1965.

Ornstein, R. E. *The psychology of consciousness.* New York: Penguin Books, 1972.

Packenham, R. *Liberal America and the third world: Political development ideas in foreign aid and social science.* Princeton: Princeton University Press, 1973.

Palmore, E. Predicting longevity: A follow-up controlling for age. *The Gerontologist,* 1969, *9,* 247–250.

Payne, J. L., & Woshinsky, O. H. Incentives for political participation. *World Politics,* 1972, *24,* 518–546.

Pervin, L. A. Performance and satisfaction as a function of individual-environment fit. *Psychological Bulletin,* 1968, *69*(1), 55–68.

Pious, R. M. *The American presidency.* New York: Basic Books,1979.

Polanyi, M. *Personal knowledge.* New York: Harper & Row, 1958.

Polanyi, M. *The tacit dimension.* Garden City, N.Y.: Doubleday, 1966.

Pool, I., & Kochen, M. Contacts and influence. *Social Networks*, 1978/1979, *1*, 5–51.

Powell, D. A., & Buchanan, S. L. Comparison of several aggression models in Long-Evans (hooded) rats: Effects of sex and isolation. *Psychological Reports*, 1978, *43*, 703–720.

Price, D. D. S. *Big science, little science.* New York: Columbia University Press, 1963.

Radnitsky, G. *Contemporary schools of metascience.* Chicago: Regnery, 1973.

Rapp, B. W. You can't manage city hall the way you manage General Motors. In F. S. Lane (Ed.), *Current issues in public administration.* New York: St. Martin's Press, 1978.

Reason, J. T. Skill and error in everyday life. In M. J. A. Howe (Ed.), *Adult learning: Psychological research and applications.* New York: Wiley, 1977.

Rein, M., & White, S. Policy research: Belief and doubt. *Policy Analysis*, 1977, *3*(2), 239–271.

Restak, R. M. *The brain: The last frontier.* Garden City, N.Y.: Doubleday, 1979.

Reychler, L. *Patterns of diplomatic thinking: A cross-national study of structural and social-psychological determinants.* New York: Praeger, 1978.

Richardson, E. Preface to special issue on HEW mega-proposal. *Policy Analysis*, 1975, *1*(2), 223–231.

Roberts, E. B. Entrepreneurship and technology. *Research Management*, 1968 (July), *11*(4), 249–266.

Roberts, E. B. Generating effective corporate innovation. *Technology Review*, 1977 (October/November), *79*, 27–33.

Rogers, C. *On becoming a person.* Boston: Houghton Mifflin, 1961.

Rokeach, M. *The nature of human values.* New York: Free Press, 1973.

Rosenthal, T., & Zimmerman, B. J. *Social learning and cognition.* New York: Academic Press, 1978.

Ross, L. The intuitive psychologist and his shortcomings: Distortions in the attribution process. *Advances in Experimental Social Psychology* (Vol. 10). New York: Academic Press, 1977.

Royce, J. R., Coward, H., Egen, E., Kessel, F., & Mos, L. Psychological epistemology: A critical review of the empirical literature and the theoretical issues. *Genetic Psychology Monographs*, 1978, *97*, 265–353.

Safire, W. *Safire's political dictionary: The new language of politics.* New York: Random House, 1978.

Sagan, C. *The dragons of eden: Speculations on the evolution of human intelligence.* New York: Ballantine Books, 1977.

Sapolsky, H. M. Organizational competition and monopoly. *Public Policy*, 1968, *17*, 355–376.

Sapolsky, H. M. *The Polaris system development: Bureaucratic and programmatic success in government.* Cambridge: Harvard University Press, 1972.

Sarason, F. G., Smith, R., & Diener, E. Personality research: Components of variance attributable to the person and the situation. *Journal of Personality and Social Psychology*, 1975, *32*, 199–204.

Schachtel, E. *Experiential foundations of Rorshach's test.* New York: Basic Books, 1966.

Schank, R. C., & Abelson, R. R. *Scripts, plans, goals and understanding.* Hillsdale, N.J.: Erlbaum, 1977.

Schelling, T. C. *Micromotives and macrobehavior.* New York: W. W. Norton, 1978.

Schon, D. A. *Beyond the stable state.* New York: W. W. Norton, 1971.

Searles, H. F. Dependency processes in the psychotherapy of schizophrenia (1955). In H. F. Searles, *Collected papers on schizophrenia and related subjects.* New York: International Universities Press, 1965. (Originally in the *Journal of the American Psychoanalytic Association*, 1955, *3*, 19–66.)

Searles, H. F. Anxiety concerning change, as seen in the psychotherapy of schizophrenic patients—with particular reference to the sense of personal identity (1961). In H. F. Searles, *Collected papers on schizophrenia and related subjects.* New York: International Universities Press, 1965. (Originally in the *International Journal of Psychoanalysis*, 1961, *42*, 74–85.)

Searles, H. F. Unconscious processes in relation to the environmental crisis. (1972). In H. F. Searles, *Countertransference and related subjects: Selected papers*. New York: International Universities Press, 1979. (Originally in *Psychoanalytic Review*, 1972, *59*, 361–374.)

Seligman, M. E. P. *Helplessness: On depression, development, and death*. San Francisco: W. H. Freeman, 1975.

Selznick, P. *Leadership in administration: A sociological interpretation*. New York: Row Peterson, 1957.

Sennett, R., & Cobb, J. *The hidden injuries of class*. New York: Random House, 1973.

Simon, H. A. On how to decide what to do. *Bell Journal of Economies*, 1978, *9*(2), 494–507.

Simon, H. A. Information processing models of cognition. In M. Rosenzweig & L. Porter (Eds.), *Annual review of psychology* (Vol. 30). Palo Alto: Annual Reviews, 1979.

Sitaram, H., Weingartner, H., & Gillin, J. C. Human serial learning: Enhancement with arecholine and choline and impairment with scopolamine. *Science*, 1978, *201*, 274–276.

Smith, M. B. A map for the analysis of personality and politics. *Journal of Social Issues*, 1968, *24*, 15–28.

Snyder, B. *The hidden curriculum*. Cambridge: M.I.T. Press, 1973.

Sproull, L., Weiner, S., and Wolf, D. *Organizing an anarchy*. Chicago: University of Chicago Press, 1978.

Starbuck, W. H. Levels of aspiration. *Psychological Review*, 1963, *70*, 51–60.

Starbuck, W. H. Organizations and their environments. In M. H. Dunnette (Ed.), *Handbook of industrial and organizational psychology*. Chicago: Rand-McNally, 1976.

Stein, M. I. *Stimulating creativity* (Vols. 1 & 2). New York: Academic Press, 1974.

Steinbruner, J. *The cybernetic theory of decision*. Princeton: Princeton University Press, 1974.

Stone, W. F. *The psychology of politics*. New York: Free Press, 1974.

Stotland, E., Matthews, K. E. Jr., Sherman, S. E., Hansson, R. O., & Richardson, B. Z. *Fantasy, empathy, and helping*. Sage Library of Social Research. Beverly Hills: Sage, 1978.

Sundquist, J. L. *A comparison of policy-making capacity in the United States and five European countries: The case of population distribution* (Brookings General Series Reprint No. 345). Washington, D.C.: Brookings Institution, 1978. (a)

Sundquist, J. L. Research brokerage: The weak link. In L. E. Lynn (Ed.), *Knowledge and policy: The uncertain connection* (Study project on social research and development, Vol. 5). Washington, D.C.: National Academy of Sciences, 1978. (b)

Szolovits, P., & Pauker, S. Categorical and probabilistic reasoning in medical diagnosis. *Artificial Intelligence*, 1978, *11*, 115–144.

Technology Review. Innovaha!tion. Cambridge: M.I.T. Press, 1979.

Thibaut, J., & Walker, L. *Procedural justice: A psychological analysis*. Hillsdale, N. J.: Erlbaum, 1975.

Thibaut, J., & Walker, L. A theory of procedure. *California Law Review*, 1978, *66*(3), 541–566.

Thomas, L. F., & Harri-Augstein, E. S. Learning to learn: The personal construction and exchange of meaning. In M. J. A. Howe (Ed.), *Adult learning: Psychological research and applications*. New York: Wiley, 1977.

Trist, E. *A concept of organizational ecology*. Invited Address, Melbourne, 1976. Unpublished.

Tushman, M. L. Managing communication networks in R & D laboratories. *Sloan Management Review*, 1979 (Winter), *20*(2), 37–49.

Vaillant, G. E. *Adaptation to life: How the best and the brightest came of age*. Boston: Little, Brown, 1977.

Van Maanen, J. (Ed.). *Organizational careers: Some new perspectives*. New York: Wiley, 1977.

Van Maanen, J., & Schein, E. H. Toward a theory of organizational socialization. In B. M. Staw (Ed.), *Research in organizational behavior* (Vol. 1). Greenwich, Conn.: JAI Press, 1979.

Vonnegut, K. Address to graduating class at Bennington College, 1970. In K. Vonnegut, *Wampeters, foma, and granfalloons (opinions)*. New York: Dell, 1976.

Warr, P. B. (Ed.). *Thought and personality*. Baltimore: Penguin Books, 1970.

Warwick, D. P. *A theory of public bureaucracy*. Cambridge: Harvard University Press, 1975.

Watzlawick, P. *The language of change: Elements of therapeutic communication*. New York: Basic Books, 1978.

Weick, K. E. Cognitive processes in organizations. In B. M. Staw (Ed.), *Research in organizational behavior: An annual series of analytic essays and critical reviews* (Vol. 1). Greenwich, Conn.: JAI Press, 1979.

Weimer, W. B. Overview of a cognitive conspiracy: Reflections on the volume. In W. B. Weimer & D. S. Palermo (Eds.), *Cognition and the symbolic processes*. Hillsdale, N. J.: Erlbaum, 1974.

Werner. H. *Comparative psychology of mental development*. New York: International Universities Press, 1948.

Werner, H. The concept of development from a comparative and organismic point of view. In D. B. Harris (Ed.), *The concept of development*. Minneapolis: University of Minnesota Press, 1957.

Werner, H., & Kaplan, B. *Symbol formation*. New York: Wiley, 1963.

Westcott, M. R. *Toward a contemporary psychology of intuition*. New York: Holt, Rinehart, and Winston, 1968.

Westin, A. F. (Ed.). *Information technology in a democracy*. Cambridge: Harvard University Press, 1971.

Wildavsky, A. *The politics of the budgetary process*. Boston: Little, Brown, 1964.

Wildavsky, A. The past and future presidency. *The Public Interest*, 1975, *41*, 56–76.

Wildavsky, A. The self-evaluating organization. In J. M. Shafritz & A. C. Hyde (Eds.), *Classics of public administration*. Oak Park, Ill.: Moore Publishing, 1978.

Wilensky, H. *Organizational intelligence: Knowledge and policy in government and industry*. New York: Basic Books, 1967.

Wilson, E. *To the Finland station*. New York: Farrar, Straus, & Giroux, 1972.

Wilson, E. O. *Sociobiology: The new synthesis*. Cambridge: Harvard University Press, 1975.

Wilson, J. Q. Innovation in organization: Notes toward a theory. In J. D. Thompson (Ed.), *Approaches to organizational design*. Pittsburgh: University of Pittsburgh Press, 1966.

Wilson, J. Q. The rise of the bureaucratic state. *The Public Interest*, 1975, *41*, 77–103.

Winters, D. *Review of political motivation*. Unpublished manuscript, 1981.

Wispé, L. (Ed.). *Altruism, sympathy, and helping: Psychological and sociological principles*. New York: Academic Press, 1978.

Witkin, H. A., Moore, O. A., Goodenough, D. R., & Cox, P. W. Field-dependent and field-independent cognitive styles and their educational implications. *Review of Educational Research*, 1977, *47*(1), 1–64.

Wohlstetter, R. *Pearl Harbor: Warning and decision*. Stanford: Stanford University Press, 1962.

Wolfsfeld, G. F. *Learning about foreign countries: A cross-cultural study of international socialization*. Unpublished doctoral dissertation, Massachusetts Institute of Technology, 1979.

Wrightsman, L. S. *Social psychology* (2nd ed.). Monterey, Calif.: Brooks/Cole, 1977.

Wyden, P. H. *Bay of Pigs: The untold story*. New York: Simon & Schuster, 1979.

Yin, R. K. Decentralization of government agencies. *American Behavioral Scientist*, 1979, *22*, 525–536.

Zacharia, F. C. Standing of public-interest litigating groups to sue on behalf of their members. *University of Pittsburgh Law Review*, 1978, *39*(3), 453–493.

Zajonc, R. B. Social facilitation. *Science*, 1965, *149*(3681), 269–275.

Zaleznick, A., & Kets De Vries, M. *Power and the corporate mind.* Boston: Houghton Mifflin, 1975.

Zaltman, G., Duncan, R., & Holbek, J. *Innovations and organizations.* New York: Wiley, 1973.

3

POLITICAL VIOLENCE
A Critical Evaluation

SHELDON G. LEVY

Introduction

The goal of this chapter is to critically evaluate research on political violence with an emphasis on data-oriented studies rather than purely theoretical presentations. In addition, an attempt will be made to present sufficient information about the research to allow the reader to independently evaluate the material. This goal, coupled with space limitations, allowed examination of only a few areas of political conflict. Further, only selected studies could be presented. In some cases, additional analyses that further examined the positions of the original author were possible based on information reported in the article. It was felt that this orientation would provide a more valuable contribution than a series of short summaries of previous investigations. Such brief summaries generally rely on the investigator's conclusions and it will become evident in many cases that questions can be raised about their validity.

If one is interested in conflict, a reasonable procedure might be first to enumerate the events of interest, then to evaluate the types or categories into which the events fall, and finally to seek variables that covary with the events. The emphasis here will be on these aspects of the field as represented primarily in quantitative macrostudies of political violence.

The striking impression of these studies in the approximately 40 years since serious quantification began is the wealth of precise data that has

SHELDON G. LEVY • Department of Psychology, Wayne State University, Detroit, Michigan 48202.

been detailed on the frequency and intensity of war. In addition, particularly for the post-World War II years, a comparable accumulation of data on societal indicators has also been achieved.

Along with this accumulation of information has been an extensive set of quantitative analyses. However, it is in this area that a number of questions arise about the methods that have been utilized. It is hoped that this chapter will provide a basis for evaluating what has been learned and for improving the validity and generalizability of the results.

The value of detailed analyses of results is demonstrated in a recent exchange between Rummel (1978) and Haas (1978). Rummel correctly indicates some obvious errors in the use of factor analysis in Haas's work. While both Rummel and Haas agree that other portions of the Haas work are valuable, the interchange also reinforces the fact that careful analysis is required if analytic errors are not to be perpetrated as empirical fact.

In addition, Gochman (1979) has examined critically five books in the field and Snyder (1978) reviewed in detail many studies relevant to this discussion. The latter article primarily focused on the logic of the analyses, including the common problem of collecting data at one level and applying it to another.

Further support for the importance of critical evaluation is provided in a recent report that three astronomers claim to have discovered a mistake in Hubble's constant. Their correction would mean that the age of the universe is 9 billion rather than 15 to 18 billion years. In addition, if their correction stands, a great deal of adjustment in astronomical theories will be required (*Ann Arbor News*, November 14, 1979, p. A-12).

In a similar vein, but closer to the area covered in this chapter, is Abelson's comments on economists: "their fallibility has expanded to include not only the inability to tell you where the economy is going but also where it is" (*Barron's*, December 10, 1979, p. 1). The problem here is not a question of methodological error but rather of the complexity of social science.

It is clear that students of political conflict, with measuring instruments far inferior to those of astronomers and no better than those of economists, are obligated to repeatedly evaluate the basis of their conclusions as well as the conclusions themselves.

Frequency of Conflict

Overview

The examination of the frequency of political conflict will be divided into three major sections. The first will deal with enumeration of large-scale events across nations. The second part will examine data on assassinations, including studies that have focused exclusively on the United States. Finally, the last section will deal with examination of political violence in the United States.

Large-Scale Conflict

It is apparent that most investigators not only collect incidents but also relate them to other variables. A number of these studies will be examined in this section.

The Sorokin (1937) and Richardson (1960b) studies represent extensive compilations of internal and external war. Sorokin's quantitative analyses dealt substantially with the frequency and the intensity of wars and with questions about the periodicity of conflict.

Richardson's analyses also examined variables that have often been presumed to lead to conflict, for example, the number of boundaries of a nation, differences in language or religion, and economic considerations.

Kende's (1971, 1978) efforts extended the enumeration of wars to the post-World War II era and also examined periodicity in regions of the world and within a typology of war.

The work of Singer and Small (1966) is also included in this section. This research examined the relationship between international alliances and war; the alliance data have been collected systematically and this structural aspect of the international system provides a complement to the war data.

Similarly, the Levine (1972) study examined the relationship between mediation efforts and war. The collection of mediations is published in Levine's article.

Modelski's work singles out global wars for analysis (1972).

Finally, Azar's research (1972, 1974) provides extensions of war occurrence data in several directions. His research examined interactions between nations. Further, the events are at many levels of both hostility and friendship. Thus, it becomes possible to examine preconflict through postconflict periods and to develop hypotheses about the nature of the conflict process itself.

Sorokin. Sorokin's (1937) monumental study represents the first modern attempt to collect data on the frequency of group conflict including revolution. His results include the study of the following countries for the indicated years: Greece (600 B.C.E. to 146 B.C.E.); Rome (509 B.C.E. to 476 C.E.); Byzantium (532-1390); France (531-1933); Germany and Austria (709-1933); England (605-1933); Italy (526-1933); Spain (407-1933); the Netherlands (678-1933); Russia (946-1933); and Poland and Lithuania (1031-1794). Altogether, 11,978 country-years were studied and 1,629 events were examined. Of these, 967 were classified as important wars.

Sorokin was well aware of the difficulty of obtaining historically accurate quantitative data, particularly for events before the seventeenth century. Nevertheless, his estimates are based on evidence from multiple sources and represent a legitimate statement on the intensity and frequency of war. The appendices list all of the events by country and by year and provide the sources from which the data were obtained. Each event is classified in terms of the major objective of the disturbance based on the following categories: (a) political; (b) socioeconomic; (c) nationalist and separatist; (d) religious; and (e) mixed, with specific objectives such as resistance to a specific law or tax.

In addition to the above classification, measures of intensity are provided for each disturbance, including the social area (local disturbance or entire country), duration, size of the masses involved, and relative amount of casualties.

Sorokin's conclusions include:

1. Casualties as a percent of the army's strength have steadily decreased.
2. For recent centuries, the order of decreasing intensity is the twentieth, then the seventeenth, the eighteenth and the nineteenth.
3. The percentage of years with war varied from 28% for Germany to 67% for Spain.
4. No systematic periodicity for war could be determined. Countries varied from less violent to more violent but the pattern was not consistent or predictable. This led Sorokin to infer that some basic processes were at work throughout history. "Disturbances have occurred not only in the periods of the decay and decline of society, but in its periods of blossoming and healthy growth" (1937, p. 495).
5. The ratio for each country of years without disturbance to years with disturbance is fairly similar, ranging from a low of 2.4 for Spain to a high of 4.7 for France, except for Byzantium which had a ratio of 8.6. This latter result was attributed to the inadequacy of historical records for this period of time.

Further, examination of the fluctuation of the magnitude of disturbances by century and by quarter century led Sorokin to conclude that the swings were

> not exceedingly wild. They indicate some permanently working forces, inherently connected with the essence of the social life itself, which do not permit either a complete elimination or the unlimited growth of disturbances. As soon as the curve of disturbances approaches either the minimum or the maximum level, a reaction sets in and sets its course in the opposite direction. (Sorokin, 1937, p. 481)

Richardson.   Richardson's (1960b) enumeration of deadly quarrels remains the most complete and objective examination of political violence available. His collection covers the years 1820 to 1949 and improves on the collections of both Sorokin and Wright (1942), although both of these collections represent a longer historical period. (Wright's list is for the years 1482 to 1939.)

Richardson argued that an objective classification of political violence could only be made if

1. Wounded were not included. Because wounds could vary from slight to severe and data were not as accurate as for deaths, only deaths should be used.
2. Data were for the whole world, not just for European nations.
3. All deaths from the hostilities were included. This would include all direct military personnel as well as relevant civilian deaths.
4. Classification was by size. In order to reduce error from historical records, the size of a deadly quarrel should be the log to the base 10 of the number that were killed so that, for example, any number of deaths between 3,162,277 and 316,228 would be classified in category $6 \pm \frac{1}{2}$.

In addition to deaths, Richardson's classification also involved the date on which hostilities ended, although there are a number of occasions for which that information is not precise. (Richardson argued against classification by who started the hostilities because of the frequent difficulty of making this determination.)

Richardson's analysis of each quarrel included attributes associated with the parties. These attributes were divided into situations (a) usually expected to make for amity; (b) expected to be ambivalent; and (c) expected to be annoyers.

It is fair to say that, in spite of a number of detailed analyses by Richardson, the wealth of information he collected remains to be exhausted.

The editors of the Richardson volume (Wright & Lienau) summarized some of the major findings in their introduction:

1. Chance accounts for the distribution of wars through time.
2. Fatal quarrels accounted for about 1.6% of the total number of deaths in the period.
3. Although population increased during the period, there was not a corresponding increase in deaths from fatal quarrels.
4. The greater the number of common frontiers, the greater the number of wars for the nation.
5. Although common citizenship does not insure peace, common

government, intermarriage, common fears, and common culture tend to be associated with fewer civil and local wars.

6. Economic factors appear to be direct causes in fewer than 29% of the wars. Further, the class conflict theory of wars was not supported.
7. Alliances are associated with fewer wars among cosigners, but the effect lessens with the passage of time.
8. Revenge is an important factor, but it too declines with time.
9. Similarity or difference in language does not appear to be an important factor. Religion is not associated with peace.
10. Most wars have been localized.

It is unfortunate that this work has not been fully extended in spite of a great deal of excellent quantitative research in the area.

International War since World War II.   Richardson's collection of wars is for the period 1820–1949 (he died in 1953). Kende's (1971, 1978) research is an attempt to extend the data to 120 wars identified during the years 1947–1976. These were waged in the territories of 71 countries and involved participants from 84 countries. The results indicated that on a typical day during those 32 years, 11.5 wars were fought, and that number increased to 15.3 during the latest 10 years. Europe has been relatively free of military involvement, and among the developed countries, capitalist countries were more frequently involved than socialist countries. Kende concluded that third world countries were the primary location for wars in the past ten years. Most of these involved internal struggles, although participants from distant countries were frequently present. He also found that the weaker parties have sometimes won the wars in their countries.

The data include some intensity factors, but the conclusions are not affected by examination of the intensity measures compared to the results based just on the number of events.

The earlier article (Kende, 1971) developed a useful classification of wars. The major distinction was based on whether there was (1) or was not (2) foreign participation. Within each of these major classifications, wars are divided into internal antiregime wars (A), internal tribal wars (B), and frontier wars (C). The classification indicates $52/97 = 54\%$ classified as A/1 (internal antiregime wars with foreign participation) and $15/97 = 15\%$ classified as A/2 (internal antiregime wars without foreign participation).

The major conclusions were: "Europe has remained outside the continents experiencing war" (1971, p. 7); Asia, Africa, and Latin America are increasingly becoming the scenes of local war; further, "since 1963, there has not been a single internal political war, type A, on earth without foreign participation" (1971, p. 16).

When individual countries were examined to determine the frequency of their intervention, the results were the United States (26), Great Britain (19), France (12), and Portugal (13) (for the four most active interventionist countries).

The widespread nature of the activity since the Second World War is indicated through the finding that 61% of the world and 75% of its inhabitants were direct participants. This compares with the 80% of the world population that participated in the Second World War.

Kende's (1971) appendix includes a complete list of wars and their classification, but it does not include intensity measures.

The data and analyses do have a number of deficiencies which should be noted. For example, the earlier article did not include intensity measures. Thus, conflicts in which only a few were killed over a few days were classified together with more severe events. Further, a large number of conflicts were omitted, and this omission is in some cases striking. These were:

1. Spontaneous uprisings and riots, even if military force was used to quell them
2. Local armed conflicts that did not extend beyond a city or a few villages
3. Massacres in which there was no organized defense
4. Conflicts in which only one of the parties used weapons
5. Border incidents (e.g., between Israel and Arab countries and between the USSR and China)
6. Crises that did not lead to armed conflict (e.g., the Cuban Missile Crisis of October–November, 1962)

In addition, his examination of the contribution of major powers to conflicts excluded involvement in terms of military aid and/or the training of military personnel from another country. Although the criteria are objective, the interpretation is affected by the particular conflicts that were chosen.

The second article (Kende, 1978) indicated some additional possible difficulties. For example, government repression was apparently not a part of the definition of a violent event. Also, events were sometimes coded into more than one category; this lack of mutually exclusive categories creates potential problems for some statistical analyses.

Finally, the changes in types of wars over time would be aided by baseline data. Thus, Kende finds decreases in the number of colonial wars in recent years. However, this could result from a change in the number of colonial countries that exist and/or actual changes in the nature of the provocations which cannot be accounted for merely by changes in the number of opportunities (e.g., the number of citizens who are dominated by a foreign power).

Two studies have identified an attribute of the international system (alliances and mediations) and related them to the likelihood of international war. Because the frequencies of these events (the alliances and mediations) have been determined, the research is included here rather than in the later section on the determinants of war.

J. David Singer has supervised a project on the correlates of war for the past 20 years. A major component of this work involves examination of the relationship between alliance formation and war (Singer & Small, 1966).

Data were collected from 1815 (the Congress of Vienna) until the end of World War II. Only political entities with a population of at least one-half million and with de jure recognition from England and France were included. The total system was divided into two parts but only for the period 1815–1920. One part consisted of peripheral nations and the second consisted of the central powers, that is, those European nations that are considered to have dominated international relations. After 1920, this distinction was no longer maintained.

Only international wars were included in the dependent measure. To qualify, at least one participant on each side had to be a member of the international system. The complete set of 41 wars is listed in Singer and Small (1966), including dates of the conflict and a number of intensity measures.

The independent variable in these analyses was alliance commitment. The 112 alliances are classified by type (defense, neutrality, and entente, i.e., an agreement for future cooperation in times of crisis), and the complete list is published in the article. Only written agreements were included. General internation agreements (e.g., the charter of the League of Nations or the constitution of the International Postal Union) were excluded. Alliances were also excluded if they "were consummated during, or less than three months before, a war in which any of the signatories participated" (1966, p. 123).

The raw data for each country on each of the twelve alliance variables and five war variables are provided.

Each of the seven alliance measures was correlated with each of five war measures across both the total number of countries (83) and the 68 members of the central system. The correlations were substantially above the statistically significant boundary (although they accounted for less than 10% of the variance).

However, there are a number of problems that occur in the analysis of this type of data. The first is that alliances may not be independent of each other. This would make it difficult to assess a correlation coefficient. The second problem is that nations entered the system at various times during the period. The data indicated that the activity of a country (i.e., length of time in the system as one measure) correlated about as highly with the number of wars as did the number of alliances. These results, therefore, strongly support the possibility that alliances are an indication of other underlying factors, that they may not be a causative factor in war.

However, the effect of activity is not totally clear. For example, Singer and Small argue that if central members alone are examined, controlling on general activity level does not appreciably reduce the correlations.

The data also suggest that the relationship between alliance commitment and war is stronger in the twentieth century than in the nineteenth. However, if those factors that lead a country to war are present, and if alliances and wars are determined by the same factors, the rate of alliance commitment and frequency of war should, of necessity, be highly correlated.

Additional research from this project will be examined later.

Levine's (1972) analysis is of mediations rather than alliances. He presents a complete list for the years 1816–1960. Altogether, he listed 322 cases involving 388 mediation efforts ("non-routine and noncooperative mediations," p. 31). Using Levine's list, it is possible to divide the time period into 13 periods of approximately 11 years each. The Spearman rank order correlation (r_s) between the time period and the number of mediations is 0.87. The striking change occurred around 1915 with r_s for the first 9 periods being 0.62.

Although Levine attempted to investigate the universe of instances, it is apparent that the list is essentially from Europe and the Americas. As is true of much data, information is more readily available for these continents. From a methodological point of view, therefore, it might be better to restrict attention to these geographical areas since the data for wars may be more readily available worldwide compared to the data for mediations. Thus, the two variables could not easily be related to each other since they would be from two different populations.

Levine did compare number of mediations to number of wars. He used the Singer and Small (1966) data for large-scale international wars and divided the data into 29 five-year periods. For the full time span, the overall correlation is close to zero. When the time span was divided into three periods (1816–1890, 1890–1920, 1921–1960) r was .40, .10, and .48, respectively. It should be noted, however, that none of these r's is statistically significant since the number of time periods is small within each of the specific divisions.

The attempt to provide data on a concept as difficult as that of mediation is extremely worthwhile. Levine provides an elaborate analysis of the concept as distinct from arbitration, judicial settlement, or authoritative action by an international organization. However, the difficulty of the definition does require some evidence of interjudge reliability of the events classified as mediation.

Finally, there is a need for baseline or control data. For example, if mediations change in frequency over time, there may be some simple explanation. Perhaps the number of nations or the number of borders is also changing. Additional information about the relative rate of conciliation or mediation is required in addition to the absolute rate. Another control deals with other processes that are similar. Levine legitimately distinguishes between mediation and arbitration or other interactions. However, the detail needed for the distinctions in itself is an argument that the processes (e.g., arbitration, mediation, judicial settlement, etc.) may have similar effects. Thus, as the frequency of mediation increases, arbitration may decrease, resulting in no net impact of mediation changes on the system. These comments are not a criticism of Levine's work, since the listing of mediations is an important contribution by itself.

Modelski's (1972) study was concerned with global wars; he identifies eight global wars since the sixteenth century. Although this is too small a number to allow statistically significant conclusions, the analyses clearly indicate the importance of great powers in war. Modelski cites the Wright (1942) and the Singer and Small (1966) data to indicate that "great power participation in wars may approach 80 per cent" (Modelski, 1972, p. 47). In addition, he extends Richardson's (1960b) material by providing a listing of all of the wars of magnitude 5 or greater that began between January 1, 1945 and December 13, 1970.

Another approach is represented in the work of Azar (1972, 1974). The basic idea is that international events involve both an acting nation and a target nation, that is, an interaction. These can occur at many levels of hostility or friendship. Azar has collected literally hundreds of thousands of events in developing the research program.

In addition to reports of actual physical events, the data also include statements made by representatives of one nation toward another. In the 1972 article, 835 interactions were selected from a data bank of 100,000 events. These represented interactions between pairs of nations among Egypt, France, and Israel between July 26, 1956 and January 11, 1957. Each citation in the data bank is coded on a 13-point hostility–friendliness scale. Thus, the most hostile code represents all-out war between nations A and B and the most friendly code is the merging of two nations into a single nation.

Signals are verbal and/or physical and include a date, an actor, a target, and an issue of international concern. A central part of the analysis is the notion that nations have a normal relations range (NRR). Azar argues that nations essentially have adapted to their NRR. It is only when they move out of this range that a new set of relationships emerge. If they move above this range, it indicates a crisis situation. If they move below the NRR, it indicates an integrative shift.

The hypotheses tested were that

1. "nations will exhibit a symmetrical signalling pattern during the escalatory phase of the conflict and a slightly asymmetrical pattern during the de-escalatory phase" (Azar, 1972, p. 187)
2. during escalation, the temporal distance between hostile signals decreases and during deescalation it increases.

Both of these hypotheses were derived from the theory and research that preceded the present investigation.

In order to establish the normal range for the nations, 320 events between May 1956 and September 1956 were used. First, an arbitrary 85% middle range, ± 1 scale point on either side of the range, was defined as the NRR. Secondly, hostile events (those classified with scores of 7–13) were simply called hostile. (It might have been better to maintain intensity differences, since there is a difference between all-out war between two nations, scale point 13, and nation A making a protest directed against nation B, scale point 8. This would have allowed the NRR to be defined as a given number of standard deviations on either side of the mean.)

To test the first hypothesis, which was concerned with symmetry, hostile signals were coded into 10-day intervals. Azar utilized the appropriate control of percent of hostile signals in a 10-day period relative to the total number of signals throughout the period. This avoids the problem of spurious correlation due only to activity level. However, the symmetry hypothesis was tested by including the period of time that was used to standardize the data. It would have been better to use nonoverlapping sets of data. Since Azar presents the data for all of the 10-day periods, it is possible to examine only the periods that occur after those used to establish the NRR. The following analyses are based on information provided in the 1972 article.

The symmetry hypothesis is strongly supported. For example, the Spearman rank order correlation between Britain and Egypt is .94. That is, if each 10-day period is given a percent score of hostile acts out of total number of acts and each nation is scored this way, it is possible to determine if two nations covaried in their percentage of hostile acts throughout the period.

The Egypt–France r_s is .97, and for Egypt and Israel it is .64. (This last relationship indicates weak symmetry between the two major protagonists.)

However, the symmetry hypothesis requires much more restrictive testing than the above. This is because there is supposed to be something special about the escalation period. If the symmetry were the same during the preescalation period, it would indicate no special support for symmetry during crisis. Azar provides seven periods during which symmetry can be examined before the crisis. Although this is a small N, it still is worthwhile to examine the correlations between the pairs of countries. The results for the precrisis period are: Britain–Egypt, $r_s = .85$; France–Egypt, $r_s = .34$; and Israel–Egypt, $r_s = .79$. There is, therefore, some weak evidence that the precrisis period was not as symmetric as the crisis plus deescalation phase.

Finally, the original hypothesis indicates that there should be greater symmetry during escalation compared to deescalation. Unfortunately, there are only six deescalation periods. Again using Azar's data, the results are: Egypt–Britain, $r_s = .77$; Egypt–France, $r_s = .99$; and Egypt–Israel, $r_s = .89$. Therefore, the evidence does not support decreased symmetry in the deescalation stages. Obviously, these results are hardly even suggestive because there are so few time periods. The basic point of this exercise, however, is to point out that to correctly test the symmetry hypotheses, data must be compared among the precrisis, escalation, and deescalation phases. (Since there are only four escalation time periods, it is very difficult to perform separate analyses, although this is critical in the above comparisons.)

Data relevant to the second hypothesis indicate that during the conflict period the hostile signals are more frequent per unit of time than during any other period. It is important not to overinterpret this particular finding since the definition of conflict is a high intensity of conflict signals.

The logic of Azar's (1974) study was to develop an early warning model. One nation's act was hypothesized to be partly determined by the action of the other party. He examined 48 Egypt to Israel and 48 Israel to Egypt events for the years 1956, 1957, 1968, and 1969. (These were selected from a data bank that included over 300,000 events. Since multiple sources were used to obtain events, duplicate citations of the same event were eliminated.)

The model accurately predicted 92.7% of the interactions (89/96). However, 90 of the 96 interactions were negative. Thus, if one had predicted negative all of the time, the accuracy rate would have been 93.75%. The handful of positive interactions do indicate that predictions are not due to chance, but the analysis of additional events is required. There is also a need for precise definition of the boundaries of an event (its beginning and end). This is necessary to avoid dividing an event into both an event and a response which would automatically lead to a relationship.

In spite of the above reservations, Azar's work must be considered an extremely valuable collection of materials, one which provides the possibility of developing empirical relationships between one nation's actions and another nation's responses and of providing a direction for testing the hypotheses.

Assassination

This section includes two systematic collections across nations of assassination attempts: those of Leiden (1970) and Feierabend (1790). Levy's

(1970b) analysis of the Leiden data is also included. These analyses dealt with frequencies of assassination attempts over time in various regions of the world. The Feierabend report also provides an introduction to the next section, since a scaling of political violence events is included. The section concludes with two collections of data within the United States, those of Simon (1970) and of Levy (1970b). Two questions examined in these articles were the motives for the attacks and the relationship between the level of the office and the likelihood of attack.

The study of assassination as a specific type of political violence can be justified on a number of grounds. First, the importance of the event is greater than many other acts because the status of the individual is often high. Secondly, even when assassination is committed by an individual for nonpolitical reasons, the political impact of the event can be quite large. Thus, assassination can both reflect underlying political tensions and may create political consequences.

Leiden's (1970) list includes assassinations worldwide for the period 1918–1968 and includes the name of the target, country, date, rank of the target, and whether or not the target was killed. Levy (1970b) analyzed the Leiden data for the higher ranks 1, 2, and 3 (heads of state, cabinet level officials, and high-ranking military officers, respectively) by region of the world for five-year periods. The data indicated a very low rate of assassination in Eastern Europe since the end of World War II and a steady increase in frequency during that period in Africa and the Middle East. Further indication of the extent to which assassination reflects general underlying political instability is the fact that Latin America shows a high frequency in the 1923–1927 period while Western Europe shows a high frequency in the 1943–1947 period.

Feierabend's (1970) list of assassinations worldwide for 1948–1967 has also been published. His coding includes the reason for the attack. Feierabend, Feierabend, Nesvold, and Jagger (1970) have analyzed the assassination data for their complete collection of 8,000 events across 84 countries.

Although the Feierabend work will be analyzed more completely in the next section, one finding in particular reinforces the study of assassination as one reasonable component of the general study of political violence. Factor analyses were performed to examine the types of polical violence that clustered together. Assassinations were correlated with guerrilla warfare and to a lesser extent with revolution. But they did not correlate with less intense forms of political violence. Then a Guttman scalogram analysis was performed which indicated four groupings (see Table 1). If a violent event in a higher group occurs in a society, events in lower numbered groups are also likely to be present. However, the reverse is not true. This analysis indicates that Richardson's approach to classification by number killed needs modification.

Table 1. Guttman Scaling of Domestic Violence

Group I	Riots, demonstrations, and boycotts
	Arrests
	Government acting against specific groups
	Sabotage
Group II	Martial law
	Coup d'etat
	Revolt
Group III	Guerrilla warfare
	Assassinations
Group IV	Executions
	Civil war

Simon (1970) has examined all attacks on officeholders in the United States. She included 81 events and came to the conclusion that the higher the office (among president, governor, senator, and representative), the greater the likelihood of attack. This conclusion is based on the number of attacks compared to the number of officeholders at each level. The finding, however, does not allow one to conclude that there is an attractive force for the higher office that leads to the attack since the constituency of the various officeholders differs greatly. The president's constituency is 435 times the constituency of a congressman and about 50 times that of a governor. If the probability that a constituent will attack an officeholder is constant, the total number of attacks at different levels should be about the same. Of course, since there are more representatives than presidents, the probability of a specific representative being attacked is far smaller than that of the president. Simon's data support this interpretation. She lists eight attacks on presidents, eight on governors, eight on senators, and nine on members of the house of representatives. It cannot, therefore, be concluded, that there is a relationship between the power of the office and the likelihood of attack.

Simon also examined the reason for the attacks. About two-thirds had specifically political motives. Of the 81 events, 29 (36%) occurred in the decade 1865–1874. These data, therefore, are consistent with the results of Levy's (1969) newspaper study of political violence throughout American history, which is discussed in the next section.

The study of assassination illustrates the difficulty in relying on a single data collection. Both definitions and sources frequently differ. Thus, Leiden's (1970) list indicates 84 incidents for the United States for 1918–1967, while Simon's (1970) indicated 24. Almost all of this discrepancy is accounted for by the inclusion of lower levels of office in the Leiden data. Similarly, an examination of the Leiden (1970) and Feierabend (1970) lists for countries that were studied by both indicates a Spearman rank order correlation of $r_s = +.80$. The ranks were assigned in terms of the number of events the investigator reported for each of the countries.

Feierabend *et al.* (1970) indicated a positive relationship between assassination and homicide on a worldwide basis. Levy (1970b) examined the relationship between homicide rates and political-assault rates in the United States for 1936–1967. The Spearman rank order correlation for the 32 years was $r_s = +0.32$ ($p < .05$). The implication is that there might be some relationship between the levels of general violence and political violence.

Levy (1970b) selected attacks on individuals from the complete set of political-violence events obtained in the newspaper study. Almost precisely the same fraction of events (2/3) were classified as politically motivated as were in the Simon data, although Levy's data included 483 events. Additional analyses indicated that 65% of the attacks resulted in no physical injury to the target.

If the marginals for degree of injury and for type of target are used to compute expected results, current officeholders (federal, state, or local) were less likely than expected to suffer physical injury as a result of an attack, while other leaders (e.g., racial, religious, business) were more likely than expected to suffer injury.

Finally, these data do indicate some relationship between the nature of the office and the likelihood of attack since federal judges, including Supreme Court justices, only provided one instance of attack while no attacks on vice-presidents were obtained in the newspaper sample.

Psychological reactions to assassination have also been examined by Levy (1970a,b, 1971a).

Conflict in the United States

This final section on frequency of conflict will examine data collections concerning the United States. R. M. Brown (1969) has enumerated vigilante movements, while Schellenberg (1970) has detailed county seat wars. These studies have particular value because they represent types of conflict whose original form has disappeared. They therefore encourage analysis of both the reasons for their emergence and the reasons for their demise (as pointed out by Schellenberg).

Brown's (1969) article provides a complete list of 326 movements on which he obtained data, including location and date of the movement, number of members, and number of people killed. He estimates that there may have been as many as 500 vigilante movements in the United States, but historical records on a number of them are lost. His list is a comprehensive one which should be of value in future investigations. His own careful historical analysis provides some insight into the reasons for the development of the movements.

Vigilantism is indigenous to the United States. Movements began in 1767 and ended about 1900 (although Brown does identify a number of activities in the 1960s that he believes are comparable to vigilante movements in some respects). The size of the movements varied from a few members to several thousand. They were prevalent in the East as well as the West and developed primarily in frontier communities where traditional law enforcement structures were unavailable. Vigilante movements usually arose in areas of the country where outlaws had taken control of a particular area and were frequently supported by the elite in the community. The great bulk (over 70%) of the movements occurred in the period 1850–1890. Altogether, Brown lists 729 deaths due to vigilante movements. Of these, 527 occurred in the western states, with the greatest number of deaths reported in Texas (140), Montana (101), and California (101).

Even where a judicial system existed, there were a number of factors that could lead to the formation of a vigilante group. These included infrequent law enforcement, corrupt juries and judges who could be bought off by criminals, inadequate jails, and ease with which criminals could use legal loopholes to escape punishment, and the expense of providing adequate formal mechanisms of law enforcement.

Vigilante movements were generally one of two kinds. In one case there was community consensus, and the group dealt frequently with a specific condition of disorder and disbanded after a short period of time. However, other vigilante movements arose without consensus and existed as separate law enforcement communities which frequently were socially destructive. Thus, even in circumstances where the legal apparatus was functioning adequately, a vigilante movement might arise.

Schellenberg (1970) studied county seat wars in the United States. His analysis involves 1,051 counties in 12 midwestern states. Altogether, 50 conflicts were identified. The majority of these occurred in the 1880s, which accords well with other indications that it was a period of high political conflict in the United States. (Actually, 40 of the 50 incidents occurred during the period 1875–1890.) Historical analysis by Schellenberg indicated that speculation over land values was a primary determinant of the wars over location of a county seat. Other historical factors cited include the general violence of the post-Civil War period and the "... weakness of conventional legal forms near the frontier" (Schellenberg, 1970, p. 351).

Schellenberg's data extend themselves to a possible examination of a contagion hypothesis, but his test does not seem as direct as it might be. The hypothesis that there might be a contagion factor is reasonable. If that were the case, adjacent counties would be more likely to have conflict than would be expected by chance. A direct test might involve the following.

Calculate the total number of pairs of counties, that is, $\binom{1051}{2}$. Next, use maps to calculate the number of pairs of adjacent counties. This number divided by $\binom{1051}{2}$ is the probability that just by chance an adjacent pair would have a county war. This number multiplied by 50 (the number of wars reported) provides the expected frequency. It can be shown that the probability that each of an adjacent pair had a county war is far greater than chance, although Schellenberg argued from his calculations that it was comparable to chance.

Suppose that each county has, on the average, seven neighbors (the actual number is probably smaller since counties on the edge might have only two or three neighbors, but any number below seven would further reduce the expected value). The number of adjacent pairs is $(1051 \times 7)/2$ (division by two is necessary to avoid counting each adjacent pair twice). The probability, therefore, that just by chance a neighbor pair would both have a county war is .006667. Since there were 50 wars reported, the expected number of wars in adjacent pairs based on chance is $50 \times .006667 = .333$. Schellenberg reported 12 such cases, far beyond chance expectation. Therefore, under the assumption that county seat wars in adjacent pairs is a result of contagion, the evidence is consistent with the contagion hypothesis.

Another attempt to examine political violence in the United States was undertaken by Levy (1969) for the period 1819–1968. Newspaper issues were sampled weekly from 1819 through 1899. For the years 1819–1850, the *Washington National Intelligencer* was the source; for the years 1851–1968, the *New York Times* was the source. From 1900–1968, only two issues were sampled each month. All sampled issues of the newspaper were read in their entirety. The full sample involved 6,000 newspaper issues and 100,000 pages.

Size of groups involved, number of injuries, number of deaths, and reasons for the violence were examined. Controls for changes in both population and newspaper size (as an index of possible increases in reporting) were used in examining both injuries and deaths.

Although the sampling procedure imposed limitations on the completeness of the data, the results do demonstrate changing patterns of violence over time. The post-Reconstruction and the most recent period had large amounts of racial violence (the battles of the Civil War were excluded) and the period from about 1873 to 1938 was high in labor violence.

Although it is always possible to examine a curve and perceive periodicity after the fact, it is probably most reasonable to conclude, as did Sorokin (1937) and Richardson (1960b), that cyclicality, if it exists, remains to be specified. The data do indicate clearly that deaths due to domestic political violence have decreased, particularly when population adjustments are made. Although the trend for injuries does not show a comparable decrease, it is unlikely that the decrease in deaths is a result of improved medical attention since, during this same period, weaponry increased in its ability to take life. The result contrasts with Sorokin's (1973); he concluded that the proportion of deaths in armies in battle was increasing over a period of several hundred years.

Finally, Lupsha and MacKinnon (1973) collected data on political violence in the United States between February 12, 1965 and September 7, 1970. Altogether, 1404 incidents were obtained from *Scanlon's Magazine* (No. 8, January 1970). A sample of the incidents was verified using the *New York Times*. The period, of course, is one in which racial violence and protests against the Vietnam War predominated.

The authors' four-stage view of political violence consists of: (1) awakening of discontent; (2) politicization of discontent; (3) mobilization of discontent; and (4) contention. They consider that their incidents cover the first two categories while others deal with the third and fourth stages. Their collection, however, does not include intensity measures or duration. In addition, they examine only attacks on government authority or symbols of such, even though a prior violent attack by the government may have been a part of the context of the event. Their report also lacks some important controls. For example, frequency of incidents in cities is not related to the population of the city.

Comment on Periodicity and Randomness

It should be noted that the major studies of worldwide conflict (i.e., Richardson, 1960b; Sorokin, 1937) do not indicate that political violence is a result of random processes. If this were true, of course, there would be little reason to engage in study except to collect instances. A seemingly random process can appear as a result of the addition of a number of nonrandom series. Thus, Richardson (1960b) found that for his collection of events, as well as Wright's (1942), the results could be accounted for by a Poisson distribution. This distribution assumes that at any small portion of time (e.g., a second, a day) there is the same small probability of an event occurring. Just by chance, some periods of time will include more of the events than others.

However, the collection is based on adding together results involving different countries and different sets of countries. Within each of these separate collections, the results might not be consistent with a random process. In fact, a number of observations indicate the nonrandom nature of human violence generally and of political violence specifically. These might include the long period of time that Sweden has been without war and the high homicide rates in the United States compared to most other industrialized countries. Similarly, the ebb and flow of a particular type of violence can be shown to be nonrandom. In addition to vigilante movements and county seat wars, lynchings of blacks in the United States might be included as examples of this.

It is evident that there are nonrandom factors that lead to these variations. One way to imagine how the addition of a set of collections, each of which is not random, can lead to an overall collection that appears to be random is to suppose that each separate collection has a pattern that is totally independent of the other patterns. The addition of the separate patterns could then result in one that contains no particular periodicity or trend.

Dimensions of Conflict

The research examined in this section represents efforts to determine the basic types of political conflict. This, of course, was the goal of the Feierabend (1970) scaling discussed earlier.

The procedure in the following studies is similar. Nations are scored for a particular time period on each of a number of conflict measures. The measures are then intercorrelated across countries and factor analyses performed to determine the clusters of conflict. Some studies score each country for more than a single time period. Each of these scores is treated as an independent value so that the number of cases in the analysis is taken as the number of countries times the number of time periods.

The Rummel (1964, 1966), Tanter (1966), and Banks (1972) articles are essentially replications of each other. Together they form a valuable basis for a typology of conflict. The first Rummel article examined both domestic and foreign conflict measures. In addition, he correlated a number of demographic variables with these. Rummel's second paper analyzed only domestic conflict. The Tanter work replicated the original Rummel research for both foreign and domestic conflict and also examined the relationship between the two. The Banks report represents a replication of the factors of domestic conflict. In addition, Banks did a factor analysis of the countries across the conflict measures to obtain types of countries. Based on this factor analysis, he related a large number of social welfare indicators to the factor loadings of the countries on the first two factors.

Finally, the Gurr and Bishop (1976) research attempted to develop a broader typology of conflict. In addition to foreign and domestic conflict, they included measures of structural violence such as coercion and discrimination.

Selected Studies

Rummel. Rummel's early study (1964) includes his own collection of data as well as data collected by Berry as reported by Rummel. The two major aspects of the research are the factor analysis of conflict measures and the relationship between indices of the society and the conflict dimensions. It will be necessary to discuss both Rummel's data and his analysis of Berry's.

Rummel collected information on nine domestic-conflict measures:

number of assassinations, number of general strikes, presence or absence of guerrilla war, number of government crises, number of purges, number of riots, number of revolutions, number of antigovernment demonstrations, and number of people killed in domestic intergroup conflict. He also collected information on 13 foreign-conflict measures: number of antiforeign demonstrations, number of negative sanctions (such as a boycott or withdrawal of aid), number of protests, number of countries with which diplomatic relations were severed, number of ambassadors expelled or recalled, number of diplomatic officials of less than ambassadorial rank expelled or recalled, number of threats, presence or absence of military action, number of wars, number of troop movements, number of mobilizations, number of accusations, and number of people killed in all forms of foreign-conflict behavior.

The data were collected for the years 1955, 1956, and 1957 from the following sources: *The New York Times Index, Keesing's Contemporary Archives, Facts on File,* and *Britannica Book of the Year.* Regression analyses were based on data from 69 countries. The possibility of systematic error was examined by measures of censorship in a country as well as a measure of world interest in the nation. In addition, Rummel used data collected by Eckstein to examine the replicability of the regressions. Eckstein's data as reported by Rummel were based only on the *New York Times Index* for the years 1946–1959. In this analysis, Rummel selected data from 66 of the 113 independent nations for which Eckstein had collected data, since Rummel's analyses indicated that colonial status for a country might be a source of systematic error.

Factor Analyses. Rummel's orthogonal rotation of the domestic-conflict measures yielded three major dimensions: *turmoil* (assassination, general strikes, major government crises, riots, and antigovernment demonstrations); *revolution* (general strikes, purges, revolutions, and domestic number killed); and *subversion* (assassinations and guerrilla warfare).

Two points should be made. First, even after rotation, two variables appear on two dimensions (assassinations and general strikes). Secondly, the clusters do not duplicate those of Feierabend (1970) reported earlier in this chapter. There are at least two reasons for this. Rummel's data are only for a three-year period. Observed clusters might change for longer periods of time. In addition, of course, the Feierabend domestic-violence variables are not the same as Rummel's.

Rummel's orthogonally rotated factor matrix of the foreign-conflict measures yielded the following clusters: *war* (protests, threats, military action, wars, mobilization, assassinations, and number killed in foreign wars) and *diplomatic* (antiforeign demonstrations, negative sanctions, severance of diplomatic reactions, and military action).

Independent Variables. Ginsburg had published data, primarily for

1955, obtained predominantly from United Nations publications such as the *Demographic Yearbook* and the *Statistical Yearbook*. Berry used these data and did a factor analysis of 43 variables for 95 countries. He found four basic patterns or clusters of variables. These were labeled technology, demography, contrast on income, and external relations and size.

Rummel used the scores for the countries on each of these clusters to predict to the violence clusters he had obtained. Technology was highly related to domestic turmoil and highly but inversely related to the foreign diplomatic cluster. The size factor was also highly related to foreign diplomatic behavior. Other than these, Rummel found no statistically significant correlations between the Berry clusters and his conflict clusters. However, as Rummel points out, "Berry's basic patterns are largely derived from economic and demographic variables and do not include political, social, and cultural characteristics" (1964, p. 100).

Further Work on Dimensions of Conflict. Rummel (1966) also examined the complete data collected by Eckstein on 113 countries for 1946–1959. Factor analysis of the variables yielded clusters that were similar to those that Rummel found in his own data, although the order of importance of the factors was different. Also, Eckstein's domestic-conflict variables were somewhat different than those of Rummel. The factors were (based on orthogonal rotation): *revolution* (including measures of mutinies, coups, plots, and administrative actions); *subversion* (warfare, extended violence, and a fairly large loading for large-scale terrorism); and *turmoil* (turmoil, riots, small-scale terrorism, and quasi-private violence).

It should be noted that the labels for the dimensions or factors in any study are subjective interpretations. Another investigator might consider the same cluster to be more adequately described by a different concept. In addition, the label itself is almost always a hypothesis about an underlying process that accounts for the cluster, and it is obviously again true that another researcher might develop a different hypothesis to explain the variables.

Tanter (1966) conducted a replication of Rummel's original (1964) study. Data were collected on 83 countries for 1958, 1959, and 1960 on the same 22 conflict variables used by Rummel. To qualify for the sample, nations had to be sovereign for at least two years and to have a population of at least 800,000 for 1958. (The 1955–1957 collection included only 77 nations.) Sources for the data were the same as in Rummel's study. High interjudge reliability for coding of events was shown.

Tanter's factor analysis of the 13 foreign-conflict measures resulted in surprising correspondence to Rummel's factors (surprising for this type of data). Tanter's factors were: *diplomatic* (number of negative sanctions, number of protests, number of ambassadors expelled or recalled, number of threats, number of lesser officials expelled or recalled, number of accusations against another country); *war* (military action, number of wars, number of mobilizations, number killed in foreign conflict); and *belligerency* (number of antiforeign demonstrations, number of countries with which diplomatic relations were severed).

In the factor analysis of the domestic-conflict measures, the turmoil dimension emerged again, but Tanter found an internal-war measure that combined Rummel's revolutionary and subversion factors. Tanter's results were: *turmoil* (number of assassinations, number of general strikes, number of major government crises, number of riots, and number of antigovernment demonstrations) and *internal war* (amount of guerrilla war, number of purges, number of revolutions, and number killed in domestic violence).

Further analysis showed the lack of relationship between foreign- and domestic-conflict measures. For example, a factor analysis of the full set of 22 variables resulted in no factors on which both domestic-conflict measures and foreign-conflict measures loaded.

In addition, Tanter examined the possibility that foreign and domestic measures were related (as had been hypothesized by a number of theorists) if time lags were considered. Time lag studies are difficult because the appropriate lag is not known. In this case, the relationships were made between the values for a country in 1955–1957 and those for 1958–1960. The most reasonable conclusion is that there was a slight increase in the relationship between foreign- and domestic-conflict measures when the time lag was considered. The average multiple R for the variables considered was .29, but the SD among the R^2 was .13.

However, there was far greater ability to predict from foreign conflict in 1955–1957 to foreign conflict in 1958–1960 and also for domestic conflict from one period to the next. Here the average R^2 was .48 with an SD of .14. It should be noted that in all of the above cases only five dependent variables were examined. Further, only three independent variables were used in each of the multiple regressions. Nevertheless, the research is a major contribution to the examination of the relationship among conflict variables.

Banks's (1972) effort expanded the work of Rummel and Tanter. His analysis was of 51 independent nations for the time periods 1919–1939 and 1946–1966. The source of the Banks data was the daily files of the *New York Times*. High interjudge reliability was shown as well as high reliability with the Rummel–Tanter 1955–1960 data. He obtained 2,177 events from the 1919–1939 period and 2,970 events from the 1946–1966 period. The totals for each country throughout the period of study are included in each of the following separate categories: assassination, general strikes, guerrilla wars, major government crises, purges, riots, revolutions, and antigovernment demonstrations.

Six separate factor analyses were performed by correlating the conflict variables across countries. The countries were scored separately for each seven-year period. (Unfortunately, Banks collapsed the original scores into 6 levels, e.g., scores of 16–32 were assigned a 5. This has the negative effect of losing some of the precision of the original scores. However, it has the positive effect of reducing the contribution of any single extreme score.)

Overall, the results were very consistent with the Rummel analyses. Three factors emerged in each analysis, although a two-factor rotation of the data across the total time period resulted in the revolutionary and subversion factor collapsing into a single internal-war factor as reported by Tanter. Table 2 indicates the variables that had their highest loading on a particular factor for each of the major analyses (i.e., 1916–1939, 1946–1966, and the total period).

In addition, Banks performed a Q factor analysis on the data. That is, countries were intercorrelated with each other across the variables. The results indicated two large clusters of nations and two smaller clusters. However, since there were only eight measures of violence, there are very few degrees of freedom for the correlations. The clusters are suggestive but only that. Most of the correlations in the matrix are determined by a few of them, which, because of the low n (i.e., small degrees of freedom) place constraints on all of the others. The clusters were nonrevolutionary Western developed states, Latin American revolutionary states, crisis states (Luxembourg, Netherlands, Finland, Norway, and Chile), and purge states (USSR, Hungary, Yugoslavia, Romania, and Bulgaria).

Finally, Banks correlated a number of social-welfare indicators from 1963 with the loadings of the countries on the first two factors in the Q factor analysis. The social-welfare indicators were (1) government revenue and expenditures per person, (2) per capita energy consumption, (3) per capita school enrollment, (4) per capita university enrollment, (5) percent literate, (6) per capita physicians, and (7) per capita gross domestic product. All of the correlations with Factor I (nonrevolutionary Western developed) were positive and statistically significant. Thus, nonrevolutionary conflict was associated positively with development. For Factor II (Latin American revolutionary) all of the correlations were negative and statistically significant indicating that revolutionary conflict was associated negatively with development.

Critique.   A brief critique of the previous research is necessary. These comments apply not only to the factor-analytic studies but also to a large number of the correlational investigations that follow.

There are two major points to consider. The first is the use of the nation as the unit of analysis and the second is the use of multiple time periods and of time lag analyses. There is a problem of activity level that applies to each of these points.

Since nations differ in size, there may be a difference in amount of

Table 2. Loadings of Domestic Violence Variables for Different Time Periods[a]

Variable	Turmoil			Revolution			Subversion		
	1916–1939	1946–1966	Total	1916–1939	1946–1966	Total	1916–1939	1946–1966	Total
Assassinations	3	1	2	1	5	2	9	6	8
General strikes	8	8	8	2	2	3	2	3	1
Guerrilla warfare	2	1	3	4	3	3	7	7	8
Major government crises	7	8	7	5	2	5	2	2	4
Purges	3	2	3	3	8	6	7	2	4
Riots	8	4	8	1	2	1	4	7	5
Revolutions	1	2	0	9	9	9	3	1	3
Antigovernment demonstrations	9	4	8	−1	−1	−1	3	8	4

[a]Numbers are in tenths with decimals omitted. The highest loadings are italicized.

activity. Large nations may engage in more war. Further, merely as a result of size, they may engage in more revolutions, assassinations, demonstrations, and so forth. As a result, correlations may be obtained that do not represent an underlying process but instead are only a function of activity.

Similarly, the relationship from one time period to the next may also be accounted for by activity level and, therefore, not represent a separate process. This, of course, means that time lag studies are also subject to the same artifact.

An example might illustrate these problems more clearly. Basketball players differ in their activity levels; that is, some players take more shots and/or play more time compared to others. If one were to correlate the number of shots that were made with the number that were missed, the result would be statistically significant. In addition, there would be a correlation across time periods because the time period activity levels are not truly independent. Players that are active at one time are likely to be active at another. The obvious standardization would be to consider the percentage of successful shots as the measure.

The analogy to political violence is direct. Instead of purges, one would examine the percentage of violent acts that are represented by purges. Another standardization would be to relate violence levels to population. One problem with percentages is that they are based on total number of events. Therefore, definitional differences would yield different percentages for the same nation on the same conflict measure. For example, one investigator might define demonstrations as part of the conflict events while another might not.

For time series data, such as the Banks study, the problem might be overcome by standardizing within a nation for each measure. For example, suppose nations are scored each year in terms of the number of wars in which they fight. Standardizing within nations (for example by using a Z score) would mean that a nation received a high score when it was active *relative to its norm.* Thus, even a very active nation could receive a low score relative to other nations.

To summarize, there are three possible problems. One is activity level due only to size. This requires adjustment to avoid spurious correlations. The second is activity level even after adjustment for size. This might be likened to the "violence energy" of a nation. Most investigators would not consider this a problem since they are attempting to discover the variables that predict to levels of activity. However, the activity level itself might be a very simple explanation of the relationship among a set of conflict measures and this requires examination before more complex alternative explanations are accepted. The third problem is that activity level could introduce spurious correlations across time periods.

The above points, including possible procedures for standardization, are only suggestive, but the problems are critical. It is not particularly valuable to know that the number of automobiles produced, gross revenues from cars, the number of autos recalled, and the number of cars involved in accidents are all highly correlated when the United States manufacturer is the unit. These measures will show a high correlation from one time period to the next across manufacturers. Obviously, since GM is dominant, the relationships are determined by its size. New knowledge is obtained only when the relationships are examined after controlling for the size of the manufacturer.

A Typology Including Structural Violence

An important question is addressed by Gurr and Bishop (1976). Their basic argument is that violence is a multifaceted concept and cannot be treated in a unitary fashion without empirical support. Of course, these ideas are present in the earlier work of Rummel, Tanter, Banks, Feierabend, and others. Gurr and Bishop, however extend the examination to structural violence, that is, violence "done to people by malign and exploitative social and political arrangements" (1976, p. 81). This concept follows the argument of Galtung, as indicated by Gurr and Bishop, and is preceded by previous work that has examined the relationship of governmental coercion to political violence (a notable example would be the work of Feierabend, Feierabend, & Nesvold, 1969).

While coercion and denial are important variables, some question might be raised as to whether they should be called violence. Too broad a use of the term violence would lessen its conceptual value. Another difficulty is that some types of structural violence, such as censorship, may be so integral a part of a system that individual acts are not reported.

Gurr and Bishop's initial typology is represented in a 3 × 4 matrix. One variable includes the nature of the entity involved in violence, that is, individual, collective, or transnational. The other dimension consists of types of violence. Physical violence consists of either private acts or official acts while structural violence includes either structures of coercion or patterns of denial. Thus, suicide, homicide, and assassination are all examples of private-individual acts. (It is unclear where a group attack on an individual political leader or an individual attack on a group, such as a mass murder, would be placed. Transnational terrorism is categorized as private-transnation. Political sanctions, including journalistically reported censorship, are official-individual.)

Data were gathered on a total of 31 indicators across 86 countries. These 31 indicators were factor analyzed and interpretations made of the typologies indicated. The factor analysis yielded eight dimensions. Four of them represented physical violence: protest, internal war, external war, and

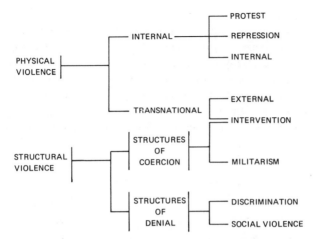

Figure 1. Empirical classification of violence.

repression. Four dimensions of structural violence were also obtained: social violence, intervention, discrimination, and militarism. The dimensions correspond closely but not precisely to the original typology. On the basis of these results, a revised typology was presented and this is replicated in Figure 1.

Gurr and Bishop scored the countries on each of the eight dimensions so that they could be compared to each other for each type of violence. Finally, measures on the four physical-violence dimensions were summed for each country and the same was done for the four structural-violence dimensions. The authors did this to compare "overall" levels of violence among the countries.

Critical Evaluations.   The critical evaluation of Gurr and Bishop's (1976) research will consider three basic points: the definition of the variables, the selection of variables for factor analysis, and the computation of overall measures of violence for the countries.

Definition of the Variables.   There is some question about the independence of some of the variables. For example, three variables that were used were homicides/100,000 population, suicides/100,000 population, and homicides/(homicides + suicides). The third measure is not independent of the other two.

Some variables are a function of activity level and may be more indicative of size than any other process. The total number of assassinations or the number of nonmilitary sanctions would fall into this category.

Some concern about the measures arises from the fact that variables were scored for different time intervals, including 1961–1965, 1948–1965, 1955–1960, 1961–1970, 1816–1965, 1948–1967, "various years during the early 60's" (p. 90), 1958–1965, 1966 only, 1965 only, 1960 only, 1958–1964. Thus, approximately 12 different time periods are used on the 31 measures. Correlations under these circumstances can be greatly affected by historical factors that override intrinsic or substantive relationships that might have emerged if only one time period were examined.

Selection of Variables for Factor Analysis. In order to completely evaluate a domain (such as one labeled violence), a universe of variables must be defined. The analysis would then proceed by using either all of the variables or a representative sample of variables. Osgood, Suci, and Tannenbaum (1957) provide a well known and excellent example of this. In the present case, the universe of possible variables could not be specified. Therefore, Gurr and Bishop proceeded in the way that was available to them. They selected a set of variables that represented possible components of the domain. In addition, they opted for a selection that appeared to be equally distributed across the domain. Thus, 16 of their variables represented physical violence and 15, structural violence. To this point the approach is quite reasonable. The problem arises in their interpretation of the factor sizes. No significance can be attached to the relative size of the obtained factors. Their weights may have arisen primarily as a function of the distribution selected for the variables, that is, equally spread through the domain. A different distribution would have yielded a different set of factor sizes. It also very likely would have yielded different factors. In fact, some other distribution might have been more appropriate. Suppose that the universe were known and that physical violence occupied two-thirds of it and structural violence one-third. This would mean that two-thirds of the variables should be physical-violence indices. Of course, since the universe wasn't known, the distribution of variables taken from the domain was made arbitrarily. However, since it was arbitrary, the relative sizes of the factors have no inherent significance.

The Overall Measure of Violence. The lack of variable independence discussed earlier is a serious problem since it creates factors as a result of artificial correlations. The overall measure of violence reported represents data for which the meaning is not readily apparent.

One major goal of Gurr and Bishop was to study types of violence. Their argument was that the types are distinctive. However, to obtain an overall violence measure they add scores on independent dimensions. Having found distinctive types, one cannot then add the types together and interpret the measure. On the other hand, the relative standings of nations on a particular dimension is valuable information.

The Gurr and Bishop (1976) article represents a very worthwhile contribution to the field of political violence. Knowledge of types of violence has been expanded, a number of key variables have been defined and data collected, and countries have been compared. However, the above discussion indicates that care must be taken in interpreting the results and in generalizing from them.

Hypotheses about Violence

Introduction

This section examines various hypotheses about conflict. It first deals with major research projects that have tested a number of hypotheses about internal violence. The Feierabend, Feierabend, and Nesvold (1969) and Gurr (1969) studies were both based on frustration–aggression theory. The research by Feierabend et al. (1969) related both uncertainties and conflicts in expectations, as well as conflicts in aspirations, to systemic frustration and aggression. The Gurr (1969) research examined a number of potential factors, including type of political system, type of culture, legitimacy of the regime, prior history of violence, institutional strength, and facilitation. The Feierabend and Feierabend (1973) paper combined three investigations and focused on attributes of force as predictors of internal conflict. The variables include the coerciveness of the regime, the legitimacy of the force, fluctuation in force, stable versus sudden changes in force, and whether the amount of force was high or low.

The second part of this section is concerned with somewhat more specialized hypotheses. Starr and Most (1978) extended the work of Richardson on the relationship between boundaries and war. The Wallace (1971, 1973) and Bueno de Mesquita (1975, 1978) studies derive directly from the Singer Correlates of War project. Wallace's first study was concerned with status inconsistency in the international system and in war and the second dealt with alliance polarization and cross-cutting relationships as independent variables. Bueno de Mesquita's research developed measures of tightness, discreteness, and power distribution in the international system. In addition, changes in the bonds among nations as well as static measures were utilized as predictors. The Köhler (1975) study restricted its attention to the role of imperial states in international conflict. Tilly's (1973) study investigated internal violence in France and tested the hypothesis that urbanization was a causative factor. Finally, Stohl (1975) and Tanter (1969) were concerned with the relationship between United States foreign and internal conflict. The Stohl (1975) paper developed some valuable (though as yet untested) hypotheses about the status of subgroups in the society and the effect of successful as compared to unsuccessful conflict on their relationships. Tanter's (1969) study was a preliminary statement about the effect of the Vietnam War on internal United States conflict.

The Feierabend Group

The basic theoretical focus of the report by Feierabend *et al.* (1969) is that frustration leads to aggression. The theoretical section specifies the social conditions that lead to frustration and, therefore, to political violence. They argue that to evaluate frustration on a collective basis, it must have been experienced collectively and simultaneously. This will occur when three criteria are met: (1) the frustration is experienced in terms of social goals; (2) it is simultaneously experienced by a number of people; and (3) it is "frustration or strain that is produced within the structures and processes of social systems" (Feierabend *et al.*, 1969, p. 635).

Four general hypotheses deal with systemic frustration:

1. Systemic frustration is a function of aspirations and expectations compared to achievement.
2. Estimates of future frustrations affect present frustration levels.
3. "Uncertainties in social expectations in themselves increase the sense of systemic frustration" (1969, p. 636).
4. Conflicting aspirations and conflicting expectations are a source of systemic frustration.

Conditions that are likely to yield high systemic frustration follow Davies's (1969) argument; specifically, these are economic (or other social) changes that lead to expectations which are unmatched by actual payoffs in the society.

Conditions relative to Hypothesis 4 are likely to be most in evidence when countries are between a traditional society and a modern one at the cultural level and are midway through the economic modernization process. (It is these midway points that are likely to produce the most conflict.)

A Guttman scaling of politically violent events was the basis for assigning scores to 84 countries for the period 1948–1965. The scale was: 0 = regularly scheduled election; 1 = dismissal or resignation of a cabinet official; 2 = peaceful demonstration or arrest; 3 = assassination (except of a chief of state) or sabotage; 4 = assassination of a chief of state or terrorism; 5 = coup d'etat or guerrilla warfare; and 6 = civil war or mass execution.

Countries were next profiled in terms of political instability using a variety of techniques: (1) by the most violent event that occurred within a particular time period (this is a particularly unstable way of classifying countries); (2) by dividing the 18-year period into three different 6-year periods and adding up the most intense event in each period; (3) by summing all scaled events throughout the time period; and (4) by summing only the politically violent events throughout the time period. The authors point out that although the profiling results correlate highly with each other, there are significant shifts for particular countries from one method to the next. Profiles for the countries using the first, second, and third methods above are presented in the article.

Various measures of modernity were used including variables such as percent literacy, radios, telephones, physicians, and GNP, as well as a composite index. The results consistently support the prediction that modern countries will be more stable politically than those that have not attained high levels of modernity. (The composite that is drawn by the authors in their discussion is not completely justified, since they did not empirically examine combinations of modernity variables. A multiple regression using the modernity values would have been most helpful.)

Political development was measured in two ways. The first was based on an Almond and Coleman classification of countries from democratic to authoritarian. The second was based on the political coerciveness–permissiveness of each country as determined by the research project. The basic finding was a curvilinear relationship between authoritarianism and political violence. The most democratic countries were also the most modern and had the least amount of political violence. The most unstable countries were those at the midlevels of coerciveness. These countries also appeared to be the least modern. The most coercive regimes (which were at midlevels of modernization) were somewhat less politically violent than those at midlevels of coerciveness.

Hypothesis 4 argued that the greatest conflict in aspirations and expectations would be associated with the greatest amount of internal political violence. Countries at midlevels of coerciveness would be expected to have the greatest conflict and/or uncertainty (Hypothesis 3) in expectations. Similarly, countries at midlevels of modernity would create the greatest conflict in expectations. The analyses of coercion and the modernity measures separately supported Hypothesis 4. However, the combination that was associated with the greatest amount of political conflict was a midlevel of coerciveness and low modernity (countries at midlevels of coerciveness tended to have the least amount of modernity).

Rates of change on socioeconomic indicators were also computed based on data from 1935–1962. "An average annual percentage rate of change for each country was calculated on each indicator and a combined rate-of-change index was developed by pooling the country's separate change scores" (Feierabend et al., 1969, p. 663). (A potential problem with this approach is that uneven changes over time can result in equivalent index scores. One country might increase steadily, for example, while another might show a large jump and then no change.) The general finding was that the higher the rate of change, the greater the instability.

Separate analysis of the transitional countries indicated essentially similar patterns. However, within these countries, the greatest instability resulted when rapid increases in education were not matched by corresponding increases in income.

In technical notes, the authors specified that some change indicators have ceilings and others do not. For example, literacy percentage cannot go above 100. Countries that are already highly literate will not be able to show large percentage increases. Other indicators, such as personal income, do not have ceiling effects. However, the nearness to a ceiling level also is related to the level of development of the country. One way in which ceiling effects were controlled was through examination of only those countries classified as transitional. In these countries, high rates of change in education were associated with political instability, but the reverse was true for measures such as telephones and income.

In later analyses another measure of political violence was developed. "Stability scores for the 84 nations were calculated on a year-to-year basis and plotted as a function of time. To characterize the time function, two measures were used—the slope of the best fit line . . . and the amplitude of change from year to year as estimated by the variance" (Feierabend et al., 1969, p. 680).

Since rates-of-change indices had previously been computed for socioeconomic indicators, it was possible to relate rates of change to political stability. Two measures of political instability were used. The static measure was based on the prior scaling of countries. The dynamic measure was based on the slope measure discussed above. Unfortunately, a combined rate-of-change indicator was used without first intercorrelating the separate indicators. If correlations among the components are low, this could reduce the ability to obtain a relationship between the rate-of-change indicator and political instability.

The results showed a positive relationship between political instability and rate of change in percentage of the population receiving primary education, and this relationship held for both the static and dynamic measures of political stability and also when a measure of population was controlled.

For rate of change in income (controlled for both level of income in one analysis and per capita GNP in another) the relationships to both the static and dynamic measures of political instability were negative.

The Feierabend and Feierabend (1973) study included three reports on results from separate studies. The first report was a review by the Feierabends of Bandura's (1973) social-learning work and of the Berkowitz (1962) and Buss analyses of aggression that led to the following hypotheses:

1. Illegitimate force leads to counterforce.
2. Legitimate use of force is more likely to act as a deterrent.
3. Fluctuation in the level of force is likely to stimulate counterforce.

4. If force at low levels is considered a source of frustration and force at high levels is considered a deterrent, the relationship between force and counterforce is postulated to be curvilinear.

5. "Sharp and sudden reversals in force levels, where the prior trend was persisting for considerable periods of time, are likely to produce an immediate rise in counter force. In the long run, however, such political systems should maintain stable levels of force and counter force" (Feierabend & Feierabend, 1973, p. 196).

Two data banks were collected. The first involved 84 nations for the years 1948–1965. Political unrest was based on data within 28 nonoverlapping categories: election, dissolution of legislature, resignation, dismissal, fall of cabinet, significant change of law, plebiscite, appointment, organization of new government, reshuffle of cabinet, severe trouble within a nongovernmental organization, organization of opposition party, governmental action against specific groups, strike, demonstration, boycott, arrest, suicide of significant political persons, martial law, execution, assassination, terrorism, sabotage, guerrilla warfare, coup d'etat, civil war, revolt, and exile. The data were obtained from *Deadline Data on World Affairs* and *Yearbooks of the Encyclopedia Britannica*.

In order to measure political instability, a seven-point rating scale was developed to assess the amount of violence. Ratings were based on the nature of the event, the number of people participating or affected, the amount of violence if any, the duration, the political prominence of the people involved, and the general impact of the event on the society. One advantage of the rating-scale approach is that it introduces an automatic, if imprecise, form of normalization since larger countries have an upper limit on the size of an event for which they are scored. The rating-scale approach does not, however, overcome the problem of very active countries disproportionately weighting the results since countries are scored for each event.

The second data bank involved the collection of data on both political aggression and political conciliation. The Feierabends identified for coding 71 discrete conflict events and 25 conciliatory acts. These latter range from discussion or conference to amnesty, repeal of martial law, and the granting of independence and regional autonomy. Targets and initiators are distinguished and the specific groups and issues for each event are identified. Post-World War II data were obtained for 130 countries and territorial units from the daily issues of the *New York Times*. The use of the event data allows countries to be profiled for political instability, government coercion, and intergroup conflict.

In addition, a separate bank was formed dealing with the coerciveness of the countries. Each country was scored on 21 variables on a six-point permissiveness–coerciveness scale. The variables were: freedom of speech, religion, and assembly, academic freedom, freedom of the arts and sciences, civil rights, freedom of minority groups, freedom from internal press censorship, external press censorship, and radio censorship, freedom of labor, of landed interests, and of business, freedom of churches, of universities, and of associational groups, opposition in the lower house, permissiveness of the executive, party opposition, absence of government participation in the economy, and suffrage.

These measures allowed fluctuation scores to be obtained for countries based on changes from one year to another. The summary fluctuation score, however, does have a potential problem because of the lack of scaling or clustering of the variables. Fluctuation in coerciveness for a country was obtained by "averaging the degree of fluctuation over the 22 years on all measures" (Feierabend & Feierabend, 1973, p. 199). The potential problem is this. A country could fluctuate a great deal but in opposite directions on two variables, so that the coerciveness level did not actually change from one year to the next. The two measures might both represent the same type of coercion and the political system could be operating on a compensatory basis; that is, changes in one area are compensated for by opposite changes in the other. All of this is to point out the ultimate importance of determining clusters or types as opposed to the use of discrete measures.

Strong support for the following additional hypotheses was claimed:

1. Regimes at midlevels of coerciveness are the most politically unstable.
2. Fluctuation in the level of coerciveness results in high political instability.

The reported results are presented in Table 3. The eta coefficients compared to the r's do indicate curvilinearity, but, of course, the shape of the curve might not be the same as predicted. However, the Feierabends examined the actual plot of the data before concluding that Hypothesis 1 was supported.

The second report (Feierabend & Feierabend, 1973) was on research by Feierabend, Nesvold, and Feierabend. The hypotheses examined were:

3. In the short run, the higher the level of coerciveness, the higher the level of political instability.
4. In the long run, the higher the level of coerciveness, the lower the level of political instability.

These hypotheses were tested using data from 10 countries that were geographically dispersed and on which data were readily available in the *New York Times*. Each country received a monthly score for each of 36 months (1959–1961) on both coerciveness and political instability. (Unfortunately, the scores were squared. This would seem to exaggerate larger or more in-

Table 3. Associations between Coercion and Instability

Variable	Product–moment correlations			Eta coefficients		
	1	2	3	1	2	3
Fluctuation of coercion	—			—		
Level of coercion	.36	—		.78	—	—
Political instability	.67	.58	—	.66	.69	—
$R_{3.12} = 0.76$						

tense events so that there is a risk of spuriously magnifying a correlation.) The countries were Argentina, Haiti, Italy, Japan, Laos, Mexico, Poland, South Korea, Spain, and the Union of South Africa.

Both simultaneous and one-month-lag relationships were obtained. The first analysis provided data consistent with Hypothesis 3 and the second provided data consistent with Hypothesis 4.

The third report (Feierabend & Feierabend, 1973) was of a study of Mullick and Feierabend. It tested the following hypothesis:

5. The higher the coerciveness of a regime, the greater the political instability engaged in by minority groups.

In this study, 25 nations were scored on a monthly basis for 60 months (1955–1959). Simultaneous time correlations were examined for the following six variables: government hostility, government conciliation, majority group hostility, majority group conciliation, minority group hostility, and minority group conciliation.

Only two correlations were found to be statistically significant. One, between majority conciliation and majority hostility, is of little consequence ($r = 0.44$). The other, between government hostility and minority hostility, was consistent with Hypothesis 5 ($r = 0.7$).

In the second and third Feierabend and Feierabend (1973) reports, each month was treated as an independent measure. Thus, n = number of countries × number of months. In the third report, $n = 25 \times 60 = 1,500$. The problem here is that months within a country are not independent with respect to conflict. Therefore, the n is exaggerated. A country's level at one month is undoubtedly a determinant of its level at another. The actual degrees of freedom in the correlation are much more likely to be closer to the number of countries than to the number of countries times the number of months. In this last study, such an adjustment would reduce n from 1,500 to 25. The correlation would still be statistically significant for $r = .71$, but the conclusions based on the second study using 10 countries would be in doubt.

Perhaps the following will illustrate the problem. Suppose one examined the stock market price as it relates to the number of people that attend the movies. Within a particular country, if one took weekly measures, there would probably not be a strong relationship between the two measures. If, however, one did the same across countries, a very high correlation might be obtained between the two variables. This is because both the stock prices within a country and the weekly movie attendance fluctuate around numbers that are relatively close to each other but consistently different from the numbers for another country. One way of overcoming the problem would be to first standardize in terms of Z scores within a country for each variable. This would eliminate a spurious correlation (except one arising from a secular trend, e.g., due to inflation over time on a worldwide basis).

Feierabend and Feierabend (1973) also provide data on coercion scores (1945–1966), fluctuation in coercion scores (1945–1966), and political instability scores (1948–1965) for each of 23 countries.

Gurr

Gurr's (1969) research on civil strife deserves careful examination. Data were collected on 114 nations and colonies during the 1961–1965 period. Only units with at least 1,000,000 people were included. The major orientation was to examine levels and types of violence in terms of the types of countries, the goals of the actions, and the factors that appeared to account for the levels of violence.

The sources for the data included *The New York Times, Newsyear,* and *African Digest.* These were supplemented by information from *The Annual Register of World Events, Africa Diary, Weekly Record of Events in Africa, Hispanic-American Report,* and country and case studies. Altogether 1,090 strife events were recorded.

Violence was measured in three ways: *pervasiveness* (participants/population); *intensity* (dead and injured/population); and *duration* (total number of days of strife).

Three classifications of countries were used. One was high, low, or medium economic development, based on the previous factor analysis results of Mary Megee for 153 nations and territories. (The factor analysis work was only somewhat utilized. Gurr combined scores on the two factors that Megee found in a way that may be only approximately accurate. Nations high on both factors were classified as high, those low on both as low, and those high on one and low on the other as medium. The medium classification, therefore, may consist of two distinct types. This distinction can be clearly seen by considering the difference between an athlete idiot and a clumsy physicist.)

The political-system classification was based on a factor analysis, by Banks and Gregg, of 115 countries with 68 variables. The classes were *polyarchic* (approximating Western democratic); *centrist* (Communist and other non-Latin American authoritarian); *elitist* (mostly newly independent African nations with modernizing elites); and *personalist* (mostly Latin American and unstable).

The geocultural classification was primarily judgmental, although a factor analysis by Russett was examined. The categories were: Latin, Islamic, African, Asian, Anglo-Nordic, Western European and Eastern European.

It should be noted that the various ways of categorizing nations overlap considerably. Further, the last classification produces small Ns in a number of categories, and this makes statistically significant results difficult to achieve. None of the analyses examined classification based on combinations of variables, although violence data is identified for each country and the classification for that country on the three variables is indicated.

Before examining the results, the operationalization of each of a number of predictor variables will be examined. Gurr relied on psychological frustration–aggression theory and its application in the theory of Davies (1969) and in the data of the Feierabends (such as that reported in Feierabend et al., 1969) to argue for relative deprivation as a major determinant of political conflict. This presentation will follow his line of argument although the major assumption of his work is not supported by much of current research in psychology. Specifically, Gurr (1969, p. 596) states that:

> Underlying the relative deprivation approach to civil strife is the frustration–aggression mechanism, apparently a fundamental part of our psycho-biological makeup. When we feel thwarted in an attempt to get something we want, we are likely to become angry, and when we become angry the most satisfying inherent response is to strike out at the source of the frustration.

The index of discontent follows the analysis by the Feierabends (e.g., Feierabend et al., 1969). Educational levels and rates of change are indices of expectations, and educational increases without corresponding changes in income indicate discontent. The results for the educational measures were not consistent with the hypotheses, although Gurr reinterprets the results to explain why.

However, measures of both short-term and persisting deprivations were developed based on the proportion of people affected. Six measures were developed and then combined into an overall measure: economic discrimination, political discrimination, political separation, dependence on foreign economics, lack of educational opportunities, and religious divisions. These measures yielded a number of statistically significant results, although Gurr mistakenly concluded, based on the correlation data, that these results showed that relative deprivation causes civil strife.

There are two notes about the analyses that deserve comment here. First, it is important to obtain evidence that within a country changes-in-relative-deprivation measures are associated with changes-in-violence measures. Secondly, and of critical concern, measures such as political and economic discrimination can be defined in such a way that they incorporate the dependent variable of civil strife. This problem will appear shortly in the definition of other variables.

Two variables examined by Gurr were history of prior violence in the country and legitimacy of the regime. Both of these variables are important, but measurement is difficult. The first variable was measured for the period of 1950–1959. However, since the Gurr study is for 1961–1965, many of the same conditions may have persisted from the first period to the second. The prediction, therefore, would not be testable since it would only indicate that the same processes were continuing through time. Further separation in time periods might be helpful, but even that would not deal with correlations that were due to activity level (although Gurr frequently adjusted for population).

The second variable raises severe questions. Legitimacy was defined in a way that it could only be high if civil strife, or at least some types of civil strife, were low. That is, by definition, attacks against the system automatically gave low scores to legitimacy. Also, the results using legitimacy were not consistent within the various types of nations.

Gurr further examined coercion, institutional strength, and facilitation as they relate to internal conflict. Two measures of coercion were used. One was the size of military and security forces relative to the population, although this might also reflect economic conditions in the country or its power position in international politics. The second measure of coercion was loyalty. Gurr concluded that "the size of forces is weakly and inconsistently related to magnitudes of civil strife." But "when coercive forces are both large and loyal, the magnitude of strife tends to be low with the apparent exceptions of Africa and Eastern and Western Europe" (1969, pp. 609–610). Aside from the exceptions, the question again arises whether the loyalty measure by definition is related to at least some types of violence.

Institutional strength was measured by the proportion of gross national product used by the central government, the number and stability of political parties, and the relative size of trade unions. The relationship between institutional strength and civil strife was not consistent within groups of countries. (Tilly, 1973, argues that institutions are prerequisites for collective action.)

Another independent measure was facilitation. This variable may also be related to civil strife by definition. That is, presence of and aid to rebels was part of the measure of facilitation. Obviously, high facilitation scores are obtained by factors that are part of civil strife. Facilitation was measured by the size and status of communist parties where they were not yet in power, the amount of isolated terrain, and "in the degree of foreign refuge, training, and supplies provided to rebels during the 1961–1965 period" (Gurr, 1969, p. 615).

Although the percentages of types of turmoil, targets, reasons for attack, and so forth, economically, politically, and geoculturally classified by country, are presented, they are difficult to evaluate since proportion of the population in these categories is not given.

Finally, a list of reasons for the civil-strife attacks is presented and should provide a useful basis for future work. They are:

1. Political objectives—(a) retaliation, (b) seizure of political power, (c) increased political participation, (d) opposition to competing political group, (e) promotion of opposition to a government policy or (f) a government act, and (g) other
2. Economic objectives—(a) retaliation, (b) seizure of economic goods, (c) change in economic distribution, and (d) other
3. Social objectives—(a) retaliation, (b) promotion of or opposition to belief systems, (c) promotion of or opposition to an ethnic, linguistic, religious, or regional community, (d) increase of social good, and (e) other

The fact that a large number of the events fell into the nonspecific categories indicates that a great amount of additional work would be advantageous here.

In summary, the Gurr (1960) article is quite valuable not only for the violence data it amassed but because of the attempt to operationalize variables such as loyalty, institutional strength, and facilitation. The fact that a great deal of work remains before the definition of these variables is adequately completed and before the relationship of civil strife to them can be determined does not reduce the importance of these attempts.

Other Studies

Starr and Most (1978) reexamined the conclusion of Richardson (1960b) that there is a relationship between the number of borders a nation has and the number of wars in which it engages. They replicated the original study using two different data sets for the years 1946–1965. The first set was based on the data from the Singer and Small Correlates of War project which "appears to tap large-scale, highly organized types of war" (Starr & Most, 1978, p. 448). The second set of data was from the Stockholm International Peace Research Institute. This set is dominated by smaller scale conflict.

In developing their analyses, Starr and Most indicated that a number of hypotheses can be developed that relate the number of borders to the number of wars. Some indicate the relationship should be positive and others indicate it should be negative. In coding the data, a sophisticated set of categories was used to determine the particular type of boundary. Two broad classes of boundaries are defined: noncolonial and colonial. Within each of these categories there are three subcategories: (a) contiguous land borders, (b) 200-mile-limit water borders, and (c) proximity zone borders. The last classification was used to include historically important frontiers between nations that did not quite meet the conditions in categories (a) and (b).

The main thrust of the analyses support the original findings that were reported by Richardson (1960b). A number of additional analyses were also reported. Generally, however, these results require care in interpretation because of statistical or conceptual difficulties. Examples are given below.

First, the coding of types of boundaries is an excellent idea. Unfortunately, there is an unresolved problem that could influence the results. The coding was symmetric. If nation A had a colonial border with nation B, nation B was coded the same way. However, nation A may have had a colony next to B and nation A's reasons for war involvement may be quite different from B's. This difference would be masked since both appear in the same boundary category. Overcoming this difficulty is not easy since asymmetrical coding leads to the placement of a single event into more than one category and many statistical analyses require mutually exclusive categories.

Second, t tests and correlations were performed by classifying nations as high or low in war involvement. The statistical effect of this must be to reduce the relationship compared to the correlation since scores on one variable are essentially reduced to a 1–0 coding.

Third, correlations were examined for differing time periods (5 years, 10 years, and 20 years). The statistical effect must be to reduce the size of the correlation for shorter time periods. This is because the range is restricted by a shorter interval. That is, the shorter the interval, the smaller is the difference between the nation with the fewest number of wars in that interval and the nation with the greatest number of wars.

Fourth, correlations within a nation must be statistically close to zero, again because of restriction of range on one variable. In this case, the variable is the number of borders, since this remains fairly constant for a particular nation over time. Further, time periods would not be independent for this measure.

Fifth, inclusion of data sets that include a large number of small countries should affect the correlation because a large number of scores on one or both variables will be at one end of the distribution. Some standardization based on size is needed.

As a final comment, it should be noted that the number of borders is a function of other characteristics of a nation, such as its size. Multiple regression techniques, therefore, would be most valuable. Similarly, once types of borders are determined, it would be valuable to know both the correlations among the types and the multiple regression of types to number of wars.

Richardson's finding of a strong relationship between the number of borders and war involvement is, however, definitely supported by this study of a more recent time period.

Wallace's (1971) study is valuable in terms of both its conceptual contributions and the inevitable methodological problems it raises. The major hypothesis is that status inconsistency, which is defined as the difference between ascribed status and achieved status, should be related to likelihood of war. To measure achieved status for the years 1820–1964, Wallace used the following indices: population, urban population, iron and steel production, armed forces available to each nation, and military expenditure. Note that the first two measures and the last two are conceptually related. Therefore, multiple regressions using all of these are subject to multicollinearity effects. Some problems might have been avoided if percent population that was urban had been used for the second index and per capita military expenditure for the last.

Ascribed status was measured using the number of nations that had diplomatic missions in each of the countries studied. The diplomatic data and the war data come from the Singer and Small project.

It is questionable whether diplomatic missions really represent ascribed status since the number of missions could be a result of size and/or economic and/or military measures. Of course, these size factors could also lead to ascribed status. However, ascribed status is only of value to prediction if it makes a contribution above that of size.

Data were aggregated for five-year periods and were normalized for the size of the system at various periods. Wallace used two important methodological controls on the data. In addition to the normalization, states had to be in the central system and had to receive diplomatic recognition from at least 30% of the members of the system to be included.

In addition, Wallace argued that status inconsistency should not necessarily have an immediate impact. Therefore, he correlated his measures with the magnitude and severity of war for time lags of 0 years, 5 years, 10 years, and 15 years. The relationships for the 10-year lag and particularly the 15-year lag appear to be statistically significant.

However, a number of questions must be raised before the findings are accepted. First, the multiple Rs are questionable since the variables are not operationally independent of each other.

Second, the status inconsistency and severity-of-war measures were evaluated for the whole system. This raises a critical problem since the hypothesis is for a single nation's status inconsistency and war. The measures that Wallace uses allow the possibility that although system measures are positively related, the relationship does not hold when individual nations are examined.

Third, although there are a sufficient number of time periods, time period data are not independent. The number of missions, population, size of army, and so forth, that exist in one time period are likely to be comparable to the number that exist at the next time period.

Finally, the data can mostly be accounted for by a secular trend. All of the measures reported by Wallace appear to be increasing through time. The one exception to this is battle deaths. (The Spearman rank order correlation between time period and battle deaths is only 0.2.)

Relevant to a point made earlier, the r_s between months in which a nation is involved in conflict during a time period and battle deaths is 0.88. Thus, the intensity measures should either be combined or only one should be used.

The correlations (r_s) for the various measures, based on information provided in the article, indicate a relationship between time and status inconsistency based on total population of 0.74, between status inconsistency based on urban population and that based on military personnel, 0.76 (for military expenditure as the second variable it was 0.72), and between military personnel and iron and steel production, 0.62. Finally, $r_s = 0.79$ between status inconsistency based on population and the same measure based on urban population.

These results indicate both that the status inconsistency measures were increasing with time and that they were very closely related to each other. It would probably have been better if the various achieved indices had been correlated with each other, an overall achievement index developed, and a single status inconsistency measure computed.

Because of the difficulties in statistical analysis and the low n's ($n = 26$ for the 15-year lag), conclusions must be tentative. Further, a single case can greatly affect the results. Thus, given the number of correlations attempted for the total time period, none can really be said to be statistically significant. Although some correlations are higher when time periods other than the total time is studied, the results are too unstable to be reliable.

In a second article, Wallace (1973) utilized the data from the Correlates of War project to examine alliance polarization and the likelihood of war. The international system between 1815 and 1964 was investigated.

In order to examine the amount of polarization, the relationships among nations were examined through their alliances, diplomatic relations (including indirect bonds through a third party), and membership in intergovernmental organizations (IGO).

For each five-year period between 1815 and 1964 a matrix was developed that indicated the diplomatic linkages of each nation with every other nation. For each 10 year period between 1865 and 1965, the same type of matrix was developed for the IGO data. (Although data were normalized for the number of countries in the system, a better normalization might have been in terms of the number of links a particular nation had. Thus, a nation with only one link would be considered strongly bonded with whatever nation it was linked. However, a nation with many linkages to different nations would not be considered strongly bonded to any single nation. It is quite possible that the analyses would not have been substantially affected by this modification, and in fact, one can argue that number of links to a country is more important than proportion of links.) The matrices were then subjected to a Lingoes–Guttman smallest-space analysis.

On the basis of the spatial relations obtained, polarization of the international system for each of the 150 years was computed. (Basically, the greatest polarization would occur when nations clustered into just two groups.) In addition, the cross-pressure a nation experienced was also obtained. "A cross-pressured nation is one whose formal military alignments bond it tightly to a different group of nations than those closely affiliated with it via diplomatic ties or common membership in the IGO" (Wallace, 1973, p. 592).

The basic findings of Wallace were negative. That is, he was unable to show substantial relations between the amount of war and alliance polarization, cross-cutting, or a combination of the two. Although curvilinear regression did account for increased amount of variance, it is difficult to argue for the importance of this unless a particular curvilinear relation had been hypothesized or unless the form of the relationship is consistent across analyses.

The inability to obtain relationships should be examined briefly. Both alliance formation and cross-cutting appear to be variables that have a high probability of being related to war incidence. Several factors might account for the failure to find these relationships: (a) a time lag may be involved; (b) the unit of time may be a critical factor—for example, a 10-year period, or even a five-year period, may be too long; and (c) the smaller nations may introduce a great deal of error into the system since changes in one linkage may introduce major changes in the evaluation of that nation.

It would be interesting to take a small set of nations such as Great Britain, France, Germany, and Russia to see if changes in their polarization levels and cross-cutting levels were associated with changes in their hostility toward each other, either simultaneously or with various time lags.

Some refinement of the polarization index should also be undertaken. It is possible that polarization of the system may not be a measure that is relevant to the war between a specific pair or set of nations.

The Wallace research is an excellent effort in both concept definition and data collection. The problems that exist are almost endemic to the field. The data and the suggestions of the theory deserve additional attention.

Bueno de Mesquita (1978) has extended the research on systemic polarization. To consider his work, a number of definitions need to be examined.

The main thrust of this research is to investigate the effect of system structure on the uncertainty of decision makers and to relate this uncertainty to the likelihood of war. However, he argues, it is not the levels but the shifts in structures that are important. And the relevant concepts, polarity, bonds among clusters, and structure shifts, are difficult to measure. (Uncertainty is not measured directly but is inferred from other measures. Validation of the measures is of great importance, particularly since the psychological literature on the effect of the variables on uncertainty and risk in decision making is not always consistent with the conclusions drawn by political scientists, for example, the risky shift as described in R. Brown, 1965).

The key variables in this analysis are tightness, discreteness, power distribution, and poles (Bueno de Mesquita, 1975).

Selection of these variables was based heavily on hypotheses about the effects of particular system states on decision makers. For example, "the level of uncertainty surrounding the outcome of any potential conflict is assumed to decrease as the number of autonomous actors in the system increase" (Bueno de Mesquita, 1975, p. 190). Certainly, hypotheses such as this one (and there are a large number of hypotheses of this type in the literature which are used to justify the development of particular variables) are amenable to experimental study. It would appear that some concerted effort should be made to develop experiments that would investigate hypotheses about human perceptions under various types of environmental constraints.

Bueno de Mesquita argues that military alliances provide the most reliable basis for evaluating the variables of interest (i.e., poles, tightness, discreteness, and power distribution). Alliances are argued to be more than just pieces of paper; that is, they represent real commitments, since "between 1815 and 1960, 64% of the nations that belonged to an alliance and that were at war found that some of their allies fought alongside them. Only 25% of the nonallied nations that were involved in wars were aided by the presence of other combatants on their side" (1975, p. 194). (It might be argued that this statistic cannot be completely evaluated until the percentages for the number of opposition nations is also determined. For example, it could be that nations that were members of an alliance also frequently found members of that alliance fighting against them.)

The Singer and Small data and alliance classification (defense, neutrality, ententes) were the basis of the investigation. The alliances were ranked in terms of the amount of commitment they required from an alliance member. Defense indicated most commitment, then neutrality, then entente, and finally no alliance.

In order to obtain measures, every dyad of nations in each five-year period was compared using a 4 × 4 matrix (the four categories of alliances). Similarity of the nations was compared using the τ-b measure for the matrix.

There are two points to consider here, both of which may be minor. First, two inactive nations can be as similar to each other as two active nations. Thus, if two nations form an alliance and have no other alliances, they are similar. Two more active nations might have 10 alliances which completely overlap and they would be considered equally similar. In addition, the measure does not directly take into account the size of the alliance, which may have some effect.

The second problem is that nations that had no alliance in a particular year were not included. This means that the set of nations differs from one year to the next. A better procedure might have been to define a set of nations over time and study the changes that occurred. This control could be important because the number of clusters might be a function of the number of nations that are aligned and, therefore, not really represent the polarity of the system. It would also allow a very important control to be examined, namely, that a nation's behavior when it is part of an alliance is different from its behavior when it is not.

The complete matrix of the τ-b values was subjected to a McQuitty typal analysis to identify the clusters of nations. (Factor analysis might have yielded greater stability to the results.) The conceptual definitions of the tightness and discreteness of the clusters are direct. A cluster achieves the maximum amount of tightness, or similarity in commitments, if the sum of the τ-bs within the cluster is equal to the number of dyads in the cluster (Bueno de Mesquita, 1975, p. 200). The tightness of total system is measured by the results across all of the clusters standardized for the total number of dyads in the clusters.

Discreteness is defined in a similar way except that it is based on the dissimilarity of the alliance commitments among members of different clusters.

Finally, the power concentration index is based on the proportion of power in a particular cluster compared to the total number of clusters. (Here, it does not appear that either the number of nations in a cluster or the relative concentration of power within a single cluster is considered. Each cluster is considered an actor.)

The complete set of clusters by year and the number of poles, discreteness, tightness, and concentration of power in the system are presented in the appendix to the article. The concentration scores are presented for each five-year period beginning in 1890.

The development of the above indices is a significant achievement. It also appears that the correlations among the various indices are low enough to justify their independent definition.

The data indicated differences between the nineteenth century and the twentieth century on discreteness but not on tightness. These analyses were further elaborated in the subsequent article (Bueno de Mesquita, 1978). The changes over time of the indicators require further evaluation because of the changes in the number of nations from one time period to another. This issue has been discussed.

In addition, the analyses have two related difficulties. The first problem, shared by a number of investigations in the area, is small n's. A number of results are reported for five-year periods ($n = 13$ and many n's = 11 in the 1978 article). These n's are so small that practically no correlation is large enough to be statistically significant.

The second is a related problem. This is the lack of independence in the cases. If measures are made on a yearly basis, for example, the results from one year to the next may not be independent. Alliances frequently last longer than a year. The numbers in the second year, therefore, will not be independent of the numbers in the first year. Similarly, the economic power of a nation (or a cluster) will not vary greatly from one year to the next (or from each five years to the next). This problem appears in a great deal of international-violence data. But it is a problem. The result of nonindependent measures is to magnify errors and treat them as consistent rather than random effects. Obtained relationships obviously may not reflect substantive relationships under these circumstances.

The problem is not easy to solve. Time and space are limited on earth. Sampling at distant points may be difficult, if not impossible, because of these limitations. The best one may be able to do is examine changes rather than levels. Even changes have problems, primarily because of possible ceiling effects. For example, if every nation belongs to the same alliance, the direction of change is constrained to move probably in the direction of a greater number of alliances rather than fewer. Nevertheless, the change measures may offer one way of dealing with a possibly severe problem.

Although sample size is still a problem, Bueno de Mesquita reports that "the correlation for tightening systems is a very substantial 0.73" (1975, p. 207). A comparable finding was not obtained for either discreteness changes or changes in power concentrations.

The second article (Bueno de Mesquita, 1978) expanded the empirical work. Overall, the results are disappointing. There are relatively few statistically significant correlations; and most are based on an n of 11 or 15 and are only significant based on a one-tailed test that predicts the direction of the result from *a priori* theory. As the excellent theoretical discussion at the beginning of the article illustrates, theory predicts either direction depending on the theorist.

The most likely candidate for a relationship is the one reported earlier between tightness changes and war. Although substantial conclusions could not be reached, the theoretical reasoning and variable definition that allowed quantification and collection of data are all valuable early steps required before more thorough understanding can be achieved.

Köhler (1975) also utilized the Singer and Small data set on alliances. He argued that the level of analysis determines many of the research questions and proposed the imperial system as one level. An imperial system is composed of a central state and a number of follower states over which it can command obedience. He considers the imperial system to be a level between the global level and the national level (the other two levels are domestic and individual). Köhler points out the differences arising in research questions that are dependent on the unit of analysis. At the global level, for example, the amount of polarization in the system may be related to the amount of war. At the individual level, questions frequently involve factors associated with human aggression.

To examine his thesis, 15 imperial powers were identified for the years 1816-1974 (nine of these were classified as major powers by Singer and Small). Köhler then examined the number of wars per decade during the imperial period and compared that result to the number of wars per decade after imperial leadership had ended. Only 7 of the imperial leaders had ended imperial leadership by 1974. For these, there was a dramatic decrease in the number of wars after imperial leadership had ended as compared to the period of imperial leadership.

Unfortunately, there are a number of problems with the analysis which leave the conclusions unclear. First, part of the process of becoming an imperial power involves the domination of follower states (Kôhler's definition). This process frequently involves military conquest. Therefore, it is not known whether the difference arises out of the process of becoming an imperial power or from the attribute of imperial power status itself.

Second, since imperial powers are frequently also great powers, there is no evidence presented that differences for great powers that change their status from great powers to former great powers would not also show comparable results. If this occurred, it would indicate that the category of imperial power provided no additional predictive capacity than that of major power.

Third, since eight of the 15 powers were still classified as imperial, data should have been examined for them over time. If they showed the same pattern as those whose imperial periods had ended, the evidence would be for a change over time that was independent of imperial status.

Köhler has presented some interesting ideas and it is possible that imperial status is a relevant variable. Some additional work along the lines suggested above would be helpful in providing a more valid basis for judgment.

Tilly's (1973) study examined data obtained within a single country (France). Altogether, 2,000 disturbances were obtained in the sample. A disturbance was "any event occurring within the country in which at least one group of 50 or more persons took part, and in which some person or property was seized or damaged over resistance" (p. 106). The events were those encountered by trained readers in scanning two national newspapers from 1830–1960. Three randomly selected months per year were studied for the period 1861–1929.

Tilly argues that there is no drastic discontinuity between routine politics and collective violence (or at least that the assumption that there is deserves to be questioned). He points out that (a) collective violence often succeeds; (b) "whether or not it succeeds in the short run and by the standards of the participants, collective violent protest is often a very effective means of entering or remaining in political life, of gaining or retaining an identity as a force to be reckoned with" (p. 101); (c) collective violence often follows a well-defined internal order; (d) its participants are frequently ordinary people (as opposed to the lunatic fringe); and (e) it tends to evolve in cadence with peaceful political action.

The critical hypothesis tested by Tilly in this study is that rapid urbanization is a cause of collective violence.

The primary analysis was for the years 1830–1832. Each department of France (*n* = 85) was scored for the amount of collective violence, adjusted for population. There were three independent variables: (a) population in cities of 10,000 or more in 1831; (b) changes (percentage) in that urban population (1821–1831); and (c) net migration into the department (1826–1831). (It is possible, but unlikely, that this last measure contains some error, since the measure of interest is not migration into the overall department but into the cities of the department.)

A multiple correlation indicated that the major predictor was the urban population. Although increases in urban population also contributed to prediction, the migration variable did not. Tilly concludes, therefore, that "whatever the effect of urban increase on collective violence, it does not operate through the unsettling arrival of uprooted immigrants" (1973, p. 113).

During this period there were also a large number of strikes. The strike activity came disproportionately from the older, established trades rather than from the expanding factory groups. Further, strikes and collective violence went together.

A specific additional analysis supports the above interpretation. In the large Parisian disturbance of 1848, the June days, records are available for 11,000 of the probable 15,000 that were arrested. These records indicate origin and occupation of the participant. The data support the notion that the disturbance involved "an amalgam of the old, politically active trades, with a few sections of modern industry" (Tilly, 1973, p. 118). Other analyses indicate that outsiders (i.e., nonnative Parisians) definitely were not overrepresented. "Again the violent masses turn out to be those integrated into the setting rather than those at the margins of society" (p. 119).

Stohl's (1975) analysis examines the relationship between external war and internal conflict based on data for the United States from 1890 to 1970. The data were obtained from the *New York Times Index*. Although Levy (1974b) has shown that there appears to be a consistent bias in the type of violence reported and the distance of the event in miles from a single newspaper source—in fact, the study was based on reporting of domestic violence in the *New York Times*—it is unlikely that these biases resulted in substantial distortions in the Stohl data.

The basis for the analysis is a quasi-experimental procedure called interrupted time series (Campbell & Stanley, 1963). The argument is that a variable that occurs intermittently can be presumed to have some effect on another variable if the second variable shows large shifts at the appropriate occasions of the intermittent variable.

The independent variable in this study consists of the occurrence of international wars (the Spanish-American War, World Wars I and II, and the Korean and Vietnam Wars). The dependent variables are the type and extent of domestic political violence that involved 20 or more people.

One contribution of the Stohl work, in addition to the examination of the possible impact of international war on domestic-conflict patterns, is the specific hypotheses that were developed to explain the changes that were occurring. The hypotheses were:

1. War mobilization enhances the economic position of subordinate groups relative to the dominant ones and, therefore, intensifies conflict.
2. Status positions change in similar ways to those of economic positions and, therefore, intensify conflict.
3. Conflict and violence are also changed as a result of war through demands for a reallocation of political demands and rewards. This hypothesis has two corollaries: (A) if the war is successful, the top segments gain most and therefore exert greater effort to maintain their gains, which increases the relative amount of violence directed downward by the dominant segments against the lower ones. (B) Lack of success in war decreases the power and prestige of dominant segments but does not provide additional goods to distribute, and thus, their inability to distribute rewards to maintain their position results in the violence downward being matched by upward violence from the lower segments who are trying to protect their gains obtained during the war.

The analyses that Stohl used were somewhat complex. However, evaluation of the work requires careful consideration of them. First, a large number of dependent indicators were measured. The number differed from period to period because of the availability of data. Thus, there were 29 indicators for the Spanish-American War, 49 for World War I, 75 for the

Korean War, and 25 for the Vietnam War. The indicators were divided into a set of categories. Intensity of the violence was measured by duration, deaths, and arrests. Further distinctions were made in terms of economic, social, and political violence and also in terms of antisystem, prosystem and nonclassifiable clashes.

The hypotheses were not directly tested so precise evaluation of them cannot be made from the article. However, the data collected do allow some future quantitative tests of Stohl's insightful propositions.

The main examination is of the possible impact of international wars on domestic violence. The key involves time series analyses. Each month is scored for a violence measure. These scores are correlated with the month itself. Thus, suppose a one-year period were examined. There would be 12 violence measures, one for each month. This would be variable X. There would also be 12 scores for the months (i.e., 1, 2, ..., 12). This would be variable Y. The correlation would allow the determination of the best-fit line and would be of the form $Y' = mX + b$, where $m = r(SD_Y)/SD_x$. The slope of the equation is m and the intercept is b. The equation allows one to predict the amount of violence at some new time in the future, say month 13.

The analyses follow essentially one of three patterns. Suppose, for the first pattern, that violence measures are taken during the months preceding the outbreak of a war. If this outbreak has an immediate impact on domestic violence, the amount that does occur in this month should be significantly different from that predicted by the equation. Stohl's results indicate some possibility that this change did occur, but the evidence is weak. Thus, there is limited evidence that the domestic violence changed dramatically in the month following the outbreak of an international war.

Suppose, for the second pattern, that the same kind of equation is developed for the months after a war's cessation. By predicting forward in time from the first equation and backward in time from the second equation, it should be possible to predict to a point in the middle of the international war. If the war had an impact on domestic violence, the actual amount of domestic violence should be different from the predicted amount. Stohl's data indicate much stronger support here for the proposition that international war affects the level of domestic violence.

Finally, if the international war has an impact, the equation for the first pattern should be different from that for the second; that is, the slopes or intercepts or overall equations should be different. Fairly strong support was found for the impact of international war on the level of domestic violence, based on this series of tests.

Unfortunately, the data do not indicate a consistent impact. Different wars yield different results. Some wars appear to have a greater impact on domestic-violence levels compared to others. Further, the type of domestic violence that is affected differs from one instance to another.

Overall, Stohl's work is a very valuable contribution to the literature. Several possible refinements should be noted. First, the variable definition should be refined. As with most investigators, measures are defined that are obviously related to each other. For example, the number of casualties is probably partially a function of the duration of the violent event. Adjustments should be made so that casualties are per unit of time if casualties are used as a measure in addition to duration.

Second, categories were not always mutually exclusive. Thus the relationships studied were not always based on independent data. For example, an event coded as social violence may also have been coded as antisystem violence, with correlations performed on both sets of data.

Third, overall measures of violence were computed without some sort of cluster analysis, such as factor analysis. Therefore, it is not possible to know if the summary measure is really based on types of violence that belong together. Of course, if the interest is in some summary measure like number of deaths, there is nothing wrong with adding deaths from a number of causes.

Fourth, regression equations are based on different numbers of months preceding the outbreak of a war or following its cessation. Further, long periods both before and after a war were used to determine the regression equations. The different numbers of months introduce extraneous factors. So does the use of long periods. The impact of any international war on domestic violence may be brief. Other changes in the society may also be important. By using long periods before and after a war, the differences obtained may not be due to the war itself but rather to other changes occurring in the society, although discontinuity in the data would argue against long-term bases.

Fifth, some regressions use a partially overlapping set of months. This would tend to reduce the likelihood that the differences between the regressions would be statistically significant. It also means that the various tests are not independent of each other.

In spite of the above comments, it should be recognized that Stohl has made a major contribution to the study of the relationship between international war and domestic conflict.

Tanter (1969) examined the relationship between external-war involvement and domestic conflict during the Vietnam War period of 1965 to 1968. His analysis of the theoretical positions taken by Quincy Wright, Simmel, and Coser indicated a general consensus that external enemies increase group cohesion and obedience to a leader.

Previous quantitative research by Rummel and by Tanter found small positive relationships between foreign- and domestic-conflict behavior, although the relationship was increased with a time lag.

The present article further examined the problem through the specific study of the Vietnam War. The focus of the analysis was on rates of change among the indicators. The external-war involvement and rates of change were measured by United States troop strength in Vietnam. The independent variables were measured by "frequencies, rates of change, and populations participating in antiwar protests, levels of urban riots, and participation in civil rights demonstrations. Secondary indicators are the number of labor strikes and levels of violent crime" (Tanter, 1969, p. 553).

The data indicated that "antiwar protests were a response to changes in U.S. forces rather than a response to their actual magnitude" (Tanter, 1969, p. 556). This result is consistent with the analysis of Milstein and Mitchell (1968) in terms of communist-troop commitments and the escalation of bombing of North Vietnam by the United States.

The above finding, however, was clouded by a number of additional facts. Although the rates of change based on the number of antiwar incidents was related to changes in forces, the finding was not supported for the rates of change of the number of participants in antiwar protests. Furthermore, during the leveling off period in Vietnam (high troop strengths but no increases in troop strength) the number of participants in antiwar protests *increased*. In addition, none of the other indicators of domestic turmoil indicate rates of change that correspond to the changes in troop levels.

The evidence, therefore, does not support a relationship between external-war changes and domestic violence on any of the measures—rates of change, levels of activity, or direction of changes. Other considerations also affect the interpretation of the results.

First, the Vietnam War continued after 1968. There were dramatic changes in antiwar protests and riots that had no corresponding changes in troop levels. The antiwar demonstrations were reduced greatly after the draft was ended, and the riots came to a substantial end after the 1968 election.

Secondly, since there is a secular trend of increasing levels of crime, this should be partialled out before other domestic-violence indicators are examined.

As Tanter's earlier (1966) research, along with that of others, indicated, there is evidence for a more general domestic-turmoil factor. This being the case, domestic turmoil indicators should be combined into a composite index.

Finally, a key ingredient was missing in the Vietnam War as it relates to hypotheses about external enemies and group cohesion. Many United States citizens did not perceive North Vietnam as either a threat or an enemy.

The relationship between domestic- and external-war indicators may, of course, be affected by the circumstances surrounding a particular event. An obvious need is for a series of studies around the occasion of other international wars, including the time period from before the war to after it has ended.

Although no conclusions can be drawn from the data in the Tanter (1969) study, it should be apparent that the question of the relationship between external turmoil and domestic turmoil, particularly as it affects group cohesion and obedience to a leader, is an important one for further investigation.

Summary

This summary consists of two major parts. First, a set of conclusions, about methodology, will be presented for the studies that have been reviewed thus far. Secondly, there will be a very brief indication of some major areas in the study of political conflict which were not included in this review.

Overall Conclusions: Macroanalyses

The field of quantitative studies of political violence has made surprising progress during the past twenty years. Not only has the collection of data been substantially extended, but there have been penetrating advances in the more difficult task of operationally defining variables which are hypothesized to be determinants of political violence. The works of Feierabend, Gurr, and Bueno de Mesquita serve as examples.

However, substantive conclusions about the actual causes of political violence must, for the most part, await additional research. The major reason for this is technical. Some of the data as well as a number of analyses require additional refinement before confidence can be placed in the validity of the relationships. Most of these difficulties have been discussed in the previous review. The following will briefly summarize the major points and occasionally suggest procedures that might overcome the problem.

1. There is some need to recognize that collections of information are based on resources that are more adequate in some parts of the world than others. While this may not be a problem for major wars, and perhaps not a serious one for smaller wars, it undoubtedly is for other variables such as mediations. This difficulty might be handled directly through separate analyses for the more complete and the less complete data.

2. The amount of information that exists is restricted by the nature of human history. As Singer (1979b) has pointed out, there have been a limited number of wars on which to base statistical analyses.

However, this problem, as well as some similar ones, might be approached through changing the variable definition from a nominal one (war or nonwar) to a continuous one (e.g., degree of hostility). Azar's research points in this direction. A blockade, a threat of war, and a shifting of troops are examples of hostile but not warring acts.

Secondly, from an objective point of view, it may be time to move

from the distinction between internal and international war and instead
to define the attributes of the conflicting segments. Examples might include differences in language and/or religion, whether disputes between
individuals are resolved by a common authority or separate ones, whether
permission was needed prior to the outbreak for transit from one group
to another, and so on.

A third point can be considered an extension of the above. Classifications of nations, great powers, imperial powers, global wars, and so
forth may not be necessary by category. Many of the attributes that distinguish members of these categories from each other are likely to be continuous (e.g., number and size of different language groups and/or religious
groups over which the central authority has domain, number of men under
arms and/or expenditures for the military, changes in time for these measures, etc.). In this way nations are not great powers or small powers; they
have a certain amount of power. Similarly, nations are not imperial or non-
imperial, but they have a certain amount of imperialism. Wars would be
more or less global.

The explanation of political conflict undoubtedly resides in a large
number of variables. To the extent that variables are categorized when
they can actually be measured on a continuous basis, predictive ability is
lost.

3.   Some problem exists in the definition of basic variables such as
wars, alliances, and boundaries; each of these can be counted at least twice
in a given study. The number of wars, alliances, and boundaries of the nations are not independently measured. The problem for wars might be handled by separating attacker from attacked, but Richardson found this determination to be difficult. Another approach would be to count casualties
within each country separately. Alliances may not be a problem, since each
country makes a separate decision and when two nations do so with each
other it is called an alliance; this is somewhat comparable to examining the
number of times individuals shake hands—when one does, so must another.
For boundaries, no immediate resolution appears.

The major point here is not that such variables as wars, alliances, and
boundaries should be examined, but rather that care be taken in statistical analyses that assume independent measurement.

4.   There is a very serious problem due to activity level which is exaggerated when a nation is the unit, resulting in the introduction of spurious
correlations. Many analyses are subject to this difficulty. It is not sufficient to standardize across units; it is also necessary to standardize within
the unit.

5.   There is frequently an inadequate amount of baseline data or control information. It is necessary to examine a particular nation's behavior
before, during, and after such events as the occurrence of a war, the forma-

tion of an alliance, or development as an imperial power in order to examine the possible impact of the variable of interest. Similarly, the absence of a trait must be compared to results when it is present.

6. The nation (and equally, the international system) are suspect as conceptual units in most analyses, since they are treated as if they have a group consciousness. Nations do not go to war; individuals within nations do. It is this problem in conceptual definition that leads to the error of analysis at one level applied to units at another level. Snyder's (1978) review is an excellent discussion of this problem.

7. Many units and variables are not independent of each other. The most common problem is with time units. Since the individual measures at various times are dependent on the level at other times, the correlations that frequently occur are a result of this artifact.

8. Analyses sometimes restrict the range on one or more variables, and this in itself may lead to smaller correlations.

9. Variables are sometimes defined so they are functionally dependent on each other. This, of course, means that the relationship is not meaningful.

10. Ceiling effects on variables are frequently not taken into account. Feierabend et al. (1969) is a notable exception to this. The ceiling of course constrains the variable so that if it is measured at or near the ceiling at one time, it is likely to move away from the ceiling at another time.

11. Variables that are empirically related to each other need to be combined into an overall index. This not only would improve the quality of the variable but would also result in less frequent analysis of each component as if new information were being provided with each analysis.

12. The reverse of the above is also a problem. Once a set of variables has been shown to consist of more than one cluster (e.g., through factor analysis) it is usually not legitimate to recombine measures in the different clusters into a composite measure.

Some Other Areas in the Study of Political Violence

This material is provided to direct individuals to some areas of study of political violence that could not be discussed in this chapter.

Other Reviews. In addition to the reviews cited at the beginning of the chapter (Gochman, 1979; Snyder, 1978), Finsterbusch (1973) has provided an excellent summary of many substantive macrostudies. The studies are compared to each other and an elaborate list of motives for political violence is presented. (Perspectives also of value include Singer, 1979a, and Tilly, 1969.)

The Study of Human Aggression. Obviously, political violence is both human and aggressive. However, the psychological studies of human aggression (e.g., Bandura, 1973; Berkowitz, 1962; Brown & Herrnstein, 1975) do not provide complete explanations of political violence. They do, however, provide a more accurate perspective on violence for the development of hypotheses about political hostility.

For example, although there are biological factors associated with aggression, these are unlikely to be the major determinants of human aggression. Lorenz's (1967) notion that aggression is a motive that increases over time and that was reduced through aggressive behavior, is unlikely to be correct. Aggression seems more similar to a drive and may provide satisfaction through the act itself. One possible source of this satisfaction is the achievement of dominance. As discussed by R. Brown (1965), dominance relationshps exist through a large part of the animal kingdom. Dominance leads to territory and territory has the advantages of access to food and mating privileges. It is conceivable that acts of aggression, as one method of achieving dominance, also bring psychological satisfaction, particularly in human beings.

Other innate factors also require careful examination. There is no inevitable link between frustration and aggression or between aversive stimuli and aggressive behavior, although these conditions may make aggression more likely. The existence of biological factors is shown, of course, through experiments such as those involving electrical stimulation of a cat's brain with resultant rage and the increase in aggression in apes after the injection of male sex hormones.

Nevertheless, the major factors leading to aggression in humans are undoubtedly under social control. Aggressive behavior occurs primarily through the experiences that govern all learned behavior—classical conditioning, instrumental or operant conditioning, and modeling.

Testing Psychological Theories in the Political Environment. The classic example of this research approach remains the work of the group headed by Robert North (Holsti, 1965; North, 1962; North & Choucri, 1968; North, Brody, & Holsti, 1964; Zinnes, 1962). The effects of stress on psychological reactions were ascertained through the examination of the literature in experimental psychology, and the hypotheses were tested by coding the memoranda of World War I decision makers. It should be noted that the hypotheses and the analyses were both at the level of the individual.

Mathematical Models. Richardson (1960a; see also Rapoport's, 1957, examination of Richardson) provided a noteworthy example of the development of formal models for the study of political violence. His *Arms and Insecurity* presented a mathematical treatment of the arms race. This work has been followed by a number of additional efforts such as that of Wallace and Wilson (1978), who examined nonlinear models. There have also been a fairly large number of other mathematical models of political violence or political relations. One example is the work of Phillips and Rimkunas (1978), who try to deal with the problem of discontinuity such as that which occurs when there is a crisis. A major problem with many of the efforts is that, unlike with Richardson, real data are not always used to test the mathematical formulation.

Action and Reaction, Including Deescalation. As Azar's (1972, 1974) research indicated, it is possible to examine international relations as an interactive system. Another excellent example is provided by Milstein and Mitchell (1968).

The examination of arms escalation was extended by Osgood (1959) through his GRIT proposal. Pilisuk and Skolnick (1974) defined an experimental situation that included a number of relevant attributes of the GRIT proposal, and Lindskold (1978) has provided an outstanding review of the experimental literature related to it. The process described in GRIT has been independently formalized in mathematical treatments by Isard (1968) and Isard and Smith (1967).

Hierarchical Considerations and the Study of Authoritarianism. Perhaps a major problem with research on political violence is the use of the nation as a unit. Not only does a nation not act (individuals do), but individuals carry different weights. Singer (1979b) clearly recognizes the importance of decision makers.

But if individuals carry different weights, hierarchical considerations may be of great importance in undersanding how groups interact aggressively with each other.

Within psychology, the line of research that has most directly addressed this problem is that dealing with authoritarianism (Adorno, Frenkel-Brunswik, Levinson, & Sanford, 1950; Rokeach, 1960; Stagner, 1936). Milgram's (1974) experimental work clearly demonstrated the effect that authority can have on individual behavior. More recently, Levy (1970c, 1971b, 1972, 1974a, 1978, 1979), through a series of survey studies, has extended the work on authoritarianism. (See also Kelman & Hamilton, 1974.)

Levy has developed and tested a theoretical formulation that argues that stress leads to a rigidification of behaviors which in turn leads to anxiety in a complex social environment. The anxiety is frequently resolved through reliance on authority. The result is an increase in group cohesion and antagonism toward outgroup members. In addition, the individual becomes less independent from authority even when the authority is oppressive toward the individual.

A number of separate links have been demonstrated in the research and writings of others. For example, stress has been shown to lead to a reduction in perceived alternatives by Holsti (1965) and in research cited in Barton (1970). Stress has also been shown to be associated with an increase in authoritarianism by Rokeach (1960), Hanson and Bush (1971), and Sales (1972, 1973).

The relationship between stress and cohesion is discussed by Berkowitz (1969) and the relationship between leadership and cohesion by Freud (1921/1960). The study by Shils and Janowitz (1954) also indicates a linkage between leadership and cohesion. Mitchell and Byrne (1973) have shown that authoritarianism is associated with punitiveness toward dissimilar others.

Tilly (1973), Gross (1970), and Horowitz (1972) indicate that resistance to oppression rises from among those who have a greater number of alternatives and/or can be considered to be under less stress since they have received a relatively greater amount of rewards in social or institutional settings.

The purpose of the Levy research has been to improve the measure of authoritarianism in individuals and simultaneously to test the relationships among several of the variables. The research is limited at this point to results obtained from questionnaire studies and from residents of the United States. Nevertheless, a few thousand individuals have been involved in the sequential series of studies that has included a dozen samples.

Documentary Material.   Unfortunately, limited use has been made in developing theories about political violence based on documentary evidence such as that represented in Prescott (1961), Levin (1968), Wells-Barnett (1969), D. Brown (1972), Solzhenitsyn (1973), Dawidowitz (1976), Begin (1978), Steiner (1968), and many others.

Concluding Comment

The focus of this chapter has been analytic rather than survey. A number of major investigations in the field of political violence could not be incorporated into this material, even to the minimal extent of citation. It is hoped that the chapter will encourage individuals to extend their knowledge while at the same time providing a background that will better enable them to do this.

References

Adorno, T. W., Frenkel-Brunswik, E., Levinson, D. J., & Sanford, R. N. *The authoritarian personality*. New York: Harper & Row, 1950.
Azar, E. Conflict escalation and conflict reduction in an international crisis: Suez 1956. *Journal of Conflict Resolution*, 1972, *16*, 183 –201.
Azar, E. E. Toward the development of an early warning model of international violence. In J. D. Ben-Dak (Ed.), *The future of collective violence: Societal and international perspectives*. Lund, Sweden: Studentlitterature, 1974.
Bandura, A. *Aggression: A social learning analysis*. Englewood Cliffs, N.J.: Prentice-Hall, 1973.

Banks, A. S. Patterns of domestic conflict: 1919–1939 and 1946–1966. *Journal of Conflict Resolution*, 1972, *16*, 41–50.

Barton, A. H. *Communities in disaster*. Garden City, N.J.: Anchor, 1970.

Begin, M. *The revolt*. New York: Dell, 1978.

Berkowitz, L. *Aggression*. New York: McGraw-Hill, 1962.

Berkowitz, L. Social motivation. In G. Lindzey & E. Aronson (Eds.), *The handbook of social psychology* (Vol. 3). Reading, Mass.: Addison-Wesley, 1969.

Brown, D. *Bury my heart at Wounded Knee*. New York: Bantam Books, 1972.

Brown, R. *Social psychology*. New York: Free Press, 1965.

Brown, R. M. The American vigilante tradition. In H. D. Graham & T. R. Gurr (Eds.), *The history of violence in America*. New York: Praeger, 1969.

Brown, R. & Herrnstein, R. J. *Psychology*. Boston: Little, Brown, 1975.

Bueno de Mesquita, B. Measuring systemic polarity. *Journal of Conflict Resolution*, 1975, *19*, 187–216.

Bueno de Mesquita, B. Systemic polarization and the occurrence and duration of war. *Journal of Conflict Resolution*, 1978, *22*, 241–267.

Campbell, D. T., & Stanley, J. C. *Experimental and quasi-experimental designs for research*. Chicago: Rand-McNally, 1963.

Davies, J. C. The J-curve of rising and declining satisfactions as a cause of some great revolutions and a contained rebellion. In H. D. Graham & T. R. Gurr (Eds.), *The history of violence in America*. New York: Praeger, 1969.

Dawidowtiz, L. S. *The war against the Jews, 1933–1945*. New York: Bantam Books, 1976.

Feierabend, I. K. Data collected by Feierabend group. In J. F. Kirkham, S. G. Levy, & W. J. Crotty (Eds.), *Assassination and political violence*. New York: Praeger, 1970.

Feierabend, I. K., & Feierabend, R. Violent consequences of violence. In H. Hirsch & D. C. Perry (Eds.), *Violence as politics*. New York: Harper & Row, 1973.

Feierabend, I. K., Feierabend, R. L. & Nesvold, B. A. Social change and political violence: Cross national patterns. In H. D. Graham & T. R. Gurr (Eds.), *The history of violence in America*. New York: Praeger, 1969.

Feierabend, I. K., Feierabend, R. L., Nesvold, B. A., & Jagger, F. Political violence and assassination. In J. F. Kirkham, S. G. Levy, & W. J. Crotty (Eds.), *Assassination and political violence*. New York: Praeger, 1970.

Finsterbusch, K. Theories of domestic and international conflict and their relationship. In H. Hirsch & D. C. Perry (Eds.), *Violence as politics*. New York: Harper & Row, 1973.

Freud, S. [*Group psychology and the analysis of the ego*] (J. Strachey, Ed. trans.). New York: Bantam Books, 1960. (Originally published, 1921.)

Gochman, C. S. Studies of international violence: Five easy pieces? In J. D. Singer (Ed.), *Explaining war*. Beverly Hills: Sage, 1979.

Gross, F. Political violence and terror in 19th and 20th century Russia and Eastern Europe. In J. F. Kirkham, S. G. Levy, & W. J. Crotty (Eds.), *Assassination and political violence*. New York: Praeger, 1970.

Gurr, T. R. A comparative study of civil strife. In H. D. Graham & T. R. Gurr (Eds.), *The history of violence in America*. New York: Praeger, 1969.

Gurr, T. R., & Bishop, V. F. Violent nations and others. *Journal of Conflict Resolution*, 1976, *20*, 79–110.

Haas, M. A response. *Journal of Conflict Resolution*, 1978, *22*, 163–164.

Hanson, D. J., & Bush, A. M. Anxiety and dogmatism. *Psychological Reports*, 1971, *29*, 366.

Holsti, O. R. The 1914 case. *American Political Science Review*, 1965, *59*, 365–378.

Horowitz, I. L. *An inventory of the terrorist as political deviant*. Paper presented at Conference on Terrorism, Office of External Research, State Department, Washington, D. C., October 1972.

Isard, W. The veto-incremax procedure: Potential for Vietnam conflict resolution. *Peace Research Society (International) Papers*, 1968, *10*, 148–162.

Isard, W., & Smith, T. On social decision procedures for conflict situations. *Peace Research Society (International) Papers*, 1967, *7*, 1–30.

Kelman, H. C., & Hamilton, V. L. Availability for violence: A study of U. S. public reactions to the trial of Lt. Calley. In J. D. Ben-Dak (Ed.), *The future of collective violence: Societal and international perspectives*. Lund, Sweden: Studentlitterature, 1974.

Kende, I. Twenty-five years of local wars. *Journal of Peace Research*, 1971, *8*, 5–22.

Kende, I. Wars of 10 years (1967–1976). *Journal of Peace Research*, 1978, *15*, 227–241.

Köhler, G. Imperialism as a level of analysis in correlates of war research. *Journal of Conflict Resolution*, 1975, *19*, 48–62.

Leiden, K. Data on assassination events. In J. F. Kirkham, S. G. Levy, & W. J. Crotty (Eds.), *Assassination and political violence*. New York: Praeger, 1970.

Levin, N. *The holocaust*. New York: Crowell, 1968.

Levine, E. P. Mediation in international politics: A universe and some observations. *Peace Research Society (International) Papers*, 1972, *18*, 23–43.

Levy, S. G. A 150-year study of political violence in the United States. In H. D. Graham & T. R. Gurr (Eds.), *The history of violence in America*. New York: Praeger, 1969.

Levy, S. G. A survey of public reaction to assassinations. In J. F. Kirkham, S. G. Levy, & W. J. Crotty (Eds.), *Assassination and political violence*. New York: Praeger, 1970. (a)

Levy, S. G. Assassination—levels, motivation, and attitudes. *Peace Research Society (International) Papers*, 1970, *14*, 47–82. (b)

Levy, S. G. The psychology of political activity. *Annals of Political and Social Science*, 1970, *391*, 83–96. (c)

Levy, S. G. Emotional reactions to six assassinations and relationships to the source. *Journalism Quarterly*, 1971, *48*, 339–343. (a)

Levy, S. G. Assassination and the theory of reduced alternatives. *Peace Research Society (International) Papers*, 1971, *17*, 75–92. (b)

Levy, S. G. Citizen responsiveness to governmental injustice. *Proceedings of the 80th Annual Convention of the American Psychological Association*, 1972, *7*, 161–162.

Levy, S. G. Governmental injustice and attitudes toward political violence. In J. Ben-Dak (Ed.), *The future of collective violence: Societal and international perspectives*. Lund, Sweden: Studenlitterature, 1974. (a)

Levy, S. G. Distance of politically violent events from a newspaper source over 150 years. *Journalism Quarterly*, 1974, *51*, 28–32. (b)

Levy, S. G. *Authoritarianism, commitment, and intolerance*. Paper presented at North American Peace Science Society meetings, Chicago, November 15, 1978.

Levy, S. G. Authoritarianism and information processing. *Bulletin of the Psychonomic Society*, 1979, *13*, 240–242.

Lindskold, S. Trust development, the GRIT proposal, and the effects of conciliatory acts on conflict and cooperation. *Psychological Bulletin*, 1978, *85*, 772–793.

Lorenz, K. *On aggression*. New York: Bantam Books, 1967.

Lupsha, P. A., & MacKinnon, C. Domestic political violence, 1965–1971: A radical perspective. In H. Hirsch & D. C. Perry (Eds.), *Violence as politics*. New York: Harper & Row, 1973.

Milgram, S. *Obedience to authority*. New York: Harper & Row, 1974.

Milstein, J., & Mitchell, W. Dynamics of the Vietnam conflict: A quantitative analysis and predictive simulation. *Peace Research Society (International) Papers*, 1968, *10*, 163–213.

Mitchell, H. E., & Byrne, D. Effects of jurors' attitudes and authoritarianism on judicial decisions. *Journal of Personality and Social Psychology*, 1973, *25*, 123–129.

Modelski, G. War and the great powers. *Peace Research Society (International) Papers*, 1972, *18*, 45–59.

North, R. C. Decision-making in crisis: An introduction. *Journal of Conflict Resolution*, 1962, *6*, 197–200.

North, R. C., & Choucri, N. Background conditions to the outbreak of the First World War. *Peace Research Society (International)Papers*, 1968, *9*, 125–132.

North, R. C., Brody, R. A., & Holsti, O. R. Some empirical data on the conflict spiral. *Peace Research Society (International) Papers*, 1964, *1*, 1–14.

Osgood, C. E. Suggestions for winning the real war with Communism. *Journal of Conflict Resolution*, 1959, *3*, 295–325.

Osgood, C. E., Suci, G. J., & Tannenbaum, P. H. *The measurement of meaning.* Urbana, Ill.: University of Illinois Press, 1957.

Phillips, W., & Rimkunas, R. The concept of crisis in international politics. *Journal of Peace Research*, 1978, *15*, 259–272.

Pilisuk, M., & Skolnick, P. Inducing trust: A test of the Osgood proposal. In P. Brickman (Ed.), *Social conflict.* Lexington, Mass.: Heath, 1974.

Prescott, W. H. *History of the conquest of Peru.* New York: New American Library (Mentor), 1961.

Rapoport, A. Lewis F. Richardson's mathematical theory of war. *Journal of Conflict Resolution*, 1957, *1*, 249–299.

Richardson, L. F. *Arms and insecurity.* Pittsburgh: Boxwood, 1960. (a)

Richardson, L. F. *Statistics of deadly quarrels.* Pittsburgh: Boxwood, 1960. (b)

Rokeach, M. *The open and closed mind.* New York: Basic Books, 1960.

Rummel, R. J. Testing some possible predictors of conflict behavior within and between nations. *Peace Research Society (International) Papers*, 1964, *1*, 79–111.

Rummel, R. J. Dimensions of conflict within nations, 1946–59. *Journal of Conflict Resolution*, 1966, *10*, 65–73.

Rummel, R. J. A warning on Michael Haas' international conflict. *Journal of Conflict Resolution*, 1978, *22*, 157–162.

Sales, S. M. Economic threat as a determinant of conversion rates in authoritarian and non-authoritarian churches. *Journal of Personality and Social Psychology*, 1972, *23*, 420–428.

Sales, S. M. Threat as a factor in authoritarianism: An analysis of archival data. *Journal of Personality and Social Psychology*, 1973, *28*, 44–57.

Schellenberg, J. A. County seat wars: A preliminary analysis. *Journal of Conflict Resolution*, 1970, *14*, 345–352.

Shils, E. A., & Janowitz, M. Cohesion and disintegration in the Wehrmacht in World War II. In D. Katz, D. Cartwright, S. Eldersveld, & A. M. Lee (Eds.), *Public opinion and propaganda.* New York: Holt, Rinehart, and Winston, 1954.

Simon, R. J. Deadly attacks upon public office holders in the United States. In J. F. Kirkham, S. G. Levy, & W. J. Crotty (Eds.), *Assassination and political violence.* New York: Praeger, 1970.

Singer, J. D. Introduction. In J. D. Singer (Ed.), *Explaining war.* Beverly Hills: Sage, 1979. (a)

Singer, J. D. From a study of war to peace research: Some criteria and strategies. In J. D. Singer (Ed.), *Explaining war.* Beverly Hills: 1979. (b)

Singer, J. D., & Small, M. National alliance commitments and war involvement, 1815–1945. *Peace Research Society (International) Papers*, 1966, *5*, 109–140.

Snyder, D. Collective violence. *Journal of Conflict Resolution*, 1978, *22*, 499–534.

Solzhenitsyn, A. I. *The Gulag Archipelago.* New York: Harper & Row (Perennial), 1973.

Sorokin, P. A. *Social and cultural dynamics* (Vol. 3), *Fluctuation of social relationships, war and revolution.* New York: American Book Company, 1937.

Stagner, R. Fascist attitudes: An exploratory study. *Journal of Social Psychology*, 1936, *7*, 309–313.

Starr, H., & Most, B. A. A return journey: Richardson "frontiers" and wars in the 1946–65 era. *Journal of Conflict Resolution*, 1978, *22*, 441–467.

Steiner, J. *Treblinka.* New York: Simon & Schuster (Signet), 1968.

Stohl, M. War and domestic political violence: The case of the United States 1890–1970. *Journal of Conflict Resolution*, 1975, *19*, 379–416.

Tanter, R. Dimensions of conflict behavior within and between nations, 1958–1960. *Journal of Conflict Resolution*, 1966, *10*, 41–64.

Tanter, R. International war and domestic turmoil: Some contemporary evidence. In H. D. Graham & T. R. Gurr (Eds.), *The history of violence in America*. New York: Praeger, 1969.

Tilly, C. Collective violence in European perspective. In H. D. Graham & T. R. Gurr (Eds.), *The history of violence in America*. New York: Praeger, 1969.

Tilly, C. The chaos of the living city. In H. Hirsch & D. C. Perry (Eds.), *Violence as politics*. New York: Harper & Row, 1973.

Wallace, M. Power, status, and international war. *Journal of Peace Research*, 1971, *8*, 23–35.

Wallace, M. D. Alliance polarization, cross-cutting, and international war, 1815–1964: A measurement procedure and some preliminary evidence. *Journal of Conflict Resolution*, 1973, *17*, 575–604.

Wallace, M. D., & Wilson, J. M. Non-linear arms race models. *Journal of Peace Research*, 1978, *15*, 175–192.

Wells-Barnett, I. *On lynchings*. New York: Arno Press & New York Times, 1969.

Wright, Q. *A study of war*. Chicago: University of Chicago Press, 1942.

Zinnes, D. A. Hostility in decision making. *Journal of Conflict Resolution*, 1962, *6*, 236–243.

4

RATIONALITY AND COLLECTIVE-CHOICE THEORY

ROBERT ABRAMS

Introduction

The term "collective-choice theory" means something quite specific in the present chapter. It refers to work which can be divided into the following categories: (a) axiomatic-choice theory; (b) spatial modeling (economic theories of politics); (c) game theory; and (d) collective- or public-goods theory.

The specialist in collective-choice theory will recognize that there is a good deal of overlap in these categories, and, in fact, it can be argued that the categories constitute the parts of a unified theory (Abrams, 1980). Nevertheless, for purposes of analysis, they will be discussed separately below.

These categories have also been described by different names. At various times, they have been referred to as "formal models," "mathematical models," or "rational-choice models." The first two terms refer to the fact that this work employs formal deduction as a methodology and that some probability theory, combinatorial theory, calculus, and set theory are employed in the theoretical analysis. The term "rational-choice models," whose implications provided the impetus for this paper, suggests that collective-choice theorists make certain assumptions about the individuals whose behavior they are attempting to model and explain. It also implies that these assumptions are different from those of sociologist and psychologist and are more akin to those of economists. In fact, the term, "political economy" has also been used to describe this field (Frohlich & Oppenheimer, 1978).

ROBERT ABRAMS • Department of Political Science, Brooklyn College, City University of New York, Brooklyn, New York 11210.

One of the misconceptions about collective-choice theory is that it not only presumes that individuals and groups strive toward rational behavior, but that such behavior is achievable. Further, the rational individual is said to be cold and calculating, more akin to the modern computer than to the passionate individual of traditional political philosophy. In this chapter, it will be argued that the results of collective-choice theory thus far tend to cast serious doubt on the very possibility of either individual or collective rationality. Further, the individual of collective-choice theory does not have to shed his or her cloak of humanity. All of the strengths, weaknesses, profundities, and absurdities of people as we know them can be taken into account. When such results are fully assimilated in the community of social scientists, the next question will be, what are the implications of such theoretical results? For present purposes, however, we will simply try to demonstrate the relationship between the collective-choice results and the notion of rationality.

Rationality

The term "rationality" has had a number of different connotations. For many traditional political philosophers, rationality, or the development of "reason," was the highest goal for humanity. The capacity to be reasonable or rational distinguished humans from animals, and the "age of reason" in the seventeenth century was characterized by a turning toward reason and away from faith in a supreme being. In that sense, reason has often been contrasted with superstition.

More recently, rationality has been frequently equated with "efficiency" in the economic sense of the term. Thus, to be rational came to mean minimizing one's costs relative to one's benefits. This notion of rational was also related to the notion of self-interest, as opposed to altruistic or community concerns. Adam Smith's butcher and baker provided society with meat and bread not out of any concern with society, but out of a desire to increase their personal gain.

With the Marxist critique of capitalist society, such rationality and efficiency were viewed as masks for the acquisition and maintenance of power by the bourgeoisie. This type of criticism reached its apogee, perhaps, at the time of the Vietnam War when Secretary of Defense McNamara brought his cost–benefit techniques from the Ford Motor Company to the jungles of Vietnam. The military and moral failure which ensued are well known.

Thus, the notion of rationality as economic efficiency has come to have a derogatory connotation among people of many political persuasions, and the idea of rational-choice models has been tainted with that same brush. This is not to say that there are not collective-choice theorists who use this limited notion of rationality, but rather that such a notion is not a prerequisite for collective-choice theory, as we will attempt to demonstrate below.

Individual and Collective Choice

The central idea in collective-choice theory is the notion of "choice." This means, quite simply, that we are concerned with situations in which we must choose between or among alternatives. There is no limit to the kinds of alternatives which the theory can consider. They can be candidates in an election, bills in a legislature, constitutions, political coalitions, public policies of various kinds, and so on. Our only limitation is that we cannot have everything. Either our resources are limited in such a way that we cannot have, say, both national health insurance and the latest missile system, or the situation is structured in such a way that the task is to select among alternatives—as when we choose a political leader, a president of a company, or someone for a job.

Moreover, it is assumed that there is more than one individual involved in the choice process. This means that each individual participates in the choice process and is affected by the outcome of that process. The exact nature of that participation and the effect depends on the particular situation.

It is also assumed that the individuals involved have preferences among these alternatives, although, as we shall see, they may be indifferent among the alternatives as well. The important problem here, however, is the *nature* of these preferences and the *grounds* for individuals having preferences.

Some philosophers have suggested a distinction between *needs* and *wants*. The latter involves human desires which tend to be somewhat superficial and certainly not essential. Although it is not completely clear what distinguishes a want from a need, it would seem that the desire for the latest automobile or a trip to Hawaii is not essential to individual welfare while rest, food, shelter, and the like are certainly essential. Most of us would also agree that a secure psychological environment, sex, and creative work are examples of things which people need in any meaningful sense of the term.

The question, then, is whether the individual preferences of collective-choice theory represent needs or wants. Some people (e.g., Braybrooke, 1968) have argued that collective-choice theory is insignificant because individual preferences can only represent wants. By this argument, there should be no normative significance in the aggregation of individual preferences into collective choices. This, of course, is simply the argument that democracy is undesirable because most individuals do not know what is good for them. As we shall see below, however, the problems raised in collective-choice theory would even apply to a society composed of individuals who had a clear understanding of human needs. In regard to our rationality discussion, the aggregation of individual preferences (wants) into collective outcomes would be irrational in the sense that it would produce results which individuals *should* not desire for their own good (i.e., not in the moral sense of "should").

By the "grounds" for an individual preference is meant the assumed reasons for individual preferences. For the most part, collective-choice theory has assumed that individuals want to maximize something called utility and that this utility is to be equated with self-satisfaction in the sense of hedonism or the Benthamite pleasure principle. As we will see, however, this is not a necessary assumption in collective-choice theory and, in fact, some interesting recent work has assumed that individuals are, to some extent, altruistic (Margolis, 1979). Nevertheless, the self-interest assumption is clearly an important part of collective-choice theory as it attempts to model the real political world.

Here again is the question of whether it is rational to be self-interested or altruistic. We can complicate the problem further by pointing out that an individual could also have preferences based on some notion of duty or right. Thus, a Kantian would choose those actions which were right in themselves and which could be universalized. That is, not only ought this individual do this act or make this choice or hold these preferences, but everyone else should do the same. Of course, if everyone knew what was right and behaved accordingly, there would be no need for politics or collective-choice theory. And, indeed, there are political philosophers who argue that the study of actions based on improper grounds is a false pursuit. Rather we should be trying to discover which actions are right or rational, in the Platonic sense of the term.

Implicit in our description of collective-choice theory is the assumption that individuals do not all hold the same preferences. This does not mean that individuals never agree, but that human nature involves conflicts of interest. This differs from the Marxist perspective in which such conflicts are limited to class societies; in the postrevolutionary classless society, such conflicts will not exist. Nevertheless, there is evidence to suggest that politics as conflict of interest will exist to some extent even in the classless society (Maguire, 1978).

Any general theory of rationality, then, must consider the relationship between the reasons for individual action, the individual action itself (in terms of either holding particular preferences or revealing those preferences in some form, such as voting), and the collective choices which emerge from those individual choices. In this chapter, however, we will simply assume that all individual preferences are rational in the sense that the individuals feel that they want some things more than others. This does not imply that we assume all preferences to be equally worthy. Ours is not an ethical relativist position. Rather, we assume that the central problem of politics is how to resolve conflict in a way which is equitable. This means that while we might consider some preferences to be outrageous, we cannot simply wish them out of existence or destroy the individuals who hold those preferences.

With this assumption, it becomes clear that the notion of rationality being used here is very much like Max Weber's *Zweckrationalität*, or means–end rationality, as opposed to his *Wertrationalität*, or value rationality. In other words, we are concerned here with the question of whether a particular individual choice (action) is the most effective in trying to achieve a particular outcome. We are also concerned with the question of whether a collective outcome is rational. By this we mean something very specific and limited—does the process by which individual choices are aggregated into a collective choice in fact product a collective choice. Our discussion below will make clear what we mean by this. We are not, then, asking whether the collective choice which does emerge is rational in the sense of being good or desirable, but simply whether there is, in fact, a determinate outcome and whether that outcome satisfies, to a certain specified extent, the individuals involved in the choice process.

Axiomatic-Choice Theory

Axiomatic-choice theory refers to the work which, in relatively recent times, begins with Arrow (1963). The best recent summary of this work is Plott (1976). In this section, we will review the so-called Arrow impossibility theorem as an illustration of this work and show the problems of rationality which it raises.

In terms of its background and origin, the Arrow work is related to welfare economics. In particular, the problem which welfare economists were considering was whether it would be possible to implement an economic system which was rationally planned in the sense that it produced and distributed goods and services according to consumer preferences. In a market system, of course, consumers are supposed to express their preferences through their purchases. Private enterprise is then supposed to respond to those preferences by producing what the consumer wants. Socialists of all kinds, however, have pointed out that such a system is not really efficient in producing and distributing the kinds of goods and services which people really need but rather only those goods and services which are profitable. In order to implement this system, a vast network of persuasion—advertising—tries to convince people that they want certain things which they would not want in the absence of such persuasion. To remedy this situation, socialist planners in the government would ascertain individual preferences in a way which would not involve propaganda and would thereby obtain "true" individual preferences. The problem for such theorists, however, was whether such a thing was possible.

The Arrow result suggests that, in general, such a goal is not possible. Moreover, since Arrow's work proceeds at a high level of abstraction, it is generally applicable to any situation in which individuals choose among alternatives and in which there is supposed to be a collective choice which emerges out of that process. This means that all of those questions which we call political are also subject to the implications of the Arrow result. Thus, the possibility of democracy itself is questioned.

Arrow's Social-Choice Theory

Arrow's central concern was whether there is a decision procedure—he called it a "social-welfare function"—which could aggregate individual preferences in such a way that a strong or weak ordering of alternatives could be produced and which would satisfy certain reasonable conditions. A strong ordering of alternatives is simply a ranking in which there are no ties. A weak ordering is a ranking which involves at least one tie. Let us illustrate this with the simple case of three individuals and three alternatives:

$$\text{Alternatives}$$

	A	$x > y > z$
Individuals	B	$x > z > y$
	C	$y > z > x$

In this case, individual A prefers x to y to z; B prefers x to z to y; and C prefers y to z to x. Now suppose that these alternatives are candidates for a public office and that only one can be chosen. If majority rule is the decision procedure, then clearly x would be chosen. For the purposes of the present example, it would not matter how z and y were ranked so long as we knew that x was the first choice. But, in other circumstances it would matter. Suppose, for example, that these alternatives were public policies and that funds were available to implement two of the three available alternatives. Then, we would want to know which two alternatives were preferred to the third. Now the problem is considerably more complicated. Consider two possible methods of determining the ordering of these alternatives: the Condorcet method and the Borda method. The Condorcet method says to compare the alternatives two at a time. The winner is that alternative which beats every other in such a pairwise comparison. In this case, individuals A and B prefer x to y, and x to z. Thus, x is the so-called Condorcet winner. In second place is y, since A and C prefer y to z. Notice that there is no majority preference for z over either of the other two alternatives, and thus z ranks last in the collective preference, which is $x > y > z$. Thus, if we had to choose two of the three alternatives, x and y would be our choices. Notice that here the social ranking of the alternatives was essential to our task.

The Borda method assigns numbers to the ranks. Thus, for example, we might give three points for a first-place vote, two for a second, and one for a third. In that case, alternative x would receive a total of 7 points, y, 6 points, and z, 5 points. The collective ordering, would be $x > y > z$, as it was when we used the Condorcet method. In this case, then, the two methods produce the same collective ordering, but this is not necessarily so.

There is another reason why it is necessary to know the collective ordering. Suppose that there was no alternative which received a majority of the first-place votes. Such a situation would occur in a primary election involving many candidates or in any situation where there was not a high level of agreement. Consider the following case:

Alternatives

	A	$x > y > z$
Individuals	B	$y > x > z$
	C	$z > x > y$

Here, no alternative receives a majority of the first-place votes, but a majority (A and C) prefers x to y, and a majority (A and B) prefers x to z. Thus, x is the Condorcet winner. Since a majority also prefers y to z (A and B), the collective ordering is $x > y > z$.

Arrow (1963) refers to the set of alternatives as the *environment*—in a political context we might refer to the environment as the agenda—and the particular group choice(s) as the *choice set*. The central problem for Arrow, then, is the selection of a choice set from an environment. For this he requires some kind of procedural mechanism, such as majority rule. The problem is how to determine which procedural mechanism to choose. This amounts to asking which procedural mechanism is best in some sense of the word. Here again we are involved in a means–end question: "best" for what? What are the criteria which any procedural mechanism must satisfy?

Arrow's theoretical strategy is first to try to establish conditions or criteria for the procedural mechanism which would not be controversial—that is, conditions which all reasonable people could accept. Presumably, after finding procedures which satisfy these weak conditions, he could then proceed to set more stringent requirements. As it turned out, there is no procedural mechanism which can satisfy even the supposedly weak conditions. That is, in essence, the Arrow impossibility theorem.

Arrow's Conditions

Connectivity. Arrow's first condition (or axiom, as he refers to it) is that for every pair of alternatives, any individual must either prefer one to the other or must be indifferent between them. He refers to this condition as connectivity. We might use the term comparability. In other words, any two alternatives must be comparable.

For purposes of Arrow's axiomatic treatment, the notion of connectivity presents no problems. It simply says that for any two alternatives, x and y, and for any individual, i, either $x\,P_i\,y$, $y\,P_i\,x$, or $x\,I_i\,y$. That is, either x is preferred to y by individual i, y is preferred to x, or i is indifferent between x and y. When we try to interpret this into real world examples, it is not difficult to see where connectivity does apply, but it is more difficult to see where it does not apply. As an example, suppose I am asked whether I prefer the moon or ice cream. Aside from the nonsensical aspect of the question, it is clear that there is no choice situation involved here. I have not been asked to choose between the moon and ice cream. I might, however, be asked whether I prefer to go to the moon or eat ice cream, at which point (assuming that going to the moon is a viable option) I have a choice and it makes sense to speak of preference and indifference. Thus, *connectivity is part of the definition of a choice situation. If two alternatives are not comparable in terms of preference or indifference, I am not in a choice situation.*

Transitivity.   The second of Arrow's axioms, transitivity, is, perhaps, the most important in terms of our discussion of rationality. In fact, the notion of transitivity may be taken as the definition of rationality in collective-choice theory. Briefly, transitivity says that if an individual prefers alternative x to y, and y to z, then that individual should prefer x to z. Transitivity, of course, is a mathematical notion which applies to numbers. In that context, it says that if one number is greater than a second number, and the second number is greater than a third number, then the first number is greater than the third.

There has been considerable debate about whether transitivity is a logical necessity in individual-preference orderings; whether it is desirable, if not a necessity; and whether, in fact, individual preference orderings in most real situations are transitive. Another problem is the relationship between individual transitivity and the transitivity of the collective-preference ordering. That is, do the transitivity requirements for individuals hold for the group as well? We will consider these issues in turn.

Intransitivity essentially means that if an individual prefers alternative x to y, and y to z, he or she prefers z to x. Now, on its face, this may not seem outrageous, or even a problem. But let us look more closely. Suppose that the alternatives are candidates in an election and that I am asked to designate one of them as my first choice. It cannot be x, since I prefer z to x; it cannot be z either, since I prefer y to z; but it also cannot be y; since I prefer x to y. In other words, if my preferences are intransitive, I cannot be said to have a first choice, and in a choice situation, I cannot act. Nor is this simply a problem of not being able to make up one's mind. Notice that I am not indifferent among the alternatives. I have very clear preferences.

The problem here is that intransitive preferences preclude an ordering of the alternatives which, as we saw, was a prerequisite for designating a choice set, or, more simply, making a choice. Thus, the intransitive ranking of the alternatives produces a *cyclical ordering: $x > y > z > x$ . . . .* It may now be clear why transitivity is tantamount to rationality in collective-choice theory. Given the goal (end) of choosing among available alternatives, transitive individual preferences are required (means). In other words, *transitivity is a rationality requirement where choosing is the goal.* In the absence of the necessity for choice, transitivity may or may not be rational, depending on the goal.

There are several more important points to make about transitivity. First, transitivity implies consistency, but only in a very particular sense of the term. That is, it does not imply that an individual does not change his or her mind about available preferences. Rather, it simply means that whatever the individual preferences, they must be transitive in choice situations. Second, intransitivity should not be confused with changing one's criterion for making a choice. To illustrate this, consider again an election involving three candidates. Suppose that in terms of foreign policy we prefer x to y and y to z, but that in terms of domestic policy we prefer z to x, and y to either z to x. What is at issue here is which criterion is more important, foreign or domestic policy. This is really a choice, then, between two different preference orders: $x > y > z$ or $y > z > x$. Moreover, if we cannot say that one of these criteria is more salient to us than the other, then, in essence, we are indifferent between x and y as our first choice. But, this is not the same as saying that our preferences are intransitive.

Some evidence has been produced which suggests a good deal of intransitivity in individual preferences (K. May, 1953). It could be that what is being observed is not necessarily intransitivity, but simply an unresolved conflict among the criteria for choice. If the conflict remains unresolved, then the chooser would be indifferent among the alternatives, as in the example above, and would either abstain from the choice process or would use some kind of random device (e.g., flipping a coin) in making a choice.

The implications of this distinction are important. If individual preferences are intransitive, and if transitivity is our definition of rationality, then those individuals are irrational. Now, there is nothing wrong with such a conclusion unless our theory presumes individually rational behavior, in which case the theory must be jettisoned. At present, however, this issue is unresolved; in fact, it is rarely confronted in the literature.

More importantly, however, the important results of collective-choice theory which we will analyze do not depend on individual preference transitivity. In fact, if individual preferences are intransitive, the results of collective-choice theory become even more firmly entrenched. In other words, *collective-choice theory has accepted the strong assumption that individual preferences are transitive or rational and has discovered that, for the most part, collective rationality or transitivity does not follow.* It is surely clear, then, that collective rationality, as defined here, could not possibly follow from individual irrationality.

Let us consider collective transitivity, since it is not clear that collective intransitivity always leads to the same problems as individual intransitivity. By "collective intransitivity" we mean a set of collective preferences which has been aggregated in some way from sets of individual preferences and which is intransitive. Consider the following famous example:

Alternatives

	A	$x > y > z$
Individuals	B	$y > z > x$
	C	$z > x > y$

Here the individual preferences of A, B, and C are all transitive. But, by the Condorcet method, x is preferred to y by A and C, y is preferred to z by A and B, and z is preferred to x by B and C. In other words, the collective preference order is $x > y > z > x$. . . , which, of course, is cyclical or intransitive. This is the famous "voter's paradox," a situation in which a set of transitive individual preferences is aggregated to produce a set of intransitive collective preferences.

Suppose this were an election. What would happen? This is not the same as a tie vote, since there is no indifference between any two of the alternatives. No matter which candidate is chosen, a majority of the voters would prefer another candidate. Clearly, such a situation would be a dilemma, since the goal of the voting process was to produce a majority choice but no such choice was forthcoming. It is in this sense that collective intransitivity is said to be irrational.

It is not necessarily the case, however, that all instances of collective intransitivity should preclude a reasonable collective choice. Consider the following example from Fishburn (1970):

Preference Orders

Number of voters for	(10)	$x > z > y$
each preference order	(10)	$y > x > z$
	(1)	$z > (xy)$ (tie vote)

Here, ten voters prefer x to z to y, ten prefer y to x to z; and one prefers z to x or y, but is indifferent between x and y. Notice that the top twenty voters have strong preference orderings (no indifference), while the lone individual in the third row has a weak preference ordering. In the previous example, we considered only strong individual preference orderings.

Using the Condorcet method we find that ten voters prefer x to y, ten prefer y to x, and one is indifferent. In other words, $x = y$, and there is collective indifference between x and y. On the other hand, twenty voters prefer x to z. Thus, we have, collectively, $x = y$, and $x > z$. Since $x = y$, then we should be able to substitute y for x and deduce that y is also preferred to z. In fact, however, 11 voters prefer z to y, while only 10 voters prefer y to z. Thus, the collective preference is $z > y$ which violates collective transitivity since, if $y = x > z$, then y should be preferred to z.

Nevertheless, it does not seem unreasonable to suggest that x should be the collective choice rather than y since 10 voters have x as their first choice and 11 voters have x as their second choice, while 10 voters have y as their first choice and only one voter has y as a second choice. This example suggests that there may be limitations to the notion of collective rationality as transitivity. There seemed to be a reasonable choice in this situation even though the collective preference was intransitive.

There are several questions which relate to the issue of individual and collective transitivity and especially to the problem of the voter's paradox. For example, why is the voter's paradox not a practical problem in the real political world, and how likely is it that the particular set of individual preferences which give rise to a cyclical majority will occur? These questions will be discussed below. For the present, we will continue our discussion of Arrow's conditions.

Unlimited Domain.   Arrow's first condition—as contrasted to the two "axioms" above—is called unlimited domain. This means, essentially, that there is to be no limitation on the way an individual can order his or her preferences. In political philosophy this might have been called, simply, freedom of choice. It is important to note here, however, that unlimited domain refers to the complete ordering of the alternatives and not simply to the selection of a first choice. Thus, it is forbidden by this condition that an individual be limited in any way (i.e., in his or her second choice, third choice, etc.). This condition applies as well to the collective choice.

This condition does not appear to be a rationality requirement. It does not seem that a limitation on individual or collective preference orders is "irrational" in any meaningful sense of the term. Of course, as we will see below, certain kinds of limitations on individual preference orderings do avoid the voter's paradox, while the unlimited-domain condition makes the paradox unavoidable. But, if a cyclical majority is an irrational outcome, then it would seem to be rational to limit individual preference orderings in order to avoid that situation. The problem, of course, is that the unlimited-domain condition represents a positive value. In the liberal democratic tradition we believe in freedom of choice. Given the irrational consequences of freedom of choice, however, we are forced to consider whether it is a rational value to hold.

Pareto Principle. Another of Arrow's conditions is the so-called Pareto principle. This is essentially a unanimity rule which says that if everyone in a group prefers one alternative to another, then the preferred alternative must be the collective choice. Another version of this rule says that if one individual in a group prefers one alternative to another, and everyone else is indifferent between them, then the preference of that one individual should be the collective preference. Again, this does not appear to be a rationality condition but rather a particular political value.

Independence of Infeasible Alternatives. This is a very complex and much debated condition, but, essentially, it says that the collective choice must be related in a direct way to the individual preferences. This is, of course, the basis of any democratic decision-making system. A more precise expression of this condition would be: If the set of individual preferences on which a collective choice is based does not change, then the collective choice should remain the same. Without going into great detail, we will simply say that this condition rules out decision procedures such as the Borda method which we described above, which use numerical indicators of utility. In other words, Arrow is an "ordinalist" in the sense that he does not believe utility can be expressed in numerical terms in a meaningful way. Rather, we are limited to ordinal rankings of alternatives.

The independence condition is also not a rationality condition. It simply expresses a very traditional belief of populist democracy.

Nondictatorship. Arrow's final condition is nondictatorship. As implied, this simply says that no individual in the group shall be the dictator. More precisely, if one individual in the group prefers x to y, while everyone else prefers y to x, then x shall not be the collective choice. This, too, is a value in democratic theory and not a rationality condition.

Arrow's Impossibility Theorem

Arrow's theorem says that the conditions described above cannot be satisfied simultaneously by any decision procedure. Put another way, there is a logical contradiction among these values. This means that we cannot satisfy some of these conditions without violating others.

In order to illustrate this point, consider the voter's paradox example above. There, the only way to come up with a collective choice is either to change the preference order of some individual or to impose the will of one individual on the other two. The first move violates the unlimited-domain condition—assuming there is not a voluntary change—while the second violates the nondictatorship condition. Thus, we cannot achieve the goal of a collective-choice process without violating one of these conditions.

The important point about the Arrow result is that it is completely general. It says that no numerical decision rule can avoid this contradiction—no form of majority rule and no form of representational decision making. This is because the theorem deals with the conditions on decision rules and because all of the conditions are meant to apply to all decision rules.

What the Arrow theorem says in terms of our rationality discussion is that it is irrational to try to implement the values expressed in the four conditions above. Notice that this is not at all the same as the traditional criticism of these conditions. For example, as we mentioned above, populist democracy has frequently been rejected on the grounds that ordinary people do not know what is best for a government to do. The Arrow analysis, on the other hand, takes populist democracy as a desirable value, but concludes that it is not implementable.

It should be pointed out that the Arrow theorem is a formal deduction from a set of axioms and conditions. It illustrates a logical contradiction. The implication for actual political practice is that if we think we are implementing these values, we are mistaken. The Arrow theorem, then, awakens us to certain basic problems about democracy of which we may not have been aware.

It is important to compare this conclusion with our discussion of the transitivity axiom. There, the task or goal was simply to make a collective choice. The absence of individual and collective transitivity would make that goal unattainable, and therefore intransitivity would be irrational. The Arrow conditions, on the other hand, represent values to be implemented in the collective-choice process. The Arrow result indicates that it is irrational to try to make a collective choice which satisfies those conditions since it is not logically possible. In both cases, there is a means–end notion of rationality.

Probability of the Voter's Paradox

The proof of the Arrow theorem depends on the set of individual preference orders which would produce a cyclical majority, as in our example above. For this reason, it is an important question whether the voter's paradox is a likely occurrence in real political situations. For if the paradox is possible but not very probable, the Arrow result remains interesting, but of little practical importance.

There is considerable difficulty in answering this question. In practice, we never see an example of a cyclical majority. Most people, in fact, have never heard the term. The reason for this is fairly simple. It is very easy to suppress the paradox or cover up its existence. For example, in most elections for political office, voters are asked only to indicate their first choice. As we saw above, a cyclical majority can only be observed if we know the preferences of individuals over an entire range of alternatives. Where there are many candidates, as in a party primary election, the usual procedure, if there is no majority winner during the initial voting, is to eliminate those candidates with the fewest votes and then hold a runoff election. It may have been that there was a cyclical majority over the candidates initially, but the elimination of some after the first round of voting means that this fact will never be known.

The two-party system also encourages the suppression of the paradox. Elaborate primaries are held in the presidential election, for example, with the idea of reducing the number of candidates to two, one for each major party. This also eliminates the possibility of the paradox, which requires at least three alternatives.

In committee settings, the paradox can be suppressed by devices such as sequential voting procedures where alternatives (policies, bills, etc.) are considered two at a time with the loser being eliminated. Consider, for instance, our voter's paradox example above. Suppose that first x and y were compared. Since x is preferred by a majority, y would be eliminated, and z would emerge as the winner since z was preferred by a majority to x. Thus, there is a winner even though the underlying preference structure would result in a cyclical majority by the Condorcet method.

In view of these practical difficulties, the strategy for studying the probability of the paradox has been to focus on the theoretical probability (Abrams, 1976; R. May, 1971; Niemi, 1969). In this case, the notion of probability which is used is the logical notion, as opposed to the relative frequency notion. That is, the probability of the occurrence of the voter's paradox is essentially the ratio of the number of times the paradox could occur—given a certain number of individuals, a certain number of alternatives, and an assumption that all possible individual preference orders over the possible alternatives are equally likely (the so-called equiprobability alternative)—to the total number of possible outcomes. For example, with three alternatives there are six possible individual preference orders ($m!$ or "m factorial," which means $1 \times 2 \cdots \times m$, where m is the number of alternatives). With three individuals and three alternatives, there are 216 different preference profiles. A preference profile is a set of individual preference orders. The formula for computing the number of possible preference profiles is $m!^n$ where m is the number of alternatives and n is the number of individuals. A cyclical majority would occur whenever the preference profile is the one in our example above, or any permutation of those three preference orders among the three individuals. Thus there are six paradox-producing preference profiles associated with that preference order. The following individual preference order also produces a cyclical majority:

Alternatives

	A	$x > z > y$
Individuals	B	$y > x > z$
	C	$z > y > x$

Associated with this preference profile are five other preference profiles (permutations of this one) which also produce cyclical majorities. Thus, there is a total of twelve paradox-producing preference profiles out of 216 possible preference profiles. The probability of the occurrence of the voter's paradox, then, for three individuals, three alternatives, and an equiprobability assumption is $12/216 = .056$. In other words, a cyclical majority would occur less than 6% of the time, a relatively low percentage.

The next question is whether this same low percentage holds as the number of individuals and/or alternatives is increased. The work in this area is relatively complex and difficult since the number of possible preference profiles increases dramatically as the number of individuals and alternatives increases. In short, however, the results with the equiprobability assumption indicate that the probability of the occurrence of the paradox does not rise above 10% with three alternatives and any number of individuals. On the other hand, as the number of alternatives increases, the pardox probability rises substantially. In fact, the paradox probability eventually approaches 1.00, or certainty, as the number of alternatives approaches infinity. The problem here, of course, is that in politics we are not interested in such large numbers of alternatives. In the more realistic political range, however, the paradox probability rises very slowly, so that even with a relatively large number of alternatives, the paradox probability is relatively low.

Such evidence indicates that the paradox probability, and hence, the Arrow problem, might not be of such importance. After all, we live in a relatively imperfect world, and a low paradox probability might be perfectly acceptable. The problem is that when we alter the equiprobability assumption, the paradox probability rises dramatically even for relatively few individuals and alternatives.

To see this more clearly, recall that the equiprobability assumption implies that any individual is as likely to have any one preference order as any other. In the real world this is highly unlikely. It means that when a set of alternatives is presented to a group, there is no *a priori* likelihood that any alternative will be favored over any other. It would be a strange society indeed which did not have certain predilections given its history and experience. To drop the equiprobability assumption means to assume that some alternatives, and hence, some individual preference orders, are more likely to be chosen than others. Suppose, for example, that alternative x in our examples above was more likely to be chosen than y. This would mean that the preference orders xyz and xzy would be more likely to occur than any of the other four preference orders.

With this nonequiprobability assumption—or "arbitrary culture," as it is called—the paradox probability is very high with relatively few individuals and alternatives (Abrams, 1976). This means that with a realistic assumption about *a priori* probabilities, the voter's paradox is likely to occur in practice, and for this reason the Arrow problem is serious and not trivial.

What this result also means is that the suppression of the paradox by the various means described above must be a pervasive phenomenon. In order to prove this with empirical data it would be necessary first to ascertain the preference orders of individuals over all of the alternatives and not simply the first choice. It would then be necessary to apply some method (e.g., the Condorcet criterion) which tries to establish a collective ordering over all of the alternatives. Sequential elimination processes would have to be avoided. The theory predicts, then, that in most cases a cyclical majority would be found.

Such a result would have devastating practical consequences. Suppose, for example, that there was a cyclical majority in an American presidential election! What would we do? Or, suppose that there were cyclical majorities for complex legislative alternatives in Congress. How would the situation be resolved? The problem is that *the theory of collective choice suggests that aggregative voting procedures cannot do what we have expected of them in the past, even when all of the manipulations of wily politicians are eliminated.* One important implication of this result is that the imposition of the values of some minority is inevitable in the political process, even in the best of all possible worlds where no one is trying to cheat or dominate anyone else. All that is required is that there be some degree of conflict of interest.

Such a conclusion is not heartening to democrats. It suggests that democracy may not be possible even in principle. In terms of our rationality discussion, then, democracy may not be a rational value to hold because it may not be implementable.

Single-Peakedness and Value Restrictedness

There are, however, ways of avoiding the paradox. We will mention two here which are related. The first is single-peakedness (Black, 1958). This is essentially a restriction on individual preference orders. More specifically, it says that some alternative shall not be the last choice for any individual. Note that single-peakedness is an alteration of Arrow's unlimited-domain condition.

In order to see what this restriction means, consider a single-issue dimension such as degree of government involvement in the economy. At one end of the issue scale is the "left" position which favors socialism and at the other end is the "right" position which favors extreme laissez-faire capitalism. The centrist position represents some combination of the two. Such a scale might be represented as follows:

x	y	z
LEFT	CENTER	RIGHT

SINGLE DIMENSION—GOVERNMENT INTERVENTION IN ECONOMY

A "leftist" would rank the issue positions $x > y > z$; a "rightist" would rank the issue positions $z > y > x$; a "centrist" would rank the issue positions either $y > x > z$ or $y > z > x$, depending on whether he or she preferred the left or right extreme as a second choice. The individual preference orders which seem to be held by no one are $x > z > y$, and $z > x > y$. This is because we have posited that the criterion for the ranking of the alternative issue positions is the degree of government intervention in the economy. By this criterion, no one of the far left or far right would have the opposite extreme as his or her second choice. Thus, when limiting the criterion for choosing among alternatives to a single dimension, the effect is to eliminate one alternative as anyone's last choice. In this case, y, the centrist position, was not the last choice of any individual. In other words, the preference orders xzy and zxy were eliminated.

When this happens, the voter's paradox cannot occur. To see this, recall that there were two basic paradox-producing preference profiles involving the six different preference orders of the three-alternative case. Moreover, the order xzy was in one of those preference profiles, while zxy was in the other. If both of these preference orders are eliminated, then the paradox cannot occur. Remember, however, that we have violated Arrow's condition of unlimited domain.

The second way of avoiding the paradox is "value-restrictedness" (Sen, 1966), which is a generalization of single-peakedness. It says that some alternative shall not be the first, second, or third choice of any individual for every triple of alternatives. In our example above, y was not the last choice of any individual. In value-restrictedness, that could apply to x and z as well. Similarly, if we eliminated x as anyone's first choice, the voter's paradox could not occur.

The point we are making here is that if Arrow's conditions are accepted, his conclusion follows inexorably. On the other hand, if there are certain alterations in those conditions, the paradox is avoidable. The important question, however, is the justification for those alterations. We have seen that the Arrow conditions represented values inherent in populist democracy, especially political equality. If we alter these conditions, suitable value justification must be offered. It is not enough to say that these new conditions are acceptable simply because they avoid the paradox. For, while that is true, they also involve a restriction of the freedom of choice which is also an important value. Nevertheless, our problem is that freedom of choice does not seem to be a rational value to hold in conjunction with Arrow's other conditions since it does not lead to determinate outcomes.

Preference Priority

One attempt to overcome the Arrow problem is Strasnick's (1976) notion of preference priority. Drawing on John Rawls's *A Theory of Justice* (1971), Strasnick argues that individuals should not be treated equally in determining the collective choice. Rather, the preference of the least advantaged individual should be given priority in any collective-choice situation. Thus, in the cyclical majority illustrated above, the impasse would be broken by determining which individual would fare worst under which outcome. The task then would be, simply, to pick as the collective choice that alternative which would maximize the benefits of the worst-off individual.

To some extent, the Strasnick solution would make voting unnecessary. All that would be required would be a determination of the individual preferences over the alternatives. The difficulty, however, is that in any preference-revealing situation there is an incentive for individuals to misrepresent their preferences in order to achieve the best results for them. In addition, it is not completely clear what the Strasnick solution would mean in certain types of situations. That is, when individuals are choosing among policies which have distributive effects built into them (e.g., a tax structure) there seems to be no difficulty. But, suppose the individuals are choosing among candidates for a job, where the beneficiary is going to be the candidate and not the choosers. In such a situation it is not clear how the notion of preference priority would be applicable. In fact, however, Strasnick's primary concern is those cases where there is a problem of distributive justice.

Cardinal Utility and the Independence Condition

As we mentioned above, Arrow's independence condition rules out the use of numerical indicators of utility. To see this, consider the following example:

Alternatives

		x	y	
	A	10	5	
Individuals	B	7	10	Utiles
	C	3	4	
		20	19	Sum of utiles

For the moment we will disregard the question of the meaning of "utile" and the very difficult question of whether the numbers given as utiles for one individual have the same meaning as the numbers for anyone else. The latter is the important question of the interpersonal comparison of utility.

In this case, x would be the collective choice since the total utility is greater than that of y. Notice, however, that x is not the Condorcet winner. Now change the utilities as follows:

Alternatives

		x	y	
	A	10	7	Utiles
Individuals	B	6	10	
	C	3	4	
		19	21	Sum of utiles

In this case, y is now the winner by the sum of utilities method and y is still the winner by the Condorcet method. In other words, the preference orderings of the individuals for x and y did not change, but the collective outcome changes. It was this situation that the independence condition was designed to avoid.

Nevertheless, by assuming only ordinal ranking of preferences, Arrow is avoiding the intensity question. He does this because a great deal of work by economists had failed to establish a satisfactory method for assigning numerical utility indicators. This is not the place to discuss the debate, but we should point out that some current theorists, such as Harsanyi (1976), do feel that the so-called von Neumann–Morgenstern utility functions are just such a cardinal indicator of utility.

The importance of this debate relates to the Arrow theorem. In some cases, cyclical majorities do not exist if cardinal utilities are used. For example, consider the following:

Alternatives

	A	x (10) $>$ y (9) $>$ z (8)
Individuals	B	y (9) $>$ z (6) $>$ x (5)
	C	z (8) $>$ x (4) $>$ y (2)

By the Condorcet criterion there is a cyclical majority. Yet, in terms of the sum of utilities, $z = 22$, $y = 20$, and $x = 19$. There is thus a clear collective-preference ordering. It is evident, then, that the question of preference intensity is crucial for the question of the paradox probability and the possibility of rational collective action. At this point, however, there is not complete agreement on whether there is a suitable cardinal indicator of utility, and there is some evidence that even with cardinal utility there are impossibility results similar to Arrow's (Schwartz, 1972).

Logrolling and Vote Trading

Some authors (e.g., Tullock, 1967) have suggested that the voter's paradox is not a serious problem because of the possibility of logrolling or vote trading (in the literature there is a distinction between the two). That is, decisions in politics are made over time, and there are many decisions to be made. This raises the possibility of logrolling, where one individual agrees to change his or her vote on a less preferred issue in return for a similar pledge from another chooser (or legislator, if we are considering legislatures). The expected result is that both traders will obtain the outcome they want on their most preferred issues, even though they do not achieve what they want on a less preferred issue.

In order to see this, consider the following example:

		Gasoline price decontrol	SALT-II treaty
Members (legislators)	A	x	y
	B	x	$-y$
	C	$-x$	$-y$
Result of majority vote		x	$-y$

Here three legislators must choose between approving or disapproving gasoline price decontrol and the SALT-II treaty. This is, of course, a simplified example for purposes of illustration, but the same analysis holds for large numbers of legislators and proposals.

In this example, legislator A supports both proposals, while legislator C opposes both proposals. Legislator B supports gasoline decontrol and opposes the treaty. In a straight vote, gasoline decontrol is passed and the treaty is defeated.

Consider now the alternatives which face each legislator. Since there is a yes or no vote on each issue, there are four alternatives: to support both proposals, to oppose both proposals, to support the first proposal and oppose the second, or to oppose the first and support the second. These alternatives can be represented symbolically as (x, y), $(-x, -y)$, $(x, -y)$, and

$(-x, y)$. Now, let us assign letters to these alternatives in order to make it easier to relate the present discussion to our previous discussion of the voter's paradox. Thus,

$$(x, y) = M$$

$$(-x, y) = N$$

$$(x, -y) = O$$

$$(-x, -y) = P$$

In other words, the two votes can be considered a package and can be represented as a single alternative. We might refer to such alternatives as *complex*, as opposed to *simple* alternatives which cannot be decomposed. For legislator A, M is the first choice, for B, O is the first choice, and for C, P is the first choice. Now, our question is, can we also indicate the second, third, and last choices for each legislator? This is a necessary step, as we will see, in determining whether vote trading is possible.

In order to determine the ranking over alternatives in this case, we must make several assumptions. First, we will assume the condition of *additivity*. Essentially, this implies that the utility for a more preferred alternative must be higher than the utility for a less preferred alternative. Thus, if (x, y) is A's first choice, then $(-x, -y)$ must be A's last choice, since either of the other two alternatives involves x or y, which have a higher utility than $-x$ or $-y$. Although this assumption appears to be logically necessary, we will see below that it is not, and that without additivity there can be very different results in our analysis.

A second assumption which we must make concerns the relative importance for each legislator of the two issues. That is, are the legislators more concerned about the outcomes on the SALT treaty or the gasoline price decontrol? Or are both issues equally important to them? This assumption determines the second and third preferences. To see this, suppose that A is more concerned about SALT than about gasoline decontrol. This means that he or she would rather see the SALT treaty passed than gasoline decontrol approved if forced to choose between the two. The preference ordering for A, then, is *MNOP*. Of course, P is the last choice since A does not obtain either desired outcome.

Now the question is whether this is a situation in which logrolling might take place. Remember, logrolling takes place only where some legislators are not satisfied with the outcome which would occur in the absence of logrolling and where there is some mutual benefit to the traders. Let us make further assumptions about the preference orders in order to create a logrolling situation. Assume that C is more concerned about gasoline decontrol than the SALT treaty and that B is equally concerned about both issues. The preference orders for B and C, then, would be $O(PM)N$ and $PNOM$, respectively. The parenthesis indicates that B is indifferent between M and P as a second choice.

The original outcome, then, $(x, -y)$, or O, is B's first choice, but it is the third choice for both A and C. The situation is obviously not satisfactory for A and C, though B is quite pleased. But, given our assumptions, it turns out that A and C can improve their positions by trading in the following way. If A agrees to vote against the gasoline price decontrol measure, and C agrees to vote for the SALT treaty, the new outcome would be $(-x, y)$ or N, which is the second choice for both A and C, but is B's last choice.

Notice that A and C can agree to alter their votes because they are both obtaining the outcome which they want on their most salient issue. In return, they are changing their vote on a less preferred alternative. At that point, however, B is in a position to offer either A or C a better deal. Suppose, for example, that B offers to vote for the SALT treaty. Then the outcome would be (x, y) which, of course, is A's first choice and B's second choice. Both legislators, then, would have improved their positions. That outcome, however, is least desirable for C. Legislator C, then, is in a position to offer B the following deal: C will vote for gasoline price decontrols and against the SALT treaty, with the result that the outcome would be $(x, -y)$, or M, which is B's first choice and C's third choice. Again, both legislators improve their position by trading.

Note, however, that outcome M is the original outcome without any trading! In other words, through a series of trades which were advantageous to the traders, the ultimate result was no different from what it would have been without trading. Of course, A and C are once again in a position where it would be advantageous for them to trade, but we now know that such trading would be futile.

What we now have here is a vote-trading cycle which is similar to the voting cycle of the voter's paradox. This is not accidental but is the result of the fact that the underlying preference profile over the alternatives is that of the voter's paradox. To see this, consider the preferences of A, B, and C over the alternatives:

Alternatives

A	$M > N > O > P$
Individuals B	$O > (PM) > N$
C	$P > N > O > M$

$M > N;\ O > M;\ N > O;\ O > P$

There is no Condorcet winner since there is no alternative which defeats every other alternative in a pairwise comparison. The cycle could be represented: $M = P > N > O > M$. In the literature (Koehler, 1975), this result has been generalized to say that an underlying preference profile which results in a cyclical majority is a prerequisite for logrolling. But this means that any logrolling under such circumstances must cycle in exactly the same way that the voter's paradox cycles. The result is an endless series of trades which could be ended only by some arbitrary device, such as a time limit, or some limitation on the trading process itself. This might be accomplished either by making vote trading illegal in some way or by preventing the communication necessary for coordinating vote trading.

The major implication of this result, however, is that vote trading or logrolling is not a way of avoiding the voter's paradox; nor is it a means of increasing the utility of all choosers involved. On the other hand, it has also been shown that the relationship between logrolling and cyclical majorities is not a necessary and sufficient one. That is, it is possible to have logrolling without an underlying voter's paradox and an underlying voter's paradox withot logrolling (Miller, 1977; Oppenheimer, 1975; Schwartz, 1977).

The Paradox of Vote Trading

Logrolling can also lead to another problem which Riker and Brams (1973) call the paradox of vote trading. In this situation, individuals trade votes in a way which increases their utility temporarily but results in less utility in the long run than would have been the case if they had not traded. Yet, if they refrain from trading, they will lose even more in the long run. We will illustrate this problem without developing the full argument.

Consider again a situation with three legislators and two dichotomous issues, but now add utility numbers as in the following:

	Proposals			
Legislators	A	x (1) $-x$ (−2)	y (1) $-y$ (−2)	
	B	x (1) $-x$ (−1)	$-y$ (2) y (−2)	
	C	$-x$ (2) x (−2)	y (1) $-y$ (−1)	
Result of majority vote		x	y	

The number in parentheses after the preferred alternative represents the utility for that member of having that preference become the majority preference. The number in parenthesis after the less preferred alternative is the cost to each member of having that alternative become the majority preference. Thus, for example, A receives a utility of 1 if his or her preferred alternative (x) is the majority choice but loses 2 utiles (whatever that may be) if $-x$ is the majority choice. In the initial vote on x, both A and B would be in the winning majority and would receive 1 utility unit, while C would lose 2. In the initial vote on y, A and C would be in the winning majority, each receiving 1 utile, while B would lose 2.

Each complex outcome, then, would be associated with a utility number which would be the sum of the utilities on each simple outcome. Thus, with the complex outcome (x, y) above, A would have a total of 2 utiles, B would have -1. Since (x, y) is the third choice of both B and C (this can be shown as in our previous example), they could trade votes. Thus, B could vote for $-x$ and C could vote for $-y$. The result would be $(-x, -y)$ which is the second choice for both B and C. At that point, A's utility outcome would be -4, while B and C would receive 1 utile each. The trade, then, resulted in an increase in utility for B and C, but a decrease for A.

It is not difficult to see that any of the three legislators could be in A's position, and the rest of the demonstration of the vote trader's paradox involves the introduction of two more dichotomous issues in which first B and then C find themselves in the position of losing utility as a result of vote trades by the other two legislators. In each case, the trades are beneficial to the traders. The result is that each player receives 1 utile in each situation in which he or she is a trader and loses 4 utiles in the one situation in which he or she is not a trader. This means that each legislator has a net loss of 2 utiles. On the other hand, if they had not traded, they would each be in A's position prior to the initial trade on one issue, and would be on the losing side twice. But the highest gain without trading is 2, while the greatest loss is only 1. Thus, there would be a net of zero utiles for every legislator without trading. This does not mean, however, that any legislators should refuse to trade, since the situation would be much worse for anyone who did so. To see this, suppose B refuses to trade on the grounds that everyone will be worse off if they trade than if they do not trade. At that point, A and C would have an incentive to trade since they would receive 1 utile each when they traded, they would receive 2 utiles when the complex outcome which was their first choice was the majority choice, and they would lose only 1 utile when the complex outcome which was their third choice was the majority outcome. The one nontrader would lose 4 utiles when the others traded, and would lose 1 utile in each of the other two situations in which the majority outcome was his or her third choice (remember, the nontrader's first choice would have been the majority choice in the case where the others traded). The traders, then, would receive a net gain of 2 utiles, whereas the legislator who refused to trade would lose 6 utiles. Here is a situation, then, in which trading does not lead to the best outcome possible, but if any one legislator tries to bring about a better outcome by not trading, the others have an incentive to improve their position by trading. The result is that the traders do well while the nontrader suffers. The legislators, then, have no choice but to make those trades which they know will make them worse off. This is the vote trader's paradox.

Notice that this is a different problem from that of the voter's paradox, where there was no collective outcome. In this case, there is a collective outcome, but it is not Pareto optimal. That is, there is another outcome which everyone would prefer.

Such an outcome can be said to be irrational on the grounds that it violates the maximizing notion implicit in the concept of preference. That is, to say that x is preferred to y means that in a choice situation, x would be chosen over y. Now let us distinguish again between individual and collective choice. In the logrolling discussion above, we saw an example of a situation where individuals preferred one alternative to another, but voted for the less-preferred alternative. Thus, a trader may have preferred x to $-x$ but in a trading situation voted for $-x$. This did not seem irrational, however, since that action was designed to maximize the individual's utility overall. Where the collective choice is one which is Pareto dominated by another, however, there is no sense in which that result can be said to be rational since everyone would be better off with the more preferred collective choice and since the postulated object of the collective-choice process is for everyone to do as well as he or she can.

Economic Theories of Politics—Spatial Models

The Arrow theorem and the work on the voter's paradox can be considered as a contribution to normative theory. We are told that certain values are inconsistent and that they cannot be implemented by any collective-decision procedure. This implies that it is not rational to try to implement such values.

Economic theories of politics, or spatial models, are concerned with the rationality of political action. They postulate rationality conditions and then ask what would rational political behavior look like. Presumably, the results of such work would be testable against behavior in the real world.

In this section, we will begin by discussing the seminal work of Anthony Downs (1957). Downs begins by postulating rational voters and rational political parties. In both cases, to be rational is to try to maximize benefits and minimize costs—a classical economic assumption applied to politics. For the voter in an election, this means that he or she will only vote if the benefits of voting outweigh the costs and will vote for one candidate over another only if the benefits which the voter can expect from the policies of that candidate are greater than the benefits which he or she can expect from the policies of any other candidate.

Notice that this is a relatively limited notion of rationality. It is similar to the notion of "role rationality" discussed by Benn and Mortimer (1976). The notion of role rationality means that an action is rational or irrational according to its appropriateness for a given role. Thus, for example, it is rational for a teacher *qua* teacher to spend extra time with students, even though that action may be irrational from the perspective of his or her activity as a scholar. Similarly, it may be rational from the viewpoint of conjugal harmony for a voter to vote as his or her spouse desires, but that is irrational in the Downsian model where the voter is attempting to maximize benefits from governmental activity.

Political parties are viewed by Downs as homogeneous teams of office seekers whose goal is to obtain the perquisites of office. In other words, Downsian parties do not seek office in order to implement certain policies but pledge to implement certain policies in order to obtain votes and win office.

It is important to remember that Downs was trying to determine what a political system would look like which had such rational voters and parties as its main components. He was not suggesting that his assumptions were realistic in the sense of being an accurate description of the way people behave. He was able to show, however, that the major components of the American political system could be deduced from such assumptions.

Note that Downs is providing reasons for preferences while Arrow would simply take preferences as given and then determine the consequences for different preference profiles and different decision rules. Downs, on the other hand, tries to provide rational grounds for certain preferences rather than others.

The basis for determining whether a voter will benefit from the policies of a particular party is the so-called policy distance. Downs uses the notion of a policy space to determine the issue position of the voters and parties. For example, a one-dimensional party space is equivalent to a single policy issue and can be represented by a single horizontal line. The famous example is the issue of governmental intervention in the economy which gives us the so-called "left-right" political divisions with which we are familiar.

LEFT   CENTER   RIGHT

If we substitute x, y, and z for left, center, and right, we have, essentially, the example used above to explain single-peakedness.

A two-dimensional model would involve both a horizontal and a vertical line. An n-dimensional model, of course, could not be represented on a two-dimensional plane.

Down's point is that individuals have a most preferred position somewhere in any policy space. The further one moves away from that most preferred position, the lower that position is in the voter's preference ordering.

With a large number of people, there will be a distribution of first preferences across the policy space. In determining their electoral strategies (i.e., what position in the policy space to adopt) the parties will try to find the single position which is closest to the first preferences of a majority of the voters.

For our purposes, it is not necessary to develop the Downsian analysis completely. Rather we will focus on those points which relate to our discussion of rationality. Perhaps the most important conclusion in Downs's analysis is that *it is not rational for his rational voters to vote in a large election*! This can be explained as follows. Even though a voter might have a clear notion that a particular party will be more beneficial to him or her than any other (putting aside the problem of whether a party's promise and performance are ever related), no single vote among a large number of votes will be of any significance. In other words, there does not seem to be a connection between the individual voter's act and the outcome which provides him or her benefits. The voter could just as easily reap the benefits without the cost of voting.

Such a result would imply that the millions of individuals who vote in American presidential elections would be irrational. While such a conclusion is plausible, it has bothered many of those who have worked on the problem. For that reason, there have been a number of attempts to provide alternative rationales for voting which allow it to be viewed as a rational act. Riker and Ordeshook (1973), for example, suggest that there is a psychological satisfaction to voting and to showing support for the political system. This may be correct, but it would not derive from the Downsian assumption that benefits come in the form of governmental policies.

Ferejohn and Fiorina (1974) suggest that there is always a possibility, however slim, that any one voter will be pivotal to the outcome of a close election. While that possibility is small, it is not nonexistent even in a large election. Therefore, given the relatively low cost of voting, it might be rational for a voter to vote on the grounds that he or she might be decisive.

Finally, it is implied in much public discussion that a voter ought to vote on the grounds that others might follow the example of the nonvoters— "what if no one voted?" While it is true that if no one voted there would not be an electoral system in this country, it does not follow that the action of any one individual has any effect on millions of others. For all intents and purposes, my vote is an independent act without consequences beyond the smallest range.

We are left, then, with the distinct impression that voting may be an irrational act; at least, that is the implication of the Downsian model. But this means that the only method available for an individual to achieve a particular end—the production of beneficial policies—is not appropriate.

Information and Rationality

In most discussions of rationality, it is assumed that an uninformed action cannot be rational. It may achieve a particular goal, but without appropriate information that would be accidental. The Downsian model makes some interesting comments on this question. First, Downs assumes that it is costly to acquire information. Therefore, the decision to become informed must involve knowledge about the relative costs of being informed or uninformed. Presumably, a voter must become informed to some extent in order to determine the issue positions of the parties; but, how much information is sufficient? For the moment, of course, we are disregarding the conclusion above that voting in large elections is not rational under any circumstances.

The difficulty is that we can never know whether we have sufficient information or whether the next fact uncovered would completely alter our judgment. For that reason, says Downs, the rational voter should be reluctant to gather information, especially since it would take time and effort away from pursuits which he or she knows all bring benefits. And, indeed, it is interesting that all of the major studies of American voters indicate an extremely low level of information. But this means that it is not necessarily irrational, or even a sign of apathy, that voters are not well informed. By the Downsian analysis, they are simply judging the relative costs of becoming informed against the potential benefits. Moreover, in a system of uncertain information, ideologies are developed as a means of obviating the need for information. That is, an ideology, as a generalized world view, gives an indication of the kinds of policies which would be implemented by parties which espoused such ideologies. It is, in other words, a kind of shorthand designed to communicate with voters and to reduce their need for information gathering.

This is, of course, a very different view of the relationship between rationality and information. It suggests that it may not be rational to increase one's fund of information in certain circumstances.

Party Strategies

While voters are trying to decide whether to vote and for whom, parties are trying to decide where the winning issue position lies in the policy space. In a world of certain information, such a position always exists when there is a single dimension and an odd number of voters. This position is the median—that is, the position which lies midway between the first preferences of the voters. In our three-person example above, the center position is the median.

The problem, then, for rational parties in a world of certain information is how to behave when everyone knows the best strategy. The answer, to some extent, is that there is no way to assure an electoral victory under such conditions without certain *ad hoc* restrictions. For example, it might be a rule that the first party which adopts the median position is the only party which can hold that position. Or, if parties are not allowed to "pass" each other along the one-dimensional issue position, then one party could take a position beyond the median, thereby preventing the other party from adopting that position.

Such limitations are stilted, however, and do not address the real problem of whether there is a rational strategy in certain circumstances. The point about this discussion, moreover, is that the difficulty in finding a rational strategy takes place in a world of complete information. Oddly, it is only the uncertainty of the real political world which induces parties to make different estimates of the distribution of voter preferences and hence to choose different strategies. Again, we are questioning the assumption that information is a prerequisite for rational action.

On the other hand, we are also aware that political parties in the United States frequently choose to imitate each other rather than to differentiate themselves from each other. One result of this is the well-known tendency of American political parties to gravitate toward the "middle of the road." The Downsian analysis predicts that this should be the case where voters and parties are rational utility maximizers and where the preference density function (i.e., the first preferences of the voters) is unimodal, that is, it has a single peak or mode. The unimodal preference density function indicates that a society is relatively homogeneous politically.

When the issue space is multidimensional, however, other problems can arise. For example, in the two-dimensional policy space, there is a possibility that a winning position may not exist. This is exactly the same as the voter's paradox result. To see this, consider Figure 1. Here, V_1, V_2, and V_3 are voters, and the curves drawn near each voter are the so-called indifference curves. The points along the indifference curves are all equidistant from the first preference of the particular voter, and for that reason are of equal utility for that voter. The indifference curve for each voter is that line

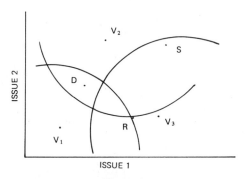

Figure 1

which is concave with respect to that voter. The voter is thus "indifferent" among these positions not in the sense that he or she does not care about them, but that he or she cares equally about them. Any point within the curve—that is, closer to the voter than the points on the indifference curve—is of greater utility to the voter; any point further away has a lower utility. Any voter prefers a position closer to him or her than farther away.

Now, suppose that this is an election involving these three voters. Which issue position—D, S, or R—is the winning position? Position R is on the intersection of the indifference curves of V_1 and V_2, while D is closer to V_1 and V_2 than the points on their indifference curve. Thus V_1 and V_2 would prefer D to R. Position S, on the other hand, is closer to V_2 and V_3 than is D. Therefore, V_2 and V_3 prefer S to D. Finally, V_1 and V_3 prefer R to S. Thus, there is a cycle: $D > R > S > D$. No matter which of the three positions was adopted by a particular party, a majority of the voters would prefer another position. In such a case, there is no rational strategy for any party.

There is another problem for party strategies when dealing with multidimensional issue spaces—how to weight a voter's position on the different dimensions. In the example above, they were weighted equally, so that V_1, for example, is simply the intersection of the lines drawn from V_1's positions on issues 1 and 2. Nevertheless, this is not necessarily the case. In the real political world, some issues are more important to us than others. For purposes of analysis, however, it is extraordinarily difficult to provide such weights, especially when there are large numbers of voters or issue dimensions.

Another approach, however, is the so-called lexicographic model (Taylor & Rae, 1971). Here it is assumed that voters in a multidimensional issue world do not meld their positions on the various issues into a single point by means of some kind of summation process. Rather, the voters first rank the issues according to their importance to them. Then, the voter considers each candidate on the issue which is most salient. If one candidate is preferred to the other on that issue, the voter will vote for that candidate regardless of the position on other issues. If, however, the candidates are equal on the most important issue, the voter will then turn to the second most important issue, and so on, until there is a clear preference.

Rae and Taylor's results are interesting for our discussion of rationality. On the one hand, they show that there are determinate outcomes (no cycles) when there are an odd number of voters, n dimensions (i.e., any number of dimensions), and when all voters have the same salience ordering of the dimensions (i.e., when all voters consider the same issues to be more important than others). This last condition does not mean that they agree on which dimensions are more important. On the other hand, when Rae and Taylor assume, more realistically, that voters do not rank the dimensions in the same way, there is generally no equilibrium point—that is, cycles prevail!

Both approaches, then, the lexicographic model, and the model of Figure 1, which assumes that all issues are of equal importance, conclude that in a multidimensional world, equilibria generally do not exist. This means that unless certain restrictions are either imposed or occur spontaneously (e.g., on the shape of individual utility functions, loss functions, lexicographic orderings, etc.), the choice of candidates will be imposed in much the same way as described in our discussion of axiomatic models above. Such results provide further evidence for the importance of the voter's paradox and for the difficulty of rational political action.

Game Theory

Some scholars believe that game theory is central to all collective-choice theory. They believe that all collective-choice situations can be cast as games—not the frivolous kind, but the kind which is the subject of the present analysis.

Game theory posits two or more *players* who are in choice situations. Each player has available *moves* or *strategies* (sets of moves) which are actions that result in *outcomes*. These outcomes involve payoffs, either positive or negative, to the players and are the result of the moves or strategies jointly by the players.

The description above is meant to be general. This allows for a wide range of applicability. Thus, players can be individuals, parties, nations, and so on. The moves and strategies which they have available can be physical action, inaction, expression of preference, or whatever. Similarly, outcomes may be states of affairs, a series of actions, or something else, all of which affect the players in some way and result in utility gain, utility loss, or no utility change.

Games in Extensive, Normal, and Characteristic-Function Form

There are several levels of analysis in game theory. At the first level are the games in *extensive form*. Such games are expressed by listing all of the players, the moves available to each, the consequences of all moves, and the ultimate payoffs to all of the players. Such games are presented in the so-called game tree seen in Figure 2.

At the next level are games in *normal form*. These games are expressed in matrix form, and include the players, their available strategies, and the payoffs for the various outcomes. Figure 3 is an example of a two-person game in normal form.

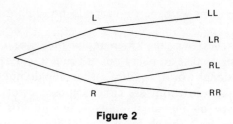

Figure 2

Finally, games in *characteristic-function form* list the possible coalitions of players, and the payoffs to each coalition, as seen in the following example:

$$v(\overline{A}) = v(\overline{B}) = v(\overline{C}) = 0$$
$$v(\overline{AB}) = v(\overline{AC}) = v(\overline{BC}) = 1$$
$$v(\overline{ABC}) = 3$$

These three levels of analysis are different essentially in the amount of information conveyed and the level of generality. Thus, games in extensive form not only list all of the players, moves, outcomes, and payoffs, but allow one to infer strategies and possible coalitions. Games in normal form do not include the particular moves available, but only the strategies. This is a more general level in the sense that games with different moves can be represented by the same matrix. Games in characteristic-function form do not include either moves or strategies, but rather the consequences of certain strategies, that is, coalitions. In game theory, a coalition is a decision by two or more players to coordinate their strategies in such a way that an outcome which they want is obtained. Thus, games with very different strategies can be represented by the same characteristic function. The interest in coalitions also means that the characteristic-function form is most appropriate for *n*-person games.

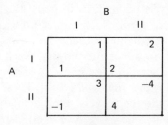

Figure 3

For a variety of reasons, game theory usually focuses on games in normal form or characteristic-function form. That is what we will do here.

Games resemble the voting situations described above in several important ways. First, the players can be seen as analogous to the voters. Second, the possible outcomes can be seen as the alternatives of voting theory. Third, the choice of moves or strategies can be viewed as the act of voting.

Generally, the outcomes of game theory are described in terms of the payoff to the players; and these payoffs are expressed in terms of cardinal utilities, although that is not necessary. The problem of choosing an appropriate strategy is similar whether cardinal utilities are used or the outcomes are simply ranked ordinally.

As in voting situations, there are individual and collective choices to be considered. And, as we will see, the problem of the relationship between individual and collective rationality which we saw in the voter's paradox arises also in game theory.

Two-Person Zero-Sum Games

At the simplest level are the class of two-person games. Such games have been classified according to the payoffs involved. In Figure 4, the numbers in the lower left-hand corner are the payoffs of player A, while the payoffs in the upper right-hand corner are those of B. Notice that the sum of the payoffs in each case are zero. It is for this reason that such games are called zero sum.

In terms of politics, such games clearly involve pure conflict. One player wins what another player loses. The appropriate analogue is a poker game, where the winning pot is filled with money from the losers.

Notice also that this is a game of *complete* information. Both players know all of the available strategies and all of the payoffs associated with all of the strategies. This is characteristic of the so-called "classical games" in game theory.

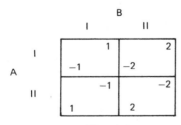

Figure 4

Individual and Collective Rationality in Games

As in voting situations, players are trying to bring about outcomes which they prefer. In so doing they must consider the outcomes and strategies available to them as well as to the other player(s). Individual rationality in game theory, then, is to choose the strategy which produces the best possible outcome for a particular player. Collective rationality means that there is no outcome other than the one chosen which would be preferred by everyone in the group.

For the two-person zero-sum game, it has been shown that there is always a "best" individual strategy and that there are no situations of collective irrationality (Von Neumann & Morgenstern, 1944). This is the so-called *minimax* result illustrated in Figure 5.

Notice that in Figure 5 if player A chooses strategy I, player B is best off choosing strategy II. If player A chooses strategy II, then B is better off choosing strategy I. Similarly, if player B chooses strategy I, then A should choose I, and if B chooses II, A should choose II. In this case there is no *dominant* strategy for either player; that is, no strategy that is best no matter what the other player does. Figure 6 is an example of a situation in which there is a dominant strategy. In Figure 6, if player A chooses strategy I, he or she receives a positive payoff of either 3 or 2. Strategy II brings a loss regardless of what B does. For that reason, strategy I is said to be a dominant strategy for player A. Player B, on the other hand, has no dominant strategy. His or her strategy choice depends completely on A's choice. Thus, if A chooses I, B is better off choosing II, but if A chooses II, B is better off choosing I. In this case, of course, since A has a dominant strategy, B can expect A to choose I, in which case B will choose II. If the rationality of one's opponent is assumed, as it is by Harsanyi (1977), then B can be sure which strategy A will choose.

Notice that B does best by choosing II only in the sense that he or she is minimizing his or her losses. It is not being claimed that the choice of strategy II produces the best outcome available for B in this game, but simply the best outcome contingent on A's expected action.

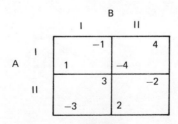

Figure 5

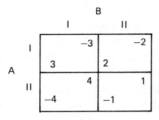

Figure 6

In our earlier example, however, there were no dominant outcomes. The question, then, is whether there is a best strategy for each player under such circumstances. The answer is yes. Moreover, the more general answer to this question is that there exists a "best" strategy for all two-person zero-sum games.

Solution Concepts

In game theory, a general rule for finding the best outcome is called a solution concept. It provides the criteria or criterion for choosing the outcome which is best for both (all) players. In terms of our discussion, the solution concept provides the rationality criterion.

The minimax notion is such a solution concept. It says that the best outcome for two-person zero-sum games is the outcome which is simultaneously the maximum of the row minima and the minimum of the column maxima. Let us illustrate this with our second example above. There, the row minima were 2 and −4. Note that these are A's payoffs. The maximum of the row minima, therefore, is 2. The column maxima are 3 and 2. The minimum of the column maxima is 2. Thus, in this case, the outcome in which A receives a payoff of 2 is the minimax solution of this game. It is simultaneously the maximum of the row minima and the minimum of the column maxima.

Mixed Strategies

This result, of course, is the result which we expected if A chose his or her dominant strategy and B made his or her best response. In this case, neither player can do better given the circumstances of this game, and, therefore, (I, II) is the best or most rational outcome for this game.

Consider our first example, however, in which the maximum of the row is −3, while the minimum of the column maxima is 1. Here there is no single best move for either player if the game is played once and if the players must choose simultaneously. Thus, A might try to obtain the highest possible payoff of 2 but runs the risk of losing 3. For this game there appears to be no intuitively best outcome.

Such games which do not have dominant strategies, however, do have best outcomes if the games are played more than once. To see this, let us consider this game without a dominant strategy. Suppose it were played many times, and suppose that each player flipped a coin before choosing a strategy. Over the long haul, each would choose strategies I and II approximately an equal number of times. This would mean that each outcome—(I, I), (I, II), (II, I), and (II, II)—would result approximately one-quarter of the time. This would mean that player A would receive a payoff of −4 (1+2−3−4) and B would receive a payoff of 4 for every four games played. In continued plays of the game, A's losses would increase while B's winnings increased. Obviously, A would not be pleased with that result.

There is, however, a way that A could improve his or her payoffs in repeated plays of the game. Strategy II produces a net loss of −1 (−3+2) while strategy I produces a net loss of −3 (1−4). Suppose, then, that A played only strategy II while B kept flipping a coin. This would mean that that outcome would alternate approximately equally between (II, I) and (II, II). Thus, A would have a net loss of −2 every four games instead of the −4 which accompanied the coin flipping. Such a result is clearly a major improvement for A.

On the other hand, B is no dummy. When it became apparent that A was playing a single strategy, B would simply play II all of the time. At that point, A would lose 4 every game. Thus, A must somehow maintain an element of uncertainty while trying to favor strategy II. In other words, strategy II must be used more than half of the time, but less than all of the time.

We will not go into detail here on the procedure for choosing the exact proportions but simply report that there is such an optimum. Once this optimum is computed, each player chooses a random device to determine when to use each strategy. For example, suppose the optimum for A is to use strategy II 70% of the time, then A would use a random device to determine what strategy to use on any particular play of the game. For example, A might fill a bowl with 30 red balls and 70 white balls and before each play of the game blindly pick a ball out of the bowl, playing II if a white ball were drawn and I if a red ball were drawn. In this way, the strategy chosen on any particular play of the game would be uncertain, but in the long haul it would be expected that II would be played 70% of the time and I, 30% of the time.

Such a procedure is known as a mixed strategy. This is in contrast to a pure strategy which involves choosing a single strategy, as in our example with a dominant strategy. A pure strategy can be thought of as a mixed strategy in which the probability of choosing one strategy is 1, while the probability of choosing the other strategy is zero.

The important result is that for every two-person zero-sum game, a "best outcome" does exist. Such an outcome, or *equilibrium* as it is sometimes called, can be achieved by the use of either pure or mixed strategies. Such a result is equivalent to the result in voting theory which says that if there are only two alternatives and an odd number of voters, there will always be a majority choice. It is important to stress, however, that this result holds for situations of pure conflict. We will see that in situations where this is not the case—for example, nonconstant-sum games, or constant-sum games which are not zero sum—such equilibria, or best outcomes, do not necessarily exist.

Prisoner's Dilemma

One famous case in which there is such an equilibrium, but in which that equilibrium is Pareto dominated by another, is the so-called prisoner's dilemma. This name comes from the original example used to illustrate this situation. In that example, two prisoners who have committed a crime are separated, and each is offered a deal by the district attorney. If they confess to the crime, there are two options. If the other prisoner has remained silent, then the prisoner who confesses is freed, while the other prisoner is virtually certain to be convicted and receive a jail term of ten years. If, on the other hand, the other prisoner also confesses, then neither is freed and both will probably be convicted and receive a sentence of five years each. If neither confesses, the district attorney has only enough evidence to convict them on a charge which carries a one-year sentence. This situation is seen in matrix form in Figure 7.

Now, what should a rational prisoner do? What is the best strategy for each? Notice that this game has a dominant individual strategy for each player, and that is to confess. This can be explained simply. Suppose

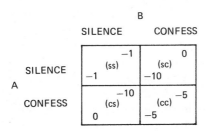

Figure 7

B remains silent. Then A can do best by confessing. But, suppose B confesses. Again, A can do best by confessing. The same is true for B. Whatever
A does, B is better off confessing. The joint outcome when both confess,
however, is five years in jail. Both prisoners would prefer the outcome in
which they went to jail for one year only. Thus, the outcome cc is Pareto
dominated by *ss*. Here is a case, then, where rational individual action
leads to an outcome which is irrational in the sense that both players prefer another outcome.

Suppose that the prisoners could communicate. Would this change
the result? For rational players, the answer is no! This is because each
prisoner would have an incentive to break the only agreement which would
come out of such a meeting—an agreement to remain silent. The dilemma
would not exist, of course, if there could be binding agreements. But, short
of that, there is no way that rational prisoners would voluntarily remain
silent.

Now, it might be that one prisoner wanted to sacrifice himself or herself for the other. In such a case, there would be no dilemma. If we are
talking about politics, however, such a situation is very unlikely. More
importantly, if one player prefers to sacrifice himself or herself for the
other, then the payoffs would not be that of the prisoner's dilemma. We
would be involved in a different game.

The prisoner's dilemma is not limited to the two-person case. In fact,
there can be *n*-person prisoner's dilemmas, as we will see below in the discussion of public goods.

N-Person Games

With more than two players, the possibility of coalitions is introduced. A coalition is simply an agreement between players to coordinate
their strategies in such a way that they both (all) benefit.

N-person game theory has focused on this question of coalition formation, and has asked what are the conditions under which coalitions
would or would not form. Such conditions are called *rationality conditions* in the literature, and are directly related to our discussion of rationality.

Rationality Conditions

In the literature on *n*-person games, certain conditions have been proposed as so-called rationality conditions. These conditions are supposed
to describe the behavior of rational individuals and to characterize rational collective outcomes.

The first of these conditions is the *individual rationality* condition
which says that an individual player in any game will not join a coalition

unless the payoff obtained is at least as great as the payoff which could be expected by not joining a coalition. Technically, the payoff which any player can assure himself or herself no matter what the other players do is referred to as that player's *security level*. For example, in a three-person prisoner's dilemma game, every player can avoid the worst possible payoff simply by playing the noncooperative strategy, just as the players in the two-person prisoner's dilemma illustrated above can assure that the maximum sentence each will receive is five years. While such a result is not desirable, it is certainly more desirable than the worst possible outcome. The individual rationality condition, then, says that no player should enter a coalition unless he or she can obtain a payoff greater than his or her security level.

In what sense is this a "rationality" condition? In our discussion of axiomatic-choice theory, rationality referred to the appropriate means for a particular end. Is this the case here? To answer this question, we must consider more closely the "payoffs" of game theory. These payoffs, expressed in numbers, are supposed to indicate relative utility. As such, they are subjective. They refer to the value of the outcomes for the players. Thus, the players could rank the outcome of a game just as they could rank the alternatives in a voting situation. In the prisoner's dilemma game above, for example, the preference orders of the outcomes would be as follows:

A	B
cs	sc
ss	ss
cc	cc
sc	cs

To say, then, that an individual should not join a coalition unless it provides a payoff higher than his or her security level simply means than an individual should try to obtain a payoff which is more preferred than one which is less preferred. In this sense, the individual rationality condition of game theory is equivalent to our assumptions in axiomatic choice theory.

The second rationality condition relates to more than one individual, that is, to coalitions of players. It says that the sum of the payoffs to the players in any coalition will be at least as great as the security level of that coalition. The notion of a security level of a coalition is analogous to that of the individual security level. It is the payoff which a coalition can assure itself regardless of the actions of the others. This is what we might call the *group rationality condition*.

Finally, if a so-called coalition of the whole (or grand coalition) forms, it is assumed that the payoff to that coalition should be the total payoff available in any particular game. For example, if the game involves splitting $100 among three players, and the players agree on a particular distribution of the money, the sum of the payoffs to the individual players should equal $100. Since there is only $100 to be distributed, the players cannot receive together more than $100. On the other hand, it would make no sense for them to distribute less—for example, to distribute $90 rather than the full $100. Remember, we are assuming that the players subjectively value these payoffs, and prefer, in this case, more money to less. If, on the other hand, the players were members of a monastic order where things of the material world were to be shunned, then the greater monetary payoffs would not be more desirable.

These three conditions seem relatively reasonable. Taken together they simply say that if an individual can bring about an outcome which he or she prefers to another outcome, it would be irrational to do otherwise. As we suggested originally, the claim that x is preferred to y is to be taken as identical to the statement that in a choice situation we would choose x over y unless by doing so we brought about outcome z which was lower than y on our preference scale.

For any game, the set of payoff disbursements to the players which satisfied these three conditions is said to constitute the *core*. The core, then, is that set of outcomes (a set can have a single element or member) which satisfies these three conditions. Such a notion is a *solution concept* in the same sense that the minimax notion discussed above is a solution concept—that is, a set of criteria for choosing among a set of possible outcomes. In that sense, the core conditions are also analogous to the Arrow conditions which we discussed above.

Expressed another way, the core is that outcome or group of outcomes which rational players would choose under conditions of complete information and with communication, bargaining, and binding agreements allowed. Ideally, we would want any solution concept to indicate a single rational outcome in order to facilitate prediction. That is, if we assume rational players and if we want to be able to predict the outcome of any game they might play, a solution concept which provided a unique outcome would be most desirable. On the other hand, if a solution concept composed of rationality conditions allowed for a number of possible outcomes, we could simply say that one member of the possible set of outcomes will be the chosen outcome. This, of course, makes our predictions probabilistic rather than determinate.

From the players' perspective, the existence of a number of rational outcomes is not of any greater importance than the existence of a single rational outcome, though it might make the bargaining more difficult and prolonged. The problem occurs when the core is empty—that is, when there is no disbursement of the payoffs which satisfies the core conditions. To illustrate the notion of an empty core, consider the game mentioned above in which $100 is to be divided. Let us now add the following rules to the game: (1) the players can bargain and make binding agreements; (2) any two of the players can split the $100 simply by agreeing to such an arrangement (of course, if two players split all of the money, the third player is left with nothing); (3) all three of the players can split the money; and (4) if the players cannot agree on a disbursement, no one receives anything. The characteristic function of such a game would be as follows:

$$v(\overline{A}) = v(\overline{B}) = v(\overline{C}) = 0$$
$$v(\overline{AB}) = v(\overline{AC}) = v(\overline{BC}) = 100$$
$$v(\overline{ABC}) = 100$$

The bar over the letters means a coalition. Thus $\overline{AB}$ refers to the coalition composed of players A and B. The "v" means the "value of" and is essentially the security level. That is, the security levels for all of the players in coalition by themselves (this is a strange notion, but it is used in game theory) is zero. This means that no matter what the other players do, each player can assure himself or herself of no loss. This can be done, of course, by simply not joining a coalition with any other player. The security level for any two-member coalition is $100. That is, by reaching an agreement, any two players can assure a total payoff to their coalition of $100 no matter what the third player does. Finally, the grand coalition also receives the available total of $100.

Now, how would this game be played? Let us assume that the players originally agree to share the $100 equally. This means that each player gets $33.33. At that point, however, any two players could improve their positions by agreeing to split the money evenly. But the third player who was left out would have an incentive to offer one of the other two players $51 and receive $49 himself. At that point, the player who would be left out would have an incentive to offer the player receiving $49 a deal in which the latter would receive $50.

Let us summarize these possible deals below.

		A	B	C
First coalition	$(\overline{ABC})$	$(33\frac{1}{3},$	$33\frac{1}{3},$	$33\frac{1}{3})$
Second coalition	$(\overline{AB})$	$(50,$	$50,$	$0\ )$
Third coalition	$(\overline{AC})$	$(51,$	$0,$	$49\ )$
Fourth coalition	$(\overline{BC})$	$(\ 0,$	$50,$	$50\ )$

It should be evident that there could be no stable outcome here so long as there is no restriction on bargaining. The deals would alternate endlessly between the second, third, and fourth coalitions above. Notice also that this situation is cyclical in exactly the same sense as the voter's paradox. For every disbursement favored by any two players, there is another disbursement which is preferred to that by another set of two players. There is thus a cyclical majority for disbursements in this situation.

Suppose, however, that the players also realized this and decided that it would be better to agree to some settlement than to continue endless negotiations. Suppose, for example, that they settled on the original even split between the three. Recall, however, that the characteristic function of the game indicated that the value of any two-person coalition was $100, whereas in the disbursement above the payoff to any two of the three players is $66.66. Thus, the payoff to any two players is less than the value of the game for any two-player coalition. But one of the rationality conditions, group rationality, said that the sum of the payoffs to the players should be at least equal to the value of the game for that coalition. In other words, by accepting the disbursement above, the players have accepted less than they could get in a coalition of two players.

Consider now any two-person coalition such as

$$(\overline{AB}, \overline{C}) = (50, 50, 0)$$

In this disbursement, the sum of the payoffs to players A and B equals the value of the game for any two-member coalition. The payoff for player C, however, is less than he or she could obtain in a two-member coalition, and for that reason, C has an incentive to try to form a coalition with one of the other players. If not, then C is accepting less as a payoff than he or she could obtain in a coalition, in violation of our second condition above.

If this example violates the rationality conditions, then there is no rational outcome to this game. But, we might ask whether it is not rational for the players to form some coalition—either the grand coalition or some two-player coalition—rather than risk endless cyclical bargaining in which no player receives anything. In this particular case, the endless bargaining would also be irrational on the grounds that it violates the group rationality condition. That is, if the disbursement is $(\overline{A}, \overline{B}, \overline{C}) = (0, 0, 0)$, this means that the players accept a payoff which is less than they could obtain in some coalition, which, as we argued above, violates the group rationality condition.

An important result in game theory is that all n-person constant-sum games such as the above have empty cores. A constant-sum game is one in which the sum of the payoffs to all possible coalitions and their complements (i.e., those players or coalitions not included in a particular coalition) is always the same.

It is not true, however, that cores do not exist. For example, the core does exist in the three-person prisoner's dilemma game. To see this, consider the characteristic function

$$v(\overline{A}) = v(\overline{B}) = v(\overline{C}) = -1$$
$$v(\overline{AB}) = v(\overline{BC}) = v(\overline{AC}) = 0$$
$$v(\overline{ABC}) = 3$$

This says that by playing alone, each player can assure himself or herself no worse than a payoff of −1 (in the three-person prisoner's dilemma, an individual always receives the worst possible payoff when trying to be "co-operative" if the other players are not "cooperative," as in the two-person case). Any two-player coalition can assure itself of a payoff of zero, while the grand coalition can assure itself a payoff of 3.

Consider now the disbursement (1, 1, 1). This means that each player receives a payoff of 1 as they would in the grand coalition. Notice that this disbursement satisfies the individual rationality condition since it is greater than the payoff which the players could receive alone; the sum of the payoffs to any two players is greater than the security level for two-player coalitions; and the sum of the payoffs for all three players is equal to the value of the grand coalition. In other words, this particular disburse-ment is in the core of the three-person prisoner's dilemma game.

The problem, of course, is that the purpose of a solution concept is to indicate a rational outcome to a game. In this case, however, the ra-tional outcome will not actually be achieved because the dominant strat-egy of each player is to choose the noncooperative strategy with its payoff of −1 for every player.

In the n-person constant-sum game, then, rational outcomes as de-fined by the core do not exist, while in the three-person prisoner's dilemma the core exists, but it is not the outcome when rational players choose their dominant strategies. It is important to stress, however, that cores do often exist in a great variety of games. Our point is simply that in a very large class of games they do not exist.

Imputations

Given the result above, the question is whether it is possible to alter the conditions of the core in such a way that the spirit of these conditions is not seriously violated—after all, they were defended on the grounds of rationality—and yet produce outcomes for all games. Moreover, as sug-gested above, the ideal result is to be able to indicate a single outcome. We have seen that just such a strategy was used to try to avoid the Arrow problem.

Which of the conditions should be altered or eliminated? It has gen-erally been argued that the condition of individual rationality is essential for any solution concept. Without this restriction, individuals could accept less than their security level. The spirit of the notion of rationality would certainly be violated were this to occur. A similar argument has been made for the condition of collective rationality involving the grand coalition. There seems to be no good reason for expecting that individuals in a grand coalition might rationally accept less than the total payoff available.

This has left the condition of group rationality involving coalitions smaller than the grand coalition. It has been argued that this condition could be eliminated with the least damage to the rationality notion. That is, it could be considered rational for an individual to accept a payoff less than he or she might obtain in a particular coalition as long as the payoff was greater than his security level. Thus, in the example above where $100 was to be divided, the outcome in which all three players shared equally violates the group rationality condition but not individual rationality or grand coalition rationality. The set of disbursements which satisfies the individual rationality condition and the grand-coalition rationality condition is the solution concept referred to as the *imputation* of a game.

The difficulty with the imputation notion is that it does little to restrict the possible rational outcomes. The imputation notion allows any one of a great number of possible disbursements to be considered rational. As a prescription for rational action, then, the imputation is of little help.

The core, then, is too stringent a requirement for rationality in a great many situations, while the imputation notion is too weak.

Domination

We might ask whether any of the possible disbursements of the imputation is superior to any other in some sense. The notion of domination suggests one way to discriminate. One outcome or disbursement is said to dominate another for a particular subset of players if the payoff to each of the members of the coalition in one of the outcomes is greater than the payoff in the other. For example, consider two of the possible disbursements in the game above in which $100 was to be divided:

$$
\begin{array}{cccc}
 & A & B & C \\
I & (50, & 50, & 0\ ) \\
II & (\ 0, & 60, & 40)
\end{array}
$$

In this case, players B and C prefer II to I since both receive a higher payoff in II than in I. Thus, II is said to dominate I via players B and C.

Suppose, however, that the disbursement

$$
\begin{array}{cccc}
 & A & B & C \\
III & (40, & 0, & 60)
\end{array}
$$

were added as a possiblity. Then, III would dominate II via players A and C. But, I also dominates III via players A and B. What we have now is essentially a cyclical majority:

$$I > III > II > I$$

In other words, the notion of domination cannot always be used to rank order all of the rational outcomes denoted by the imputation notion since it is subject to intransitivities in exactly the same way that we observed in the case of the voter's paradox.

The Shapley Value

The discussion above should not be interpreted to mean that there are no solution concepts in game theory which produce determinate and, hence, rational outcomes. One example of such a solution concept is the Shapley value (Shapley, 1953). The Shapley value applies to those games where the grand coalition is expected to form and does not, therefore, apply to all games; nor does it overcome the problems illustrated above. We will not illustrate the computation of the Shapley value in detail here. Rather we will simply say that it is a unique disbursement of payoffs whose computation is based on the security levels of the individual players. Essentially, the Shapley value assumes that if one player's security level is higher than that of another, then the player with the higher security level should receive a greater share of the payoff in the grand coalition.

The Shapley value also assumes that the grand coalition would be formed in stages, with a series of coalitions between players, beginning with a two-person coalition and gradually expanding to include all of the players. It is also assumed that all coalitions smaller than the grand coalition are equally likely to form and that it is equally likely that any one player will solicit any other player to form a coalition.

The disbursement which constitutes the Shapley value is the expected value of the particular game for all of the players. It is not necessarily the disbursement which would form in fact, but is, according to Shapley, an estimate of the players' average payoff prospects. That is, while the Shapley value may not be the actual disbursement in any particular game, it is likely to be the average of the disbursements of that game played many times by different players.

In terms of our rationality discussion, the notion of *expected value* is the key concept in the Shapley value. Let us now illustrate this notion. Suppose that two players, A and B, in a particular game, can obtain payoffs of 2 and 4 respectively without joining any coalitions. These are, then, their security levels. Suppose also that in a coalition together A and B could obtain a payoff of 8. Now the question is, if A and B did form this coalition, how should the payoff be divided? Shapley makes several assumptions. First, he assumes that the player who approaches the other to form a coalition is more anxious for the coalition than the player approached. This means that the initiator should expect less in the coalition. But how much less? The exact figure depends on many factors such as the bargaining ability of the players, the alternative coalitions available, and so on. Nevertheless, the individual rationality condition which we described above is accepted, so neither player will accept less in a coalition than his or her security level. Thus, the limit of any player's expected payoff in any coalition—that is, the maximum that any player could expect—would be the total payoff to the coalition less the security level of the other member of the coalition. In our example, A's maximum expectation would be 4 (8–4), while B's maximum expectation would be 6 (8–2). These maximum expectations, of course, would only apply to situations in which the player was approached by another to form a coalition. We might say, in more colorful terms, that the courting player receives less than the player to whom court is paid!

The same analysis applies to the next stage of coalition formation where a particular two-player coalition approaches a third player. That is, the third player, say C, can expect a maximum payoff which is the difference between the total payoff to the three-member coalition $\overline{ABC}$, and the security level of the two-member coalition $\overline{AB}$. Thus, suppose the payoff to the coalition $\overline{ABC}$ is 12, and C's security level is 6. Then, C's maximum expected payoff is 6 (12–6).

The Shapley value, then, involves the computation of the maximum expected payoff for every player at every stage of the game. It then assumes that every possible coalition sequence is equally likely. This means, in a three-player game, that every player will be solicited twice to form a two-player coalition, and that every player will also be solicited twice to form a grand coalition. In addition, every player will also be the initiator of the grand coalition on two occasions for which he or she can expect to receive only his or her security level. The Shapley value, then, is the sum of these maximum expectations, each of which has been multiplied by the proportion of times that each can be expected. For example, with three players there are six different sequences by which a grand coalition can be formed. Each player will be the last solicited member of the grand coalition in two of those instances. Thus, the maximum expectation for being the solicited third member of the grand coalition must be multiplied by one-third. The same applies to the maximum expectations for the two-member coalitions.

For purposes of our discussion, the important point is that the Shapley value is always a unique disbursement and, unlike the core, always exists. This, then, is an example in which rational collective action can be expected.

On the other hand, the Shapley value applies only to situations in which the grand coalition is expected to form. Notice also that the rationality conditions of the core notion involve *minimum expectations*, while the Shapley value employs the notion of *maximum expectations*. It is not clear whether this difference is related in any way to the fact that the core does not exist in certain classes of games.

Nash Equilibrium

While the Shapley value applies only to games with the grand coalition, the Nash equilibrium (Nash, 1950) applies to any two-player bargaining situation. If it is a bargaining situation, of course, we are not dealing with zero-sum games in which bargaining is not possible for obvious reasons. Thus, the Nash equilibrium applies to two-person non-zero-sum (or, variable-sum) games (see Figure 8).

In this game (Figure 8) both players have an incentive to avoid the outcomes (I, II) and (II, I). On the other hand, player A does better than B in (I, I), while B does better than A in (II, II). We could also say that in (I, I) player A has his or her way, while in (II, II) player B has his or her way.

Suppose, however, that the players were able to bargain and make binding agreements. Assume further that the game was played many times. This raises the possibility that the players could agree on, or at least negotiate about, the number of times each player should have his or her way. The question, then, is whether there is a particular proportion of times either A or B should have his or her way.

One solution to this bargaining problem is to simply say that the players will each have their way an equal number of times, Suppose, however, that one of the players objects. At that point a bargaining problem has arisen.

There are really two ways, then, of looking at this question: either as an arbitration or ethical problem (i.e., finding the "fair" solution) or as a power game (i.e., what either player can impose on the other). Here we will be concerned only with the latter.

In terms of power, the question is whether either player has the ability to force the other player to accept an outcome because of a threat. For example, A might say: "If I do not get my way at least 60% of the time, I

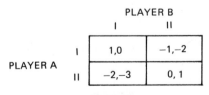

Figure 8

will only play strategy I." This would force player B to either choose strategy I all of the time, and receive nothing, or to counter with a threat—that is, to say to A, "If you play only I, I will play only II." Thus, while B would lose 2 every game, A would lose 1. Presumably, A would rather reduce his or her demand than lose 1 every game; but the question is, by how much?

The "rationality" question here is, what agreement would be reached by rational bargainers trying to maximize their own payoffs? The Nash solution takes the *threat potential* as the status quo in trying to determine the equilibrium point for such a game. That is, each bargainer must begin by considering the damage which the other bargainer could inflict if he or she were to carry out his or her threat. Thus, in the example above, A begins from the possibility that he or she could lose 1 in every game, while B must consider that he or she could lose 2 in every game. Clearly, A is in the stronger position. On the basis of this reasoning, Nash concludes that the rational outcome for this game, when played repeatedly, should be some combination of (I, I) and (II, II) which reflects the fact that player A has less to lose if both players carry out their threats.

In fact, in this situation A is in a position to demand the full payoff of 1 in every game according to the Nash solution. This rather unusual result comes from Nash's proof that there is a unique point which satisfies certain rationality axioms. That point is the maximum product of the difference between the conflict point and the utility of the two players. Figure 9 shows this more clearly. The point $(-1, -2)$ in Figure 9 is the conflict point; that is, the payoffs which would result if both players carried out their threats. For Nash, that is the status quo. The point $(0, 1)$ is equivalent to (II, II) in our matrix above. It is the point where player B receives 1 and A receives nothing. Consider now the distance from that point to the conflict point for each player. For A, the distance is $(0 - (-1)) = 1$, and for B it is $(1 - (-2)) = 3$. The product of those differences is $3(1) = 3$. Consider now the point $(1, 0)$. The distance from A's payoff to the conflict point is $(1 - (-1)) = 2$, while for B the distance is $(0 - (-2)) = 2$. The product of

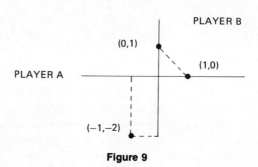

Figure 9

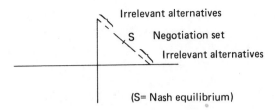

Figure 10

the differences is 4. As you can easily verify, there is no point along the line connecting (0, 1) and (1, 0) which produces a higher product than 4. Thus, the point (1, 0) is the Nash equilibrium. This means that player A is in a position to rationally demand that he or she receive a payoff of 1 every time the game is played, and that B should rationally accede to this demand rather than lose 2 every game.

Nash proposes this point as a solution to the game because it is the only point which satisfies four rationality criteria. First, the solution of the game should not depend on the way the players are labeled. Thus, if we reversed our labels "A" and "B" above it would not affect the outcome of the game, except in the sense that it would be B who would receive the payoff of one rather than A. This is also referred to as an *anonymity* condition. Second, the solution ought to be in the negotiation set. The negotiation set is that set of payoff points in which both players can do better than they can in any other set of points in that particular game. Thus, in our example above, if A and B choose any other payoff than one on the line connecting (0, 1) and (1, 0), they both receive negative payoffs. Third, the solution should not be affected by a linear transformation of the payoffs. This means that if the payoffs of either player are changed by applying a linear transformation [e.g., multiplying all of the payoffs by $(2x + 1)$] the solution should not change. Finally, suppose the status quo point remains unchanged, but that additional payoff pairs become available. This is somewhat difficult to see in Figure 9, but it would be clearer if the end points in the negotiation set were represented by payoffs greater than zero. In any case, this condition, which has also been called *independence of irrelevant alternatives* (compare the Arrow condition above of the same name) says that if both players have rejected an alternative, that alternative shall not affect the outcome of the negotiation provided that it does not alter the status quo point. Another way of intuitively understanding this point is to picture players rejecting a series of points near the end points of a negotiation set and then moving toward a midpoint solution. The direction of that movement will not be altered if the endpoints from which the players began are extended, as seen in Figure 10.

The Shapley Solution

L. S. Shapley, whose value solution concept we discussed above, has also proposed a solution concept for the two-person bargaining game. It differs from the Nash solution primarily in its choice of a status quo point. Shapley proposes that the status quo point be the security level of the two players. In certain cases, the security level for both players might be zero. For example, suppose the players had the option of not playing. Then neither player would win anything, nor would either lose. In such a case, the only settlement which could be negotiated would be one in which each player got his or her way half of the time. The threat potential in such games can be ignored because neither player is in a position to impose damage so long as the other can avoid that by simply refusing to play.

On the other hand, suppose that the "not play" option is simply not available. It is most likely, in fact, that real-life political bargaining games do not admit the "not play" option. Consider, for example, what it would mean for the United States not to play in the SALT game! In such cases, the security level would be determined by the payoffs of the particular game.

For example, in our game above, it can be shown that A's security level is $-.5$, while B's security level is -1.0. This can be achieved when each player uses a mixed strategy in which each strategy choice (i.e., I or II) is played an equal number of times, though the particular strategy in any particular game is chosen at random.

After computing the security level, Shapley then proceeds to find the solution as we did for the Nash equilibrium. In this case, then, the Shapley solution would be $(.75, .25)$. That is, player A would have his or her way three-quarters of the time, while player B would have his or her way one-quarter of the time. In other words, the Shapley solution makes the payoff more nearly even than the Nash solution. This is because the security level produces a higher possible payoff than the conflict result.

Our question, of course, is which of these solutions is more rational? In the context of the game theory literature this question is not answered. But this is an important omission since these solution concepts purport to be prescriptive. That is, they propose to tell us how rational players should behave in game situations. Presumably, however, the rational player would have to ask himself or herself whether he or she thought an opponent was making a Nash or Shapley assumption! In other words, it would not be clear whether a failure to reach an agreement would result in the kind of damage associated with the implementation of threats, or whether a player could count on achieving at least his or her security level. Our point, then, is that while the Nash and Shapley solutions are determinate for two-person bargaining games, it is not clear which approach rational players would choose.

On the other hand, a player's security level is, by definition, the payoff which he or she can assure himself or herself no matter what the other player does. But this would mean that either player can avoid the damage of a threat from the other player simply by mixing strategies in an appropriate way. Thus, in our example above, if B carried out his or her threat to use strategy II all of the time, then A could assure himself or herself a payoff of −.5 (his or her security level) by alternating between strategies I and II. (Actually, if B uses II all of the time, A can do even better by also using II; but this would reward B with a payoff of 1 every game.) With A mixing strategies that way, B can assure his or her security level either by using strategy II all of the time or by mixing strategies. Thus, the worst damage is done only if both players use their threat strategies. This means, however, that the security level is the more likely candidate for the status quo point.

Harsanyi's Risk–Dominance Relations

In an important recent book, John Harsanyi (1977) has extended the work of Nash (1953) and Frederik Zeuthen (1930) as it relates to the problem of two-person bargaining. Harsanyi shows that the Nash and Zeuthen theories are mathematically equivalent. Zeuthen was concerned with the process of the bargaining itself, especially the conditions which determine whether, at any particular stage, one player or the other should make a concession. If we think of the Nash equilibrium point in our example above, the Zeuthen analysis shows the process of arriving at that point through a series of proposals and counterproposals.

Harsanyi's contribution to this analysis is to show that the application of the so-called Bayesian rationality postulates provides determinate outcomes for all such games. In fact, he goes further and argues that the use of such postulates provides determinate solutions for all "classical" games.[1] This analysis is complex, however, and too detailed for present purposes. For that reason, we will concentrate only on Harsanyi's contribution to the two-person bargaining game which we have been discussing.

Suppose that our players A and B above are negotiating and that A proposes an alternative along the negotiation set as the payoff point. The problem for B is to determine whether he or she should accept or reject

---

[1]A "classical" game is one with the following characteristics: (1) complete information; (2) fully cooperative or fully noncooperative (i.e., players must be permitted to make firm and enforceable agreements before playing the game or they must not be permitted to make such agreements at all); (3) the game must be representable in normal form—Harsanyi has shown that there are games which are fundamentally altered when converted to the normal form and such games are not "classical."

the proposal, come up with a new proposal, or repeat any previous proposal which he or she has made. Harsanyi suggests a way for determining who should make a concession at any point. Essentially it involves first determining the status quo point as discussed above. That is, if there is no agreement and neither player is willing to make a concession, then each player would use his or her threat strategies, or security level strategies, as discussed above. The task for each player is to make subjective probability estimates of the likelihood that the other player will either make a concession or revert to his or her security level. Harsanyi calls the outcomes associated with the use of threat strategies the *conflict point*.

Since the players are proposing alternatives along the negotiation set, we know that any proposal from either player will be preferable to the conflict point. But we do not know for certain that the opponent will in fact use his or her threat strategy. That is, if one player refuses to make any concession from a particular demand, the other player must either accede to the demand or carry out his or her threat. In probability terms, if the probability of making a concession is p, then the probability of not making a concession is $1-p$. Each player, in Harsanyi's analysis, must make subjective estimates of those probabilities in determining whether to make a concession or stick to his or her demand. For Harsanyi, a player should stick to the demand if the probability of obtaining a concession from one's opponent (i.e., having one's way) times the utility associated with that outcome, plus the probability of having one's opponent refuse the demand and implement the threat strategy times the utility of the conflict point which would result is greater than or equal to the utility associated with acceding to one's opponent's demand. In symbols,

$$(1 - p_{ji}) \cdot U_i(A_i) + p_{ji} \cdot U_i(C) \geqslant U_i(A_j)$$

where p_{ji} is the probability that one's opponent will not accede to your demand; $(1 - p_{ji})$ is the probability that he or she will accede to your demand; $U_i(A_i)$ is the utility for player i when his or her opponent accepts his or her demand; $U_i(C)$ is one's utility for the conflict outcome; and $U_i(A_j)$ is one's utility for the opponent's demand.

Harsanyi then invokes Zeuthen's principle which says that the player who is more willing to risk the consequences of a possible conflict, as shown by the formula above, should not make a concession. Conversely, the player who is less willing to take such a risk ought to be the one who makes the concession. If, on the other hand, both players are equally willing to risk conflict, then both players should make concessions. The culmination of this process, says Harsanyi, is the Nash equilibrium.

For purposes of our discussion, several points should be noted about the Harsanyi analysis. First, the probabilities are all subjective. This means that the issue of whether such probabilities are "true" does not arise. Second, the utilities are also subjective, as they always are in utility theory. On the other hand, once these probabilities and utilities are given, it is an objective question as to which player should make concessions. In other words, we do not judge the players' rationality in determining the probabilities and utilities; but once these are given, we can then determine whether a particular concession was or was not rational.

The subjective probabilities to which Harsanyi refers are not simply groundless guesses on the part of the players. There are, in fact, certain "rationality postulates" which Harsanyi puts forward as the foundation for a rational theory of subjective probability. In particular, it must be assumed that one's opponent is rational in the same way that one is. Nevertheless, Harsanyi does admit the possibility that not all players will be rational, in which case "our theory will need appropriate modifications in order to enable each player to take full advantage of—and at the same time also take full precaution against—any irrational behavior that he might anticipate on the part of the other players" (1977, p. 19). Harsanyi does stress, however, that the choice of such subjective probabilities in a game situation where the strategies and payoffs are all known is considerably less difficult than in decision making in general (1977, p. 292, note 7).

There is, however, an important problem here. Recall that the Zeuthen analysis and the Nash analysis were shown to be formally equivalent. This means that we could expect the result of a bargaining situation to be the Nash equilibrium. On the other hand, the bargainers are employing subjective probabilities in determining whether to accede to demands. This raises the possibility that the bargaining would end either at a point on the negotiation set which was not a Nash equilibrium, or that players could retreat to their security levels. Harsanyi himself recognizes this possibility: "in a true bargaining game the solution will tend to lie in the middle range of the negotiation set (except if the two players' utility functions, i.e., their attitudes toward risk, are very dissimilar)" (1977, p. 186). This caveat is difficult to understand. If the two players are rational, if there is a rational solution (Nash equilibrium), and if everyone has complete information, why would the players "bargain"? Why wouldn't they simply sit down and figure out the Nash equilibrium?

In any case, Harsanyi's rationality postulates are similar in spirit to the rationality postulates which we have discussed before. In addition to the postulate of "mutually expected rationality" above, he assumes that rational players will always prefer strategies yielding higher payoffs to those yielding lower payoffs; that rational players will be indifferent between strategies yielding equal payoffs; and that rational players will not be satisfied until they have found strategies which yield the maximum possible payoff.

The Nash–Zeuthen–Harsanyi work, then, does indicate that determinate outcomes exist under particular conditions. For these theories, rational collective behavior is possible. The strictures necessary to achieve these results, however, are formidable: there must be complete information; it must be possible to make binding agreements; and the players must be averse to risk in approximately the same measure. Clearly, such requirements limit the applicability of this work.

Collective Goods

The theory of "collective goods" (also called "public goods") has been developed primarily by economists, even though the applications have proven most relevant to politics. A collective good is one whose benefits can be enjoyed simultaneously by more than one individual. It is contrasted with a private good, which benefits only one individual at a time. Collective goods need not be supplied by governments. A system of trust among acquaintances can be considered a collective good for them. At the national level, collective or public goods include things like clean air, national security, political stability, and so on.

The discovery of the notion of collective goods in economics can be attributed to Mazzola, Sax, and Lindahl (see Musgrave & Peacock, 1958). It became immediately apparent that the analysis of collective goods differed in important respects from the analysis of private goods. In particular, it became necessary to deal with the question of the appropriate "share" of the "production costs" of the collective goods to be borne by the members of a group. Economists such as Lindahl argued that an individual share of the costs should depend on the (subjective) valuation which an individual placed on a particular level of supply of the collective good. The so-called Lindahl equilibrium, then, is the point at which each individual paid a share of the costs of the collective good which reflected the benefit enjoyed by each.

In relation to our previous analysis, such an equilibrium is equivalent to a choice set in the axiomatic choice analysis, a "winning position" in spatial modeling, or a dominant outcome in game theory. As in these analyses, the existence of such a collective equilibrium represents a rational outcome while the absence of such an equilibrium represents an irrational outcome. As we will see below, the problem in the collective-goods theory is that although these equilibria exist, they are Pareto dominated by other outcomes. In this sense, they share the rationality problem of the prisoner's dilemma.

Free Riders

Since collective goods are available to everyone in a particular group if they are available to anyone, there is an incentive for each individual to try to enjoy a good without paying for it. Sometimes "payment" may be in monetary terms, as when a community wants to build a road. (We will discuss below the role of government taxation in this process.) At other times, however, the costs may simply be action or inaction on the part of individuals. For example, the absence of crime can be seen as a collective good. One way to combat crime is to pay for police, jails, courts, and so on. Another way, however, is to induce individuals not to commit crimes. For those individuals contemplating a life of at least some crime (here we include not only street violence but also white-collar crime), refraining from such activities represents a cost—an "opportunity cost" as economists would say. Now, if everyone was a criminal, the result would be detrimental to everyone. After all, a criminal's benefit depends, to some extent, on the fact that most others obey the law. In a law-abiding society, then, a criminal is a *free rider*, obtaining the benefits of such a society without contributing to its maintenance.

The notion of a free rider, and its implications for the voluntary provision of collective goods, was developed by economists such as Samuelson (1954), Buchanan and Stubblebine (1962), and Olson (1965). Olson, in particular, pointed out that in large groups, no individual had an incentive to contribute to the provision of the collective good for several reasons. First, since the group was large, the individual's single contribution would not make a significant difference. He or she could not assure the provision of the collective good by his or her contribution, nor could his or her failure to do so undermine the efforts of others. Second, the actions of a single individual in a large group would go unnoticed. Thus, there would be no praise for a positive role and no blame or opprobrium for the failure to contribute. Finally, the individual who did receive the collective good without paying for it would be in a better position in terms of costs and benefits than the individual who had paid for it.

The difficulty is that if everyone reasons that way—and Olson argues that such reasoning is individually rational—then there would be no voluntary provision of collective goods in large groups. Of course, it might just be that everyone in the group feels that it would be wrong to be a free rider. In such a case, there would be no free-rider problem. It is important to note, however, that if the individual free rider is rational, then the individual who is not a free rider is either irrational or rational under some other definition of the term. For example, Benn (1979) argues that the "consequentialist presuppositions" in Olson's model are not the only basis for rational action. He suggests that an action is individually rational if it is somehow expressive of an individual's values and is consistent with the character of that individual.

What is at issue in this debate, however, is not the definition of rationality. We are more interested in the consequences of certain assumptions about individual behavior for the process of collective choice, whether those assumptions are seen as rational or irrational. Thus, if individuals

<table>
<thead>
<tr><th></th><th colspan="2">COLLECTIVE</th></tr>
<tr><th></th><th>CONTRIBUTE</th><th>NOT CONTRIBUTE</th></tr>
</thead>
<tbody>
<tr><td>CONTRIBUTE</td><td>Collective
Good</td><td>No Collective
Good</td></tr>
<tr><td>NOT
CONTRIBUTE</td><td>Collective
Good</td><td>No Collective
Good</td></tr>
</tbody>
</table>

INDIVIDUAL

Figure 11

want to obtain the greatest benefit for the least costs, then we must confront the free-rider problem. If however, they are concerned only with whether a particular act is right or wrong, then there may be no free-rider problem. Which of these assumptions is correct at any particular time and place, however, is a matter for empirical verification.

Free Rider and Prisoner's Dilemma

Hardin (1971) pointed out that the free-rider problem was structurally the same as an n-person prisoner's dilemma. In order to see this, consider the game of "individual vs. collective" in Figure 11.

Here, the dominant strategy for the individual is to "not contribute," regardless of the actions of the "collective." The problem, of course, is that if everyone reasons that way, no one will contribute anything and the collective good will not be provided. Here again, we have a situation in which there is an equilibrium outcome (no one pays) but that outcome is dominated by another outcome (everyone pays) which everyone prefers. This is true on the assumption that everyone prefers the outcome in which the collective good is provided and everyone contributes to the outcome in which no one contributes and the collective good is not provided. Do not forget, the collective good is, by definition, something which everyone in the appropriate group wants. The problem is a strategic one: Is it necessary for an individual to pay in order to obtain it?

Hardin points out that if this were a voting situation, in which the possible outcomes in the cells above were the alternatives, the outcome in which everyone contributed would be a weak Condorcet choice. It is for this reason that a government would be justified in taxing citizens in order to provide a collective good which everyone wanted but which could not be provided voluntarily (i.e., without governmental intervention) for the strategic reasons which we have described above.

Problems of Preference Revelation

If a government is justified in trying to provide a collective good which is generally desired and which cannot be provided by the market mechanism or a voluntary collective process, it still faces an important problem. It must determine the tax share which each individual must pay. In our system, we give lip service to the notion of "progressive" taxation in which those who can afford more are taxed more. In practice, of course, this does not necessarily work out, and there are, moreover, "regressive" taxes such as social security and sales taxes. Nevertheless, the principle remains.

Another principle of "just taxation," however, is that individuals should pay for benefits received according to the value of those benefits to them. Thus, one individual pays a higher tax share than another if the value of the benefits provided is greater. The problem here is that everyone has an incentive to underestimate the value of the benefit received in order to reduce his or her tax share. This problem has received a great deal of attention in the literature (e.g., the special issue of *Public Choice*, 1977) and there have been some ingenious attempts to overcome it. Nevertheless, it remains relatively intractable. This means that neither voluntary collective action nor governmental intervention can provide solutions to the free-rider problem. Of course, government can simply impose taxes in any way it wants and provide collective goods. This is obviously a "solution" to the free-rider problem, though an undesirable one.

Noncooperation without Prisoner's Dilemma

In terms of our rationality discussion, the free-rider problem represents an irrational collective situation because an outcome is chosen which is not most preferred but where maximizing behavior has been assumed. It should be pointed out, however, that not all instances of noncooperation are to be viewed in these terms (see Figure 12). Here both A and B have dominant strategies—that is, the noncooperative strategy. For purposes of illustration we are using the example of pollution. Notice, however, that the two individuals here do not have a mutual preference for the mutually cooperative strategy, since A is better off with the mutually noncooperative strategy (N, N). This situation, therefore, is not a prisoner's

| | | B | |
		NOT POLLUTE (cooperation)	POLLUTE (noncooperation)
NOT POLLUTE (cooperation)	2	(C, C) 3	(C, N) 4 / 1
POLLUTE (noncooperation)	4	(N, C) 1	(N, N) 2 / 3

(A labels the rows)

Figure 12

dilemma. In such a situation, there would be no justification for governmental intervention on the grounds that strategic reasons prevent the individuals from achieving their goals.

Altruism

It has also been suggested that individuals are not motivated solely
by self-interest and that altruistic behavior would make the free-rider
problem irrelevant (Margolis, 1979). Altruistic behavior refers to the attempt on the part of any individual to bring the maximum possible benefits to others rather than to himself or herself. Under such an assumption,
an individual would refrain from polluting the air or committing crimes
or would contribute to public television or the neighborhood security
patrol because of the benefits which such actions would bring to others.

The problem with this approach, however, is that it ignores the peculiar difficulty of the large group. That is, in a large group, where the collective good benefits everyone and where the cost of the good is very large
relative to the income of any one individual (e.g., the cost of providing
clean air is far beyond the resources of any one individual), the increment
of the cost which any individual provides (or, conversely, the absence of
such an increment in the free-rider case) is so small that the increment (or
reduction) of the collective good associated with that payment is also small
—in fact, infinitesimal. For example, suppose that I wanted to reduce the
pollution problem (clean air is a collective good) by using unleaded fuel
rather than leaded fuel in my car. Of course, if everyone did that, the air
would be much cleaner; but the increment in air cleanliness associated
with my individual act is minuscule. Thus, any benefit, whether to myself
under the self-interest assumption or to others under the assumption of
altruism, must also be very small. In fact, under either assumption, it
would be more rational to focus on private acts rather than collective action. An altruist would do better by expending resources on goods for one,
or at most, a few other individuals rather than on collective goods. It might
even be the case that if everyone were altruistic and no one contributed
directly to the provision of collective goods, the result would be a collective good anyway! Perhaps we have here an altruism market in which
each individual, while trying to provide a good to a limited "other," would,
by means of an "invisible hand," produce a collective good for all!

Conclusion

In this chapter I have attempted to show that the major results in
collective-choice theory point to the difficulty in achieving rational collective action. This view differs from that of many scholars outside the

field who have mistakenly assumed that "rational choice" models show how groups and individuals should be rational.

It should be stressed that not all results in collective-choice theory show the limits of rational collective action. We have given certain examples to show that under certain circumstances rational collective action is possible. We have pointed out, however, that such situations usually require certain restrictions which either violate certain values or require relatively unrealistic assumptions. If we made an analogy between collective-choice processes and a highway, we might say that while the highway does exist, it is extraordinarily bumpy and in some places there are great craters. In order to traverse such a road, it would be necessary either to tread very warily, avoiding certain sections, or to do a massive repair job. The results of collective-choice theory, however, indicate that the road may be irreparable, in which case we may either have to try another mode of travel or stay where we are!

References

Abrams, R. The voter's paradox and the homogeneity of individual preference orders. *Public Choice*, 1976, *26*, 19–27.

Abrams, R. *Foundations of political analysis: An introduction to the theory of collective choice.* New York: Columbia University Press, 1980.

Arrow, K. *Social choice and individual values* (2nd ed.). New Haven: Yale University Press, 1963.

Benn, S. I. The problematic rationality of political participation. In P. Laslett & J. Fishkin (Eds.), *Philosophy, politics, and society* (Fifth Series). Oxford: Basil Blackwell, 1979.

Benn, S. I., & Mortimer, G. W. *Rationality and the social sciences.* London: Routledge & Kegan Paul, 1976.

Black, D. *Theory of committees and elections.* Cambridge, England: Cambridge University Press, 1958.

Braybrooke, D. Let needs diminish that preferences may prosper. *American Philosophical Quarterly Monographs.* 1968, *1*, 86–107.

Buchanan, J., & Stubblebine, W. C. Externality. *Economica*, 1962, *29*, 371–384.

Downs, A. *An economic theory of democracy.* New York: Harper & Row, 1957.

Ferejohn, J., & Fiorina, M. The paradox of not voting: A decision theoretic analysis. *American Political Science Reveiw*, 1974, *68*, 525–536.

Fishburn, P. The irrationality of transitivity in social choice. *Behavioral Science*, 1970, *15*, 119–123.

Frohlich, N., & Oppenheimer, J. *Modern political economy.* Englewood Cliffs, N.J.: Prentice-Hall, 1978.

Hardin, R. Collective action as an agreeable *n*-prisoners' dilemma. *Behavioral Science*, 1971, *16*, 472–481.

Harsanyi, J. *Essays on ethics, social behavior, and scientific explanation.* Dordrecht, The Netherlands: Reidel, 1976.

Harsanyi, J. *Rational behavior and bargaining equilibrium in games and social situations.* Cambridge, England: Cambridge University Press, 1977.

Koehler, D. Vote trading and the voting paradox: A proof of logical equivalence. *American Political Science Review*, 1975, *69*, 954–960.

Maguire, J. *Marx's theory of politics*. Cambridge, England: Cambridge University Press, 1978.

Margolis, H. Selfishness, altruism, and rationality: An essay in the theory of public choice. Cambridge: Center for International Studies, M.I.T., 1979.

May, K. Intransitivity, utility, and the aggregation of preference patterns. *Econometrica*, 1953, *22*, 1–13.

May, R. Some mathematical remarks on the paradox of voting. *Behavioral Science*, 1971, *16*, 143–151.

Miller, N. Logrolling, vote trading, and the paradox of voting: A game theoretical overview. *Public Choice*, 1977, *30*, 51–73.

Musgrave, R. A., & Peacock, A. *Classics in the theory of public finance*. New York: MacMillan, 1958.

Nash, J. The bargaining problem. *Econometrica*, 1950, *18*, 155–162.

Nash, J. F. Two-person cooperative games. *Econometrica*, 1953, *21*, 128–140.

Niemi, R. Majority decision-making with partial unidimensionality. *American Political Science Review*, 1969, *63*, 488–497.

Olson, M. *The logic of collective action*. Cambridge: Harvard University Press, 1965.

Oppenheimer, J. Some political implications of "vote trading and the voting paradox: A proof of logical equivalence." *American Political Science Review*, 1975, *69*, 963–966.

Plott, C. Axiomatic social choice theory: An overview and interpretation. *American Journal of Political Science*, 1976, *20*, 511–596.

Public Choice, 1977 (Spring), *29*.

Rawls, J. *A theory of justice*. Cambridge: Harvard University Press, 1971.

Riker, W., & Brams, S. The paradox of vote trading. *American Political Science Review*, 1973, *67*, 1235–1247.

Riker, W., & Ordeshook, P. *An introduction to positive political theory*. Englewood Cliffs, N.J.: Prentice-Hall, 1973.

Samuelson, P. The pure theory of public expenditures. *Review of Economics and Statistics*, 1954, *36*, 387–390.

Schwartz, T. Rationality and the myth of the maximum. *Nous*, 1972, *6*, 97–117.

Schwartz, T. Collective choice, separation of issues, and vote trading. *American Political Science Review*, 1977, *71*, 999–1010.

Sen, A. A possiblity theorem on majority decisions. *Econometrica*, 1966, *34*, 491–499.

Shapley, L. S. A value for n-person games. In H. W. Kuhn & A. W. Tucker (Eds.), *Contributions to the theory of games, II* (Annals of Mathematics Studies 28). Princeton: Princeton University Press, 1953.

Strasnick, S. The problem of social choice: Arrow to Rawls. *Philosophy and Public Affairs*, 1976, *5*, 241–273.

Taylor, M., & Rae, D. Decision rules and policy outcomes. *British Journal of Political Science*, 1971, *1*, 71–90.

Tullock, G. *Toward a mathematics of politics*. Ann Arbor: University of Michigan Press, 1967.

Von Neumann, J., & Morgenstern, O. *The theory of games and economic behavior*. New York: Wiley, 1944.

Zeuthen, F. *Problems of monopoly and economic warfare*. London: Routledge & Kegan Paul, 1930.

5

POLITICAL SYMBOLISM

ROZANN ROTHMAN

Introduction

Symbols are manifestations of the deeply felt human need to order what Henry James called "the blooming, buzzing confusion" of experience and endow this order with meaning. Order is socially cued and of human construction. Symbols are the artifacts or objectifications of this search for meaning; they are value and emotion laden. Symbols become part of the day-to-day realities we know so well that we are not conscious of their compulsions and demands. At the same time, these social constructs are subject to the constant pressure of changing experiences.

Politics, especially power relations, are the raw material of the symbol-making function. The life of every citizen is shaped by the actions of the state and the idea of the state. Governments raise taxes, declare war and make monetary policy that fuels inflation or leads to recession. In such cases, the import of government action is obvious, though interpretations of such actions may differ. In other instances, government can have a role in shaping perceptions, and the import of its action will be only dimly suspected. In either case, symbols function as vehicles of communication and the means to strengthen group cohesion. But if symbols are recognized as symbols, their use is perceived as manipulation and they may undermine group cohesion.

The student of political symbolism assumes that any political relationship, as well as the perception of the relationship, is a mixture of symbolic, instrumental, and rational aspects. Human beings have speech and

ROZANN ROTHMAN • Center for the Study of Federalism, Temple University, Philadelphia, Pennsylvania 19122. With the assistance of Robert L. Henderson of the University of Illinois.

are by nature symbol makers and symbol users. But humans and the symbols they use are shaped by the patterns of interaction among beliefs, values, persons, categories, groups, masses, elites, and government that prevail in the society in which they are located. Our task is to explore these patterns, determine the meaning of symbols and how they shape perception, and assess the import of symbols.

The analysis of political symbols tends to be eclectic and multidisciplinary, and the study makes certain demands on its practitioners. First, the data are multifaceted and do not lend themselves to quantitative analysis. For some mathematicians, semigroups may seem more real than tables and chairs, but most people do not share this perception. The clauses of the United States Constitution may seem more compelling for some politicians than for others. Hypotheses can be developed about the political needs and interests which underlie the devotion, but the devotion itself is a political fact and has symbolic import. Ernst Cassirer (1953) defined a symbol as something that becomes charged with meaning. Susanne Langer argued that symbols

> are *vehicles* for the conception of objects. . . . it is the *conceptions, not the things, that symbols directly "mean."* Behavior toward conceptions is what words normally evoke; this is the typical process of thinking. (1948, p. 61, Langer's italics)

From the myriad events, actions, and accidents that shape the history of a nation, some are selected to endow that experience with meaning and define that people's location in time, space, and history. A symbol has public, communicable meanings which are derived from a society's culture and tradition and are shaped by the degree of unity and differentiation present in the society. But perceptions of culture and tradition are subject to change and the meaning of a symbol is related to to the particular context in which it is used. Lee (1954/1964, p. 81) noted that

> the symbol thus gets its meaning through participation in the concrete situation; and it grows in meaning, and even changes in meaning, with each participation. . . . [The symbol] . . . is a thing in process, containing and conveying the value which has become embodied in it, and communicating it in so far as there is a community of experience between speaker and hearer.

Consistency and flexibility are two main attributes of integrative political symbols. The raw material of political experience is laced with contradictions. The grand conceptions—liberty, equality, authority, class, power—constantly need to be reconciled with the concrete experiences of communal existence. Symbols possess the capacity to transform acts of violence and heroism, accidents and tragedy into landmarks of meaning for individuals and societies. To perform this function, integrative symbols (i.e., symbols that enhance group cohesion) must be ambiguous. They must be broad enough to transcend idiosyncratic differences and sufficiently universal to express and contain common fears and channel common yearnings and aspirations. These symbols evoke clusters of intertwined and interdependent meanings, but meaning is always dependent on participation in the concrete situation and thus is entwined with a specific context. Because circumstances and participants change, the cluster of meanings is susceptible to interpretation and reinterpretation.

Symbols shape individual and communal responses but the symbols themselves are shaped by the traditional, historical, linguistic, and societal constraints which inhere in every social context. In other words, symbols and their uses are socially cued. Depending on the context, a symbol such as the American Constitution can be perceived as a guarantee of order or a covenant with death. For this reason, social facts must be considered problematic; they are vulnerable constructs which remain subject to interpretation.

There is a dialectical relationship between the fundamental opposites of social experience; they mutually imply one another and are inextricably linked so that they can neither exist nor be understood except in relation to one another (Burke, 1954, pp. 21–58; for a sociological interpretation, see Cole, 1966). Acceptance of the dialectical approach to social experience offers the means to encompass the contradictions of political experience, the alternations between hope and fear, optimism and pessimism about the future, unity and diversity, alienation and integration. Symbols objectify and ameliorate the tension between fundamental opposites and reconcile us to them. Theory and practice diverge and the dialectic bridges the gap. The dialectic of conceptualization has its particular logic, but the dialectic of experience is a stunted dialectic. Actions fail to reach their stated goals and we are caught up in a mesh of unintended consequences. Individuals act purposefully, but they do not know the script, they misread the lines, they misinterpret the cues, and, in short, they act without knowledge of the total scope, implications, or motivations of action.

The American Constitution serves as an example of an integrative symbol that exhibits both consistency and flexibility. The Constitution was quickly accepted as fundamental law, and it has been perceived ever since as the symbol of an encompassing order. But the Constitution filled this role only because elites and masses used its clauses, commandments, and prohibitions to explain and justify political decisions and actions. As noted above, from the myriad events, actions, and accidents of history, something becomes charged with meaning. That something must possess some degree of appropriateness in terms of the times and the context. If it does, acceptance of the symbol shapes perception of future events. The strength of constitutional symbolism in American history is demonstrated by the inability to effect fundamental political change despite widespread social and economic change (Lasch, 1969; Rothman, 1972). American radicals have not been able to escape the boundaries imposed by widespread acceptance of an overarching symbol that promises stability and predictability in social and political relationships. Reform rather than revolution has seemed mandated by societal norms, and even radicals have acquiesced, albeit at times grudgingly. Examples of integrative symbols such as the Constitution suggest the significance of symbols in the development and maintenance of social order.

It is ironic that integrative symbols are most effective when their symbolic functions go unnoticed. Then they appear as natural as the other artifacts of communal existence and are taken for granted. Berger and Luckmann (1967, pp. 21–22) analyzed the strengths that accrue from this kind of acceptance.

> I apprehend the reality of everyday life as an ordered reality. Its phenomena are prearranged in patterns that seem to be independent of my apprehension of them and that impose themselves upon the latter. The reality of everyday life appears already objectified, that is, constituted by an order of objectives that have been designated as objects before my appearance on the scene. The language used in everyday life provides me with the necessary objectifications and posits the order within which these make sense and within which everyday life has meaning for me.

When a bill is enacted by the Congress of the United States, the process symbolizes and reaffirms the original federal bargain. But the clash of interests, regularized legislative procedures, and established political habits deflect attention from the symbolic aspects of the process. The symbolism is implicit and its effect is both pervasive and persuasive. Deep, unexamined beliefs in God, country, and the flag are more potent motivators of communal action than scholarly analysis of the uses of symbols in enhancing societal cohesion. The latter may engender or increase skepticism about political incumbents or the workings of the system and inadvertently function to undermine social cohesion. Furthermore, attempts to strengthen or rationalize taken-for-granted political symbols are likely to expose their banality. Law Day was never accepted as a satisfactory substitute for May Day in the United States.

In contrast to the strengths that inhere in "taken-for-grantedness," Sapir (1934b, p. 494) noted that

> it is important to observe that symbolic meanings can often be recognized clearly for the first time when the symbolic value generally unconscious or conscious only in a marginal sense, drops out of a socialized pattern of behavior and the supposed function, which up to that time had been believed to be more than enough to explain it and keep it going, loses its significance and is seen to be little more than a paltry rationalization.

In any society, some individuals are more aware than others that instrumental functions tend to atrophy, and widespread awareness that supposedly instrumental functions are symbolic may be significant indicators of marginality and alienation. A. Cohen (1976, p. 8) discussed this problem in his analysis of the intellectual and emotional paradoxes that create dilemmas for scholars who are "personally caught up in the same body of symbols which they try to decode."

The fact of human selectivity also complicates the study of political symbols. Omniscience is not a human characteristic and the raw materials of existence are overwhelming. Language, culture, history, philosophy, tradition, and habit coalesce to provide a framework for interpreting and utilizing the material of experience. The selective focusing of interest and attention is a factor in the study of all social action. The question is on what attention is focused and how this focus affects the interpretation of the data. Sperber (1975, Chaps. 1–3) discusses some intricacies of selectivity and recognizes the element of arbitrariness in expositions of symbolic action. Erikson (1964) placed subjectivity at the center of clinical inquiry and argued that *disciplined* subjectivity functions to control the biases of patient and psychologist as well as to inform and deepen their relationship. Edelman (1977, p. 15) stressed the problematic nature of social facts and quoted Hannah Arendt, that "in politics more than anywhere else, we have no possibility of distinguishing between being and appearance. In the realm of human affairs, being and appearance are indeed one and the same." This assumption mandates self-conscious examination of both the selective character of observation and the reflections of that selectivity in social research (Edelman, 1977, p. 13). For these reasons, the student of political symbolism must be cognizant of his or her preconceptions and of the need to control and utilize them.

One consequence of selectivity is that approaches to the study of symbols differ; the researcher may be interested in the definition of a symbol, its meaning, its function, or its ramifications for communal existence. The differences are related to whether the student is an anthropologist, a political scientist, a psychologist, or a sociologist. The differences are also related to where the researcher cuts into the data. The same symbol can function as an integrative force or recognition of the symbol can signify increased alienation. An empirical investigation of the context is needed before any determination can be made, but as noted above, the factor of selection affects the design of the research and its conclusions.

Given that the subject of this essay is political symbolism, the survey of research was restricted to work that stresses communal rather than individual responses to symbols in anthropology, political science, and sociology. The survey of the literature is representative rather than comprehensive. For example, some works of Kenneth Burke and Harold Lasswell were analyzed in depth, but a compendium of all their writings was not prepared. In the section on applications, works were surveyed that represent the diversity of application rather than the complete explication of any particular trend of application. This strategy was adopted because the diversity of application appears in sharp contrast to the consensus on theory. The consensus on theory includes the following points:

1. People are symbol makers and symbol users; their role is active rather than passive.
2. The structures which order existence are socially cued and constructed.
3. These constructions are shaped by the context, with its constraints, in which the individual is located.
4. Because construction takes place in a context and is socially cued, there is intersubjectivity. Individual constructions overlap the constructions of others and the meanings of symbols are common and accessible.
5. Because individuals differ and circumstances change, symbolic action must be conceptualized as dialectical. Social existence is conceived as a process and the ambiguity of social facts is recognized.

To summarize, the student of political symbols assumes that language, role, social cuing, and selective perception are the crucial elements in the construction of a social world. Research focuses on the interaction between these elements, and an exploration of the meaning of interaction is required. But the objective can be reached by diverse, even disparate methods and strategies.

The review of the literature undertaken in the next sections emphasizes the common assumptions that underlie the theory, notes the reasons for theoretical divergence, and sketches the diversity of application. The diversity of application, despite the consensus on assumptions, symbolizes the dialectical aspects of social and political experience and suggests the significant role of context and relationships in the determination of meaning.

Sources of the Research Focus

This section will examine the seminal assumptions that underlie the study of political symbols. The generative ideas have come, for the most part, from philosophy, but they have been elaborated on and applied by anthropologists, political scientists, psychologists, and sociologists. Symbols lend themselves to disparate interpretations and the list of elaborations and applications reflects this eclecticism. In his classic essay on symbolism, Edward Sapir (1934b, p. 492) sketched the evolution of the term to cover a variety of dissimilar models of behavior and concluded that gradual broadening of the concept has meant that the terms "symbol" and "symbolism" include not only trivial and well-established representations but also those objects and devices which are not necessarily important in themselves but which point to ideas and actions of great consequence to society.

Sapir suggested various uses of symbols and identified two common characteristics of all symbols. First, because a symbol is always a substitute for some more closely intermediating type of behavior, "all symbolism implies meanings which cannot be derived directly from the contexts of experience." Second, the symbol "expresses condensation of energy, its actual significance being out of all proportion to the apparent triviality of meaning suggested by its mere form" (1934b, p. 493).

Symbolic theory has been developed primarily within the humanistic rather than the scientific tradition. In the section on applications, the empirical studies in symbolism will be discussed, but this section will concentrate on the development of the assumptions and insights that provide the framework for the study of political symbols. Although symbols can be studied as explanations of individual responses or societal attitudes, the literature on individual responses will not be reviewed unless it pertains to or has bearing on societal attitudes and responses. The debate concerning the way that symbols mediate the relationship between individuals and society is ongoing. Clarification of concepts, however, has remained an elusive goal, in part because of the inherent ambiguity of the material and also because symbols only have meaning in terms of their appropriate context. But as Sapir claimed, common characteristics can be discovered in all symbols and identification of these characteristics is the prerequisite for analysis.

Although approaches differ, all students of political symbolism assume that symbols and their uses are socially cued. A symbol is something that for some individual or group has been differentiated from the generalized chaos which is pristine reality and that has been charged with significance. Again, although scholars disagree about the extent of manipulation of symbols by elites, there is agreement that the human response is constructive rather than passive. Moreover, there is agreement that contexts and the relationships that develop within these contexts must be explored in order to assign or assess meaning. Finally, there is recognition that ambiguity is a central characteristic of symbols and that the researchers must accept its pervasiveness in human thought and action. Kenneth Burke (1954, pp. xii–xiii) argued for terminology that would "clearly reveal the strategic spots at which ambiguities necessarily arise." Transformations occur at these spots to create the distinctions that shape social relations and infuse symbols with compelling power.

Philosophic Concepts of Symbolic Systems

Before reviewing Burke's contribution to the study of political symbols, the philosophic foundations of the research focus will be sketched.

Ernst Cassirer was a leading expositor of the philosophy of symbolic forms. He argued that there is unity in human consciousness and sought to build a general theory of culture.

> The various products of culture—language, scientific knowledge, myth, art and religion—become parts of a single great problem-complex; they become multiple efforts, all directed toward the one goal of transforming the passive world of mere *impressions*, in which the spirit seems at first imprisoned into a world that is pure *expression* of the human spirit. (1955, pp. 80–81, Cassirer's italics)

The study of symbols offers insight into the diverse forms that branches of culture assume in order to impart their distinctive truths. Cassirer built his theory of symbolic forms on the presupposition that humanity is the creator of its worlds. There may be multiple realities, but each is accessible because symbols and their uses are socially cued. The key to understanding symbols lies in recognizing that symbols do not exist in pure form but inhere in social relationships and contexts. Meaning is public but a particular meaning may be shared by only a few. Consequently, lack of familiarity with the imaginative universe that nurtures particular meanings may prove an obstacle to understanding. Or conversely, too close association with a culture can hamper realistic assessment of its strengths and weaknesses (Cohen, 1976; Geertz, 1973, p. 13; Langer, 1948, pp. 49–51). But the caveats underscore the need to explore relationships, contexts, and meanings for the clues to assess how and why political symbols are effective and what their import is.

In the *Myth of the State*, Cassirer deals most directly with political symbols and offers an analysis of the myths that cluster around the concept of the state. Myths are not simply an emotional state; the function of myth is the expression of emotion which transforms a passive state into an active process (1946, p. 52). Symbolic expression is a process of intensification and condensation. "In language, myth, art, religion, our emotions are not simply turned into mere acts; they are turned into 'works' . . . [which] are persistent and durable" (1946, p. 56). Symbolic expression has the power of objectification and solidification and "myth is an objectification of man's social experience, not of his individual experience" (1946, p. 57). Against this background, Cassirer analyzed the struggle against myth in the history of political theory. The twentieth century, however, has shown that the "triumph" of rationality cannot eliminate the power of myth. Nazi success with the most blatant symbols of the *Volk* indicates that myth is in some sense invulnerable. "It is impervious to rational arguments; it cannot be refuted by syllogisms" (1946, p. 373).

The rise of Naziism and the use of psychological warfare during World War II sparked new interest in symbolism for some American intellectuals. The early years of the Cold War added impetus to the study of American symbols; they were to be shaped and honed to do battle in the ideological wars. These developments will be discussed in the section on applications, but they are noted here because they suggest the easy movement from theory to application and the strong practical motivation that often accompanies the study of political symbols.

Susanne K. Langer elaborated many of the basic themes of symbolism in *Philosophy in a New Key*, which placed the ability to symbolize at the center of distinctively human activity. Although ours is an age that responds to facts,

> between the facts run the threads of unrecorded reality, momentarily recognized, wherever they come to the surface, in our tacit adaptation to signs; and the bright twisted threads of symbolic envisagement, imagination . . . [gives form to] the whole creative process of ideation, metaphor, and abstraction that makes human life an adventure in understanding. (Langer, 1948, p. 236–237)

Language is *the* symbolic structure par excellence and "speech is, in fact, the readiest active termination of that basic process in the human brain which may be called symbolic transformation of experience" (1948, p. 48). Ritual and magic are also symbolic transformations of experience that other mediums fail to express (1948, p. 52). In other words, symbolic transformations provide the artifacts which literally support the framework of human existence.

The most characteristic human function and asset is the ability to conceptualize. For this reason, "our most important assets are always the symbols of our general orientation in nature, on the earth, in society and in what we are doing: the symbols of our Weltanschauung and Lebensanschauung" (Langer, 1948, pp. 241–242). Political symbols such as the American Constitution (Burke, 1954; M. Lerner, 1937; Rothman, 1974) and the coronation of the Queen in England (Shils & Young, 1953) are included among the symbols of general orientation and their aura of rightness and legitimacy infuses these integrative symbols with compelling power. However, a change in political, social, and economic conditions can open these symbols to criticism. The disparity created by the gap between expectations and the realities of existence can produce new perceptions of integrative symbols so that they appear as obstacles to a more equitable future. During the debate over the role of the Supreme Court in blocking social legislation, Max Lerner (1937, pp. 1293–1294) attacked the fetish of constitutionalism. The "Constitution and Supreme Court are symbols of an ancient sureness and a comforting stability," but they had become stumbling blocks to social progress, and social forces were slowly preparing the way for the emergence of new symbols.

Intellectual and practical analyses of the uses of symbols and their role in unifying societies, securing mass quiescence, or fanning the flames of revolution will be discussed more fully below. Here the point is that critics of symbol manipulation also admit the centrality of symbols in the maintenance of political order. The difference in conclusions is attributable to the different emphases of a critical approach and does not signify disagreement about the fundamental assumption—that the contexts and relationships that endow events, ideas, and beliefs with meaning must be explored.

Kenneth Burke's contribution to the study of symbols provides certain key assumptions for the examination of political symbols. Acceptance of ambiguity and the stress on clarification of the resources of ambiguity alert the researcher to the interrelations and subtle shifts in the complex matrix that is the source of political action and rhetoric. In *A Grammar of Motives* (1954), Burke offers five terms (act, scene, agent, agency, purpose) as the generating principles of a dramatist perspective and offers this perspective as a means to encompass the subtleties of human action.

> Certain formal interrelationships prevail among these [five] terms by reason of their role as attributes of a common ground or substance. Their participation in a common ground makes for transformability. At every point where the field covered by any one of these terms overlaps upon the field covered by any other, there is an alchemic opportunity. . . . From the central moltenness where all the elements are fused into one togetherness, there are thrown forth, in separate crusts, such distinctions as those between freedom and necessity, activity and passiveness, cooperation and competition, cause and effect, mechanism and teleology." (Burke, 1954, pp. xiii–xiv)

The symbol-making functions (language and thought) are conceived as modes of action and the emphasis is on process, transformability, and the dialectical relationships that inhere in transformations. The researcher must recognize the antinomies of definition which make transformations possible and investigate the subtle and complicated motivational shifts that spark shifts in perceptions and attitudes. For example, Burke notes that there are directional "moments" that "summarize the foregoing and seminally contain the subsequent. But in themselves they 'just are,' being an 'eternal present' that has wound up the past and has the future wound up" (1954, p. 32).

Burke's insight into the shifting, at times tumultuous interplay of human motivation provides the linguistic tools for the sophisticated analysis of political symbols. Naming is a linguistic tool with significant political ramifications. "To tell what a thing is, you place it in terms of something else. This idea of locating, or placing, is implicit in our very word for definition itself: to define, or determine a thing is to mark its boundaries" (1954, p. 24). There is also the phenomenon of compensatory naming in which something is named not for what it is but for what it is hoped it will become (1954, p. 54).

Anselm Strauss (1959) elaborated this insight into the significance of naming in his work on identity. Naming not only indicates but also identifies an object as some kind of object. To accomplish this feat, classification comes into play. A background of relationships is assumed and defining a class means relating it to systematically associated classes. Classification thus makes it feasible to organize activity in society in an "orderly" and "sensible" manner. This analysis has political relevance when it is realized that the direction of group activity is shaped by the group's ability to develop a common or shared terminology which in turn depends on the particular ways that the group classifies objects (Strauss, 1959, pp. 15–25). The examples are myriad, ranging from Nazi ability to define Jews as vermin and to develop intense cohesion and loyalty in the elite divisions of the S.S., to the devotion of Southern politicians to states' rights, to the cohesion and dedication of students in a high-school play.

Burke also explores specifically political relations in the chapter on "The Dialectic of Constitutions" (1954, p. 323–401). This chapter is a paradigm of the utility and versatility of the dramatist perspective and includes analytical sketches of certain aspects of American politics—judicial review, the Constitution and laissez-faire, and money as "God Term." Political rhetoric is presented as a form of secular prayer, a way to reassure audiences as to the import and consequences of policy, and the characterizations highlight the ironies of political stratagems (pp. 393–394).

Work in phenomenology intersects the study of symbolism and provides additional philosophical structure. The philosophic framework of phenomenology was expounded by Edmund Husserl (1962) and Martin Heidegger (1962). Phenomena are conceived as mind dependent; and mind exerts its potential for selective control. Albert Schutz interpreted many of the concepts of phenomenology for the social sciences and introduced the concept of multiple realities. In his essay, "Symbol, Reality, and Society," Schutz sought to bypass the controversies concerning the definition of what a symbol is and the origins and uses of the symbol-making functions. He stressed instead the common denominator of the various theories on significative and symbolic relations—that the object, fact, or event called sign or symbol refers to something other than itself. Schutz used Husserl's concept of appresentation, or analogical apperception, to clarify the role of symbols in perceiving and transcending the multiple realities of existence. The world of everyday life is an intersubjective world; shared with others and interpreted by others, significative and symbolic relations furnish the tools of communication that make transcendence possible. The individual participates in the intersubjective world and experiences transcendence; he or she shuttles back and forth between these experiences on the links forged by symbolic relations. What A affirms, B might disavow, but the socially shared symbol, notwithstanding the possiblity of disparate interpretations, is the means of communication and passage (Schutz, 1954/1964, pp. 135–202).

Symbolic-interaction theory deals with the same motifs as the theory of political symbols, and assumptions and insights are often shared. George Herbert Mead (1934) laid the framework for the development of symbolic interaction, but his insights are scattered in lecture notes, fragmentary manuscripts, and first drafts of unpublished manuscripts. Bernard Meltzer (1967) took up the task of systematic presentation of Mead's philosophy. Mead viewed human behavior as social behavior and human acts as social acts and assumed the prior existence of society as the context within which selves arise. Through language the child learns the symbols of his or her groups and comes to internalize its definition of events and things. Human behavior involves responses to interpreted stimuli, and human beings respond to one another on the basis of their interpretation of the intentions or meanings of gestures. The gesture is a symbol; when it has a shared, common meaning, it is designated as a "significant symbol."

Mind emerges out of the organic life of human beings through communication and is viewed as a process. The individual interacts with him or herself and uses significant symbols to do so. However, the process is more complex than a stimulus–response process. Stimuli are not the initiators of activity—they are elements selected by the organism to further its activity. Although the mind is social in origin and function, it is an active participant in the process and not a passive factor. However, the individual controls his or her activity by reference to the definitions provided by others and the social function of mind is manifest. To obtain a standpoint from which to converse with him or herself, the individual "takes the role of the other." The other is "the generalized other," the system of common symbols and meanings that surrounds and constrains the individual in society. This brief summary of Mead's philosophy illustrates the interrelatedness of his concepts of symbolic interaction, role-taking, meaning, mind, and self; each term involves the other terms, and consequently Mead's theory has an organic unity (Meltzer, 1967, pp. 5–20).

Although Mead's concepts have been criticized as ambiguous and vaguely conceptualized, these defects were a catalyst which resulted in refinement of the concepts. For example, Herbert Blumer (1967) clarified and elaborated Mead's concepts and stressed the characteristics of process in human behavior. He began with Mead's presuppositions concerning the basis of symbolic interaction: that human society is made up of individuals who have selves, that individual action is the result of the individual noting and interpreting features of the situation in which he or she acts, and that group or collective action consists of the aligning of individual actions brought about by the individuals interpreting or taking into account each others' actions. Blumer contrasted symbolic-interaction theory with other sociological theories. The individual is not a vessel through which the forces of history are poured. Instead, the social actions of individuals in society are constructed by these individuals through a process of interpretation. Empirically, it is clear that human society consists of acting units and that actions are formed or constructed from human interpretations of situations. "Group life consists of acting units developing acts to meet the situations in which they are placed" (1967, p. 143).

Social organization (culture, social stratification, social roles) furnishes the framework and sets the conditions for action, but acting units act toward situations as they have defined them. Social organization supplies fixed sets of symbols which people use to interpret their situations, but the possibility of social change is always present. By definition, interpretation opens up the possibility of change. Recognition of the potential of interpretation gives this perspective the ability to handle the prospect of change (Blumer, 1967, pp. 146–148). Blumer's interpretation of the origins of social action illustrates the relationship between symbolic-interaction theory and the philosophical assumptions that underlie the system of political symbolism. In both, the social characteristics of action are recognized, but the emphasis is on the individual as actor, and his or her actions are viewed as constructive. The assumptions of symbolic-interaction theory parallel philosophic conceptions of the symbol-making function; both stress that the function is active and constructive.

This type of interaction between disparate theories is fairly typical. Theorists in the social sciences have refined and elaborated assumptions derived from philosophic investigations of symbols and used them to construct behavioral theories. No unified theory of symbolic function for the social sciences has developed; rather theorists have stressed those aspects of symbolic function that are relevant to their respective disciplines. However, assumptions and insights are shared and there has been a kind of cross-fertilization. The works of Edward Sapir, Clifford Geertz, Mary Douglas, Dan Sperber, Victor Turner, Abner Cohen, Harold Lasswell, Murray Edelman, Robert Nisbet, and Albert Salomon reflect this cross-fertilization. These scholars use similar assumptions, and their conclusions are generally applicable to the broad range of questions raised by the problems of political or societal order and stability; but their respective disciplines shaped the thrust and defined the limits of the theories.

Contemporary interest in political symbols was sparked by the traumas of World War II and its aftermath. There was a new awareness of the role of symbols in shaping behavior and a heightened fear of the virulence and intractability of the affective power of symbols. The lessons of history—that flags, icons, and slogans were capable of mobilizing the devotion and energies of individuals even though such devotion typically proved costly in terms of individual well-being—were, for the moment, obvious. Researchers sought to explore the question of why symbols had such power. Could the compelling aspects of symbols be identified, and if so, how? What were the costs of the use of symbols? Could the study of political symbols provide explanations of why individuals or societies behaved in certain ways? At the least, the study of political symbols promised a more sophisticated insight into the subtleties and intricacies of human interaction. Furthermore, symbols seemed to be more accessible to empirical investigation than values or beliefs. Salomon (1954/1964, p. 106) claimed that "symbols refer to the objective significance of acts, objects, events and ideal images which represent a living and concrete pattern for the context of a social whole." There is a public quality to a symbol; for it to be effective, it has to be accepted. Acceptance implies a shared meaning, and that meaning in turn is accessible to all members of the given culture. Idiosyncratic interpretations of a common symbol are possible and often have significance for a given society, but the relationship of the idiosyncratic to the common meaning is usually manifest. There appears to be a consensus among scholars regarding the public character of symbols and their influence on human action, but there is disagreement over the question of how symbols shape and mediate the relationship between individuals and society.

Such disagreements, particularly the controversy over whether symbols are primarily integrative forces, the source of rationales to legitimize power, or devices to secure mass quiescence, are as irresolvable as the controversy over the rationality of symbols. In general, more fruitful approaches to the study of symbols stress the meaning of the symbol for those who recognize it. Acting units define the situation in terms of their perception or interpretation of the situation. In the process, meanings are attributed to the symbols, but meaning is dependent on the specific situation. Thus, depending on the context and its specific relationships, the same symbol can serve integrative purposes or function to mystify the masses. Context and the relationships that develop between categories in that context are the important variables for the analysis of symbolic import.

Linguistic and Anthropological Approaches to Symbolism

Edward Sapir's essay on language (1934a) contains several seminal insights concerning the significance of context and relationships. As noted previously, language is the perfect example of a symbolic system, and Sapir argues that language forms predetermine for us certain modes of observation and interpretation. Thus, language both helps and retards us in our exploration of experience. More significantly, language may report, or refer to, or otherwise substitute for direct experience, but "it does not as a matter of actual behavior stand apart from or run parallel to direct experience but completely interpenetrates with it." Language creates "that world of the potential intergrading with the actual that enables human beings to transcend the immediately given in their individual experience and to join in a larger common understanding. This common understanding constitutes culture" (Sapir, 1934a, pp. 156–157). Language thus mediates between idiosyncratic interpretations of the situation and the conventional symbols of a society. The flow is always both ways. Language serves primarily integrative and conservative functions, but at the same time it provides the means for identification of specific symbols with particular groups, societies, or individuals. One scrap of colored cloth is charged with meaning for the British and a different scrap of colored cloth represents the nation for Americans. The assignment of meaning may be arbitrary, but a symbol possesses the power to motivate and mobilize those who accept it.

Sapir divides symbols into two classifications: referential and condensation. The former classification includes the more concrete, objective, and observable systems which "are agreed upon as economical devices for purposes of reference." The latter "is a highly condensed form of substitute behavior for direct expression, allowing for the ready release of emotional tension in conscious and unconscious form" (1934b, p. 493).

Political symbols appear to be a mixture of referential and condensation components. As Geertz (1964) noted, so-called cognitive and so-called expressive symbols or symbol systems share a common characteristic: "they are extrinsic sources of information in terms of which human life can be patterned—extrapersonal mechanisms for the perception, understanding, judgment and manipulation of the world" (p. 62). Symbol systems provide the templates for the organization of social and psychological processes, and this organization, in turn, controls the relations of the materials to each other and shapes the way the materials are utilized to constitute an ordered system (1964, p. 62). The political symbol performs this function; it is a configuration of complex and ambiguous meanings that possesses the expressive power and the rhetorical force to engender loyalty and sacrifice in return for the identity of citizen. If the symbol is accepted, it serves to organize the experience of a people. For example, a constitution can become

> the concise and hallowed expression of man's complex and ambivalent attitudes toward others: his wish to aggrandize his goods and powers at the expense of others; his fears that he may suffer from powerful positions of others and their predations; his seeking for an encompassing principle that will introduce stability and predictability into this explosive clash of interests. (Edelman, 1964, p. 19)

The affective component of the political symbol infuses it with compelling power. This aspect is most vivid and probably dominates when the relationship of the event, behavior, institution, or process with the symbol has just emerged. For example, if the symbol emerges during the height of revolution, its affective import is obvious. If the symbol is a legacy from the long distant past, habit and the accretions of time seem to dim its emotional compulsion. But then the symbol appears as natural in its context and this naturalness has its own compulsions. If a symbol lacks this compulsion, it fails. When Richard Nixon appeared on television in 1973, at the beginning of the Watergate revelations, the flag, the Seal of the United States, and a bust of Abraham Lincoln were obviously displayed. But the attempt at association was both blatant and banal and proved unpersuasive. Reminders of presidential power and greatness were inadequate to the task of dispelling or counterbalancing perceptions of corruption.

Not all attempts at symbol construction are effective and this fact highlights the selective aspect of the symbol-making function. Dan Sperber (1975) has discussed some aspects of the selection process. The individual constructs a grammar or symbol mechanism by selecting from empirical data those that are relevant to his or her purposes (1975, p. 85). In other words, the symbol-making function is constructive in that the human process of selection is the determinant of significance. The process becomes politically relevant when a symbol is accepted by a specific group or society. Once accepted, the symbol provides the map for organizing relationships, in part because symbolic thought utilizes statements about the world to establish relations between categories. The pervasiveness and import of the selective acceptance of symbols was illustrated by Robert Nisbet (1969) in his discussion of western theories of development. All that we can see in social life is mixed facts of persistence and change—migrations, wars, revolutions, technological innovation, or decline. Nevertheless, in order to understand or assimilate the facts, western thought has resorted to the "oldest, most powerful and encompassing metaphor," the metaphor of growth. Utilization of the metaphor immediately changes the perspective of the observer. Instead of random and adventitious change, the reference is to change "that is intrinsic to the entity," to change that has direction, that is, a trend or longitudinal shape (Nisbet, 1969, pp. 3–11). It is no exaggeration to suggest that the metaphor of growth has shaped the western view of history by supplying pattern and structure for an ambiguous process. The example clarifies both the utility and the danger of the use of metaphor in social thought. Or as noted above, language both helps and retards us in our explorations of experience.

Clifford Geertz recognized these nuances in his analysis of the organizing function of symbols. "Thick Description: Toward an Interpretive Theory of Culture," the introduction to *The Interpretation of Culture* (1973), and "Ideology as a Cultural System" (1964) are representative of his theory of cultural interpretation. Geertz advocates a semiotic concept of culture because man is an animal suspended in webs of significance he himself has spun (1973, p. 5). The webs are defined as interworked systems of construable signs or symbols and culture is the product of this interaction. Culture is not a power; social events, behavior, institutions, or processes cannot be causally attributed to it. Rather culture is a context; something within which social events, behavior, institutions, or processes can be intelligently or thickly described (1973, p. 14). Thick description consists of sorting out the structures of significance and determining their social ground and import (1973, p. 9).

The theory of culture is developed primarily for use by anthropologists, who are urged to develop ethnographic descriptions grounded in material complexity. This emphasis differentiates Geertz's approach to cultural analysis from more abstract conceptions. Cultural analysis involves "guessing at meanings, assessing the guesses and drawing explanatory conclusions from the better guesses," in contrast to discovering "the Continent of Meaning and mapping out its bodiless landscape" (1973, p. 20). Anthropologists confront the same grand realities—power, change, faith, oppression, authority, violence—that historians, economists, political scientists, and sociologists confront. However, for the anthropologist, these realities are discovered in obscure and homely contexts. Geertz eschews theoretical formulations that are stated independently of their applications because they seem commonplace or vacant. The essential task of theory building is not the codification of abstract regularities but the creation of the possibility of thick description (1973, p. 26). Thick description encompasses both the hard surfaces of life—the biological, political, economic, and stratificatory realities—and the symbolic dimensions of social action which structure and pattern perceptions of these realities.

In the earlier article (1964) Geertz explicated his conception of the symbolic dimensions of social action. The paucity of theoretical conceptualizations of ideology and also the practical difficulties of utilizing the term were attributed to the inadequacies of interest and strain theories of ideology. Interest theory, although plausible, is oversimplified, and strain theory, although offering a more sophisticated analysis of motivation, provides primarily adventitious explanations.

> A pattern of behavior shaped by a certain set of forces turns out, by a plausible but nevertheless mysterious coincidence, to serve ends but tenuously related to those forces. A group of primitives sets out, in all honesty to pray for rain and ends by strengthening its social solidarity. (1964, p. 56)

The concept of latent function is invoked to cover such anomalies, but it serves only to name the phenomenon. Interest and strain theories of ideology fail because they ignore the autonomous processes of symbolic formulation; they "go directly from source analysis to consequence analysis without ever seriously examining ideologies as systems of interacting symbols, as patterns of interworking meanings" (1964, p. 56).

Ideologies should be explored as systems of interacting symbols so that a more comprehensive understanding of their roles and functions can be obtained. Meaning is socially rooted and the success or failure of attempts to utilize symbols as ideological templates is determined by stylistic mechanisms and those hard surfaces of human existence, the biological, political, economic, and stratificatory realities. War is hell, or war is the father of creation and the mother of culture—each slogan is effective in the appropriate context, and each fails totally if the contexts are reversed. "It is thus not truth that varies with social, psychological and cultural contexts, but the symbols we construct in our unequally effective attempts to grasp it" (1964, p. 59).

What is socially determined is not the nature of conception but the vehicles of conception. These vehicles are symbol systems which possess public meanings and are accessible to systematic examination. The utility of symbolism is demonstrated by the capacity to provide a better understanding of ideology. Ideologies become crucial as sources of sociopolitical meanings and attitudes when neither the society's general cultural orientation nor its pragmatic ones adequately explain or legitimize contemporary realities.

> It is a loss of orientation that most directly gives rise to ideological activity, an inability for lack of usable models to comprehend the universe of civic rights and responsibilities in which one finds oneself located. . . . And it is, in turn, the attempt of ideologies to render otherwise incomprehensible social situations meaningful, to so construe them as to make it possible to act purposefully within them, that accounts both for the ideologies' highly figurative nature and for the intensity with which, once accepted, they are held. (1964, p. 64)

A systematic exploration of the symbolic dimensions of social action is the key to more adequate theoretical conceptualizations of the structure and role of ideology.

Mary Douglas (1970) also focuses on the organizing function of symbols. She analyzes the role of dirt or impurity in society. The analysis extends to the diverse means that societies devise to cope with the ambiguities and anomalies that engender perceptions of impurity.

> Dirt is essentially disorder. There is no such thing as absolute dirt: it exists in the eye of the beholder. . . . There is nothing fearful or unreasoning in our dirt-avoidance: it is a creative movement, an attempt to relate form to function, to make unity of experience. (1970, p. 12)

Culture is described as the public, standardized values of a community which mediate the experience of individuals. Any classification system gives rise to anomalies, and any culture must devise means to cope with the challenge posed by aberrant forms. The relativity of the idea of dirt is the source of its symbolic import. Pollution rituals derive from human antipathy to ideas or objects that are likely to confuse or contradict cherished classifications. The reaction may be exaggerated, but the threat of anomaly is perceived as real. Human classifications are human defenses against the chaos of shifting, unstable impressions and pollution rituals constitute an array of barricades (1970, pp. 48–53).

Douglas relates the rituals and communal beliefs of various primitive communities in light of the above assumption and notes the connection of the habitual practices and pragmatic experience of the community with the prevailing belief structure. Pollution rituals arise from the recognition that power and "danger lies in transitional states; simply because transition is neither one state nor the next, it is undefinable" (1970, p. 116). Ritual functions to unify experience and, in doing so, contains and channels the costs and consequences of marginality. Rites of passage serve this function. But more significantly, for our purposes, the development of ritual is a recognition of the crucial role of "naming." As noted above, naming is a major component of identity, and conversely, the lack of name or status appears as a threat, albeit ill-defined, to the cherished classifications of the community. Marginality, even in secular society, seems to pose threats out of all proportion to an objective estimate of the ability of the marginal person. Ex-prisoners and released mental patients have severe reentry problems because they have been on the margins of or outside society (1970, p. 117).

In the primitive universe, the interplay of the ideas of form and formlessness is the source of ideas about power in society. This assumption probably holds true for secular society also. Douglas assumes that most of the experiences of human beings are held in common—drought is drought, hunger is hunger, calamity is calamity—"but each culture knows a distinctive set of laws governing the way these disasters fall" (1970, p. 119). This same assumption about the interplay between unity and diversity is found in Geertz and is one of the reasons that anthropologists emphasize context. The symbol-making function is constructive; individuals, groups, and societies create particular worlds and each universe must be grasped in its full particularity if sense is to be made out of its symbolic structure.

The idea of society is a powerful image which has form—external boundaries, margins, and internal structure—and serves as a defense against formlessness. According to Douglas, the idea of the body is even more potent and is probably the primary image. The body

> is a model which can stand for any bounded system. . . . The functions of its different parts and their relation afford a source of symbols for other complex structures. . . . [We must be] prepared to see the powers and dangers credited to social structure reproduced in small on the human body. (1970, p. 138)

The interpretation of body symbols must be related to the interpretation of social symbols. It is not individual psychoses that are the source of bodily symbols, but societal preoccupations with guarding the margins. Any structure of ideas is vulnerable at the margins. All margins are dangerous

> if they are pulled this way or that the shape of fundamental experience
> is altered. . . . Each culture has its own special risks and problems. To
> which particular bodily margins its beliefs attribute power depends on
> what situation the body is mirroring. (1970, p. 145)

In summary, then, bodily symbols and the rituals which develop around them reflect society's concerns and its perceptions of threat. However, these perceptions, and in fact the very perception of margins and marginality, depend on the progress of differentiation. The reaction to dirt is a consequence of differentiation. The attitude to dirt, to those rejected bits and pieces of experience, goes through two stages. First, these pieces are recognizably out of place and a threat to good order. They are in this condition as long as they retain some identity; at this stage they are dangerous. In the second stage, they have disintegrated and dirt is totally undifferentiated. "In its last phase, then, dirt shows itself as an apt symbol of creative formlessness" (1970, p. 190). The phases through which dirt passes symbolize people's common urge to make a unity of all their experience (1970, p. 200), but each culture devises its own version of the common drama. Each culture's beliefs, fears, and preoccupations are the source of the symbolic system it devises to cope with the human need for certainty in a problematic universe.

Victor Turner (1974), like Mary Douglas, explores the function and powers of marginality. He uses the term "liminality" to convey the centrality of the concept of marginality. A view of society as in process is the result, and Turner stresses the need to analyze the dynamic aspects of society. He uses the term "social drama" as a unit of aharmonic or disharmonic process arising in conflict situations (1974, p. 37). The structure of society provides the framework for social drama, and conflict is the other side of cohesion. Cohesion depends on "interest" which binds the individual to structural rights and obligations, imperatives and loyalties, and that other bond—communitas—which unites people over and above their formal bonds (1974, p. 43).

The stress on process makes it necessary to use the metaphor of "becoming." As noted above, Nisbet sketched the dangers of this metaphor, particularly its organic implications, but Turner must utilize it. "Cultural systems . . . depend not only for their meaning but also for their existence upon the participation of conscious, volitional human agents and upon men's continually and potentially changing relations with one another" (Turner, 1974, p. 32). This is the "humanistic coefficient," a basic assumption in Turner's theory.

Social dramas represent sequences of social events and arise because there is a shifting, changing universe. But the structural frame in which social dramas are enacted includes "atemporal structures," models of what people "believe they do, ought to do, or would like to do." These structures and systems are revealed in the intersubjective, collective representations of the group. They are carried in people's heads and nervous systems and "have a steering function, a 'cybernetic' function, in the endless succession of social events, imposing on them the degree of order they possess and indeed dividing processual units into phases" (Turner, 1974, p. 36).

This use of atemporal structures as a stabilizing element in a shifting universe parallels Kenneth Burke's use of "directional moments" that sum up the past and seminally contain the subsequent, but in themselves just are. The interplay of change and structure gives form to the intersubjective world. Despite the prevalence of change, certain norms and relationships (it doesn't matter whether they are crucial or trivial) persist. Systematic analysis of processual units and temporal structures combined with awareness of phases and atemporal systems provides a blueprint for the study of persistence and change.

Turner's theory points to the need to explore particular universes or contexts. To accomplish this task, an understanding of symbols, especially ritual symbols and root metaphors, is needed. Symbols are multivocal; they have the "capacity to resonate among many meanings at once like a chord in music." Root metaphors imply

> a certain kind of polarization of meaning in which the subsidiary subject is really a depth world of prophetic, half-glimpsed images, and the principal subject, the visible, fully known (or thought to be fully known) component, at the opposite pole of it, acquires new and surprising contours and valences from its dark companion. On the other hand, because the poles are 'active together' the unknown is brought just a little more into the light of the known. (Turner, 1974, p. 50)

The similarity between this depiction of the role of metaphor and the one used by political scientists will be discussed below. Here, the point is that symbols, especially ritual symbols, offer the means to transcend partial experiences and to participate in a unity of cultural and social experience. For this reason, Turner refuses to treat symbols as epiphenomena, and accords them ontological status (1974, p. 57). As noted above, Schutz argued that the individual participates in the intersubjective world but shuttles back and forth between experiences of transcendence on links forged by symbolic relations. The socially shared symbol furnishes the means of communication and passage. Although there is no unified theory of symbols for the social sciences, the separate contributions to symbolic theory should not be viewed as unrelated. As this review of the theorists in the social sciences proceeds, the assertion that assumptions are shared and that there is cross-fertilization between the theories will be demonstrated. Then perhaps the theories developed for the respective social sciences can be viewed as important variations on or adaptations of a central theme.

The work of Abner Cohen, a political anthropologist, provides a bridge to the study of specifically political symbols. For Cohen, "symbols are objects, acts, concepts or linguistic formations that stand *ambiguously* for a multiplicity of disparate meanings, evoke sentiments and emotions, and impel men to action. They usually occur in stylized patterns of activities" (1976, p. 13, his italics). In society, power relations are found in almost all social relationships. Politics is broadly defined and consists of the processes "involved in the distribution, maintenance, exercise and struggle for power" (1976, p. iii). These broad definitions are applicable to all the social science disciplines and in fact, parallel the definitions of Lasswell and Kaplan (1950; see below, pp. 308–309).

Cohen's approach to the material is rooted in the anthropological tradition, but the cornerstones of his theory are the common assumptions of symbolic theory. First, symbols can be created by individuals, but once adopted by a group they become objective. They exist outside individual psyches and constrain individual behavior. Second, symbols are a mixture of cognitive, agitative, and conative elements. Third, symbol formulation is an autonomous process, and symbolic forms and action are the source of social relations. Thus, symbolization underlies the whole phenomenon of institutionalization. Finally, symbolic action is dramatic. There is a dialectical relationship between the structures of society and the autonomous process of symbol formulation; the one is incomplete without the other. Human needs—the struggle to achieve personal identity, the continuing confrontation with the problems of existence, and the fear of chaos—create symbols and are the source of their compelling power (A. Cohen, 1976, pp. 4–5, 14).

Symbolic forms and symbolic function are not the same and their interaction reinforces the dialectic. The same function can be performed by a variety of forms (A. Cohen, 1976, p. 26) and changes in symbolic form do not necessarily imply changes in symbolic function (1976, p. 29). Old symbolic forms perform new functions and new symbolic forms perform old functions (1976, p. 139). The flag and First-Amendment guarantees are distinct symbolic forms, but each can function as an integrative mechanism (Rothman, 1978).

Symbols are the vehicles of change because they stand ambiguously for a multiplicity of disparate meanings. The dialectical relationship between symbols and the structures of social life initiates and moderates change and makes an ordered social life possible. Symbols are a mixture of cognitive and affective elements, and symbolic formulations are created

by the continuous interaction between the hard surfaces of existence and
the human's need to confront the problems of existence. The meaning of
the symbol is derived from perceptions of this interaction.

Theories of Political Symbols

The work of Charles Merriam is important for the development of a
specifically political theory of symbols. Merriam's insight into the interaction between human needs—the fear of chaos and the compulsion to assign
meaning to the accidents of existence—and various legitimizations of power
led to his classification of the "credenda" and "miranda" of power. *Miranda*
is the general term for things to be admired and *credenda* is the term for
things to be believed. Credenda and miranda are

> cornerstones of the power situation. Power seeks to project itself into
> prestige and prestige to transform itself back into power. Ideology,
> symbolism, the club are never far apart: and they reinforce each other
> in many ways. (Merriam, 1934, p. 132)

Merriam's analysis is based on the common assumptions of symbolism
theory; existence consists of webs of significance spun by people and perceived as interworked systems of construable signs or symbols. The relevance of this assumption is obvious in Merriam's assessment of power.

> Power becomes both beauty and duty; and whether it brings death or
> life may matter little, in comparison with the warm and vivid reality of
> the splendid moment in the span of one's existence, the moment trans-
> cending the life of the individual and carrying him out on the golden
> sea of sacrifice, devotion, participation. (1934, p. 132)

Credenda and miranda are more than legitimizing devices; they are
the artifacts of the search for meaning in the political realm. Consider only
that the political realm has appropriated more days for itself than any other
realm (except the ecclesiastical). Or note the proportion of territorial space
appropriated for public use and the number of streets, ways, and places that
are endowed with power group names and generally equipped with monumental advertisements of power (Merriam, 1934, p. 105).

Merriam illustrates the pervasiveness of these webs of significance by
the role of legality. "There is in 'legality' a symbolic value of high importance in social relations. To be 'legal' is to bear the proud banner which
rallies to its support great numbers of almost any community or tends to
do so" (1934, p. 12). The symbolic value of legality is most obvious in periods of crisis and transition. Although rebels attack particular holders of
the power of legality, they do not attack legality itself. "The old symbols of
departing rulers may be discarded but new forms and colors will promptly

appear, reminders of the new holders of old powers" (1934, p. 12). The domestic crises of the 1960s in the United States seemed to offer verification of this insight. In this period, the function of law as an ordering force contrasted sharply with the perception of law as an instrument of class or social domination. In spite of, or perhaps because of, this juxtaposition, the desire for order persisted and the quest for a new aura of validity was visible even in those who attacked the system (Rothman, 1972, p. 50). Or as noted above, Mary Douglas has argued that dirt or disorder easily became apt symbols of creative formlessness.

However, a critic sees the above process differently, and the difference illustrates the ambiguity and flexibility of symbols. As A. Cohen (1976, p. 37) noted, "the same symbolic form may have different shades of meaning to different individuals, and at different times to the same individual. It is given to different interpretations by different people and under different circumstances." The events of the 1960s led Robert Paul Wolff (1965) to a critical analysis of the boundaries of American tolerance. Wolff discovered the chasm between insider and outsider and found that "the territory of American politics is like a plateau with steep cliffs on all sides. . . . On the plateau are all the interest groups which are recognized as legitimate; in the deep valley all around lie the outsiders" (1965, p. 45). Wolff stressed the costs of the climb to the plateau, not the results of accomplishment, and this perspective makes the difference in interpretation.

Merriam influenced the next generation of political scientists and Harold Lasswell used the notions of credenda and miranda for a scientific rather than a humanistic approach. Lasswell also focused on power relations and his most comprehensive effort to analyze power was *Power and Society* (1950), which was coauthored with Abraham Kaplan. This work presents several contrasts to the theories discussed above. Although their approach is similar to the approaches of Cohen and Merriam in that interest in symbols is sparked by the roles they play in setting up, altering, or maintaining power practices, the work of Lasswell and Kaplan is distinguished by its concentration on the function of political symbols.

Political symbols are defined as "symbols that *function* to a significant extent in power practices" (1950, p. 103, italics added). Political symbols must be studied because they serve an important function in clarifying our understanding of the concept of power. "Power itself is classified as formal and effective, into authority and control, according to the role of symbols (perspectives) with which it is associated" (p. 103). The emphasis on the function of symbols rather than on their properties severely restricts the scope of inquiry. In order to clarify function, a series of classifications are developed. Depending on the circumstances surrounding their use, symbols may be global or parochial, general or special, universal or particular. Again dependent on circumstances, symbols have latent or manifest content and there can be expansion or contraction of their scope and appeal (pp. 104–105).

The second contrast to other theories of symbols is that this approach is self-consciously scientific. Lasswell and Kaplan defined the basic concepts and hypotheses of political science, and only "the empirical propositions of political science" were explicitly formulated (1950, pp. xi–xiii). Richard McKeon (1954/1964) noted the dangers of this kind of restriction. The distinction between cognitive and noncognitive language, though useful, has limited theoretical scope and practical utility. The arbitrary restriction placed "on the 'cognitive' translates all rational and causal uses of language in practical action and esthetic construction into problems of emotion and power accessible to cognition only at the removal from which science views them" (McKeon, 1954/1964, p. 15).

The consequences of this restriction are evident in Lasswell and Kaplan. Abstract regularities of behavior were noted and considerable effort was expended on the formulation of precise definitions. But only the functions of symbols were analyzed; their meaning was ignored. It is ironic, but if the problem of meaning is excluded, the omission hinders attempts to clarify function. The most general statement of the function of symbols is that symbols evoke a response from individuals or groups. Because symbols do not appear to have intrinsic meaning, neither interpretation of a symbol nor the evocation of response is automatic. Rather, both interpretation and response are the result of dynamic interactions between the context of a symbol and the relationships that develop within this context. These are the variables which determine meaning and meaning is the clue to function. If a wink is really a tic, extended discussion of its function is meaningless.

This dynamic interaction is accessible to empirical investigation. Thick description, an alternative theoretical concept developed by Geertz (1973), sorts out significant structures and determines their social ground and import. It is possible to discover which acts, events, or works come to symbolize what to whom. But the empirical task cannot be undertaken, let alone accomplished, unless there is theoretical clarity about what is to be studied. To concentrate on the function of symbols and ignore their meaning results in a species of reductionism.

For this reason, Lasswell's contribution to the study of symbols is found in the area of application rather than theoretical conceptualization. His definition of key symbols, his efforts to define and to operationalize the notions of political myth and political doctrine, and his stress on the scientific analysis of political language (Lasswell, 1949) were developed and refined by students of propaganda and content analysis. However, from the perspective of theory, insight rather than scientific precision is the crucial variable. Thus, Charles Merriam's overview of the role of the credenda

and miranda of power was probably the more fruitful approach, if only because its scope was wider.

Murray Edelman's theoretical work has been influential, in part because the scope of his work is also broad. A review of his theoretical contribution will conclude this section. Edelman's work was influenced by
Lasswell, but it quickly moved beyond the restrictions of a narrowly scientific approach. The difference was made explicit when Edelman (1964,
p. 43) argued that "the 'what' of Lasswell's famous definition is a complex
universe in itself." The shared assumptions of symbolic theory are the tools
for exploration of this complex universe. Meanings are not in symbols but
in people. "Political symbols bring out in concentrated form those particular meanings and emotions which the members of a group create and reinforce" (1964, p. 11). There is nothing in a symbol that requires it to stand for
any one thing. In democracies, institutions such as elections, legislative
debates, and enactment of laws can be analyzed not only in terms of their
instrumental function, but for their role in reinforcing belief in the reality
of citizen participation (1964, pp. 11–12). A society emphasizes certain
themes about its government, and these themes tell us what people want to
believe about themselves and their states (1964, pp. 190–192). In other
words, "groups of people create their worlds in a common image and develop common political interests" (1964, p. 187).

The myths and emotional compulsions of mass responses to politics
are juxtaposed to the cool and oftentimes successful efforts of the few to
secure money, prestige, or power. The difference between politics as a spec-
tator sport and the political activity of organized groups that seek specific
tangible benefits must be explicated (Edelman, 1964, pp. 5–6). Government
confers benefits on some while its forms function to placate or arouse spec-
tators (1964, p. 12). The complex, ambivalent, and ambiguous relationship
between the individual and the state, the alternating current of threat and
reassurance, provides the raw material of symbol formation (1964, p. 1).
The remoteness of political acts from the realities of everyday life blurs or
minimizes the significance of realistic details that could weaken the symbolic import of political acts (1968, p. 8). For this reason, our widely held
beliefs about how government operates resemble myths. A key characteristic of myth is that it is generally unquestioned, widely taught and believed.
Political acts easily become condensation symbols which evoke emotions
and reinforce mythic understandings of politics. Elections are one example.
They appear as verifications of our most deeply held value, that government is based on the consent of the governed. But empirical studies show
that elections have little impact on policy and it seems evident that elections
function primarily to reinforce the common social beliefs which hold a
community together (1964, pp. 33–36).

Elections could not serve this ritual function if commonly held social

beliefs were widely questioned. This last point suggests an important quali-
fication of the utilization of political symbols. As noted above, the symbol-
making function is selective and there are obstacles to deliberate manipulation. The symbols with the greatest affective potential are those which are
taken for granted; that is, those which are most rooted in the realities of
everyday life (Berger & Luckmann, 1967). But the analysis of embedded
symbols requires either Olympian detachment or the condition of marginality. As Sapir (1934b, p. 494) noted, "symbolic meanings can often be recognized clearly for the first time when the symbolic value, generally unconscious or conscious only in a marginal sense, drops out of a socialized pattern of behavior and the supposed function . . . loses its significance and
seems to be little more than a paltry rationalization." Political symbols,
and especially their potential for manipulation, are more evident in transitional or crisis periods than in periods of relative peace. This observation is
confirmed by all students of symbols. A. Cohen (1976, p. 8), for example,
notes that symbols are essential for the development and maintenance of
social order and that they do their job most effectively when they are unnoticed. If this function becomes known to the actors, symbols lose much of
their efficacy. At the same time, we know that symbols are manipulated by
interest groups for their own benefit and we fear that we are being exploited
without our knowledge. This problem is inherent in any political symbolism analysis and the tension generated by the paradox is the motivation
for such analysis.

Edelman's *The Symbolic Uses of Politics* (1964) was criticized because
it "debunked" the myths of American politics, instead of focusing on "how
symbolic forms give meaning to the social order" (Zald, 1966, p. 90). It
must be pointed out that the critical perspective is not a function of the theory; rather, it should be attributed to the institutions and material that
were the subject of analysis. Edelman's thesis was that the notion of evaluating a political system as an instrument which more or less reflects what
people want is too simple.

> The very question of what man *is*, let alone what he wants, is in part a
> product of the political system, and in turn conditions the system. The
> nature of man and the functioning of the system are part of a single
> transaction. The expressive and symbolic functions of the polity are
> therefore central: not simply a blind for oligarchic rules, though they
> may sometimes be that too. (Edelman, 1964, p. 19, Edelman's italics)

If the expressive and symbolic functions of the polity are central, it becomes necessary to explore meanings of, for example, the acts and gestures
of leaders, the settings in which political acts occur, and the language styles
and phrases that permeate political discussion and action. In addition, it is
necessary to grasp the relationship between these meanings and the re-

sponses they evoke in the larger public (1964, p. 20). If this results in debunking, so be it. What is debunked in any specific case depends on the context in which the symbol is perceived. What may appear to one as a key integrative symbol, appears to another as an obstruction to contemporary needs. Different people interpret the same symbol differently; the ambiguity of symbols provides the flexibility that makes an ordered social life possible.

Edelman offered a symbolic interpretation of the administrative system, political leadership, and political quiescence, and his interpretations highlight the complexity of political interactions. His interpretation of language has relevance for theory. Politics is talk and the employment of language to justify action differentiates politics from other methods of allocating values; human needs and emotions make talk potent, culture shapes vocabulary, and individuals respond to verbal cues. "To the political scientist, the patterning or consistency in the contexts in which specific groups of individuals use symbols is crucial, for only through such patterning do common meanings and claims arise. . . . Accuracy is not the important characteristic of political language, but the appraisals common to members of a group" (Edelman, 1964, p. 115). Language serves this function because it reifies the abstract and focuses attention and passion on the remote and the symbolic. Abstractions simplify grossly, but not randomly (1964, pp. 117–119). The abstraction becomes a condensation symbol and takes on compelling connotations. The use of language is the product of social role talking. "Once a term becomes a vehicle for expressing a group interest . . . it is in no sense descriptive, but only evocative" (1964, p. 125). A term such as "government regulation" has different meanings to the president of General Motors and to a consumer advocate. Group use of a term gives a clue to group values.

Edelman analyzed four styles of language—hortatory, legal, administrative, and bargaining—and the interaction of language form and response to verbal cues was explored. The meanings of the styles of political language are the persistent political meanings and offer clues to "the precise dynamics by which political stability and popular consensus are maintained concurrently with wide freedom of policy maneuver for elites" (1964, p. 133).

In summary then, the basic assumptions of Edelman's theory are: there is a transactional tie among language, experience, and meaning, and recognition of the tie opens the door to analysis of political dynamics (1964, p. 150). People create their worlds; language and role taking make these worlds common. Mass publics respond to symbols; "not to 'facts,' and not to moral codes embedded in character or soul, but to the gestures and speeches that make up the drama of the state" (1964, p. 172). Finally, "the themes a society emphasizes and re-emphasizes about its government may not accurately describe its politics; but they do at least tell us what men want to believe about themselves and their state" (1964, p. 191). Such beliefs hold people together and help maintain an orderly state (1964, p. 192).

The richness of Edelman's perspective is attributable in part to the disparate and appropriate examples that he used to illustrate his major themes. Certain of these examples will be discussed in the section of applications. His later work, *Politics as Symbolic Action: Mass Arousal and Quiescence* (1971) and *Political Language: Words that Succeed and Politics that Fail* (1977), refined and elaborated the themes presented in the earlier work. However, each of the two later works also contributes to theory.

Politics as Symbolic Action is an inquiry into the dynamics of mass arousal and quiescence. The symbolizing ability with which people adapt their world to their behavior and their behavior to their world is the motivational core of political dynamics. Political beliefs, demands, and attitudes are not fixed and stable but sporadic in appearance and fluctuating in intensity. "Public policies and processes themselves serve as cues that evoke particular changes in the direction and intensity of political cognitions" (1971, pp. 3–4). The theory which underlies this assertion is based on the distinction between information and meaning. Meaning is different from information and is incompatible with it. "Meaning is associated with order—with a patterned, cognitive structure that permits anticipation of future developments" while "information involves complexity or lack of order; inability to foresee" (1971, p. 31). Political symbols make it possible to align experiences with meaning which reinforces social order; receptivity to information carries the potential of disruption. This insight, as well as the assumption that fear, hope, language cues, role, self-conception, and mythic assumptions coalesce into the complex transaction that is politics, governs Edelman's interpretation of the data.

The role of language is central to the process. "Language forms perform a crucial function by creating shared meanings, perceptions and reassurances among mass publics" (1971, p. 65). There is an extended discussion of metaphor and it is again clear that language both helps and retards us in our exploration of experience. Several of the themes of language are treated more extensively in *Political Language*. But the stress in all of Edelman's work is on the notion that political perceptions, beliefs, norms, and demands are multifaceted, ambivalent, and changeable and that changes are systematic and patterned. The patterns arise from interaction with others and the result is the creation of common conceptions and beliefs about the external world. In *Politics as Symbolic Action*, the stress is on the role that government plays in shaping cognitions about political issues; and the implications are far-reaching. Institutions of government do not so much reflect the people's will as shape it (1971, pp. 172–175). This perspective is critical and the criticisms become more pointed in *Political Language*. But the central theme of symbolic theory remains the motivation for analysis:

"the eternal human search for meaning and for status can be counted on to fuel the problematic interpretation" (1977, p. 63).

Edelman's critique of elite manipulation of symbols is sparked by the perception that in history the search for meaning has all too often resulted in accommodation and conformity. Elites have the resources to use symbols to serve their purposes and can convincingly portray their purposes as the common or public purpose. But symbols are inherently ambiguous and knowledge of their role as well as their relation to a group's beliefs, hopes, and demands can engender a more sophisticated search for meaning with less oppressive consequences.

The theories that have been discussed in this section illustrate the cross-fertilization and shared assumptions of students of symbolism, regardless of whether they are linguists, anthropologists, sociologists, or political scientists. There is no unified theory of symbols in the social sciences, but the work of theorists in all the disciplines demonstrates the autonomous role of the symbol-making function. Language, role, and social cuing are essential to the creation of a common world. Out of the chaos of pristine reality, something becomes charged with meaning and lo and behold—there is structure and pattern in the common world. The symbol-making function is selective, which accounts for the ambiguity of symbols and makes all interpretation problematic. But human beings seek meaning and the quest is a process. Exploration of the many facets of the process is the name of the game, whether it is called thick description, symbolic-interaction theory, phenomenology, or the symbolic uses of politics.

A Survey of Applications of Symbolic Theory

This section reviews applications of symbolic theory in the social sciences, primarily political science and sociology. Anthropologists, particularly those discussed above, have made extensive use of symbolic theory in ethnographic studies with excellent results. Such studies illustrate the heuristic value and utility of the symbolic perspective, particularly its insight into the motivational springs of nonwestern, nonindustrialized society. However, the pervasive role of symbols in "modern" society (i.e., a society which takes pride in its rational foundation and attitudes) is less obvious. Moreover, in that more familiar context there are radical disparities in how symbols are interpreted and used. To illustrate and compare these differences, our analysis will be confined to studies of the uses of symbols in "modern" society.

As noted earlier, the rise and success of Nazi Germany with its propaganda and blatant symbolism shocked and horrified "rational" man. In Cassirer's *The Myth of the State* (1955a), the fact of Nazi Germany evoked a certain fatalism. The optimism engendered by nineteenth-century theories of progress could not prevail against the new forces of darkness, and humanity had to learn to cope with the power of myth. Much of the early interest in symbolism was sparked by renewed fear of the potency of myth and should be understood as attempts to hold back or at least contain the forces of "darkness." The interest in symbolism was evident in two symposia—"Symbols and Values" and "Symbols and Society"—held in the early 1950s. Several of the participants reflected concern with the destructive power of political symbols and these articles illustrated the connection between the time and interest in the use of symbols. These symposia were interdisciplinary and included papers on symbols and religion, semantics and symbols, the arts (including architecture) and symbols, the symbols of folk culture, and of course, symbolism in politics and society. Only the latter will be reviewed here, and related or later elaborations of similar themes will be compared with the symposia articles.

Harold Lasswell discussed "Key Symbols, Signs and Icons" (1954/ 1964) in order to obtain a better understanding of the general social function of symbols. The basic perspectives of the group were termed "myth"; these are "the basic themes that are standardized in the communications of group members with one another" (1954/1964, p. 199). Key signs foster "sentiments that may transcend limitations of culture, class, organization and personality" (p. 201). In the life of society key signs provide "*economic cues for communication*" (p. 200, Laswell's italics). These cues "are able to 'trigger' common responses by evoking perspectives which are widely shared" (p. 200). Key terms permeate the process of policy formation and application. Because key signs are cues to collective action, they appear to play a conservative, standardizing role in society. But the converse is that standardization of perception may engender anomalous or anachronistic perceptions which block adjustment to changed circumstances. Key signs produce either result because they are condensations "of salient allusions to a critical context," such as "the configuration of incidents in a crisis, or the fundamental values and practices of a society" (p. 204).

Lasswell focused attention on the common experience condensed by a symbol and its integrating function and sketched the role played by symbols in policy formation. He also noted that symbols, if they produce false perceptions, block adjustment to change. Shils and Young (1953, pp. 72–79) used the theme of integrative symbols in their analysis of the coronation of Elizabeth II. Popular participation in the coronation was analogous to participation in a religious ritual. During the event, British society had intensive contact with its sacred symbols and the result was an act of national communion which renewed and reaffirmed the bonds of obligation in the society.

In contrast, Charles Frankel (1954/1964) was concerned with the illusions and delusions spawned by symbols. Political symbols are potent in generating and sustaining collective behavior, but if they symbolize "dead idols," they are an obstacle to communication and understanding. Frankel defended liberalism against the charge that it destroyed warm and civilizing symbols, rooted in family, home, native land, and ancestral religion, and replaced them with symbols such as "liberty" and "equality" that were too rational, material, and abstract. The major criticism of liberal symbols was that they lack "the sense of discipline and of the limits of human achievement which symbols descended from the past convey; [they] lack the power to elevate or ennoble or to lift men to a sense of membership in a community larger than the circle of their own personal ideas and interests" (1954/1964, pp. 364–365). Because Frankel feared that symbols of dead idols were obstacles to the development of human autonomy, he championed liberalism, which spent its efforts freeing people from enslavement to symbols.

Frankel recognized that his society was ambivalent and confused about its symbols; inherited symbols had lost their potency and failed to evoke common emotions or produce communion (p. 68). But the failure was predictable: "the power which symbols have to move us is *borrowed* power. And when what they stand for changes or disappears, they live on borrowed time" (p. 370, his italics). Frankel was concerned that the attempt to reinvigorate worn-out symbols would result in shoddy symbols. The choice was clear: it was better to live in a world devoid of symbols or a world where symbols were realistically appraised than to live in bondage to dead idols.

Concern about the potential of symbols to generate false perspectives could produce, as the Frankel article indicates, a defense of liberalism. It could also be used to legitimize a scientific or behavioral approach to the study of symbols. Finally, it might become the source of a critical perspective.

With respect to the scientific approach to symbols, two examples are offered. Daniel Lerner (1954/1964) argued that a science of symbols could and should be used to strengthen the American position in the world. Given the Cold War, the United States could not afford to lose the neutrals. If the behavioral perspective was used to study symbols, it would enable us to cut through the fogs surrounding our values and find their usable elements. The United States had failed after World War II "to elaborate a symbolism commensurate with the magnitude of its acts, a symbolism that would clarify the meaning of these acts in such a way that people of the Free World would feel themselves to belong to a more righteous and powerful community as a result of participating in these acts" (1954/1964, p. 379). Unfortunately, the key symbol—"democracy"—was ambiguous, and its disparate uses increased Western ambivalence about the term. If the operational specifications of democracy were discovered, knowledge could be joined with power to bring "enlightenment with governance, in the services of democratic preferences" (p. 381). People with knowledge have a special responsibility. They must bring the fruits of their knowledge to bear on the outcomes of politics (p. 382).

The exhortation was powerful, it offered unlimited vistas to the knowledgeable. But it was dictated by the circumstances of ideological confrontation. And with changes in circumstances, the exhortation appears to be at best naive. Conscious attempts to reinvigorate symbols and to utilize them as props for controversial policies or leaders weaken the force and power of integrative symbols. When experience contrasts sharply with expectations, efforts to use symbols to cover the discrepancies are more likely to engender cynicism than reaffirmation. Despite the purity of his purposes, Lerner's approach reeks with the temptation to manipulate symbols to produce desired policy goals. Such a strategy fails in so far as it ignores the interplay of context and meaning and the relationships which develop from this interplay.

A more neutral empirical approach to meaning was developed by Ithiel de Sola Pool (1954/1964, p. 350): "For an empirical study of meanings the problem is to determine and specify the meanings which men in any given context embody in a given symbol." Utilization of this approach bypassed the problems of finding the philosophical truth of a value or determining what learned people meant by it (pp. 350–354). For a social scientist, the meaning of a symbol to a certain person is defined "as the sum of the contexts in which the person will use that symbol" (p. 354). The task is analogous to, although more sophisticated than, that of the modern dictionary maker or grammarian. "Where men feel a word applies and where they feel it does not is their definition of it" (p. 355). But because most values are ambiguously applied, there are technical problems connected with the empirical study of value-laden language. "But with the aid of precise analysis of linguistic constellations, they [technical problems] are not insurmountable" (p. 359).

Karl Deutsch (1954/1964) also utilized an empirical approach to the symbols of political community. He saw political symbols as indicators, their statistical distribution informing us about the flow of messages and, in turn, the flow telling us "something about the context in which political meanings are perceived, remembered and recalled. . . . Thus they help us understand political meaning and political perception at different times and in different communities" (p. 23). In other words, if a symbol is an indicator, circumstances determine the trends of usage and both are accessible to empirical investigation.

Symbols can also be classified as "regulators" or instruments of political control. Then the task is to determine what symbols do to further or hinder the integration of political communities. Again this is an empirical question. Successful integration of political communities seems to be the result of a multiplicity of integrative symbols, their mutual interrelatedness and mutual reinforcement (Deutsch, 1954/1964, pp. 36–39).

The work of Pool and Deutsch offers excellent examples of the utility of empirical approaches to symbols; each has stimulated the work of other scholars. But the empirical approach has limitations. It neglects the fact that symbols are a mixture of cognitive and affective elements. Neither determinations of the frequency of use nor specification of the contexts in which symbols are used reach the affective aspects of symbols and their import. The categories of context are not neat and the association of symbols and values is complex, not pat. The commutability and compatibility of symbols, as well as the consequence of commutation and compatibility, engender erratic and unpredictable results. Symbolic theory and what we know of the use of symbols in history suggest that there is a relationship between the success of a symbol and its ambiguity or flexibility. The empirical studies cited above fail to pay attention to the potential for transformation and the dialectical relationships that are the source of transformation.

Research on symbols during the 1950s reflected the issues and the times. Although there was concern over the condition of American symbols and increased alienation, symbols were studied primarily as integrative forces. William C. Mitchell's (1962) analysis of the American polity illustrates the emphasis on symbols as integrative forces but goes beyond "the facts" and thus serves as a bridge to the more critical analyses of the 1960s. Mitchell used a structural-functional approach but also examined the components of belief systems (values which specify what is considered good or valuable and norms which are prescriptions of behavior). Political culture is the general term for the sets of beliefs and operative norms in a given society. Culture shapes inputs to the polity, particularly demands on the system, expectations about the system, and support for the system (Mitchell, 1962, p. 22). The belief system constitutes a way of perceiving and evaluating the world. In every society, some set of beliefs tends to dominate and the dominant set typically constitutes a defense of society and its political system as a just one (see McIntosh, 1963). Mitchell (1962, pp. 4–23) also noted that the appeal of symbols was based primarily on the affective or emotional and esthetic needs of people.

Mitchell designated liberalism as the American belief system. It consisted of collections of ideas as to what politics are and what they ought to be. These collections were (and are) not neat, logical, or lucid; rather they were composed of "generally fuzzy, unclear and frequently illogical connections of ideas" (1962, p. 106). Nevertheless, American perceptions of power were shaped by these collections of ideas.

Power is regarded as a tool to be used for special, clearly defined purposes. Power is also regarded as an evil, although at times a necessary evil. It is also conceived as a "thing" which has to be limited in quantity. Power typically is perceived as the possession of one group rather than another; thus, one group gains power at the expense of another. This belief system shapes the perceptions of political scientists as well as those of citizens. American political scientists are primarily concerned with the patterns of distribution of power and the allocation of values by the polity (Mitchell, 1962, p. 110). This ambivalence about power is not a new development; it was articulated at the Constitutional Convention in 1787. Ratification of the Constitution legitimized this collection of beliefs, and over time they have become embedded in the American psyche (Rothman, 1974). Mitchell described this ambivalence—the belief that power is evil and should not be exalted coexisting with secret pride in the use of power and the acts of power holders (1962, p. 110).

This ambivalence is also reflected in our use of public space. Greek or baroque architecture is used in many of our public buildings to symbolize the grandeur of the authority of government. On the other hand, the shabby, slightly deteriorated buildings of local government reflect our suspicions about power and express our desire to keep it limited. We may succumb to the temptations of power but we also demand that the financial and psychological costs be minimized (Mitchell, 1962, p. 125).

American concentration on the rational legal foundation of authority is probably the most significant factor in shaping our perceptions of power and is the major means of controlling power. To be legitimate, power must conform to the criteria of rational legal standards (Mitchell, 1962, pp. 111–113). The emphasis itself is significant; it suggests the contemporary need for the reassurances of rationality and the fears that symbols are potent sources of false perceptions and delusions. The history of the twentieth century is a constant reminder of the havoc that false symbols create. An emphasis on rational legal standards makes a neat contrast to the forces of unreason and sharpens perceptions of the alternative. Rational legal standards appear capable of containing the forces of darkness. The primacy of rational, legal authority in our Weltanschauung and its role in checking power serve as an excellent example of the potency of implicit, or taken-for-granted, symbols.

Peter Hall (1972) also used the assumptions of symbolism theory and symbolic-interactionist theory to construct a theory of society as a "negotiated order." His model has particular relevance for American politics. Hall assumed that "the basis for joint action is the establishment through interpretive interaction of common definitions of the situation." But his stress was on the

> numerous contingencies, ambiguities, constraints, problems and conflicts which require new or changing definitions. Thus the quality of social life is characterized by greater degrees of uncertainty and requires stronger conscious effort than normally described. (1972, p. 41)

Because "values, goals, rules, roles, collective vs. individual interest, new situations, resource constraints and courses of action" are all problematic, joint action is a "complex process involving all the manifestations of bargaining and negotiating." The negotiated-order model of society is "characterized by a complex network of competing groups and individuals acting to control, maintain, or improve their social conditions as defined by their *self*-interests" (1972, p. 45).

In the political arena, power processes are central, but the bases or resources of power have not been systematically studied. Hall sketched an analysis of some of the processes of power (e.g., manipulation of symbols, control of the flow of information, and dispensing conditional rewards) and justified this focus with the contention that the basic element of politics is talk. The social scientist must be concerned with political impression management. "Control over the conduct of others is achieved by influencing the definition of the situation in which all are involved" (1972, p. 51). Given these assumptions, a dramatistic perspective modeled on the theory of Kenneth Burke was used to analyze the compelling quality of the interdependencies that constitute the definition of the situation. "The manipulation of symbols takes place in the context of existing sets or symbols or a political culture." However, the notion of political culture does not imply a

cohesive, coherent, integrated, consensual belief system because that is not the reality of the situation. Rather what exists are numerous values and beliefs which are only partially integrated, partially conscious and often in contradiction with one another. (Hall, 1972, p. 53)

Definitions of the situation are constituted and reconstituted from arrangements and rearrangements of these elements. Various aspects of defining the situation were discussed by Hall, and the political relevance of this process was obvious. "In general, people who have degrees of control or influence seek to have situations defined so that they impressionistically transform power into authority" (1972, p. 69). The investigation of integrative symbols is at the center of the analysis, but the perspective is critical and the emphasis is on the management and manipulation of symbols. Recognition of the types of manipulation offers insight into the internal processes of society and illustrate the ways that people establish their social worlds by constituting them conceptually (Hall, 1972, pp. 70–72).

Hall's conception of a negotiated order was influenced by the work of Erving Goffman and Murray Edelman. Goffman's *The Presentation of Self in Everyday Life* (1959) examines the complex interactions that constitute the definition of a situation. The arts of impression management are based on moral claims.

> Society is organized on the principle that any individual who possesses
> certain social characteristics has a moral right to expect that others will
> value and treat him in an appropriate way. Connected with this prin-
> ciple is a second, namely that an individual who implicitly or explicitly
> signifies that he has certain social characteristics ought in fact to be
> what he claims he is. (Goffman, 1959, p. 13)

These reciprocal claims are the basis for predictable social interaction.
To supplement this base, individuals employ various stratagems to enhance their positions. For example, it is in the interest of the individual to
control the conduct of others.

> This control is achieved largely by influencing the definition of the situ-
> ation which the others come to formulate, and he can influence this
> definition by expressing himself in such a way as to give them the kind
> of impression that will lead them to act voluntarily in accordance with
> his own plan. (Goffman, 1959, p. 4)

The insight is as applicable to the behavior of elites and government officials as it is to an analysis of individual behavior. Goffman treated the
material as matters of fact and presented it as the motivations of routine
behavior. Edelman examined these interactions and was critical of the outcomes. Hall's treatment of symbol manipulation was influenced by Edelman's critical analysis of the process of power as well as by Goffman's
approach to human interactions.

Kantor (1972) criticized the negotiated-order model because it made
self-interest the motivating force of social action, thus neglecting the influence of institutional constraints and the ties of community. Hall, however, explicitly framed his theory for the American political system, and
his analysis may be appropriate in that context. As Mitchell asserted, American perceptions of power are ambivalent and idiosyncratic. If liberalism
is the prevalent American belief system, it too stresses the "happiness" of
the individual and tends to diminish the constraints of traditional order. If
that is the case, the evocation of the symbols of traditional society does not
constitute a criticism of the negotiated order. Rather, this evocation establishes alternative symbols as primary values and confronts one postulated
order with another. For this reason, Kantor's critique can be viewed as another illustration of how the symbols of our weltanschauung shape our
definitions of the situation.

W. Lance Bennett (1979) carefully examined the power of integrative
symbols in his work on civil religion. Although the evils of manipulation
were recognized, the accomplishments of civil religion, its "creation of an
unquestionable pattern of social relations and civil obligations," outweighed the possible risks (1979, p. 109). The success of civil religion in
secular society is related to its core symbols; they "must be ambiguous

enough to accommodate divergent initial perceptions of events and to obscure . . . differences in emphasis and private concern. . . . Ambiguity in the usage of basic political principles breeds consensus" (1979, p. 116). Participation in public rituals is an implicit citizenship trait and the "collective, consensual and validational aspects of imitation within ritual context" create "what is taken for objective political facts on which the stable operating procedures and legitimacy of a state depend" (1979, p. 115). According to Bennett, however, the incorporation of public morality into the rituals of civil religion in secular society is fraught with danger. Tragedy and nightmare are as likely outcomes as a great awakening of public spirit. But fear of the consequences of manipulating symbols should not deter us from studying and understanding the moral bases of modern society.

Utilizing a different approach because they assume that symbols play an integrative role, Cobb and Elder (1972) examine possible uses of symbols in the political process. The many uses of symbols are detailed; for example, they influence onlookers and relevant decision makers and enhance group commitment (1972, p. 142). Symbol manipulation produces disparate effects: arousal, provocation, dissuasion, demonstration of strength of commitment, and affirmation (pp. 145–150). Cobb and Elder also recognize that the manipulation of symbols is a central fact of mass society, in part because direct contact between leaders and followers is minimal or nonexistent.

This review suggests that recognition of the integrative role of symbols does not preclude differences in the perception of the phenomenon. The integrative symbol may serve noble purposes or it may mask elite control of the tangible rewards of the polity. The interpretation depends on the eye of the beholder, but the difference is illustrated by a comparison of Gusfield's analysis of the temperance movement and the research of Murray Edelman. Gusfield (1963) examines the role that government plays in the distribution of status. Political action that affects the allocation of instrumental rewards is distinguished from political action that affects the distribution of values through symbolic acts. The latter shapes perceptions of status because the dramatic, symbolic meanings of politics shape much of our response to political events (1963, p. 167).

There are two major forms of political symbolism, according to Gusfield (1963, pp. 171–172): gestures of cohesion and gestures of differentiation. The former "fix the common and consensual aspects of society as sources of governmental support." The latter "point to the glorification or degradation of one group in opposition to others within the society." Gestures of differentiation lie at the root of status allocation and the conferral of deference. The stratagems of the temperance movement over time were shaped by consideration of changing allocations of status. Originally, temperance forces were culturally dominant and the movement sought to persuade the weaker members of society to reform themselves. Later, when cultural dominance became problematic, the movement turned to governmental action to secure and establish their values. "The need for symbolic vindication and deference is channeled into political action. What is at stake is . . . their [human] ideals, the moralities to which they owe their public allegiance" (p. 177).

Gusfield cautions against viewing symbolic action either as irrational or as merely expressive behavior and criticized Edelman for excessive reliance on the notion of "psychological reassurance." Because Edelman assumed that psychological reassurance of symbolic action led to mass acceptance of the disparate distribution of instrumental rewards, he minimized the real questions of status allocation that were at stake in status politics (Gusfield, 1963, p. 182). Gusfield argued that status conflict is an integral part of the study of politics in a society where class conflict is weak and status is problematic. Although status conflicts are difficult to institutionalize, the quest for an honored place in society persists, and social change continually upsets old hierarchies and generates new aspirations. "Status politics is neither a new nor a transient aspect of American society" (1963, p. 188). Gusfield's emphasis on the persistence of status politics has been restated in the work of cultural historians such as Robert Kelley (1979), who described the persistence of status conflict in American party politics.

A recent empirical study compared self-interest and symbolic politics as explanations of white opposition to school busing and concluded "that it is apparently the *symbolism* evoked by the prospect of any white children's forced intimate contact with blacks, rather than the *reality* of one's own children's contact, that triggers opposition to busing" (Sears, Hensler, & Speer, 1979, p. 382). Moreover, "it seems likely that whites' perceptions of the hazards of 'busing' are generally based more on what it symbolizes than on what it actually is" (Sears et al., 1979, p. 383). The seeds of status conflict inhere in the symbols that shape perception of contemporary issues and status conflict continues to be a significant aspect of American politics.

Edelman's perspective differs from Gusfield's in its emphasis on psychological reassurance, but it is misleading to interpret this emphasis as neglect of the reality of status conflict. Edelman cuts into the material differently and his perspective is more critical. His approach is related to the critical analyses of Max Lerner (1937), Thurman Arnold (1962), Harold Lasswell (1930), and George Orwell (1962). Orwell's classic essay "Politics and the English Language" (1962) presented examples of political language and concluded that their imagery was stale and lacked precision. This degradation of language was not accidental: "in our time, political speech and writing are largely the defense of the indefensible" (p. 153). Political language "is designed to make lies sound truthful and murder respectable, and to give an appearance of solidity to pure wind" (p. 157). We must defend ourselves from these temptations if language is to become respectable again.

Lerner, Arnold, and Lasswell focused on elite manipulation of symbols and indicated the frustrating effects of adherence in periods of change to symbols inherited from a different past. Or as Sapir (1934b) noted, the recognition that the symbol has dropped out of its rational framework is one source of the critical perspective. However, Edelman's work is more theoretical and comprehensive than the earlier critiques. The theory is wide ranging, with appropriate political examples used to illuminate the import of symbolic action. The material that is explored, not the theory, leads to the conclusion that symbol manipulation typically results in mass quiescence and the reinforcement of the status quo. This conclusion is reached by contrasting rhetorical commitments and beliefs with policy outcomes. The result is a realistic, albeit critical appraisal of the potency of the symbols of our Weltanschauung.

According to Edelman, several psychological processes interact and function to justify maintenance of the status quo. These processes include:

> personification of fears and hopes, so that particular public figures symbolize them; perception of real human beings as objects; condensation of diverse issues and observations into a single symbol, promoting cognitive confusion; categorizations that unconsciously evoke elaborate structures of dogmatic belief. (1977, p. 144)

The psychological process that provides the most effective defense of the status quo is the ability to resort to different and contradictory sets of cognitions to justify conforming behavior and "to rationalize the failure of authorities to achieve their goals." Because leaders and institutions come to symbolize hopes and fears, symbols can be used to "justify established authorities and their policies while also rationalizing inequalities, deprivations and ineffective courses of action" (Edelman, 1977, p. 144).

Language is completely intertwined with these psychological processes, as well as with justifications and the rationalizations of politics. "We must recognize that it is language about political events rather than the events themselves that everyone experiences" (1977, p. 142). The use of language styles—hortatory for public messages and bargaining for insiders (1964, pp. 130–151)—and the distinction between meaning and information (1971, pp. 31–52), as well as the critical analysis of the language of the helping professions (1977, pp. 57–75), suggest how language masks the exercise of power. The language of "politics creates a way of living with social problems by defining them as inevitable or as equitable" (1977, p. 141). The typical outcome of symbolic action is reinforcement of the viability of the polity.

This outcome may be typical but it can threaten the cherished values of the polity. The people's right to know is threatened by the central role government plays in the diffusion of political information. Modern governments are in a position to use facts to justify their policies even though the logical connection between fact and policy is dubious, problematic, or nonexistent. The symbolism of democratic government shapes public expectations and "predisposes the public to accept government's part in gathering, shaping and presenting the facts. As long as the actions of government conform to expectations, there is little likelihood that government's role in the formation of communications will be perceived, let alone criticized" (Rothman, 1977, p. 75). The routine operation of government shapes beliefs about which data are relevant, and the implications of data and this unrecognized power offer greater control over the information marketplace than the techniques of secrecy and propaganda (Rothman, 1977, p. 76).

Claus Mueller (1973) also developed a far-reaching critique of the role of communication in modern society. "Language codes and socialization can obscure the perception of social needs and societal problems" (p. 23). Mueller described three main types of distorted communication (1973, pp. 24-87): directed, arrested, and constrained. Directed communications occur primarily in totalitarian countries but traces can also be found in democracies. Arrested communication is the result of the impoverished language codes of the lower classes. Constrained communication is communication "between the government and the public and public communications regarding societal problems which are subject to the systematic bias of governmental and private interests" (pp. 86-87). Because information is the crucial prerequisite for political control, distortions of communication must be exposed. Impression management offers the possibility of control and constrained communication gives officeholders greater control over the management of public issues.

However, the language code of the middle and upper-middle classes encourages reflective responses to political events (Mueller, 1963, p. 172) and a confluence of factors has resulted in a delegitimization of government. Traditional verities are no longer honored and efficiency and rationality appear to be the sole remaining legitimizers of government. Unfortunately, efficiency and rationality offer insufficient support and "the absence of effective legitimizing rationales constitutes a problem to which the political system has no answer" (1963, p. 182).

Mueller was pessimistic about the possibility of replacement symbols because distortions of communications adversely affect the development of adequate symbols and the middle and upper-middle classes are likely to become increasingly alienated. His analysis recognized the role and the potency of legitimizing symbols but ignored the strength of inertia and the power of even declining symbols to sustain the polity. The middle class can be persuaded of the legitimacy of authority as easily as the lower classes if they are convinced that cherished values are at risk.

Dan Nimmo's (1970) analysis of political communication is a hard look at the techniques of modern election campaigns which recognizes the influence of symbols of political perceptions. The changed circumstances of political campaigns and the low or noninvolvement of the mass public have altered the purposes of political persuasion. Efforts are no longer directed at changing the attitudes of the committed; they are directed toward shifting the perceptions of voters with low involvement. Here the qualities of the mass media, particularly television, highlight the form of the message rather than its content; imagery becomes crucial. "It is important that the content of a message or the qualities of a product or candidate be sufficiently ambiguous so that members of an audience can project into it the percepts relevant to their own cognitive needs" (1970, p. 181).

Although less-involved citizens do not receive information from the mass media during political campaigns, they do derive entertainment.

> [Media] communications are symbolic in that they capture the outlines of any event or message in simple, easily grasped concepts. That conceptualization implies subjective selection and interpretation by newsmen, public relations personnel, media specialists and others. The overall process results in a refraction or reduction of fidelity in the transmission of context. (Nimmo, 1970, p. 188)

A political environment is structure which can be perceived only through the media. "People perceive in the televised political campaign precisely what the media have led them to believe should be there." Consequently, the media "shape predispositions about what politics is about (crisis and conflict) and the preferred qualities of political leaders (credibility and trustworthiness)" (1970, p. 187).

Professionally mediated campaigns influence voting behavior and the invasion of professional managers, pollsters, and image-makers changes if not skews the electoral marketplace. The new technology increases the likelihood of systematic deception (1970, pp. 193–195), but this outcome is not necessarily attributable to the increase of conscious manipulation. Technicians can make a candidate appear to be what he is not so that in the technological era appearance counts for more than reality. Technology has unbalanced the relationship between politics and persuasion and professionally mediated campaigns "reinforce and extend the symbolic dimensions of American elections" (1970, p. 198).

Nimmo also described and analyzed the composition and functions of political images in *Popular Images of Politics* (1974). He discussed theories of political imagery and reaffirmed the crucial role of symbols in the creation of political images. Nimmo also argued the need for a dramatistic perspective.

> *Politics is dramatic action* and the images through which we play our roles . . . are sometimes authentic and sometimes illusory. Political competence begins with our willingness to recognize the difference between the authentic and the illusory and explore the subtle ways that political action arises from a combination of the actor's rational understanding of the nature of politics and his emotional responses to the political situation. (1974, p. 155, Nimmo's italics)

The rhetoric in defense of the Vietnam War increased American sensitivity to the use of language to defend the indefensible. Skidmore's *Word Politics* (1972) is a collection of critical articles detailing this new sensitivity. He presented various examples of the way that language is perverted and used to further interests and enhance commitment. Additional knowledge of the resources and stratagems of language usage was obtained from the distinction between deep and surface political issues.

The most powerful political issues are probably composed of condensation symbols in configurations which produce masked images (Bennett, Harris, Laskey, Levitch, & Monrad, 1976, p. 111). Masked images are ambiguous symbolizations that evoke more than directly related images. Gerald Ford's advocacy of amnesty presents an example of the introduction of masked symbols. There were two levels to Ford's rhetoric: at the first level, the symbols were fairly concrete; at the second level, abstract images were used to shape audience dispositions about broader political concerns. When Ford used the words, "binding the nation's wounds," the reference was to the aftermath of Watergate as well as to the aftermath of Vietnam. "The contexts of 'unity,' 'binding wounds,' and 'healing' provided a subtle focus for a litany of absolution for the era" (Bennett *et al.*, 1976, pp. 116–117). If abstract images are used to transmit deep political images, the actor must be capable of maintaining control of the message format. Ford maintained control in the early stages of the debate on amnesty but lost control when he granted a pardon to Richard Nixon. The loss of control points up the significance of fit among variables as a determinant of whether a given political issue or action can "serve as a vehicle for the transmission of deeper political issues" (1976, p. 125–126).

Although the applications discussed above dealt primarily with aspects of American politics, the diversity of the applications is an indication of the utility of the perspective. The focus on symbols offers insight into the dynamics of language and communication, administration, leadership, political parties, elections, and the making and implementation of policy. The applications may be disparate, but the core of the focus is consistent; the dynamics or processes of politics must be explored. There is a dialectical relationship between symbolic action and power relations (Aronoff, 1977; A. Cohen, 1976; Turner, 1974). Definitions of the situation shift and the stage is set for transformations, but the consequences of the relationship are bounded and contained by the specific institutional structure in which it is located. Symbols primarily serve integrative functions, but if circumstances change the symbol drops out of its socialized pattern. Then recognition of its symbolic function can increase marginality and contribute to alienation. This is the source of the critical focus; criticism results from empirical investigation of the data and is not inherent in the theory.

To conclude this section on applications, two subareas will be briefly sketched. The first subarea is law as a symbol system. Although work in this area overlaps the more general applications of symbolic theory, it will be separately treated because most of this research is more critical than the main body of applications. Dissonance is generated when law, which is typically perceived as the source of our perceptions of an overarching order, is found to have dropped out of its socialized pattern. This discovery has broad implications; the concept of law is so encompassing that exploration of law as symbol opens an area of social and political relationships with a scope as extensive and complete as language.

The second subarea is the renewed interest in metaphors. This area might have been included in the theoretical section, but the emphasis on metaphor, though not a pragmatic exercise, derives from the theoretical perspective. Perhaps the insight of Mary Douglas, that pieces which are out of place yet retain identity are perceived as threats to good order, should be applied to metaphors. The insight might explain both the attraction of the uses and the dangers of the misuses of metaphors.

Law as a Symbol System

Max Lerner's (1937) work on the fetish of the Constitution illustrates the impact of the perception that law is a symbol system. According to Lerner, the crisis of the depression and the resultant human misery made social change imperative, but the Supreme Court used the symbols of the past to obstruct the needed change. When the realization became widespread, the common people would again have the opportunity to be both symbol breakers and symbol makers. The search for economic security would lead "*necessarily through new forms of social construction and therefore through the creation of new myths*" (M. Lerner, 1937, p. 1319, his italics). The conclusion is ironic. Awareness that inherited symbols are used to block social change does not lead to freedom from symbols; it leads to the replacement of one set of symbols by a more adequate set.

A critical approach to legal symbols is also predominant in the work of Julius Cohen (1954/1964). The lawyer starts with facts and uses symbols, but the latter are value charged. The symbols of the law are weapons of combat between competing claims as well as instruments for ordering and creating. They are the primary means for maintaining or changing human relations. Of necessity, these symbols are as competitive as the interests in whose defense they are used. Clarity about value-charged symbols must be "the starting point of an inquiry into the meaning of a conflict situation . . . and of the merits of the policy decision." If, as is often the case, clarity is lacking, the value system becomes the "concealed terminal point of the decision itself" (J. Cohen, 1954/1964, p. 439).

Edelman argued that since much of statutory law is amended or emasculated by administration, its primary function must be to reassure the public that their interest is protected (1964, pp. 37–38). He also noted that there are two kinds of law enforcement; the difference between them amounts to the difference between mutual threat (command) and mutual role taking (the game) (1964, pp. 47–49).

Michael Barkun's (1968) perspective is less critical; he focuses on the integrative role of legal symbols—how they provide a framework for human interaction. The human need for order is pervasive and is the source of law even in such unlikely places as primitive society and the international arena. Recognition of this basic need produces a different model of law, one which recognizes the behavioral regularity that is the prerequisite of social organization. Law is a set of interrelated symbols which are more or less complex, relative to the complexity of the society. "Law as a symbol system is a means of conceptualizing and managing the social environment" (Barkun, 1968, p. 151). It should be viewed as preemption rather than prescription because "it narrows the number of ways in which something can be done until, ideally, there are only two alternatives, which we think of as obeying or disobeying the law" (p. 157). The most useful aspect of law is its flexibility. The ambiguities of law, especially in complex society, provide "a means for maintaining change within humanly acceptable limits, for allowing innovation by increments while keeping the general scheme of things within accustomed tracks—for perpetually altering the status quo while perpetually preserving it" (p. 166).

Scheingold (1974) also explored the use of legal symbols to contain conflict, but from a more critical perspective.

> Legal symbols are used to persuade those involved in the conflict that it makes sense to think of the problem in terms of rights and obligations— thus tapping that latent sensibility to the need for rules and, at the same time, framing the issue in readily comprehensible fashion. Lurking behind the appeal to everyone's common sense, however, is the machinery of government . . . which can produce an authoritative determination. . . . The underlying purpose of the debate is to channel dispute into established institutions. (1974, p. 50)

My own work on legal symbols has focused on stability and change in a legal order. The language of law is the language of social control. People's need for order and for maps to serve as criteria of political choice have shaped a rhetoric of justification which masks the language of social control (Rothman, 1972, p. 40). Because the public believes that the legal system symbolizes a just order, legal symbols channel societal conflict. Even when there is widespread skepticism about whether a particular order is right and just, the human need for order and the tendency to reify existing rules are still manifest and the drive for order continues unabated. Legal systems thrive on the perception of their inevitability. "The removal of the component of inevitability may destroy a particular order, but it does not destroy the quest for order. The pieces will be resorted, rearranged and reestablished and a new aura of validity will be created" (Rothman, 1972, p. 50).

A different aspect of the integrating power of symbols is revealed when the symbolic import of the First Amendment is contrasted with the ambiguous prescriptions derived from it. The First Amendment is perceived as the symbol of American commitment to the free marketplace of ideas. But there is continuing tension between this commitment and the threat that dissidence poses to security and order. The legal arguments over interpretation of the First Amendment legitimize both the commitment and the fears and bind the passion of dissent with the chains of rationality. As the precedents of case law evolve into ritualistic patterns, the public is reassured that law can contain dissent, regardless of the outcome of specific cases, and the process contributes to the viability of the polity (Rothman, 1978).

Although the research on law as a symbol system recognizes the integrative power of symbols, the focus seems to have removed the aura of authority and legitimacy from the law. If the symbols of law are as competitive as the interests they represent, then the analysis of legal symbols confronts and contradicts cherished notions about order. The new awareness may engender skepticism, more realistic appraisals of the ambiguities of social order, or demands for new, more compelling symbols.

The Relation of Metaphor and Political Symbolism

The use and abuse of metaphors is a constant reminder of the problematic nature of social order. Metaphor is a linguistic device that springs from the complexity and ambiguity of human existence. Nisbet argued that

> metaphor is a way of knowing . . . a way of proceeding from the known to the unknown. It is a way of cognition in which the identifying qualities of one thing are transferred in an instantaneous, almost unconscious, flash of insight to some other thing that is, by remoteness or

complexity, unknown to us. . . . Metaphor is our means of effecting in-
stantaneous fusion of two separated realms of experience into one il-
luminating, iconic, encapsulating image. (1969, p. 4)

Edelman (1971, p. 67) emphasized the pervasiveness of metaphor. "Thought
is metaphorical and metaphor pervades language, for the unknown, the
new, the unclear and the remote are apprehended by one's perceptions of
identities with the familiar."

Although the use of metaphor is ingrained in language, metaphors are
feared because they are the stuff of illusion. The possibility of adherence to
false symbols is also feared for this reason. The propensity of people to accept the illusions generated by metaphor, imparts urgency to pleas to har-
ness and chain the powers of metaphors and symbols. In addition, the
dominance of science in modern times, with its emphasis on precision in
research, militates against the conscious use of metaphor in the social sciences. There is irony in "scientific" attempts to simplify the language of
politics and social action. Both experience and language are rich, complex,
and ambiguous. To strip language of its complexity and still hope to encap-
sulate the complexity of political action is self-defeating. The result of
simplifying language is a narrowing of the political focus.

In addition, try as we may, the use of metaphor is inevitable, even in
science. Furthermore, metaphor is so pervasive that even attempts to explain the concept depend on the use of other metaphors. For example, Max
Black (1962) explicated an interaction view of metaphor, but to explain
his concept he needed to use the notion of a lens or filter. This is clearly a
metaphoric use of language. Black claimed that a metaphorical statement
had a principal and a subsidiary subject. These subjects are systems of associated commonplaces or sets of standard beliefs or multivocal symbols. In
other words, each subject brings into relation ideas, images, sentiments,
values, and stereotypes. The associated commonplaces of the subsidiary
subject become the filter or lens through which the principal subject is
viewed. In this way, the metaphor selects, emphasizes, suppresses, and or-
ganizes features of the principal subject by relating it to the subsidiary subject (Black, 1962; Turner, 1974; Zashin & Chapman, 1974).

Turner utilized the interaction view of metaphor as a foundation for
his analysis of symbolic behavior. He saw the meaning of a metaphor as a
result of the interaction of the two subjects that it joins (1974, p. 29). But
Turner also recognized that metaphors have the power to engender illusions. A particularly potent example of this power is the illusion spawned
by organic metaphors (Turner, 1974, p. 24; see also, Nisbet, 1969). Turner
recognized the indispensability of metaphors but chose them carefully for
"appropriateness and potential fruitfulness" (p. 25). Metaphors and models
provoke thought, provide new perspectives, and are exciting because they

offer alternative perspectives and insights. Scholars should use them, "provided that one is aware of the perils lurking behind their misuse" (p. 31).

The meanings created by metaphor are dependent on multivocal symbols and thus are part of the fabric of symbolic action. Mary Douglas (1973) sketched how these interrelationships operate. Recognizing that the goal of identifying natural symbols had a paradoxical aspect, she nevertheless sought common patterns in symbol use in order to transcend the constraints of culture. She argued that there is concordance between symbolic and social experience and identified four distinctive systems of natural symbols derived from images of the body. A social system uses its image of the body to reflect and enhance each person's experience of society. One of the systems conceives the body as an organ of communication; this conception is reflected in taboos, rituals, and behavior. A second system conceives the body as a vehicle of life and is concerned about the boundaries of the body and its intake. There is also the pragmatic view of the body, and finally there is the image of the body as evil. In the last case, spirit and body are sharply distinguished and spirit is the focus of attention and yearning (Douglas, 1973, pp. 11–18). Needless to say, none of the images could be conceived, let alone constructed, without the use of metaphor.

Politically, the importance of metaphor is demonstrated by the central role of language in the process of generating, reinforcing, or changing cognitions (Edelman, 1971, p. 67). A political metaphor

> intensifies selected perceptions and ignores others, thereby helping one to concentrate upon desired consequences of favored public policies and helping one to ignore the unwanted, unthinkable or irrelevant premises and aftermaths. . . . Metaphor is therefore an instrument for shaping political support and opposition and the premises upon which decisions are made. (Edelman, 1971, pp. 67–68)

Metaphors shape factual premises as well as create and filter value premises. The effects are pervasive and they must be explored if a more comprehensive grasp of the processes of politics is the objective. If the use of metaphors is not examined, the typical result is that they are used to create conformity and contribute to the maintenance of the status quo.

Walzer (1967) and Zashin and Chapman (1974) have analyzed some political uses of symbolic thought and metaphor and analogy. Walzer argued that symbolic thought serves as a bridge between periods of stability, thus inserting continuity into periods of upheaval. Although shifts in reference systems dissolve the evocative power of old symbols, they retain some affective power. The political theorist reshapes the decaying, emotive symbol so that it is congruent with the new reference system. He saw the work of Thomas Hobbes as an example of how this process functions. Walzer's article suggests that metaphor is important in that it constitutes the bridge between the known and the unknown.

Zashin and Chapman's study is more comprehensive than Walzer's and therefore more broadly applicable. They disagree with current attempts to create "a political vocabulary with clear observational predicates, stripped of the multiple and ambiguous meanings attached to words in conventional discourse" (1974, pp. 293–294). A multifaceted language is the prime requisite of comprehensive knowledge about the political realm. Lack of a rich language minimizes our ability to grasp the complexities of political action. We must again become aware of the importance of the devices of metaphor and analogy, which are the workhorses of a rich language and which "establish relationships which were not previously apparent, either through creating a context of similarities and differences or by organizing one realm through the categories of another and carrying over the relationships of the latter to the former" (1974, p. 317).

Metaphors derive meaning from their environmental setting just as symbols derive meaning from the context in which they are located. However, "the distinctive structure of metaphor is its *anomalous assertion of identity.* . . . [Recognition of the anomaly] creates a tension which leads us to search for a basis of identity . . . thereby shaping or reshaping, our understanding of the thing to which the metaphor refers" (Zashin & Chapman, 1974, p. 300, their italics).

The present focus on "scientific" language has resulted in neglect of the traditional concerns of political theory. Consequently there has been a decline in the vitality of public discourse. A crisis of legitimacy has developed as the institutional domains of society have become

> more opaque to those outside them and even to those playing subordinate roles within them. The totality is beyond the comprehension of most individuals and no unifying meaning system *intelligible to the great mass of the population* is available to legitimate the society seen as a system. (Zashin & Chapman, 1974, p. 323, their italics)

The decline has been in part the result of the poverty of political language. Lacking a richness of language and unwilling to make use of metaphor, political scientists are no longer capable of handling the topics that create the symbols of community. But as Frankel noted, "the power that symbols have to move us is *borrowed* power. And when what they stand for changes or disappears, they live on borrowed time" (1954/1964, p. 370, his italics). Although the malaise may be more intractable than is suggested by the neglect of metaphor, it seems obvious that any prospect of rejuvenation depends on a revival of interest in and concern with metaphor.

Miller's (1979) approach to metaphor differs in that he criticizes extant approaches and constructs a bridge between them. The verificationist view (advocated by M. Landau and K. Deutsch) holds that metaphors when developed as explicit models play a role in the search for political knowledge, but insists that "the analogy or likeness that is presumed to exist between model and thing must be subject to verification" (Miller, 1979, p. 158). In contrast, the constitutivist view of political metaphor holds that language does not mirror political reality; rather, language creates reality by organizing the complexities of experience. Metaphor creates political reality by shaping perception of both facts and values. M. Edelman is cited as an advocate of this view. The difference between the views is that

> verificationism holds that any claim of metaphors, analogies, or models to have cognitive meaning must be tested by a factual knowledge of political reality. It assumes that political facts, as we know them from sense perception, are somehow prior to and independent of metaphorical speech and thought. Constitutivism denies that political reality can be recognized or its meaning understood independently of some metaphorical interpretation. One's understanding of the facts is shaped by the metaphor, so the facts cannot provide an independent means of verifying or falsifying the metaphor. (Miller, 1979, p. 162)

Miller finds that each approach contains some truth and has some problems. (pp. 162–168). He advocates a manifestationist view in order to utilize the truths of the disparate approaches. It contends that metaphor "can be a way after knowledge that leads somewhere, a path that takes us beyond the familiar experience of everyday life to knowledge of political things as they are" (Miller, 1979, p. 169). The language used by Miller, as well as that used by other students of metaphor, appears to demonstrate that the use of metaphor is inevitable in spite of the fears engendered by the prospect of abuse.

In summary, metaphor has been treated here as a separate facet of application; the set of common concerns with its use and abuse have been reviewed. The selections recognize the significance and utility of metaphor and provide demonstrations, at times inadvertent, of how it creeps into the language of politics. The arguments can be summarized by the caution to be wary—metaphors shape perception and are easily abused. The approaches, however, diverge after this caution. But the selections illustrate the relevance of metaphor for the study of political symbolism. Symbols are things which have been charged with meaning. They are public and accessible and this accessibility is made possible by the communion of language. Metaphor as a linguistic device contributes to the expansion of intersubjectivity by identifying the unknown with the known, thus facilitating recognition and acceptance of the patterns of social interaction.

Conclusion

It is difficult to comprehend, let alone analyze, the pervasive influence of political symbols on value and status allocations as well as on decision making and policy formulation. If, as Edelman asserts, what we experience about political events is language rather than the events themselves, then there is no escape from the influence of symbols. As Sapir noted, language is heuristic and completely interpenetrates experience. Or as Langer claimed, symbols are vehicles for the conception of objects and this constitutes the process of thinking. Behavior toward these conceptions is what words evoke.

Political symbols are most potent when they are embedded in the frameworks of experience, including the social and institutional fabric of society. Such symbols convey both rational and emotional attitudes, values and legitimizations. The values and attitudes that are encapsulated in any symbol are amorphous, inchoate, complex, and somewhat contradictory. However, when a symbol is entangled in the webs of everyday realities, the response it evokes is typically uncritical and the symbol serves an integrative function. This function appears so natural that the process itself can only be observed by an outsider, someone who has escaped from the webs that constitute everyday reality.

Some examples from American history illustrate the strength of constitutional symbolism as well as its integrative function. Americans have been called a people of paradox.

> We are comfortable believing in both majority rule and minority rights, in both consensus and freedom, federalism and centralization. It may be perfectly reasonable to support majority rule with reservations, or minority rights with certain other reservations. But this has not been our method. Rather we have tended to hold contradictory ideas in suspension and ignore the intellectual and behavioral consequences of such "double-think." (Kammen, 1972, p. 280)

Americans throughout their history have juggled the somewhat contradictory cluster of conceptions that surround the symbols "liberty" and "equality." The meaning of equality was debated with particular intensity in antebellum days, during the Civil War and Reconstruction, and in the 1960s and 1970s. A definitive definition has not been achieved and with good reason. Definitiveness would not be sufficiently broad to encompass the complexity of disparate and inchoate beliefs. Our arguments about the proper role of government present a similar pattern. Laws are enacted to preserve equality in the marketplace, but in the name of liberty such laws are often emasculated. Nevertheless, the fact of their passage shapes public expectations concerning the responsibilities and capacities of government and legitimizes further expansion of the government's role in the marketplace. For most of our history, we have been able to devise neat formulas which obscure the contradictions of our belief system so that Americans can easily believe themselves to be both free and equal.

These examples suggest that integrative symbols arise from the human need for order. Somehow individuals must reconcile their experience of the intractable problems of existence with the expectations and ideals that give meaning to communal existence. Political symbols, when they appear embedded in everyday reality, perform this ameliorative function. They also enhance group cohesion in that they provide ready legitimizations for political acts and decisions.

Although integrative symbols are interpreted and reinterpreted as times and participants change, they must appear to be consistent over time if they are to serve as props of communal solidarity. Because they are ambiguous, they become a magnet for the diffuse and disparate fears and hopes of individuals and serve to transform and channel these emotions into communal molds. Selectivity is an offshoot of ambiguity—anything can be charged with meaning and become symbolic or changed expectations can generate reassessments and reinterpretations of established communal symbols. But integrative symbols prove effective only if they are widely accepted and constantly utilized by elites and masses to explain and justify political decisions and actions. Once the symbol is accepted in this way, its function goes unnoticed and its use is routine and ritualistic.

In contrast to the integrative function, symbols also serve as measures of differentiation. Used this way, they enhance the cohesion of one group by glorifying or denigrating other groups. The Nazi emphasis on Aryan blood, the Southern white belief in segregation, and the use of apartheid in South Africa have enhanced the cohesion of dominant groups at the expense of the denigrated group.

In either case it is clear that symbolic structures derive coherence from social experience. In other words, symbols derive their meaning from the context in which they are embedded. A political symbol takes its particular meaning from its relationship to the other symbols of the polity and the patterned whole which the symbols constitute. Even universal symbols derive meaning from their practical applications. The American quest for equality would surely be misunderstood by a Russian whose own quest for equality is shaped by the particular political structure in which he or she is located. Similarly, the American conception of the meaning of federalism diverges sharply from the Yugoslavian concept of this governmental form. For this reason, cultural environments and social and institutional structures should be viewed as sources of differentiation which spark different cultural interpretations of symbols. What this means in practical terms is that the analyst of political symbols, in order to determine meaning, must pay close attention to the empirical context in which the symbol is used.

Close attention to context is also mandated by the fact that circumstances and actors change and the meaning of a symbol varies accordingly. A symbol appears to serve integrative purposes in one period and at other times it seems to serve as an opiate of the masses. The same symbol serves as the rallying cry of revolution or the linchpin of order. Or, as Geertz noted, the anthropologist must know the difference between a wink and a tic before he embarks on an analysis of the meaning of wink. The need to explore context is illustrated by the survey of applications of symbolic theory. As noted above, most of the applications appear to be shaped by the period in which they were written. In the early 1950s, interest in symbols was sparked by Nazi success, by the use of psychological warfare during World War II, and by fears of communist strength and expansion. In the United States, research on symbols focused on their integrative function. In the 1960s, against the background of racial conflict and confrontations over Vietnam policy, it no longer seemed self-evident that American symbols performed primarily integrative functions. The critical perspective of the 1930s, spawned during a different crisis of legitimacy, again became salient. But critics who stressed the manipulative potential of symbols also delineated the relationship of symbol and context. The insight into the manipulative potential of symbols was based on the recognition that symbols were used intentionally or unconsciously to reinforce problematic beliefs that favored the status quo. The perception that publicly recognized symbolic structures had lost coherence was related to changing perceptions of the role of government, its responsibilities, and its capacities.

Research in the 1970s was more mixed. Some studies focused on whether self-interest or symbolic politics played the greater role in political decision making. There were also studies of the symbolic and ritualistic functions of political institutions which maintain societal cohesion in the face of historical change and political conflict. The last topic became more salient because opinion polls indicated that although Americans were increasingly distrustful of incumbent political officials, this distrust had not shaken belief in the viability and value of American political institutions and ideals.

Applications of symbolism theory in anthropology, political science, and sociology reflect its wide-ranging perspective. There is a theoretical consensus on basic assumptions which stresses that human beings are symbol makers and users, that the structures which order experience are socially cued and constructed, and that symbols express communicable, public meanings. There is also agreement that if our knowledge of symbols is to be increased, language, role, norms, social cuing, and selective perception as well as the interrelationship of context and meaning must be explored in depth. Discovery of the influence of symbols may be due to alienation and marginality and research into symbols may be particularly significant in a world where ideology no longer attracts enthusiastic partisans. Or it may be that awareness of symbols and their uses is the prerequisite for revisionist studies of the past or psychobiographical studies of political leaders. Or recognition of the significance of symbols may increase awareness of the factors that produce stability or result in mass quiescence amid the conflicts and tumult of politics. In this last instance, the study of symbols focuses on the values and the webs of relationships that unite, bind, and constrain the members of a society.

In summary, symbols bridge the gap between ideals and expectations and our experience of the confused and contradictory outcome of politics. Exploration of the pervasive effects of political symbols and their ramifications offers insight into the problematic relationships that we systematically construct to order our worlds. Given the complexity and ambiguity of the political realm, the need for in-depth analysis of these fundamental relationships and their meaning is imperative.

References

Arnold, T. *The folklore of capitalism.* New Haven: Yale University Press, 1962. (Originally published, 1937).

Aronoff, M. J. *Power and ritual in the Israel Labor Party.* Assen, The Netherlands: Van Gorcum, 1977.

Barkun, M. *Law without sanctions: Order in primitive societies and the world community.* New Haven: Yale University Press, 1968.

Bennett, W. L. Imitation, ambiguity, and drama in political life: Civil religion and the dilemmas of public morality. *Journal of Politics,* 1979, *41,* 106–133.

Bennett, W. L., Harris, P. D., Laskey, J. K., Levitch, A. H., & Monrad, S. E. Deep and surface images in the construction of political issues: The case of amnesty. *Quarterly Journal of Speech,* 1976, *62,* 109–126.

Berger, P. L., & Luckmann, T. *The social construction of reality: A treatise in the sociology of knowledge.* Garden City, N.Y.: Doubleday Anchor Books, 1967.

Black, M. *Models and metaphors.* Ithaca: Cornell University Press, 1962.

Blumer, H. Society as symbolic interaction. In J. G. Manis & B. H. Meltzer (Eds.), *Symbolic interaction: A reader in social psychology.* Boston: Allyn & Bacon, 1967.

Burke, K. *A grammar of motives.* New York: Prentice-Hall, 1954.

Cassirer, E. *An essay on man.* New York: Doubleday Anchor Books, 1953.

Cassirer, E. *The myth of the state.* New York: Doubleday Anchor Books, 1946.

Cassirer, E. *The philosophy of symbolic forms* (Vol. 1). New Haven: Yale University Press, 1955.

Cobb, R. W., & Elder, C. D. *Participation in American politics: The dynamics of agenda building.* Boston: Allyn & Bacon, 1972.

Cohen, A. *Two-dimensional man: An essay on the anthropology of power and symbolism in complex society.* Berkeley: University of California Press, 1976.

Cohen, J. The value of value symbols in law. In L. Bryson, L. Finkelstein, R. M. MacIver, & R. McKeon (Eds.), *Symbols and values: An initial study.* New York: Cooper Square Publishers, 1964. (Originally published, 1954.)

Cole, R. Structural functional theory, the dialectic and social change. *Sociological Quarterly,* 1966, *7,* 39–58.

Deutsch, K. W. Symbols of political community. In L. Bryson, L. Finkelstein, H. Hoagland, & R. M. MacIver (Eds.), *Symbols and society.* New York: Cooper Square Publishers, 1964. (Originally published, 1954.)

Douglas, M. *Purity and danger: An analysis of concepts of pollution and taboo.* Harmondsworth, England: Pelican Books, 1970.

Douglas, M. *Natural symbols.* New York: Vintage Books, 1973.

Edelman, M. *The symbolic uses of politics.* Urbana: University of Illinois Press, 1964.

Edelman, M. *Politics as symbolic action: Mass arousal and quiescence.* Chicago: Markham Publishing, 1971.

Edelman, M. *Political language: Words that succeed and politics that fail.* New York: Academic Press, 1977.

Erikson, E. H. The nature of clinical evidence. In E. Erikson, *Insight and responsibility.* New York: W. W. Norton, 1964.

Frankel, C. Liberalism and political symbols. In L. Bryson, L. Finkelstein, R. M. MacIver, & R. McKeon (Eds.), *Symbols and values: An initial study.* New York: Cooper Square Publishers, 1964. (Originally published,1954.)

Geertz, C. Ideology as a cultural system. In D. Apter (Ed.), *Ideology and discontent.* New York: The Free Press, 1964.

Geertz, C. *The interpretation of culture.* New York: Basic Books, 1973.

Goffman, E. *The presentation of self in everyday life.* Garden City, N.Y.: Doubleday Anchor Books, 1959.

Gusfield, J. R. *Symbolic crusade: Status politics and the American temperance movement.* Urbana: University of Illinois Press, 1963.

Hall, P. M. A symbolic interactionist analysis of politics. *Sociological Inquiry,* 1972, *42,* 35–76.

Heidegger, M. [*Being and time*] (J. MacQuarrie & E. Robinson, trans.). New York: Harper & Row, 1962. (Originally published in 1935.)

Husserl, E. [*Ideas*] (W. R. B. Gibson, trans.). New York: Collier, 1962.

Kammen, M. *People of paradox.* New York: Alfred A. Knopf, 1972.

Kantor, R. Symbolic interactionism and politics in systemic perspective. *Sociological Inquiry,* 1972, *42,* 77–92.

Kelley, R. *The cultural pattern in American politics: The first century.* New York: Alfred A. Knopf, 1979.

Langer, S. K. *Philosophy in a new key.* New York: Mentor Books, 1948.

Lasch, C. *The agony of the American left.* New York: Alfred A. Knopf, 1969.

Lasswell, H. D. *Psychopathology and politics.* Chicago: University of Chicago Press, 1930.

Lasswell, H. D. The language of power. In H. Lasswell (Ed.), *Language of politics: Studies in quantitative semantics.* New York: G. W. Stewart, 1949.

Lasswell, H. D. Key symbols, signs and icons. In L. Bryson, L. Finkelstein, R. M. MacIver, & R. McKeon (Eds.), *Symbols and values: An initial study.* New York: Cooper Square Publishers, 1964. (Originally published, 1954.)

Lasswell, H. D., & Kaplan, A. *Power and society.* New Haven: Yale University Press, 1950.

Lee, D. D. Symbolization and value. In L. Bryson, L. Finkelstein, R. M. McIver, & R. McKeon (Eds.), *Symbols and values: An initial study.* New York: Cooper Square Publishers, 1964. (Originally published, 1954.)

Lerner, D. Strategy of truth: Symbol and act in world propaganda. In L. Bryson, L. Finkelstein, R. M. MacIver, & R. McKeon (Eds.), *Symbols and values: An initial study.* New York: Cooper Square Publishers, 1964. (Originally published, 1954.)

Lerner, M. Constitution and court as symbols. *Yale Law Journal,* 1937, *46,* 1290–1319.

McIntosh, D. S. Power and social control. *American Political Science Review,* 1963, *62,* 619–631.

McKeon, R. Symbols, myths and arguments. In L. Bryson, L. Finkelstein, R. M. MacIver, & R. McKeon (Eds.), *Symbols and values: An initial study.* New York: Cooper Square Publishers, 1964. (Originally published, 1954.)

Mead, G. H. *Mind, self and society.* Chicago: University of Chicago Press, 1934.

Meltzer, B. N. Mead's social psychology. In J. G. Manis & B. N. Meltzer (Eds.), *Symbolic interaction: A reader in social psychology.* Boston: Allyn & Bacon, 1967.

Merriam, C. E. *Political power: Its composition and incidence.* New York: McGraw-Hill, 1934.

Miller, E. F. Metaphor and political knowledge. *American Political Science Review*, 1979, *73*, 155–170.

Mitchell, W. C. *The American polity.* New York: The Free Press of Glencoe, 1962.

Mueller, C. *The politics of communication.* New York: Oxford University Press, 1973.

Nimmo, D. D. *The political persuaders: The techniques of modern election campaigns.* Englewood Cliffs, N.J.: Prentice-Hall, 1970.

Nimmo, D. D. *Popular images of politics: A taxonomy.* Englewood Cliffs, N.J.: Prentice-Hall, 1974.

Nisbet, R. A. *Social change and history: Aspects of western theory of development.* Oxford: Oxford University Press, 1969.

Orwell, G. Politics and the English language. In G. Orwell, *Inside the whale and other essays.* Harmondsworth, England: Pelican Books, 1962.

Pool, I. de S. Symbols, meanings and social science. In L. Bryson, L. Finkelstein, R. M. MacIver, & R. McKeon (Eds.), *Symbols and values: An initial study.* New York: Cooper Square Publishers, 1964. (Originally published, 1954.)

Rothman, R. Stability and change in a legal order: The impact of ambiguity. *Ethics*, 1972, *83*, 37–50.

Rothman, R. *Acts and enactments: The constitutional convention of 1787.* Philadelphia: Center for the Study of Federalism, 1974.

Rothman, R. The symbolic uses of public information. In Y. Galnoor (Ed.), *Government secrecy in democracies.* New York: Harper Colophon Books, 1977.

Rothman, R. The First Amendment: Symbolic import-ambiguous prescription. In R. J. Simon (Ed.), *Research in law and sociology* (Vol. 1). Greenwich, Conn.: JAI Press, 1978.

Salomon, A. Symbols and images in the constitution of society. In L. Bryson, L. Finkelstein, H. Hoagland, & R. M. MacIver (Eds.), *Symbols and society.* New York: Cooper Square Publishers, 1964. (Originally published, 1954.)

Sapir, E. Language. In E. R. A. Seligman (Ed.) *Encyclopedia of the Social Sciences* (Vol. 9). New York: Macmillan, 1934. Pp. 155–169. (a)

Sapir, E. Symbolism. In E. R. A. Seligman (Ed.) *Encyclopedia of the Social Sciences* (Vol. 14). New York: Macmillan, 1934. Pp. 492–495. (b)

Scheingold, S. A. *The politics of rights: Lawyers, public policy and political change.* New Haven: Yale University Press, 1974.

Schutz, A. Symbol, reality and society. In L. Bryson, L. Finkelstein, H. Hoagland, & R. M. MacIver (Eds.), *Symbols and society.* New York: Cooper Square Publishers, 1964. (Originally published, 1954.)

Sears, D. O., Hensler, C. P., & Speer, L. K. White's opposition to 'busing': Self-interest or symbolic politics? *American Political Science Review*, 1979, *73*, 369–384.

Shils, E., & Young, M. The meaning of the coronation. *American Sociological Review*, 1953, *1*, 63–81.

Skidmore, M. J. *Word politics: Essays on language and politics.* Palo Alto: James E. Freel, 1972.

Sperber, D. *Rethinking symbolism.* Cambridge, England: Cambridge University Press, 1975.

Strauss, A. L. *Mirrors and masks: The search for identity.* Glencoe, Ill.: The Free press, 1959.

Turner, V. *Dramas, fields and metaphors: Symbolic action in human society.* Ithaca: Cornell University Press, 1974.

Walzer, M. On the role of symbolic thought in politics. *Political Science Quarterly*, 1967, *82*, 191–204.

Wolff, R. P. Beyond tolerance. In H. Marcuse, B. Moore, Jr., & R. P. Wolff, *A critique of pure tolerance.* Boston: Beacon Press, 1965.

Zald, M. N. Politics and symbols: A review article. *Sociological Quarterly*, 1966, *7*, 85–91.

Zashin, E., & Chapman, P. C. The use of metaphor and analogy: Toward a renewal of political language. *The Journal of Politics*, 1974, *36*, 290–326.

INDEX

Accountability and review systems, 129–130, 143
Action mood theory, 115–116
Additivity condition, 245
Aggression, theories of, 217–218
  by Freud, 91
  frustration and, 191, 192, 199
Alliances and war, 170–171, 204–205, 206–208
Allport, F. H., 4
Altruistic motivation, theory of, 91, 102, 282
  opposing views, 91, 92–93
Ambiguity and social comparison, 12, 14
Amnesty, Ford's advocacy of, 327
Anthropology, political, 306. *See also* Culture
Antiwar protests, 214
Anxiety and social comparison, 12, 13–14
Arrow impossibility theorem, 229–237
  conditions in
    connectivity, 231–232
    independence of infeasible alternatives, 236
    nondictatorship, 236
    Pareto principle, 236
    transitivity, 232–235
    unlimited domain, 235–236
    violation of, 236–237, 240–244
Artificial-intelligence models, 117

Assassination, study of, 175
  by Feierabend, 175, 176–177
  by Leiden, 175, 176–177
  by Levy, 175, 177
  by Simon, 176
Associationism, 96
"Atemporal structures," Turner's concept of, 305
Atmosphere in small groups, 19
Attitude change theory, 107
Attraction, social, 7–11
Authoritarianism, studies of, 219–220
Aversive motivation, 111–113, 141
Avoidance, in social-learning theory, 98–99
  of boredom, 101–102
Axiomatic-choice theory, vote trading, 244–249. *See also* Arrow impossibility theorem; Voter's paradox
Azar, E., study by, 172–174

Banks, A. S., political-conflict study by, 181, 184–185, 186
Barkun, Michael, 329
Bay of Pigs decision makers, 27–28
Bayesian rationality postulates, 275
Belief systems
  contradictions within, 335
  Mitchell's view of, 318–319, 321
Bennett, W. Lance, 321–322

"Best and Brightest" team, Kennedy's, 27–28

"Big Team," Nixon's, 31

Bishop, V. F., political-violence study by, 181, 188–191

Black, Max, 331

Blumer, Herbert, 296–297

Body, symbolism of, 303–304, 332

Body state encoding, 117–118

Boldness shift, 94

Borda method for ordering alternatives, 231, 236

Borders and war, relationship between, 201–203

Boredom avoidance, theory of, 101–102

Brain
  limitations, 139
  physiology, 118

Brainstorming groups, 5

Brown, R. M., vigilantism study by, 177–178

Bueno de Mesquita, B., studies by, 191, 206–209

Burke, Kenneth, 291, 294–295, 305

Burnout, 113

Busing, symbolism of, 323

Campaigns, election, Nimmo's view of, 326

Cardinal versus ordinal utility, 236, 242–244

Cassirer, Ernst, 286, 292, 314

Chapman, P. C., 333

Chess, learning from experience in, 116–117

Choice. See Collective-choice theory

Choice-shift (risky-shift) literature, 5–7, 54–55

Civil religion, Bennett's view of, 321–322

"Classical" game, defined, 275n.

Classification, views of
  by Douglas, 302–303
  by Strauss, 295

Coalitions, in game theory, 256, 262–264, 265–267
  and Shapley value, 269–271

Cobb, R. W., 322

Coercion–compromise model of managerial system, 36

Coerciveness, political, 193, 195–196, 200
  and instability, 196–197

Cognitive process modeling, 116–117

Cohen, Abner, 289, 297, 306, 308, 311

Cohen, Julius, 328–329

Cohesiveness in small groups, 19, 21, 22–23, 28–29
  with factionalism, on Nixon team, 31, 33
  Kennedy team, 27–28
  MARTA groupings, 36, 37

Collaboration–consensus model of managerial system, 36

Collective-choice theory, 225–283
  axiomatic-choice theory, vote trading, 244–249. See also Arrow impossibility theorem; Voter's paradox
  collective (public) goods, 278–282
  economic theories of politics (spatial models), 249–255
  game theory. See Game theory
  individual preferences, 227–229
  rationality in. See Rationality

Collective-goods theory, 278–282

Colson, Charles, 32, 33

Commonality in social attraction, 8–9

Communication distortion, Mueller's view of, 325

Communication flow theories, 120–121

Comparison, social, 11–14, 17

Competition, effects of, 4

Conceptual modeling, 105

Condensation versus referential symbols, 299

Conditioning approach to learning, 99–100

Condorcet method for ordering alternatives, 230, 231
  and collective intransitivity, 234, 235
  in "individual versus collective" game, 280
  numerical indicators versus, 231, 243, 244

Conflict
  need for, theories of, 107, 108–109
  See also Political violence

Conflict point
  in Harsanyi analysis, 276
  in Nash equilibrium, 272

Connectivity, Arrow's axiom of, 231–232

Conservative shift in groups, question of, 6

Constitutions as symbols, 299
  American, 287–288, 293, 328
    First Amendment, 330

Constitutivist view of political metaphor, 334

Context embeddedness, 96–97

Contract evaluation research, 127–128

Core, in game theory, 264
  alteration, 267–268
  empty, 264–266
  Shapley value versus, 270–271
  in three-person prisoner's dilemma, 266–267
Coronation, Elizabeth II's, integrative symbolism of, 293, 315
County seat wars, study of, 177, 178–179
Creativity, 81
Credenda of power, 307
Cross-pressured nations, 205
Culture, theories of
  by Cassirer, 292
  by Douglas, 302–304
  by Geertz, 300–301
  organizational culture, 121
  by Turner, 304–305
Cyclical majority, in game theory, 266, 269.
  See also Voter's paradox

Decision making, political, 44
  Kennedy team, 27–28
  theoretic framework for microanalysis, 26
  See also Policy formation
Dependency theories, 115, 143–144
Depersonalization, 112
Deprivation and political conflict, 199–200
Deutsch, Karl, 317–318
Development, political, measurement of, 193
Developmental theories of learning, 102–109, 141
Differentiation
  in intellectual development, 77, 78, 103
  in symbolism, 304, 322, 336
Dirt, Douglas's view of, 302–303, 304
Discreteness in international system, 207–208
Dominance, aggression and, 91, 218
Dominant strategy, in game theory, 258
  lack of, 259–260
  noncooperation as, 280, 281
  in prisoner's dilemma, 261–262, 267
  "individual versus collective," 280
Domination, in game theory, 268–269
Douglas, Mary, 297, 302–304, 332
Downs, Anthony, 249, 250–251, 252, 253
Dramatistic perspective, 294, 295, 320, 327
Drug use in government, 118

Economic theories of politics, 249–255
Economics
  collective goods in, 278, 279
  rationality, 138, 226
  welfare economics, 229
Edelman, Murray, 289, 297, 299, 310–314, 321, 323, 324, 329, 331, 332, 334
Effectiveness, as criterion of learning, 77, 78–79
Ego development, 104
Egypt, interaction study involving, 172–174
Elden, M., on work organization, 49, 50, 51–52
Elder, C. D., 322
Elections
  campaigns, Nimmo's view of, 326
  ritual function of, 310–311
  See also Voting behavior
Emotional drives, fixed, theory of, 90–91
Empathetic mirroring, 107
Equiprobability assumption, 238, 239
  abandonment of, 239–240
Erikson, Erik, 114, 289
Evaluation studies, problems with, 127–128
Executive-branch learning. *See* Government learning
Expectancy–instrumentality–valance theory, 100–101
Expected value, notion of, 269–271
Experience, learning from, 116–117
Exposure and social attraction, 10
Extinction of responses, 100

Facilitation
  and civil strife, 200–201
  social, versus inhibition, 3–7, 12–13, 21
Familiarity, attraction as, 10
Fear–security debate, 108
Feierabend, I. K. and R. L., political-violence studies by, 175, 176–177, 182, 191, 192–198, 199
Festinger, Leon, 11–12, 13
Finifter, A., 29–30
First Amendment as symbol, 330
Force, attributes of, as predictors of conflict, 191, 194–195
Ford, Gerald, 327
Forecasting, problem of, 139
Foreign policy
  knowledge, trends in, 89
  small-group analysis, 27–28

France, studies involving
  interaction, 172–174
  internal disturbances, 209–210
Frankel, Charles, 315–316, 333
Free riders, in collective-goods theory, 278–
  280, 281, 282
Freud, Sigmund, theories of, 92, 94, 97, 108,
  112
  aggressive drives, 91
Frustration–aggression theory, 191, 192,
  199
Funding of knowledge activities, 86

Game theory, 255
  coalitions, 256, 262–264, 265–267
    and Shapley value, 269–271
  imputations, 268
    domination, 268–269
  levels of analysis, 255–257
  n-person games, 262–271
  prisoner's dilemma in, 261–262
    "individual versus collective," 280
    noncooperation, 281–282
    three-person, 263, 266–267
  solution concepts, 259
    Harsanyi analysis, 275–278
    mixed strategies, 259–260
    Nash equilibrium, 271–273, 275, 277–
      278
    Shapley solution, 274–275
    Shapley value, 269–271
    See also Core
  two-person zero-sum games, 257
    "best" strategy, 258–261
Geertz, Clifford, 297, 299, 300–302, 309
Genetic component of drives/aptitudes,
  possible, 94
Global wars, study of, 172
Goal-setting theory, 102
Goffman, Erving, 320–321
Government learning, 73–145
  accountability and, 129–130, 143
  agendas, 84–86
  barriers to, 111, 112, 113–114
  criteria for, 77–79
  as dependent variable, 135
  developmental theories and, 105, 106,
    107, 108
  diagnosis of problems, 75–76
  drugs and, 118
  fixed-nature theories and, 90–91, 92–94

Government learning (cont.)
  lobbying and, 129
  "mode of production" and, 123–124
  news media and, 130
  normative issues, 86–88
  organizational, 83–84
  organizational memory and, 83, 108,
    121–122
  policy formation and. See Policy forma-
    tion
  problem types and, 135–140
  reasons for, 73–74
  recommendations, 142–145
  recruitment and, 118–119
  "smart" organization theory and, 119–
    121
  social-learning theory, 97–99, 101
  social scientists, relevance to, 74
  time structures and, 128–129
  trends in, 88–90
  and unconscious motivation, 114–115
Grand coalition, 263–264, 267, 268
  and Shapley value, 269, 270, 271
GRIT proposal, 219
Group theory. See Small-group study
Groupthink, 28, 33
Growth, metaphor of, 300
Gurr, T. R., political-violence studies by,
  181, 188–191, 198–201
Gusfield, J. R., 322–323
Guttman scaling of violence, 175, 176, 192

Haldeman, H. R., 31, 32
Hall, Peter, 319–320
"Hardball politics" analysis, 131–132
Hardin, R., 280
Harsanyi, John, 275–278
"Humanistic coefficient," Turner's concept
  of, 304

Id, 92
Ideology
  in decision making, 145
  Geertz's views of, 301–302
  and information-need reduction, 252
  interest and strain theories, 301
Imagery-encoding theory, 96–97, 115
Imaginal concrete level, 104
Imaginal scanning, 104–105
Imitation of high-status people, theory of,
  97–98

Impact statements, 87
Imperial systems, Köhler's theory of, 209
Impression management, 320–321
Imputations, in game theory, 268
    domination, 268–269
Incoherent-policy problems, 140
Independence of infeasible alternatives, 236
    numerical indicators ruled out by, 242–243
Independence of irrelevant alternatives, 273
Indifference curves, 253–254
Information
    dissemination by government, 87, 325
    meaning versus, 313
    and rationality, 251–252
Inhibition versus facilitation, social, 3–7, 12–13, 21
Innovations, government, 89
Instability, political, 192–193, 194, 195
    coerciveness and, 196–197
Instincts, theories of, 90–91
Institution creation strategies, 125–126
Institutional strength and civil strife, 200
Integration
    in intellectual development, 78
    structural, 20–21
    into work group, 29–30
Integrative symbols, 318, 335–336
    attributes, 286–287
    Constitution as, 287–288, 293
        First Amendment, 330
    coronation, 293, 315
    legal, 329, 330
    perception of, 293, 322
    "taken-for-grantedness," 288
Interaction view of metaphor, 331
Interactions, international, studies of, 172–174, 219. See also War, international
Interest theory of ideology, 301
International relations
    foreign-policy making, 27–28
    as interactive system, 172–174, 219
    See also War, international
Interrupted-time series, defined, 211
Intransitivity, 232–233
    collective, 234–235
        in game theory, 266, 269. See also
        Voter's paradox
Intuition, 80–81
Israel, interaction study involving, 172–174
Issue space (policy space), 250, 252–254

Janis, I., "groupthink" concept of, 33
    and analysis of Kennedy team, 27–28, 31
Jaques, E., developing-work-capacity theory
        of, 104–106
Judiciary, small-group analysis of, 42–43, 45, 46

Kantor, R., 321
Kaplan, Abraham, 308–309
Kende, I., war study by, 168–169
Kennedy, John F., "Best and Brightest"
    team of, 27–28

Key signs, Lasswell's concept of, 315
Known-answer problems, 137
Köhler, G., 209

Langer, Susanne K., 286, 293
Language
    cognitive and noncognitive, 309
    metaphor, 300, 304, 305, 330–334
    naming, 294–295, 303
    as symbolic structure, 293
    views of
        by Edelman, 312, 313, 324
        by Mueller, 325
        by Orwell, 323–324
        by Sapir, 298–299
        by Skidmore, 327
Lasswell, Harold, 297, 308–309, 315, 324
Law, symbolism of, 307–308, 328–330
Law of association, 96
Leadership
    necessity for, 97
    in small groups, 19
    judiciary, 45, 46
Learning
    "action mood" for, 115–116
    agendas, 84–86
    barriers to
        aversive motivation, 111–113, 141
        burnout, 113
        resistance to rethinking, 113–114
        stress, 109–111, 141
    definitions
        analytical, criteria in, 77–79, 80
        descriptive, 76
    diagnosis of problems, 75–76, 140–142
    executive-branch. See Government learning
    from experience, 116–117

Learning (*cont.*)
  images of, 109
    developmental, 102–119, 141
    fixed nature, 90–95, 141
    passive reactive, 95–102, 141
    individual. *See* Learning, images of;
      Learning, types
  organizational, 82–84
  pathologies of, 75–76, 98
  physiology of
    body state encoding, 117–118
    brain, 118
  secularization/orthodoxy and, 134–135
  small groups, 15, 18
  truth-telling and, 133–134
  types
    assessment, 84
    creativity, 81
    intuition, 80–81
    scientific, 79–80
    skill, 81
    wisdom, 81–82
Legal standards, rational, and power, 319
Legal symbolism, 307–308, 328–330
Legislators
  logrolling (vote trading), 244–249
  norms, 45
Legitimacy, regime's, and civil strife, 200
Leiden, K., assassination study by, 175,
    176–177
Lerner, Daniel, 316–317
Lerner, Max, 293, 328
Levine, E. P., war study by, 171–172
Levy, S. G., political-violence studies by,
    179, 211, 219, 220
  of assassination, 175, 177
Lexicographic model, 254–255
Liberalism, 316, 318, 321
Libidinal inertia, 92
Lindahl equilibrium, 278
Lobbying, 129
Loevinger, Jane, 104, 108
Logrolling (vote trading), 244–247
  vote trader's paradox, 247–249
Lupsha, P. A., political-violence study by,
    179–180

McKeon, Richard, 309
MacKinnon, C., political-violence study by,
    179–180
Magruder, J. S., 32, 33

Managerial systems, kinds of, 35, 36
Manifestationist view of political meta-
    phor, 334
Marginality, views of
  by Douglas, 303, 304
  by Turner, 304
MARTA (Metropolitan Atlanta Rapid
    Transit Authority), small-group
    technology in, 35–37
Masked images, 327
Maslow, A. H., motivation theory of, 100,
    103–104, 108
Mass theory, inadequacies of, 42
Mathematical models, of political violence,
    218–219. *See also* Collective-choice
    theory
Mead, George Herbert, 296
Media, effects of, 130, 326
Mediations and war, 171–172
Memory, organizational, 83, 108, 121–122
Merriam, Charles, 307–308, 309–310
Metaphors, 300, 304, 330–334
  root metaphors, 305
Metropolitan Atlanta Rapid Transit Au-
    thority (MARTA), small-group
    technology in, 35–37
Milgram, S., studies by, 15, 16–17
Miller, E. F., 333–334
Minimax notion, in game theory, 258, 259
Miranda of power, 307
"Missing middle" in mass theory, 42
Mitchell, John, 31–32, 33
Mitchell, William C., 318–319
"Mode of production," executive branch's,
    123–124
Modelski, G., war studies by, 172
Modernity, correlates of, 193
Moral learning, 82
Moral sensitivity, government's, 89
Most, B. A., war study by, 201–203
Motivation, theories of
  action mood, 115–116
  altruism, 91, 102, 282
    opposing views, 91, 92–93
  aversive, 111–113, 141
  boredom avoidance, 101–102
  in collective-choice theory, 228, 282
  meaningful work, 102
  by Maslow, 100, 103–104
  unconscious, 114–115
Mueller, Claus, 325–326

Myth, views of
  by Cassirer, 292
  by Edelman, 310

Naming, significance of, 294–295, 303
Nash equilibrium, 271–273, 275, 277–278
Nazi Germany and symbolism, 292, 314
Needs versus wants, 227
Negotiated-order model of society, Hall's,
    319–320
  criticism of, 321
News media, effects of, 130
Nimmo, Dan, 326–327
Nisbet, Robert, 297, 300, 330–331
Nixon, Richard M.
  symbols, use of, 300
  "Young Team," 31–34
Nondictatorship condition, 236
Normal-relations range (NRR), interna-
    tional, 172, 173
Norms
  low salience, 138–139
  in small groups, 19, 45–46
  strong, systems with, 138

Obedience studies, Milgram's, 15, 16–17
Olson, M., 279
Operational definitions, in small-group
    analysis
  list, 19
  variations in, 24, 56
Opportunism, intellectual, 93
Ordinal versus cardinal utility, 236, 242–244
Organization development (OD), 34–35
  in MARTA, 35–37
Organization theory, "mode of production"
    in, 123–124. *See also* Policy forma-
    tion; "Smart" organization theory
Organizational learning, 82–84
  pathologies of, 75–76, 98
Organizational memory, 83, 108, 121–122
Orthodoxy, issue of, 134–135
Orwell, George, quoted, 323–324
Overconfidence, government, 93–94, 145
Overload, problem of, 144

Pareto domination, 236, 249
  in prisoner's dilemma, 261, 262
    collective-goods theory, 278, 280
Parties, political, strategies of, 252–254
Perceptual-motor concrete level, 104

Personality
  in small groups, 19, 49
  views of, in learning theories, 92–95, 101
Phenomenology, 295
Philosophic concepts of symbolic systems,
    292–298
Physical appearance, influence of, 8
Physiology
  of knowledge and learning
    body state encoding, 117–118
    brain, 118
    time required, 140
  of stress, 110
Polarization, alliance, 204–205, 206, 207
Policy formation, theory of, 124–125
  contract evaluation research, 127–128
  institution creation strategies, 125–126
  professionalism, 126–127
  social-science research, use of, 126
Policy space, 250
  and party strategies, 252–254
Political behavior
  "hardball politics" concept, 131–132
  organized groups, question of, 132
  uniqueness, 130–131
  See also Government learning
Political culture, 318, 320
Political economy. *See* Collective-choice
    theory
Political symbols, 285–338
  applications of symbolic theory. *See* Sym-
    bols, application of theory
  foundations of study, 290–291
    linguistic/anthropological, 298–307
    philosophic, 292–298
  integrative. *See* Integrative symbols
  problems of analysis, 286, 289
  recent interest, 292–293, 297–298, 337
  theories
    consensus, 290, 291, 337
    by Edelman, 310–314
    by Lasswell and Kaplan, 308–309
    by Merriam, 307–308
Political violence, studies of, 163–220
  aggression perspective, 217–218
  authoritarianism research, 219–220
  frequency
    assassination, 174–177
    large-scale conflict, 165–174
    randomness question, 180–181
    in United States, 176, 177–180

Political violence, studies of (*cont.*)
  GRIT proposal, 219
  hypotheses
    by Bueno de Mesquita, 191, 206–209
    by Feierabend *et al.*, 191, 192–198, 199
    by Gurr, 191, 198–301
    by Köhler, 209
    by Starr and Most, 201–203
    by Stohl, 191, 211–213
    by Tanter, 191, 213–214
    by Tilly, 209–210
    by Wallace, 191, 203–206
  mathematical models, 218–219
  problems, summary of, 215–217
  stress, role of, 218, 219–220
  types, 181
    by Banks, 181, 184–185, 186
    critiques of, 185, 187–188, 189–191
    by Gurr and Bishop, 181, 188–191
    by Rummel, 181–183
    by Tanter, 181, 183–184
Politics
  economic theories of (spatial models),
      249–255
  relevance of group theory to, 24–26
    benefits from, 37–53
    cases, 26–37
  self-transformation capability, 132–133
Polling, public opinion, 88–89
Pollution rituals, 303
Pool, Ithiel de Sola, 317
Power, views of
  by Cohen, 306
  by Hall, 320
  by Lasswell and Kaplan, 308
  by Merriam, 307
  by Mitchell, 318–319
Preference priority, 242
Prisoner's dilemma
  in game theory, 261–262
    "individual versus collective," 280
    noncooperation without, 281–282
    three-person, 263, 266–267
  in small-group analysis, 5–7
Problem conceptions, 85, 137–138
Problem sequencing, 107
Problem solving, 79
  problem types, 135–140
Professionalism, 126–127
Program evaluation studies, problems with
      127–128

Psychoanalytic theory, 92
Psychological reassurance, Edelman's con-
      cept of, 323
Psychotherapy, processes in, 107, 108
  truth-telling, 133–134
Public good, knowledge as, 87
Public-goods theory, 278–282
Public-opinion polling, 88–89

Rational-choice models. *See* Collective-
      choice theory
Rational legal standards and power, 319
Rationalist (developmental) theories of
      learning, 102–109, 141
Rationality, 226
  in collective choice theory, 228–229, 282–
      283
    collective goods theory, 278, 279, 281
    conditions not required for, 235–236,
      237
    economic theories of politics, 249–255
    transitivity as, 232, 233–234, 235
    in vote trading, 249
    See also Game theory
  myth versus, 292
  role rationality, 249–250
Raven, B. H., analysis of Nixon team by,
      31–33
Readiness, "action mood" as, 115–116
Realpolitik analysis, 131–132
Recruitment, government, 118–119
Referential versus condensation symbols,
      299
Reinforcers, 100
Religion, civil, Bennett's view of, 321–322
Resource-dependent problems, 136–137
Responsibility diffusion in groups, theory
      of, 7
Reward systems, alternative, 99
Richardson, Lewis F., political-violence
      studies by, 167–168, 218
Risky shift, study of, 5–7, 54–55
Ritual, Douglas's view of, 303, 304
Ritual symbols
  elections as, 310–311
  Turner's view of, 305
Role rationality, 249–250
Role constellation theories of organizations,
      120
Role styles in small groups, 19, 46
Root metaphors, 305

Rummel, R. J.
on Haas work, 164
political-conflict studies by, 181–183

Sapir, Edward, 288, 290–291, 297, 298–299, 311, 324
Schachter, Stanley, 12, 13–14
Scheingold, S. A., 329
Schellenberg, J. A., study of county seat wars by, 177, 178–179
School busing, symbolism of, 323
Schutz, Albert, 295–296, 305
Scientific learning, 79–80
Scientific method in problem solving, 138
Secrecy penetration problems, 139
Secularization, issue of, 134–135
Security level, in game theory, 263, 265
and Shapley solution concepts, 269, 270, 274–275
Selectivity
in study of symbols, 289
in symbol-making function, 300
Self-managed/democratic alternative for work organization, 50, 51–52
Semiconfused thinking, 106
Shapley, L. S., solution concepts of
Shapley solution, 274–275
Shapley value, 269–271
Similarity, in social attraction, 8–9
Simon, R. J., assassination study by, 176
Singer, J. David, war study by, 170–171
Single-peakedness, 240–241
Skill, definition of, 81
Small-group study, 1–64
applied component, 34–35, 52–53, 58–60
in MARTA, 35–37
in professional development and teaching, 47
misunderstandings
about bases of attraction, 22
about boundaries, 23–24
about cohesion, 22–23
about operational definitions, 24
about relevance to politics, 24–26
political analysis, 26–27
of auto-worker groups, 29–30
of Kennedy team, 27–28
of MARTA groupings, 35–37
mistaken emphasis, 24–26, 40–41
of Nixon team, 31–34
theoretic framework, 25

Small group study (*cont.*)
political scientists, benefits for, 37
applied component, 52–53
methodological advantage, 38–39
in research on individual-to-system linkages, 47–52
separation of "is" from "should," 39–40
in traditional areas of concern, 41–47
properties of groups, 18–20, 45–46
lack of attention to, 59, 60–61
relations of, 20–21
See also Cohesiveness
research trends, 1–2, 16, 18, 24, 57, 58, 59–60
stuckness, 53–54
assumptions leading to, 54–56
consequences, 60–61
overcoming, 62–63, 64
reasons, 57–60, 63–64
severity of, 61–62
themes, major, 2–3
attraction, 7–11
comparison, 11–14
control, 15–17
facilitation/inhibition, 3–7
"Smart" organization theory, 119
culture formation theories, 121
organizational-process theories, 120–121
people theories, 120
Social attraction, 7–11
Social comparison, 11–14, 17
Social control, small group's role in, 15–17
Social cueing, in symbolism, 287, 290, 291, 292
Social drama, Turner's concept of, 304, 305
Social facilitation/inhibition, 3–5, 12–13, 21
risky shift, 5–7
Social indicators, 88
Social-judgment theory, 107
Social-learning theory, 95–102
Social psychologists and small-group study, 2
Socialist theory, 229
Socioeconomic indicators, 88, 185
rates of change, 193–194
Solution concepts. *See* Game theory, solution concepts
Sorokin, P. A., war study of, 165–166
Spatial models (economic theories of politics), 249–255
Sperber, Dan, 289, 297, 300

Starr, H., war study by, 201–203
Status allocation, Gusfield's view of, 322–323
Status conflict, 323
Status inconsistency and war, 203–204
Stohl, M., study by, 191, 211–213
Strain theory of ideology, 301
Strasnick's preference priority concept, 242
Strauss, Anselm, 295
Stress, 109–111, 141
Strong-norm-system problems, 138
Structural integration, 20–21
Structural violence, 188, 189
Subordination, psychology of, 111–113
Suffering theory of growth, 109
Supreme Court, United States
  and small-group variables, 46
  and symbolism, 293, 328
Symbolic-interaction theory, 296–297, 319
Symbols
  application of theory, 314–334, 337
    by Bennett, 321–322
    by Cobb and Elder, 322
    by Deutsch, 317–318
    by Edelman, 323, 324, 329, 331, 332
    by Frankel, 315–316, 333
    by Goffman, 320–321
    by Gusfield, 322–323
    by Hall, 319–320, 321
    by Kantor, 321
    by Lasswell, 309, 315
    law as symbol system, 328–330
    by Lerner, 316–317
    metaphor, analysis of, 330–334
    by Mitchell, 318–319
    by Mueller, 325–326
    by Nimmo, 326–327
    by Pool, 317
  and metaphors, 300, 304, 305, 330–334
  political. See Political symbols
  theorists
    Blumer, Herbert, 296–297
    Burke, Kenneth, 291, 294–295, 305
    Cassirer, Ernst, 286, 292, 314
    Cohen, Abner, 289, 297, 306, 308, 311
    cross-fertilization, 297, 305–306, 314
    Douglas, Mary, 297, 302–304, 332
    Geertz, Clifford, 297, 299, 300–302, 309
    Langer, Susanne K., 286, 293
    Mead, George Herbert, 296
    Sapir, Edward, 288, 290–291, 297, 298–299, 311, 324

Symbols (cont.)
  theorists (cont.)
    Schutz, Albert, 295–296, 305
    Sperber, Dan, 289, 297, 300
    Turner, Victor, 297, 304–305, 331–332
    See also Symbols, applications of theory; Political symbols, theories

T-groups, 58–59
Tanter, R., political-conflict studies by, 181, 183–184, 191, 213–214
Taxation, in collective-goods theory, 280–281
Teaching, small-group applications in, 47
Team building, in MARTA, 35–36
Technology-dependent problems, 136
Temperance movement, Gusfield's view of, 322–323
Thick description, Geertz's concept of, 301, 309
Threats
  common, and social attraction, 9
  in game theory, 271–272, 276
Tightness in international system, 207–208
Tilly, C., 209–210
Time-constraint problems, 140
Time series, 88
  analyses, equations in, 212, 213
  interrupted-time series, defined, 211
Time structures in government, 128–129
Transitivity, Arrow's axiom of, 232–235
Triplett, N., 4
Truth theory, 133–134
Turner, Victor, 297, 304–305, 331–332

Unconscious motivation, 114–115
Unlimited domain, 235–236
  violation of, 236, 240–242
Urbanization and collective violence, theory of, 210
Utility
  additivity, 245
  cardinal versus ordinal, 236, 242–244
  in Harsanyi analysis, 276–277
  indifference curves, 253–254
  in paradox of vote trading, 247–248

Valance–instrumentality–expectancy (VIE) theory, 100–101
Value-restrictedness, 241
Values, study of, 82
Verificationist view of political metaphor, 333–334

VIE. *See* Valance-instrumentality- expectancy theory.
Vietnam War and United States domestic violence, 213–214
Vigilante movements, study of, 177–178
Violence, political. *See* Political violence
Vonnegut, K., 134–135
Vote trading (logrolling), 244–247
  paradox of, 247–249
Voter's paradox, 234, 235, 236–237
  logrolling and, 244, 246–247
  probability of, 237–240
  unlimited domain and, 235
  ways of avoiding, 240–242, 243–244
Voting behavior
  collective intransitivity, 234–235
  deviant, and work-group integration, 29–30
  economic theory, 249, 250–252, 253–255
  game theory compared to, 257

Wallace, M. D., war studies by, 191, 203–206
Walzer, M., 332
Wants versus needs, 227
War, international, studies of, 165
  by Bueno de Mesquita, 206–209
  correlates
    alliances, 170–171, 204–205, 206–208
    borders, number of, 201–203
    imperial systems, 209
    internal conflict, 211–215
    mediation, 171–172
    status inconsistency, 203–204

War, international, studies of (*cont.*)
  by Kende, 168–169
  by Köhler, 209
  by Levine, 171–172
  by Modelski, 172
  problems, summary of, 215–217
  by Richardson, 167–168
  by Singer, 170–171
  by Sorokin, 165–166
  by Starr and Most, 201–203
  by Stohl, 211–213
  by Tanter, 213–214
  by Wallace, 203–206
Wars, county seat, 177, 178–179
Welfare economics, 229
Werner, Heinz, on intellectual development, 77, 103
Wisdom, components of, 81–82
Wolff, Robert Paul, 308
Work capacity, developing, theory of, 104–106
Workplace
  group integration and political deviation, 29–30
  organizational forms, 49–52
  social comparison, 14

Yerkes-Dodson Law, 110–111
"Young Team," Nixon's, 31–34

Zashin, E., 333
Zeuthen, Frederik, 275, 276, 277–278

C